D1380529

THE FRENCH INTIFADA

Andrew Hussey

The French
Intifada

The Long War between France and its Arabs

GRANTA

Granta Publications, 12 Addison Avenue, London, W11 4QR

First published in Great Britain by Granta Books 2014

A CIP catalogue record for this book is available from the British Library

9 8 7 6 5 4 3 2 1

ISBN 978 1 84708 147 6

www.grantabooks.com

Typeset by Avon DataSet, Bidford on Avon, Warwickshire

Printed an͏   0 4YY

To Carmel
With all my love as always
More than ever

And to my parents John and Doreen
Dawn, Gas, Leila and Gaby
Love to the whole tribe

'These are not natural events;
they strengthen from strange to stranger.'

The Tempest, Act V, Scene 1

Contents

Part Three: In Morocco

Part Four: Tunisia, Made in France

Part Five: Prisoners of War

THE FRENCH INTIFADA

NORTH AFRICA

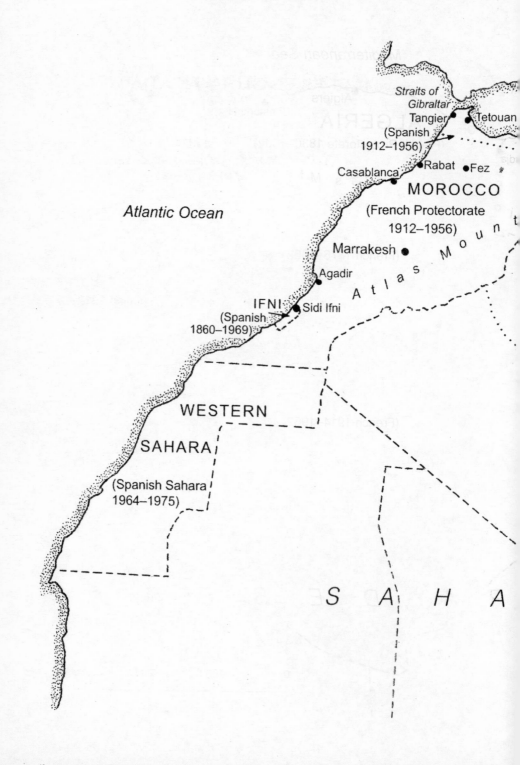

Atlantic Ocean

Straits of
Gibraltar
Tangier
(Spanish
1912–1956)
Tetouan

Casablanca
Rabat
Fez

MOROCCO
(French Protectorate
1912–1956)

Marrakesh

Agadir

IFNI
(Spanish
1860–1969)
Sidi Ifni

Atlas Mount

WESTERN

SAHARA

(Spanish Sahara
1964–1975)

S A H A

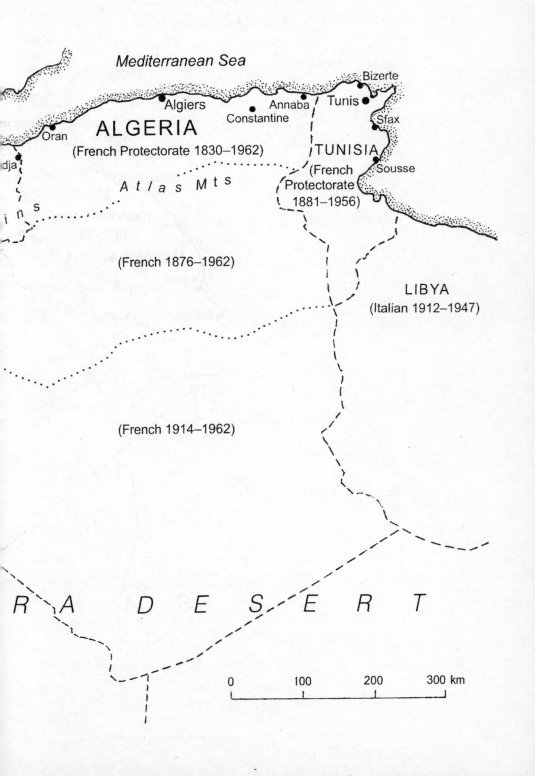

Mediterranean Sea

Bizerte

Algiers   Annaba   Tunis

Constantine

Oran   **ALGERIA**   Sfax

(French Protectorate 1830–1962)   **TUNISIA**

dja

Atlas Mt^s (French

Protectorate

i n s   1881–1956)

Sousse

(French 1876–1962)

LIBYA

(Italian 1912–1947)

(French 1914–1962)

R A   D E S E R T

0   100   200   300 km

PARIS
ARRONDISSEMENTS AND BANLIEUES

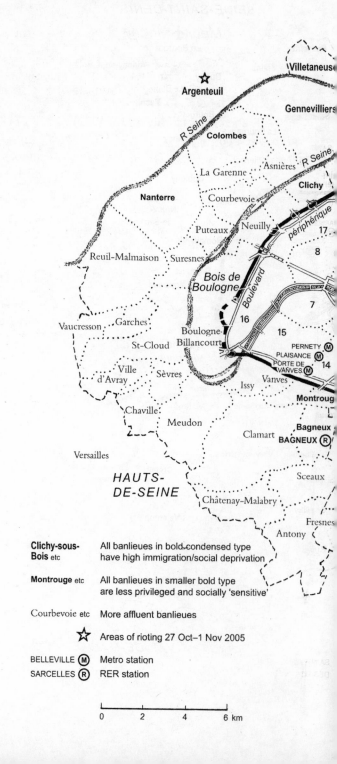

Villetaneuse

Argenteuil

Gennevilliers

R Seine   Colombes

La Garenne   Asnières   R Seine

Clichy

Nanterre   Courbevoie

périphérique   17

Puteaux   Neuilly   8

Reuil-Malmaison   Suresnes

Bois de
Boulogne   7

Vaucresson   Garches   16   15

St-Cloud   Boulogne-
Billancourt   PERNETY Ⓜ
PLAISANCE Ⓜ
PORTE DE
VANVES Ⓜ   14

Ville
d'Avray   Sèvres   Issy   Vanves

Montroug

Chaville   Bagneux
Meudon   Clamart   BAGNEUX Ⓡ

Versailles

Sceaux

HAUTS-
DE-SEINE   Châtenay-Malabry

Fresnes
Antony

**Clichy-sous-
Bois** etc   All banlieues in bold-condensed type
have high immigration/social deprivation

Montrouge etc   All banlieues in smaller bold type
are less privileged and socially 'sensitive'

Courbevoie etc   More affluent banlieues

☆   Areas of rioting 27 Oct–1 Nov 2005

BELLEVILLE Ⓜ   Metro station
SARCELLES Ⓡ   RER station

0   2   4   6 km

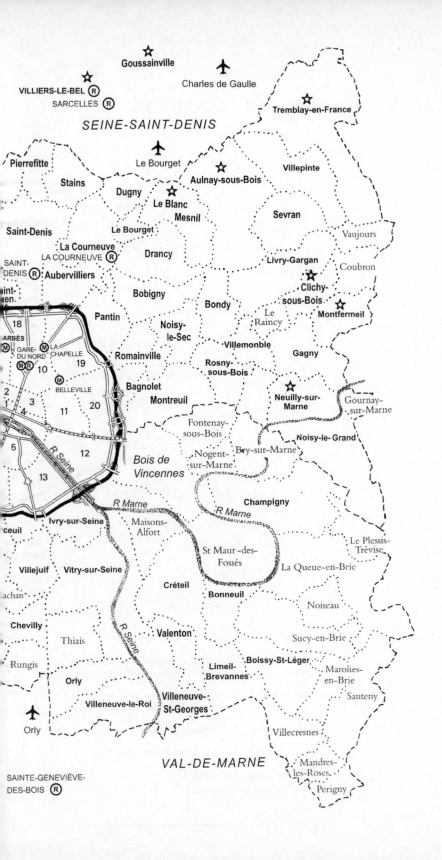

Goussainville ☆

Charles de Gaulle ✈

VILLIERS-LE-BEL ⓡ ☆
SARCELLES ⓡ

Tremblay-en-France ☆

SEINE-SAINT-DENIS

Pierrefitte

Le Bourget ✈

Villepinte

Stains

Dugny

Aulnay-sous-Bois ☆

Le Blanc
Mesnil

Sevran

Saint-Denis

Le Bourget

Vaujours

La Courneuve
LA COURNEUVE ⓡ

Drancy

Livry-Gargan

Coubron

SAINT-
DENIS ⓡ Aubervilliers

Clichy-
sous-Bois ☆

int-
en

Bobigny

Bondy

Le
Raincy

Montfermeil ☆

18

Pantin

Noisy-
le-Sec

Villemonble

Gagny

ARBÈS

GARE- ⓜ ⓜ LA
DU NORD CHAPELLE

Romainville

Rosny-
sous-Bois

ⓜ
ⓜⓡ 10 19
2
1 3 ⓜ BELLEVILLE
4

11 20

Bagnolet

Montreuil

Neuilly-sur-
Marne ☆

Gournay-
sur-Marne

Fontenay-
sous-Bois

5

12

Bois de
Vincennes

Nogent-
sur-Marne

Bry-sur-Marne

Noisy-le-Grand

13

R Marne

Champigny

R Marne

Ivry-sur-Seine

Maisons-
Alfort

ceuil

Le Plessis-
Trévise

St Maur -des-
Fossés

Villejuif

Vitry-sur-Seine

La Queue-en-Brie

Créteil

Bonneuil

Noiseau

achan

Chevilly

Valenton

Sucy-en-Brie

Thiais

R Seine

Rungis

Boissy-St-Léger

Limeil-
Brevannes

Marolies-
en-Brie

Orly

Villeneuve-le-Roi

Villeneuve-
St-Georges

Santeny

✈
Orly

Villecresnes

VAL-DE-MARNE

Mandres-
les-Roses

SAINTE-GENEVIÈVE-
DES-BOIS ⓡ

Perigny

Introduction

'Fuck France!'

In the late afternoon of 27 March 2007, I was travelling on the Paris metro, heading home after a day's work in the east end of the city. I got off at the Gare du Nord to change trains. In a trance – lost in the music on my headphones – I automatically made for the shopping mall which connects the upper and lower levels of the station. This was where I would normally buy a newspaper and a coffee and then catch a train south to my flat.

But this was no ordinary evening. As I walked up the exit stairs I could smell smoke and hear shouting. The corridors were a tighter squeeze than usual and everyone a little more nervous and bad-tempered than the average rush-hour crowd. As I got nearer the main piazza of the mall, smoke stung my eyes and nostrils, and the shouting grew louder. I could see armed police and dogs. Still, there didn't seem to be too much to worry about. My only real fear was how to get through the tide of commuters, which by now had come to a dead halt, and on to my train home.

I pushed my way through the crowd, burst into the empty piazza, and found myself in dead space, caught in a stand-off between two battle lines – on one side police in blue-black riot gear, drumming batons on their clear, hard shields, and on the other a rough assembly of kids and young adults, mainly black or Arab, boys and girls, dressed in hip-hop fashion, singing, laughing, and throwing stuff. You could tell from their accents and manners that these were not Parisians; they were kids from the *banlieues* – the poor suburbs to the north of Paris, connected to the city by the trains running into the Gare du Nord. One African-looking kid was swinging an iron bar and shouting. The bar crashed into a photo booth and a drinks machine. A few yards further on, a fire had been started in a ticket office.

The atmosphere was strangely festive. Behind the reinforced steel and glass of the Eurostar terminal, new arrivals from London were ushered into Paris by soldiers with machine guns – the glittering capital of Europe now apparently a war zone. They looked on the scene with horror. But it was exhilarating to watch kids hopping over metro barriers, smoking weed and shouting, walking wherever they wanted, disobeying every single one of the tight rules that normally control access to the station. It was also frightening, because these kids could now hurt you whenever they wanted. They had abolished all the rules, including the rule of law.

There is no word in French or English which expresses the opposite of the verb 'to civilize': the concept does not exist. But this was *anti*-civilization in action – a transgression of every code of behaviour that holds a society together. Like a terrorist attack or a football riot, the act of anti-civilization is a total experience: it undermines everything all at once. This is not an intellectual concept; it is a feeling. These kids were taking on the whole world around them – the police, the train authorities, passers-by – wrecking the station, the shops and the offices. And they knew exactly what they were doing.

I stumbled back into the pack of commuters, all transfixed by the spectacle of real, raw violence. No one spoke much. There was nervous laughter but everyone was frightened too. No one could say where this was heading, or where it was going to end.

In fact, the battle went on for another eight hours. I walked most of the way home and then watched the news reports on French television. With the shots of helicopters, flares and paramilitary troopers, these seemed like dispatches from the front line of a distant war rather than an early-evening riot in a commuter railway station only twenty minutes away. And yet the journalists' demeanour was mainly calm and unsurprised. This was a level of violence that would have shaken most European governments, but here in France the incident seemed unremarkable, even banal.

Over the next few days, I read the press. Most reporters and eyewitnesses agreed on the chronology. At half past four in the afternoon, a young Congolese man, already known to the police, had been arrested while trying to dodge the ticket barrier. The arrest was heavy-handed and as the cops started hammering the guy, passers-by waded in to support the underdog. Guns were pulled out, batons drawn, and soon enough a riot was in full swing.

But how did this happen? What made the Gare du Nord such a powder keg that the arrest of a ticket dodger could, within minutes, make it the most ungovernable part of French territory? This is where the interpretation of events became confused. In the pages of *Le Parisien*, the chronicle of daily life in the city, the events were described as *'une émeute populaire'* (a popular riot). The tone was one of mild approval. *Le Parisien* is not particularly left-wing, but it is always on the side of the 'people' – that most cherished of Parisian myths. This language placed the events at the Gare du Nord in a long tradition of popular uprisings in the city – from the days of La Fronde through to the French Revolution and the Commune, these have been a defining feature of Parisian history. Several other newspapers, including the right-wing *Le Figaro*, reported the same facts with a shiver of horror, adding that the crowds had been chanting *'A bas l'état, les flics et les patrons'* ('Down with the state, the coppers and the bosses'), thereby domesticating the riot as part of the Parisian folklore of rebellion.[1]

But the problem was that none of these accounts was true. The kids I saw didn't give a fuck about the state or the 'bosses'. Most of them didn't have jobs anyway. And although they did hate the police, they would never have used an old-fashioned slang word like *flics*, which belongs to the Parisian equivalent of the Krays' generation. For the rioters, the police were either *keufs* or *schmitts*. The chanting I heard was mostly in French: '*Nik les schmitts*' ('Fuck the cops'), and sometimes in English: 'Fuck the police!' But there was another slogan, chanted in colloquial Arabic, which seemed to hit hardest of all: '*Na'al abouk la France!*' ('Fuck France!'). This slogan – it is in fact more of a curse – has nothing to do with any French tradition of revolt.[2]

These days France is home to the largest Muslim population in Europe. This includes more than 5 million people from North Africa, the Middle East and the so-called 'Black Atlantic', the long slice of West Africa which stretches from Mali to Senegal. A short walk around the Barbès district in northern Paris, where almost all of these nationalities are represented in the same tiny, overcrowded space, provides both a vivid snapshot of the diversity of this population and a neat lesson in French colonial history

The Gare du Nord, at the heart of this district, is frontier territory. It is the dividing line between the wretched conditions of the *banlieues,* the suburbs outside the city, and the relative affluence of central Paris. It is where young *banlieusards* come to hang out, meet the opposite sex, shop, smoke, show-off and flirt – all the stuff that young people like to do. Paris is both near and distant; it is a few short steps away, but in terms of jobs, housing, making a life, for these young people it is as inaccessible and far away as America. So they cherish this small part of the city that belongs to them.

This is why the Gare du Nord is a flashpoint. The area is generally tense but stable: everyone in the right place, from the police to the dealers. But when the police come in hard, it can feel like another display of colonial power. So the battle cry of '*Na'al abouk la France!*' is also a cry of hurt and rage. It expresses ancestral emotions of loss, shame and terror. This is what makes it such a powerful curse.

The rioters at the Gare du Nord or in the *banlieues* also often describe themselves as soldiers in a 'long war' against France and Europe. To this extent, they are fighting against the very concept of 'civilization', which they see as a European invention. The so-called 'French intifada', the guerrilla war with police at the edges and in the heart of French cities, is only the latest and most dramatic form of engagement with the enemy.

This war began with Napoleon's cynical aggression in Egypt in the early 1800s, marking the start of a French lust for all things Oriental that culminated in the acquisition – by force – of Algeria, Tunisia and Morocco (the territories of the Maghreb). All of this was conducted in the name of the '*mission civilisatrice*' (civilizing mission), the historical destiny of the French Republic: to export the universal values of liberty, equality, fraternity – to *civilize* the world.

In return, the spices, drugs, architecture, music and religion of the 'exotic East' were imported into France throughout the nineteenth century. This is when 'Orientalism' became a favoured motif in French art and literature. Poetry in particular came under the Orientalist spell; from Baudelaire to Nerval to Mallarmé, French poets dreamed of an East that they saw as sensual, sexual and outside the everyday demands of the modern capitalist world.

As France colonized the Arab world, the French government began describing itself as '*une puissance musulmane*' (a Muslim power). As well as signalling that France would look after the interests of Catholics in Muslim countries, this meant in the first instance that France saw itself as the protector in the Middle East of Catholics and Muslims against the encroaching Protestants of the British Empire (it was on these grounds that France extended its powers in Syria and Lebanon in the 1920s). More recently, the term *'une puissance musulmane'* has been evoked by a succession of French foreign ministers to buy goodwill in the Arab world by hinting at a shared mistrust of the United States and Israel (the French have never been afraid to invoke the spectre of anti-Semitism in their dealings with Arab states).

The real rivalry between Britain and France in the nineteenth and twentieth centuries was about commercial and political power. They sought to achieve their aims, however, in very different ways. The British were mostly interested in money and therefore mainly indifferent to the cultures of the 'natives' they colonized, subjugating them by force of arms when and if necessary. The French, in contrast, controlled their colonies by pursuing the 'civilizing mission', effectively seeking to make their subjects culturally French. Of course the French plundered where they could, but there was an added strategic urge to extend the concept of 'Frenchness' across the world.

Furthermore, under the rigidities of the French educational system, there could be no argument about what this identity meant. The absurd end-point of this policy was Berber Muslim students in the hills of Algeria, who had never been to France, reading about their 'Gaulish ancestors'. The comedy soon turns tragic when this cultural cosh splinters individual identity; as we shall see, such psychic trauma is the key to understanding not just the killing-jar of Algeria but the entire French sphere of influence in the Arab world.

The subtitle of this book refers to 'France and its Arabs'. There is a deliberate emphasis on the sense of ownership that France has felt and still feels towards the Arab world. It is this ambiguous relationship – which has more in common with a dysfunctional family structure than with colonialism in pursuit of profit – that shapes the story and explains present-day tensions.

In November 2005, eighteen months before the riot in the Gare du Nord, the tensions in the *banlieues* had again spilled over into violence and, for one spectacular moment, threatened to bring down the French government. The catalyst was a series of confrontations between immigrant youth and the police in the Parisian *banlieue* of Clichy-sous-Bois. As the fighting between police and the *banlieusards* intensified, riots broke out in major cities across France. This was when the term 'French intifada' was first widely used by the media and by the rioters themselves.

The violence began on 27 October 2005, when two young men were electrocuted while trying to escape police by fleeing through an electricity substation. This incident was followed by almost a week of rioting every night, during which thousands of cars were burned. Then it began to spread to other French towns and cities. President Jacques Chirac declared a state of emergency, effective from midnight on 8 November. This gave the government and police special powers of arrest, the power to order a curfew and conduct house-to-house searches. But this only seemed to intensify the situation. On 11 November there was a blackout in part of Amiens when a power station was attacked – to the alarm of the police, this was to become a common and effective tactic. Churches were also firebombed.

The riots finally subsided after two weeks. But this was no easy victory for the police – quite the opposite in fact. The violence was partly fuelled by aggressive police tactics and by the belligerence of Nicolas Sarkozy, then Minister of the Interior, who declared 'zero tolerance' and said that he would clean the streets of '*racaille*' (scum). Such inflammatory words only served to increase anger in the *banlieues* – it was clearly the language of war. By the end of November, with the French government in disarray, the riots across France had demonstrated that the youth of the *banlieues* could take on the authorities whenever they wanted to, and win. Since then the troubles in the *banlieues* have been sporadic but have never gone away.

The events of 2005 inevitably provoked an almost ceaseless flow of articles, books and debates in France. For all the noisy rhetoric, however, there were several important points of consensus on the Right and the Left. First of all it was generally agreed that the severity of the crisis had been exaggerated by the English-speaking media, who knew little of France and used the news of the French riots as a distraction from their own problems with immigration and immigrants in their own countries. This is, of course, the traditional role of the perfidious Anglo-American world in the French imagination.

Secondly, there was broad agreement that the riots had little or nothing to do with Islam or the historical French presence in parts of the Islamic world. Leftist intellectuals, in the pages of *Le Monde* or *Libération*, fell over themselves to distance the riots from any connection with the same anger that radicalized Islamists. According to these journalists, the riots were caused by a '*fracture sociale*' and lack of '*justice sociale*'. Even the French intelligence services, the Renseignements Généraux, joined in, producing their own report, which described the riots as a 'popular insurrection' and downplayed the role of Islamist groups and the immigrant origins of the rioters. In this way the riots of 2005 were domesticated and made part of a traditionally French form of protest. There was an almost complete denial that what was happening might be a new form of politics that was a direct challenge to the French state.

There is, however, a very real conflict in contemporary France between the opposing principles of *laïcité* and *communautarisme*, which is being played out in the riots. The term *laïcité* is difficult to translate; put simply it means that under French law it is illegal to distinguish individuals on the grounds of their religion. Unlike the Anglo-American model of the secular state, which seeks to hinder state interference in religious affairs, the

French notion of *laïcité* actively blocks religious interference in affairs of state. This dates back to the Revolution of 1789 and is traditionally understood to be a way of controlling and disciplining the Catholic Church. The Dreyfus affair, which led to the formal separation of church and state in 1905, is still held up as an example of why the Catholic Church needs to be policed in this way. As a specifically anti-religious concept, *laïcité*, it is argued, guarantees the moral unity of the French nation – the '*République indivisible*'.

In recent years this core value of the French Republic has been opposed by *communautarisme*, which sets the needs of the 'community' against the needs of 'society'. Again, the loose Anglo-American model, where 'difference' – whether of sexuality, religion or disability – is tolerated or even prized, does not apply in France, where 'difference' is seen as a form of sectarianism and a threat to the Republic. The most acute problem for the recent generations of Muslim immigrants to France is that the proclaimed universalism of republican values, and in particular *laïcité*, can very quickly resemble the 'civilizing mission' of colonialism. In other words, if Muslims want to be 'French', they must learn to be citizens of the Republic first and Muslims second; for many this is an impossible task, hence the anxieties over whether Muslims in France are *musulmans de France* or *musulmans en France*.

But this conflict is not just about politics or religion. It is also about extreme emotions. More than death, most human beings fear annihilation. This is a process familiar to psychiatrists who treat patients for disorders such as schizophrenia and depression. Part of the process of mental disintegration which characterizes these illnesses is the experience of partial or total alienation. When a person loses all sense of authentic identity, all sense of self, to the extent that they don't feel that they properly exist, they then become literally strangers to themselves.

Historically this is what happened in France's territories during the colonial era and what is happening now in the *banlieues*. This is why it is almost impossible for immigrants to France from its former colonies to feel authentically 'at home' there. For all their modernity, these urban spaces are designed almost like vast prison camps. The *banlieue* is the most literal representation of 'otherness' – the otherness of exclusion, of the repressed, of the fearful and despised – all kept physically and culturally away from the mainstream of French 'civilization'.

This is an argument made by the political scientist Gilles Kepel in his 2012 book *Quatre-vingt-treize*, a title which alludes to Victor Hugo's great novel of the Terror of 1793, and to the notorious Seine Saint-Denis district of Paris, which is known as 'Ninety-three', after its postcode. In his book Kepel conducts a forensic examination of the recent history of this district, concluding that although several varieties of Islam are at war with each other, they are all united in their hostility towards the secular French state.

Kepel is also convinced that the one of the crucial conflicts in the *banlieues* is the challenge to the French Republic from the 'outside', by which he means both the *banlieues* and France's former territories in the Muslim world. Most importantly, unlike many of his peers, he sees the recent changes in French society as intimately connected to events in the Arab world which are little understood in the West. 'Many French political commentators are blind,' he told me in his cramped office just off the boulevard Saint-Germain. 'They do not want to see the world beyond France. And so they do not understand that what happens here is because of our relationship with the Arab world, and our history there.'[3]

Kepel insists that the present tensions in France cannot be separated from the so-called 'Arab Spring' – the wave of rebellions which spread across the Muslim world in 2011. More specifically, the Arab Spring has led to a severe shake-up of all accepted truths about North Africa, which until now has normally been known to the world through French eyes.

None of this is straightforward. The Tunisian revolution of 2011, which sparked the Arab Spring, was hailed as a triumph by Tunisians in France. At the same time, as the régime was swept away, the true extent of French duplicity with the corrupt Ben Ali government was properly revealed. This, of course, only deepened the suspicion of Tunisians in France towards the French government, while in Tunisia there has been a growing number of Salafis (this is the word currently used for radical Islamists) who have specifically targeted France as their enemy. I saw this for myself on my last trip to Tunisia in 2012, when I spoke to Salafis who called for 'a new war of liberation' against France.

The mood is the same in Morocco and Algeria, where the unpopular governments reinforce their power with French arms and money. The largest section of this book is devoted to Algeria. This is not only because Algeria is the biggest country in the region – a potential regional superpower – but also because it is where the French fought an out-and-out war against a Muslim population. Although there was also strong resistance to the French presence in Morocco and Tunisia, it never reached the same level, and for this reason it is the spectre of Algeria, the memories of its bloody war with France, which still figure most heavily in the French and Muslim imagination.

At the time of writing, as Syria collapses into carnage and chaos, it seems as if the Arab Spring may well become the 'Arab Holocaust'. The French, of course, do not want this to happen, but as they struggle to maintain order there is growing disorder in their own *banlieues*; the anger and violence is matched and mirrored on both sides of the Mediterranean.

This is the view of the philosopher Alain Finkielkraut, who gave a controversial interview in the immediate wake of the riots to the Israeli newspaper *Ha'aretz*,[4] in which he made the more nuanced point that the rioters were rising up against 'France' rather merely protesting for social reform. The interview was reported in *Le Monde* and suddenly Finkielkraut became a hate figure for the Left. He was denounced in *Le Nouvel Observateur* as a 'neo-reactionary' and even accused in other quarters of serving Jean-Marie Le Pen's Front National and inciting racial hatred.[5]

I discussed this claim with Finkielkraut, who dismissed it as obvious nonsense. But what it did reveal was the barely veiled anti-Semitism which still contaminates French political discourse on the Left as well as the Right — it was implied or argued that because Finkielkraut comes from a Jewish background he has a vested in interest in provoking divisions between France and its Arabs. (Kepel, too, has been frequently attacked for his alleged 'Jewishness'.) This usefully blurred the argument that Finkielkraut was making: that there is a clear distinction between protest and sedition. According to Finkielkraut, the rioters were burning schools and institutions of the state 'not because they had been thwarted by an uncaring society' but because they had declared war on the state. This, he says, is the true voice of the rioters and it must be listened to as the real preliminary to any political response. Most importantly, he says, they do not see themselves as victims but rather as agents of history. This is why they describe themselves as 'soldiers'.[6]

Writing any history of France is to enter an arena of conflict and confrontation. The French have very fixed ideas of what historiography is or should be and are extremely wary of an Anglo-Saxon challenging or subverting these ideas. A history of France and its Arab colonies by a non-French writer is, following this logic, doubly contentious.

One of the key arguments put forward in this book is that the abrupt and sudden break-up of the nineteenth-century European empires following the Second World War will have a defining effect on the twenty-first century. Until now most historians have focused on the Second World War as the key event of the past hundred years. The number of books on Hitler, Churchill and Stalin that appear on the bestseller lists each year testifies to the lingering fascination with the political and cultural schisms of this period. Similarly, the Cold War – which historians now sometimes refer to as the Third World War – is considered the significant conflict of the post-war period.

This book, in contrast, is a tour around some of the most important and dangerous front lines of what many historians now call the 'Fourth World War', from the *banlieues* of France to Algeria, Tunisia and Morocco, and back again to the *banlieues* and the prisons of France. This war is not just a conflict between Islam and the West or the rich North and the globalized South, but a conflict between two very different experiences of the world – the colonizers and the colonized. It is necessarily a war of shifting frontiers, elusive enemies and ever-changing tactics, because of the ambiguous complicity that defines this relationship under the colonial order. The process of decolonization is dangerous because it is fraught with these ambiguities and psychological conflicts. This is nowhere better demonstrated than in Algeria, which is still experiencing the endless trauma of a nation in mourning for the loss of its parent figure.

The recent histories of Morocco and Tunisia have been defined by fear of Algeria and the French. Both countries gained their independence in the late 1950s, and although Tunisians and Moroccans sympathized with their Muslim brothers and their struggle, they were worried that the Algerian conflict would spill over into their territory. They were also terrified that, should this happen, the French would be provoked into the kind of massive military action that was taking place in Algeria. (Although the conflict was known at the time as the 'secret war', the rumours of torture and massacre by the French were common currency in Tunis and Rabat.)

The same fears have lingered on through the 1990s to the

present day. During the years of the Second Algerian Civil war, Algerian borders were closed and the only traffic was smuggling contraband or people. In 2007 al-Qaeda du Maghreb established its North African base in Algeria, declaring that Tunisia and Morocco were 'infidel states'. Meanwhile, France has retaken its position as the dominant economic power in all three countries.

The tension in this region has barely eased since 1957, when the French built La Ligne Morice (the Morice Line, named after Defence Minister André Morice) – a fence which ran for hundreds of kilometres from the Tunisian border with Algeria down to the Sahara and the Moroccan border. This was an incredible if sinister feat of military engineering which was matched only by the Maginot Line, the doomed wall which the French built along the German border in the run-up to the Second World War. The Morice Line was electrified and along its length it was strewn with the pathetic corpses of sheep, dogs, goats, donkeys and shepherds.

Despite its enormous expense and the hundreds of French troops who manned its checkpoints, the Morice Line simply did not work. Algerian rebels quickly learned how to use wire-cutters and it was in any case an impossible task to police the Sahara. The barrier only succeeding in making Algerians feel as if they were living in a massive concentration camp, while their fellow Muslims were prevented from helping them. The same emotions are alive today in Ramallah and Gaza, and it is these feelings of imprisonment and exclusion that flare up in the French *banlieues*.

The specific aim of this book, then, is to examine the major role that French colonial wars in North Africa have played in the worldwide process of decolonization. Torture, collective killings and ethnic cleansing were all deployed by the French in North Africa as weapons of war. On the Muslim side, insurgency, terrorism and assassination were legitimized as tools against the European oppressor. From this point of view, this book becomes the new story of an old nation whose identity as the world capital of liberty, equality and fraternity is at every step challenged and confronted by antagonisms with its cultural opposite – the secular Republic against the politics of its dispossessed colonial subjects.

From this dual perspective, my argument will be that France was not – as most French historians like to think – the sole agent of history during its colonial period, but that the countries of the Maghreb also had a direct influence on the twists and turns of French history. And that this process, largely ignored by contemporary French intellectuals, still continues in the *banlieues*.

However much the French media or intellectuals try to reduce the problem to familiar domestic issues, the fact is that France itself is still under attack from the angry and dispossessed heirs to the French colonial project. As long as this misunderstanding persists, the 'long war' will endure: '*Na'al abouk la France.*'

Andrew Hussey, Paris, 2013

Part One

STATE OF DENIAL

1

Murder in the Suburbs

A few short months after I had watched the riots at the Gare du Nord in 2007, on a cold evening in late November, I left my flat in southern Paris, took the metro to Saint-Denis, a suburb to the north of the city, and then a bus to an outlying council estate, or *cité*, called Villiers-le-Bel. The journey took little more than an hour but marked a sharp transition between two worlds: the calm centre of the city and the troubled *banlieue*.

'*Banlieue*' is often mistranslated into English as 'suburb', but this conveys nothing of the fear and contempt that many middle-class French people invest in the word. In fact it first became widely used in the late nineteenth and early twentieth centuries to describe the areas outside Paris where city-dwellers came and settled and built houses with gardens on the English model.

One of the paradoxes of life in the *banlieue* is that it was originally about hope and human dignity. To understand the *banlieue* you should think of central Paris as an oval-shaped haven or fortress, ringed by motorways – the *boulevards périphériques* (or *le périph*) – that mark the frontier between the city and the suburbs or *banlieue*. To live in the centre of Paris (commonly described as *intra-muros*, within the city walls, in language unchanged from the medieval period) is to be privileged: even if you are not particularly well off, you still have access to all the pleasures and amenities of a great metropolis. By contrast, the *banlieue* lies 'out there', on the other side of *le périph*. The area is *extra-muros* – outside the city walls. Transport systems here are limited and confusing. Maps make no sense. No one goes there unless he or she has to. It's not uncommon for contemporary Parisians to talk about *la banlieue* in terms that make it seem as unknowable and terrifying as the forests that surrounded Paris in the Middle Ages.

The *banlieues* are made up of a population of more than a million immigrants, mostly but not exclusively from North and sub-Saharan Africa. As the population of central Paris has fallen in the early twenty-first century so the population of the *banlieues* is growing so fast that it will soon outnumber the two million or so inhabitants of central Paris. The *banlieue* is the very opposite of the bucolic *sub*-urban fantasy of the English imagination: for most French people these days it means a threat, a very urban form of decay, a place of racial tensions and of deadly if not random violence.

The day before I set off for Villiers-le-Bel, two teenagers of Arab origin had been killed at La Tolinette, one of the toughest parts of this tough neighbourhood, after their moped crashed into a police checkpoint. They had been on their way to do some rough motocross in an outlying field. No one in the area believed that this was an accident but rather a *bavure* – the kind of police cock-up that regularly ends with an innocent person dying or being injured. Within an hour gangs of youths pulled up their hoods, covered their faces with scarves and went on to the streets to hurl petrol bombs and stones at the police. A McDonald's and a library were burned down. Streetlights were smashed or taken out so that the only light came from the flames of burning cars. The mayor of Villiers-le-Bel, Didier Vaillant, had tried to negotiate with the gangs but retreated under a hail of stones. A car dealership was set alight. By daybreak as many as seventy policemen had been injured. President Sarkozy, in Beijing, was alerted to the fact that a small but significant part of French territory was beyond control.

By the time I arrived in the *banlieue* the next day, the scene was set for another confrontation. 'See, they treat us like fucking *bougnoules*,' said Ikram, a young man of Moroccan origin who lived nearby, pointing at the police lines that were blocking access to certain areas. *Bougnoule* is a racist French term for Arabs that is as offensive as 'nigger' and dates back to the Algerian War of Independence, 1954–1962, when the French military used torture and terror against Algerian insurgents. The term *bavure*, meaning a police fuck-up, also comes from the same period. (The most infamous *bavure* was the so-called Battle of Paris, in October 1961, when a skirmish on the Pont de Neuilly between demonstrating Algerians and police led to a riot that ended with more than a hundred North Africans dead. Their bodies were thrown into the Seine by the police, under the orders of the Prefect of Police Maurice Papon, whose special brigades were known as 'les BAVs'. Papon had previously been involved in the deportation of Jews during the German occupation of the early 1940s but was not prosecuted for his crimes until the 1990s.)

At around 5 p.m. it was getting dark and the mood and atmosphere changed in Villiers-le-Bel. Drinkers in the café where I was sitting began smoking harder. Civilians – that is to say, non-rioters – were hurriedly leaving the scene and then, quite without warning, the area was occupied entirely by the police and their opponents. I watched as the gangs moved in predatory packs around the road, the car parks and the shops. I had heard on many occasions their stated aim of shooting a policeman. The rumour was that this time the gangs were armed, with cheap hunting rifles and air pistols. But the only weapons I saw belonged to the police.

Later, on returning to my flat and watching the surprisingly dispassionate television coverage of what was going on in the *banlieue*, I reflected that Paris had become hardened to levels of violence that, in any other major European capital, would have threatened the survival of the government. The French were used to violence, to mini-riots and clashes between police and disaffected youth. Even in my own neighbourhood, the quiet district of Pernety, armed police regularly sealed off parts of the *cité* adjacent to the RER railway lines (the RER is the fast commuter train that connects the *banlieues* with the centre of Paris). Across the city, there were regular battles with police at the Gare du Nord, where an unnamed Algerian had recently been shot during another police *bavure* in the metro.

Outsiders

In the winter of 2007/8 I set out to learn more. I started by visiting the area around Bagneux, to the south of Paris. This is far from being the worst part of the *banlieues*: Courneuve and Sarcelles to the north are much more run-down and dangerous. These districts were portrayed in the 1995 film *La Haine*, in which a black, an Arab and a Jew, all from the *banlieues*, form an alliance against society. I found the film unconvincing, because I suspect that a Jew could never be friends with blacks and Arabs in this way. Also, although I know plenty of Jews in Paris, I don't know a single Jew who lives in the *banlieues*, even though at one time the Jewish community flourished in the suburbs – there are still synagogues in Bagnolet and Montreuil which date from the 1930s.

Much more realistic, to my mind, were the intrigue and shocking violence of Michael Haneke's film *Caché* (2005). This is a story of murderous revenge in which a middle-class French intellectual is disturbed by memories from a deeply repressed and violent past. His fears are related both to his mistreatment of an Algerian child adopted by his parents and to his complicity as a Frenchman in crimes committed by the French state against

Algerians. *Caché* is set in the southern suburbs of Paris, not too far from Bagneux, the centre of which is much like any small French town. There is a church, a small market, cafés and green spaces. The architecture is not uniformly 1960s brutalism: there are cobbled streets and small, cottage-like houses.

The original meaning of *banlieue* dates back to the eleventh century, when the term *bannileuga* was used to denote an area beyond the legal jurisdiction of the city, where the poor lived. In the late fifteenth century, the poet and bandit François Villon described how Parisians feared and despised the *coquillards*, the army deserters and thieves who lived on the wrong side of the city wall. As Paris grew larger during the eighteenth and nineteenth centuries, the original crumbling walls of the Old City, which marked the city limits, became known as *les fortifs* or *la zone*. This was marginal territory, with its own folklore and customs, a world of vagabonds, rag-pickers, drunks and whores. It was also the fertile ground that later produced street singers such as Fréhel and Edith Piaf, who dreamed and sang of *le Grand Paris* or *Paname* (slang for Paris), of the rich city centre only a few kilometres away from where they lived but which was as distant and alien as America.

In the 1920s and 1930s, as France began to industrialize rapidly, the population of the *banlieues* swelled with immigrants, mainly from Italy and Spain. The *banlieues rouges* (red suburbs), usually led by a Communist council, were key driving forces in the Front Populaire (the Popular Front), the working-class movement that swept to power in May 1936. This was the first truly left-wing government in France since the days of the Commune of 1871 (when a rag-bag of anarchists and workers' groups held the city between March and May), and its success changed France for ever, with the introduction of paid holidays, a working week of forty hours and the sense that, for the first time, the workers were in control. During the *trente glorieuses*, the period of rapid economic growth that occurred between the

1950s and 1970s, other major towns across France adopted the Parisian model of building estates far outside the centre. The first developments of the new *banlieues* were sources of pride to the Parisian, Lyonnais and Marseillais working class, who were often grateful to be evacuated there from their slums in the city centre. Once, long ago, the *banlieue* was the future.

I remarked on this to Kevin, a rangy black lad of twenty who, with his mate Ludovic (roughly the same age), was showing photographer Nick Danziger and me around Bagneux. 'I can't imagine this as anyone's future,' Kevin said, gesturing at the car parks and boarded-up shops. 'All anybody wants to do here is to escape.'

Both of them were obsessed with football, especially with the English Premier League. They were impressed that I had met and interviewed the French footballers Lilian Thuram, who is black, and Zinédine Zidane, who is from an Algerian family. Kevin himself was a footballer of average ability; he had a trial with Northampton Town in England. 'I hate France sometimes,' he told me. 'And, at other times, I just stop thinking about it. But the real thing is that here, when you are born into an area and you are black or Arab, then you will never leave that area. Except maybe through football, and even that is shit in France.'

I asked him about his English name. 'I like England. And, like everyone here, I don't feel French, so why should I pretend?' Ludovic, who has a more conventionally Gallic name but is originally from Mauritius, joined in: 'They don't like us in Paris, so we don't have to pretend to be like them.' By 'them' he means white French natives – *Gaulois* (Gauls) or *fils de Clovis* (Sons of Clovis – one of the first kings of France) in the language of the *banlieue*.

It is this Anglophilia, transmitted via the universal tongues of rap music and football, which explains why so many kids in the *banlieues* are called Steeve, Marky, Jenyfer, Britney or even Kevin. They don't always get the spelling right, but the sentiment is straightforward: *we are not like other French people; we refuse to be like them.* As we walked and talked we soon entered a dark labyrinth of grey, crumbling concrete. This was 'Darfour City', a series of rectangular blocks of mostly boarded-up flats where the local drug dealers gathered. The police call it a *quartier orange*, largely a no-go area for the police themselves as well as for ordinary citizens.

DARFOUR CITY was scrawled across a door at the entrance to a block of flats. As we wandered deeper into the estate, there was more graffiti, in fractured English: FUCK DA POLICE; MIGHTY GHETTO. Halfway down the street we were hailed by a pack of lads, all black except for one white. They were all smoking spliffs. These were the local dealers, a gang of mates who, according to Kevin, could get you anything you wanted. They delighted in selling dope and coke at wildly inflated prices to wealthy Parisians. They were pleased to hear that I was English. 'We hate the French press,' said Charles, who is thin and tall and of Congolese origin. 'They just think we're animals.' They then looked at me with suspicion. 'No one comes here who isn't afraid of us,' said another, Majid. 'That's how it should be. That's how we want it.' The gang tired of me and my questions and I understood it was time to go.

Modern Warfare
In January 2006 a mobile-phone salesman named Ilan Halimi, aged twenty-three, was kidnapped in central Paris and driven out here to Darfour City. Halimi, who was Jewish, had been invited out for a drink by a young Iranian woman named Yalda, whom he had met while selling phones. It turned out that it was her mission to trap him and lure him away from safety. Yalda later described how Ilan had been seized by thugs in balaclavas and bundled into a car: 'He screamed for two minutes with a high-pitched voice like a girl.'[1]

Three weeks later, Ilan was found naked and tied to a tree

near the RER station of Sainte-Geneviève-des-Bois. He died on the way to hospital. His body had been mutilated and burned. Since being kidnapped, he had been imprisoned in a flat in Bagneux, starved and tortured. Residents of the block had heard his screams and the laughter of those torturing him, but had done nothing. Fifteen youths from the Bagneux district were arrested. They were members of a gang called the Barbarians, a loose coalition of hard cases, dealers and their girls, who shared a hatred of 'rich Jews'. The alleged leader of the Barbarians, Youssef Fofana, went on the run to the Ivory Coast. He was later arrested and extradited and is now serving a life sentence in Clairvaux prison in the east of France. In the spring of 2012 he defied the French authorities by smuggling out from his cell videos in which he praises al-Qaeda and describes his capture as a 'symbolic trophy for the Zionists of New York'. During his trial he described how he had dowsed Ilan in petrol and set fire to him with a cigarette lighter. He said he was 'proud' of what he had done.

Theories about the motives for the crime were initially confused. Was it a bungled kidnap? A *Clockwork Orange*-style act of pure sadism? Or was it the work of hate-fuelled anti-Semitism? The police were, at first, reluctant to admit this possibility. But Yalda, who turned out to be a member of the Barbarians, said in her testimony that the gang had specifically told her to entrap Jews. Her confession was widely reported, as was the fact that she called Fofana 'Osama', in homage to Bin Laden.

At the same time, out in the *banlieues* themselves, the murder took on a skewed new meaning: the word was that what had begun as a heist and kidnap to extort a ransom from 'rich Jews' had become a form of revenge for crimes in Iraq and, in particular, for events at Abu Ghraib prison. Bizarrely, in the view of some, this transformed the torturers into martyrs – soldiers in the 'long war' against the white Western powers. The kids of Bagneux accordingly gloried in their own 'intifada'.

They openly identified with the Palestinians, whom they saw as prisoners in their own land, like the dispossessed of the *banlieues*.

One afternoon back in central Paris, I visited the rue des Rosiers, the Jewish quarter at the heart of the Marais. This is like a little Tel Aviv, a place where French-Israeli waitresses, dressed in combat fatigues, serve up beer and schawarma. It was from here, during the occupation, that French Jews began the final journey to the death camps of eastern Europe or, closer at hand, to the Vél d'Hiv, the sports stadium to the south of Paris where, rounded up the French police and the German authorities, thousands died because of squalid conditions (there was no food and little sanitation: diarrhoea and dysentery arrived swiftly; death was not far behind). The cries of the dying in the stadium, like those of Ilan, were ignored by their Parisian neighbours.

In a coffee shop near the rue des Rosiers, a place owned by Moroccan Jews, I spoke to Myriam Bérrebi, herself a Tunisian Jew, about the killing of Ilan. 'I have never known such terror and anger in this neighbourhood,' she said, 'not since the shootings at Jo Goldenberg's Deli.'

She was referring to the massacre by Arab gunmen in 1982 of six diners at Goldenberg's, just across the street from where we were sitting. 'But, you know,' she continued, 'there were other echoes too – especially of the Nazi period, when Jews died and everybody pretended everything was all right.'

After the murder of Ilan, to the anger of many Parisian Jews, the Chirac government dissembled about 'social problems' in the *banlieues*. Only Nicolas Sarkozy, then an ambitious Minister of the Interior, whose mother was a Sephardic Jew, denounced the murder of Ilan as 'an anti-Semitic crime'. With Sarkozy's intervention the terms of the debate were changed. Was the killing of Ilan the isolated act of individuals, or was it a political murder in the largest sense: an act that expressed a collective hatred? Did it belong to individuals, or the whole community?

Despite the murders and the riots, good work is going on in
the *banlieues*. I was discussing this with Hervé Mbuenguen as
we sat in his flat in Vache Noire, in what is meant to be a less
impoverished neighbourhood of Bagneux. 'Good stuff happens
in bad places,' I said. 'That is a very quaint idea,' he replied.
'Nowadays the *banlieue* only means one thing: trouble.'

Hervé's family is originally from Cameroon but he has lived
in the *banlieues* all his life. He is educated and articulate, a
graduate of the Ecole Normale Supérieure, and makes a living
as a computer engineer. 'If you live here, if you speak with a
banlieusard accent, you are condemned as an outsider in Paris
and in fact in all French cities. It is a double exile – you are
already an outsider because you are black or Arab. But then you
are an outsider because you are a *banlieusard.*'

Yet he has chosen to live here. 'The *banlieue* is my home. I
cannot feel comfortable anywhere else.' Hervé's block of flats
was rotten; the walls of the lift-shaft were falling apart on the
inside. But his apartment was tidy and organized. This was a
place where a full, hard-working life was being lived. His flat
is the headquarters of Grioo, a website devoted to the African
diaspora in France (*grioo* is a mild corruption of the West African
term *griot*, meaning 'storyteller'). The success of the website is
a testament to the positive side of the *banlieues*. The only taboo
subject between us was that of the Jews. I had asked, innocently,
why there were so few, if any, Jews left.

'They cannot live here,' Hervé said.

Hervé is not an anti-Semite but his remark reflected a
shameful reality about the prevalence of anti-Semitism in the
suburbs, a reality that makes even open-minded people like him
feel awkward.

During several weeks exploring Bagneux, I chatted to hip-
hop kids, footballers, football fans and self-proclaimed *casseurs*
(wreckers, or rioters). I met and talked to them in cafés, at bus
stops, in shops and sports centres. It was mostly entertaining

and enlightening; there is a lot of serious laughter and benign mischief in the *banlieues*. But the more time I spent there, the more I began to pick up on the casual references to synagogues, Israelis and Jews, like a secret code being revealed. These references would be refracted through the slang of the *banlieues*. So phrases such as *sale juif, sale yid, sale feuj, youpin, youtre* (this latter term dates from the 1940s and so, with its echoes of the Nazi deportations, contains a special poison), all racist epithets, were widely used. I heard all about the crimes of the Jews, yet it was hard to find anyone who had met a Jewish person. 'We don't need to meet Jews,' I was told by Grégory, a would-be rapper and Muslim from La Chapelle. 'We know what they're like.'

But that was the problem: nobody did actually know what 'they' were like. It seemed to me that hating Jews – like supporting Arsenal or listening to the rap band NTM – had become a defining motif of identity in the *banlieues*.

Hatred of the Jews: this is one of the oldest traditions in Paris, dating back, like the very notion of the *banlieue*, to the medieval period. In *Portrait of an Anti-Semite*, written in the wake of the German occupation of Paris, Jean-Paul Sartre was searching for an explanation for his compatriots' complicity in the crimes against the Jews. From a specifically French perspective, he describes the typical French anti-Semite as driven by his own sense of 'inauthenticity'[2] – a sense of existential and psychological unreality which at once challenges and undermines the anti-Semite's identity as a middle-class Frenchman. Unconvinced of his own true place in society, he none the less finds comfort in the reality of his Jew-hatred.

Anti-Semitism in France is a phenomenon of the political Left as well as of the Right, of the underclass as well as of the ruling élites. This in part explains, if it does not justify, the writings of Louis-Ferdinand Céline, the great chronicler of Parisian working-class life in the twentieth century. Céline hated Sartre.

In response to Sartre's accusation that he had been paid by the Nazis to write anti-Jewish propaganda, Céline retorted with fury that he did not need to be paid to feel hatred for Jews: his hatred was authentic enough. Rather, it was his identity as a petit bourgeois, a member of a class forged in the late nineteenth century and already sinking into history, that felt unreal.

Céline describes the *banlieues* to the north of city as a kind of inferno. Rancy, the imagined suburb of his 1932 novel *Journey to the End of the Night*, is as dank and polluted as the Wigan described by George Orwell in *The Road to Wigan Pier*. But Céline's *banlieue* is infected by a particular kind of metaphysical misery: 'The sky in Rancy is a smoky soup that bathes the plain all the way down to Levallois. Cast off buildings bogged down in black muck. From a distance, big ones and little ones look like the fat stakes that rise out of the filthy beach at the seaside. And inside it's us!'[3]

Céline was a pessimist, obsessed by disease and filth. He saw no hope for the poor of the *banlieues*. In the end, he blamed nearly everything on the Jews. 'War in the name of the bourgeoisie was shitty enough,' he wrote in one of his pamphlets, 'but now war for the Jews! . . . half negroid, half Asiatic, mongrel pastiches of the human race whose only aim is to destroy France!' In recent years, Céline has become an inspiration for rappers in the *banlieue*, who admire his use of stylized slang and street language. The rapper Abd al Malik has devoted a song on his latest album to Céline. 'Céline revolutionized literature because he was very close to real people, like us rappers today,' he said in an interview on his blog. 'That's generally a good thing, but there's a danger about being so close to the people; you can start to embrace all the things that are wrong with society.'[4]

Today the literary heir to Céline as the chronicler of the Parisian underclass is novelist Michel Houellebecq. His vision of the *banlieue* is of a failed utopia, a district that has now reverted to wilderness. Houellebecq gives voice to this view in the novel *Platform* as the businessman Jean-Yves Espitalier muses on the rape of a female colleague by Arab and black youths on a 'dangerous railway line' between Paris and the *banlieues*. 'As he was stepping out of his office, Jean-Yves looked out over the chaotic landscape of houses, shopping centres, tower blocks and motorway interchanges. Far away, on the horizon, a layer of pollution lent the sunset strange tints of mauve and green. "It's strange," he said, "here we are inside the company like well fed beasts of burden. And outside are the predators, the savage world."'[5]

Extremists

One afternoon I visited Jean-Claude Tchicaya, a black official in the *mairie*, the local town hall. I had read an interview with him in which he had spoken of knowing the murderers of Ilan Halimi. Tchicaya was dressed in a smart suit with a black leather gilet draped over his back. In his office, amid old copies of *Jeune-Afrique* and *Libération*, there were portraits of Martin Luther King and Nelson Mandela. Wasn't it a contradiction to admire these 'heroes of peace' when the reality of the struggle for racial equality had also involved so much death and conflict?

'Struggle doesn't just mean violence,' Tchicaya said. 'It also means dignity.' I asked him how he knew the murderers of Halimi. 'This is not my milieu,' he said, 'but everyone in Bagneux knows everyone.'

Then I asked him if he knew the Tribu Ka, a group of black militants, resident in Bagneux, who openly declared that they hated Jews and had issued messages in support of the Barbarians who had killed Ilan Halimi. 'Look,' Tchicaya said, 'all extreme situations create extremists. It's the pattern of history. But I don't want to know about those people.'

Out on the street, the Tribu Ka is in fact a hard-core political movement of black supremacists led by Kémi Séba, whose real name is Stellio Capo Robert Chichi. He was born in Strasbourg in 1981 into a first-generation immigrant family from Benin. Kémi was a clever, restless, angry young man who, at the age of eighteen, began his apprenticeship in radical politics with Nation of Islam's Parisian chapter, based in Belleville, the traditionally working-class district in the north-east of the city. Founded by Elijah Muhammad in the 1930s and now led by Louis Farrakhan, Nation of Islam has only a tangential relationship with 'authentic' Islam. It preaches that the black races are descendants of the Tribe of Shabazz, the lost tribe of Asia.

Nation of Islam gave Kémi a cause and philosophy, but he was determined to lead his own political group. He travelled to Egypt in his twenties, and there he began to construct his own world view, a mix of Islam, black power and revolutionary politics. Kémites are the chosen race of God, or Allah, and will lead the black race out of slavery to their rightful position as masters of the world. The non-violent methods of Martin Luther King (a betrayer of the black race, according to Kémi) and Gandhi (an enemy of Muslims and agent of the British crown) are denounced as ineffectual.

Even when Kémi was imprisoned for five months, in 2007, for inciting racial hatred, he placed his faith in Allah and called himself a martyr. During his most recent prison sentence, in the jail of Bois d'Arcy, to the west of Versailles, until his release in late 2012, Kémi's blog was regularly updated on his website and his supporters spoke of his being *embastillé* (locked up in the Bastille).

The Tribu Ka are regarded as the real masters of the Bagneux. 'Those guys are mad fuckers,' I was told by Kevin, my guide through the *banlieues*. And they are having a discernible impact on France: if you are hassled by tough black kids in the Les Halles shopping centre in central Paris, they will often be wearing the Tribu Ka's colours of black, red and yellow, or the insignia GKS (Génération Kémi Séba). This is less than a kilometre away from the rue des Rosiers where, in May 2006, the Tribu Ka marched, chanting anti-Semitic slogans, and launched 'a declaration of war against Jews', while attacking anyone in their path with baseball bats. Two months later, they launched a raid to 'take back African treasures' from the new museum of colonial history at Quai Branly.

Tribu Ka are now banned, but Génération Kémi Séba is effectively the Tribu Ka, reinvented and well organized, but with a new media-friendly profile; on their website rappers such as ragga star Princess Erika and Orosko Racim of Ghetto Fabulous Gang profess their support. Another of Kémi's defenders is the mainstream black comedian Dieudonné, who was once as mild and inoffensive, and as popular, as the black British comic Lenny Henry. Now, Dieudonné is widely known for his virulent anti-Semitism.

Kémi's website continues to publish his speeches on the end of the white and Jewish races. He still lives in Paris and remains an accomplished public speaker and a master of double-talk. His interviews and speeches on YouTube are models of chilling self-righteousness, and he is seldom seen without two menacing guards at his side. Kémi has a variety of modes of dress, ranging from Afrocentric gear to suits in the style of Afro-American intellectuals of the Black Panther generation. For several weeks I tried to arrange a meeting with him. I was told by an intermediary that 'Kémi will speak soon. But he doesn't want to speak to the white press you represent. His time will come later. This will be when the white press is no more.' I was then told that they knew who I was and it might be wise to leave them alone. Or stay out of Bagneux.

'I understand Kémi,' I was told by a friend, a young black woman. She has a degree, a good job in publishing and a white boyfriend, who is a lawyer. 'Only if you are black or Arab in France can you understand the contempt people feel for you, and the hate and desire for revenge that this inspires in you. Kémi is nasty but I understand his appeal. He is about war and violence. What angry young man in the *banlieues* doesn't feel the same at some point? It's the same for the Taliban as for the youth in the *banlieues*: they are fighting to let us know that they exist and that they hate society as it is. They feel that the Jews rule the world, and from one point of view it can look that way. They see Iraq and Gaza and Rwanda and Kenya and the Jews of Paris or New York who have profited from their pain. To them, it all makes sense.'

2

The Secrets of Lyons

For ordinary French people as well as the authorities, one of the most terrifying aspects of the riots of 2005 was that they were not confined to Paris. In the last days of October, violence spread through the Ile-de-France region, stretching police resources to their limit. On 3 November, trouble was reported in fifteen towns and cities across France. These included not only major centres such as Lyons, Marseilles, Strasbourg, Toulouse and Lille, but also small and medium-sized places such as Dijon, Roubaix, Arras, Rennes, Tourcoing, Belfort, Cambrai, Amiens and Saint-Etienne. Conflict between the *banlieues* and the police was not new to these places but it had never occurred with such concerted ferocity and all at the same time. By 9 November, 119 cities, town and villages had reported serious violence.

What really scared everyone was that the police and government were totally wrong-footed by the sheer scale of what was happening. There seemed to be no pattern, no connecting point between these geographically and culturally separate locations. It was if some hidden force had suddenly unleashed itself on the nation, with no warning signs. In truth, however, the signs had been there for all to see for several decades; it was rather that no one wanted to acknowledge them.

There had, for example, been long-established divisions

between France and its new immigrant population from its former colonies. Traditionally France prides itself on its cultural diversity – travelling from north to south or from east to west across the country, you always encounter a variety of dialects, cuisines and cultural practices. For this reason the non-Parisian French usually define themselves as the product of their *terroir* – the word which means the unique combination language, land and climate that gives such a distinctive and individual flavour to regional identity in France. A French person is therefore always an Auvergnat, a Breton, a Marseillais or a Bordelais before being 'French'.

Since the sixteenth century the expression '*de souche*' has been used to describe this authentic identity of a French person, the direct product of the *terroir*.[1] (A *souche* is the part of a tree-trunk which is most stubbornly rooted to the land.) In recent years the term has been used particularly in right-wing circles to distinguish 'truly French' citizens from newcomers.

The riots of 2005 stood in direct contradiction to this long-standing cultural narrative. The rioters did not care about their geographical location any more than they cared about 'France' or being French. They just wanted to fight. Their enemy was France in all its official and unofficial forms, including the *souchards* – a word which soon became a term of abuse in the *banlieues*, and had been used during the first riots fought in France in 1981. Intriguingly, these had taken place not in Paris but in Lyons. This had a deep impact on the nation's psyche. Trouble could always be expected in Paris, which many non-Parisians consider barely a French city at all, but a cosmopolitan mix heaving with anti-French dissidents.

The question was asked then and now: why Lyons? In a few short weeks during the summer of 1981, the *banlieues* of Lyons were turned into a battleground where the police were obliged to fight with paramilitary tactics and weapons on French soil. There had been trouble in Lyons before, but this was the first time that fighting had been on such an intense scale and gained nationwide media coverage. The French public was stunned.

What was so special, so weird, about this city?

Deep, Dark France

For most foreign visitors to France these days, Lyons is known as little more than the gateway to the South of France – famous for its gastronomy, middle-class good-living, some Roman ruins and not much more. A short afternoon stroll from the handsome Place Bellecour down to the newly gentrified Old Town, via the swish restaurants of the rue Mercière, does little to contradict this perception and is enough to convince the casual visitor that this is definitely one of Europe's more civilized backwaters.

Lyons is France's second city but has a difficult relationship with the capital. Historically it has always looked to the south and east, to Provence, Italy and Switzerland, as a focus for trade. It has accordingly represented itself as a kind of anti–Paris – the first major town of the south. Most importantly, Lyons sets up itself as the capital of *La France profonde* (Deep France) – this is the 'real' France of rural or bourgeois provincial virtues, the France of *le terroir* and *de souche* regional identities – the very opposite of cosmopolitan and untrustworthy Paris.

The Lyonnais are also proud of their reputation for discretion to the point of furtiveness. This is seen as a virtue at odds with the showing-off associated with Paris and the Parisians. Oddly for a second city in a major European country, Lyons does not sell itself much to the outside world – unlike, say, Barcelona, Birmingham or Munich, it does not attract much tourism or actively seek it out. Arguably, Marseilles, Nice or Bordeaux are much better known to the world outside France than this inward-looking and insular place. One of the secrets of Lyons is that it is one of the most 'Algerian' cities in France, as a result of a massive influx of Algerians feeling Algeria in the 1960s.

Somewhat bizarrely, Lyons also has a long-standing reputation for occult activity, including necromancy and Satanism. In 1993, this made the cover story of the news journal *Le Point*, which called it '*Lyon, Capitale de L'Etrange*' ('Lyons, Capital of the Strange')[2] and painted a portrait of the quiet provincial capital as a secretive and sometimes sinister place. Figures associated with the city include Nostradamus and, in the nineteenth century, the spiritualist Allan Kardec and the mystic Maître Philippe. J. K. Huysmans set his novel *Là-Bas* (*Down There*, or *The Damned*) partly in Lyons, basing his Satanic priest Dr Johannes on a real figure, l'Abbé Boullan – a priest from Lyons notorious for his 'holy sodomy' and rumours of child murder. On its publication in 1891, the book was banned from sale in railway stations across France.

In fact, so many occultists, alchemists and prophets were attracted to Lyons for the purely rational reason that it had some of the finest and most sophisticated printing equipment during the late Renaissance and early Enlightenment. Later, in the nineteenth century, its working classes refused to accept the 'machine-civilization' of rationalism which was then sweeping across France and transforming the cities into huge factories. As artisans who had highly specialized skills, the silk weavers known as 'les Canuts' preferred secret, local forms of knowledge to the spreading cult of reason. This deep link between industrial practices and occultist beliefs led the historian Jules Michelet to describe Lyons as the most '*mystique et matérieliste*' city in France.[3] Unsurprisingly, Freemasonry flourished in Lyons, as the perfect hidden form of resistance to the iron laws of technology and progress. Although Catholics were forbidden by the Church to be Freemasons, the various Lodges based in Lyons had no problem in admitting Catholics, who in fact made up most of their population. It was also significant that Lyons has always been home to some of the most fanatical and mystical strains of Catholicism, which allows the Lyonnais to cultivate an image of themselves as superior to

Parisians, representing the deep, holy heart of France and its true religious capital.

The city's proletariat has also always been angry and Romantic. This was the first city in Europe where the black flag of anarchy was hoisted against a government. The Russian anarchist Mikhail Bakunin came to Lyons in 1868 to lead the workers' uprising. With his comrades, he proclaimed a revolutionary commune in what is now Place des Terreaux, setting off insurrections down the Rhône valley to Provence.

This is where the shiny new opera house now stands. The dark, thin streets which run alongside it are emblematic of the sharp social and racial divisions in Lyons. During the Second World War, members of the Resistance used these alleys and passageways (known locally as 'traboules') to dodge the Nazi forces. This was the historical background to the trial of the Gestapo commander Klaus Barbie, which convulsed Lyons in 1986. Barbie was notorious as the so-called 'Butcher of Lyons', who sent over 14,000 people to their deaths in the Hôtel Terminus in Lyons. He had also used new techniques of torture, including electroshocks and sexually abusing prisoners with dogs. His defence, conducted by the maverick lawyer Jacques Vergès, was that this was no more nor less than what the French did during the Vichy régime and the colonial régime in Algeria. The Lyonnais who accused Barbie were now suddenly the accused. They backed off and many of the charges against him were dropped. This was one of the rare times that Lyons made the international stage; its reputation was not enhanced.

Nowadays the police rarely enter the area around Place des Terreaux, which, by night and by day, has mostly become a drugs supermarket. The heart of Lyons is, however, still relatively calm compared to the districts of Vaulx-en-Velin and Vénissieux, the outlying *banlieues* where the riots took place in the 'hot summer' of 1981.

'Brixton en France!'

Throughout that summer, cars were regularly set alight by immigrant youths who declared war on the police and called this kind of entertainment 'rodeos'. The epicentre of the violence was the *cité* (housing estate) in Vénissieux called les Minguettes, which had been hastily thrown up from 1965 and designated a *Zone à urbaniser à priorité* (ZUP – a Priority Zone for Urbanization) in order to provide cheap housing for the anticipated influx of immigrants, mainly from North Africa and the former French colonies.

The word *cité* can be misleading. It originally meant a fortified encampment and eventually a real city, in the sense of an urban centre, hence the *Ile de la Cité*, the island in the Seine which was the original centre of Paris. In the late twentieth century the word *cité* was applied to the new building developments which were grafted on to the outskirts of French towns and cities. These developments are the equivalent of English council estates or American housing projects; the point is that they are disconnected from the real life of the city and their inhabitants feel that they live marginal lives, entirely separate from the rest of society.

All of France was perturbed by the nightly confrontations between the youth of les Minguettes and the police during the summer of 1981. Most French people had never visited such places, nor indeed were they aware that they existed, and what they found most surprising and disturbing was that these events started only a few months after François Mitterrand had been elected, in a surge of enthusiasm for the first truly Socialist president of the post-war period. At this point, the whole of left-wing France was in a state of exaltation. It seemed as if the generation of May 68, which had fought so hard against the paternalist constraints of 'Old France', would finally make good its promises of freedom for all.

All of this was called into question by the events in Lyons. One of the most immediate challenges faced by the government and the authorities was that no one knew how to explain the disturbances or what to call them. There had already been a long trail of violence in this part of Lyons, and in other similarly deprived parts of France, throughout the 1970s. These disturbances were largely attributed to the so-called 'second generation' of immigrants, the children of those who had come to France from North Africa in the 1960s. They were often referred to as '*génération Beur*' – *Beur* was backwards slang for the word *arabe* and was used in immigrant communities and beyond with a positive value.

This generation of Arab youth was both angry and optimistic. They were angry about what they perceived as a racist society bent on excluding them from the mainstream, but they also accepted the essential correctness of French left-wing values. These young people were largely uncontaminated by radical Islam. They believed in the right to speak their own languages and have their own cultural practices. They also believed in the right to smoke dope, drink alcohol, chase girls of all ethnic extractions, and form rock bands. In other words, tradition and modernity could be friends on the same terms.

This was, for example, the experience of Rachid Taha, who was born in Algeria, moved to Lyons and is now one of the most respected and loudest Arab voices in French culture. In the 1980s Taha was a fan of traditional Arab music, French pop music and British punk rock. Taha founded a club scene in Lyons, which was then briefly touted as the new 'capital of French rock'. He had a band called Carte de Séjour (named after the document immigrants needed to stay in France) which brought these influences together. In 1983 the group took part in the 'Marche des Beurs', the great left-wing march from Marseilles to Paris which brought thousands of young North Africans together to protest against racism and police violence.

But although the *Beurs* could proudly identify themselves in this way – on the model of young Black Americans – the authorities did not want to recognize this identity. Or worse still, they did not want to acknowledge the fact that it was also *Beurs* who were fighting the police in les Minguettes. During the first really serious wave of trouble in 1981, when over 200 cars were burned, the first point of reference was the riots which had torn across Liverpool, Brixton and other fault lines in the UK that same year. On 17 April 1981, a week after the worst rioting in London, *Le Monde* published a full-page open letter protesting at the French government's immigration policy. It ran under the menacing rubric, *'Brixton en France?'*[4]

But for all the cross-cultural traffic via music and pop culture, there were massive political and cultural differences between the revolts in England and France. For one thing, the uprising in Brixton had been unmistakably a race riot, an upsurge of anger from the mainly West Indian community at heavy-handed and racist policing methods. The riots in Liverpool were a much more multiracial affair. They were sparked off in the black community around Granby Street in Toxteth but soon involved the black and white youth of Liverpool, usually a very racially divided city.

I was there and can remember travelling on the bus into town with other pale white lads, pouring in from the council estates of Speke and Netherley, all of them buzzing to pile in against the police and do some robbing. Most importantly, the riots in Brixton and Toxteth (and other parts of England) were explicitly political: a wave of hatred against the government of Margaret Thatcher. Fittingly, the soundtrack to that summer of trouble was the Specials' 'Ghost Town', a gloomy slow ska tune which perfectly caught the atmosphere of simmering rage.

This was not at all the same mood that I found when I went to France later that summer. This was my first extended trip to the country and somehow I ended up working at a leftist commune just outside Lyons, alongside political refugees, mainly from Chile and South-East Asia. The whole enterprise was basking in the afterglow of Mitterrand's recent victory. In the evening we watched 'instructive' films by Costa-Gavras or Godard. (It was in this vaguely euphoric atmosphere that I celebrated my A Level results with a recently acquired Vietnamese girlfriend and a crate of East German lager.)

Everybody knew what had been happening in les Minguettes and that the violence was serious. But no one really understood it. It was entirely separate from the mood in the rest of the country. One afternoon I caught a bus out to les Minguettes and found myself in a reasonably functioning suburb of high-rise flats. Everything was modern and clean, a long way from the jagged and broken slums of Liverpool or the grimy streets of Brixton. I noted that nearly everyone was of North African origin; but at the time, naïvely, I equated this with a kind of 'Frenchness'.

The mainstream French press described the rioters as 'delinquents' but used rather quaint, outdated words such as *voyous* or *loubards* (hooligans, ruffians). It was as if there was no language to express what was happening. The right-wing press, however, was unafraid to use openly racist language and pointed the finger at 'Arabs who are going to steal our cars and violate our daughters' (*Le Quotidien de Paris*).

In 1984 France was shocked by even more violent disturbances across Vénissieux, which led to the week-long occupation of the area by more than 4,000 armed police officers. People who lived in or near the area talked of a 'new French civil war'. At this stage, François Mitterrand himself turned up on a surprise visit to les Minguettes, declaring grandly that something had to be done.

The rioters couldn't have cared less. By now they had no interest in either revolution or reform. They were simply angry and wanted to cause as much damage as possible. They certainly did not align themselves with the leftists who came their way pouring sympathy and support. 'It's only afterwards that leftists and intellectuals turned up to try and explain to the guys the true meaning, as they said, of the rodeos. For us it was bullshit and anyway we didn't get it,' commented Farid, one of the first rioters. 'They weren't the ones in deep shit ... Some of them even got slapped in the face. You have to understand we were fed up with everybody.'[5]

Negationists

To anybody who knew Lyons from the inside, the 1980s riots in les Minguettes could hardly have come as a surprise. The tension had been building for years, ever since the first wave of immigrants from North Africa in the 1960s were housed in *bidonvilles* (shanty towns) outside the city. These were makeshift villages, with huts built out of cardboard and corrugated iron, and little sanitation or electricity. Some of these *bidonvilles* still existed in the 1970s, as central Lyons grew ever more prosperous. During this period tens of thousands of North Africans were cut out of the life of the city. There were some immigrant enclaves in the centre, around the area of La Guillotière and down towards the rue de Marseille, but mainly Lyons remained as solidly white and right-wing as it had ever been.

In keeping with its eccentric nature, Lyons has always had a very strange political culture and has never had a mainstream political identity. Although today's mayor is the relatively benign figure of Gérard Collomb – a Parti Socialiste deputy – the spectre of far-right politics has never been far away. A classic example was Collomb's predecessor, Raymond Barre – an arrogant neo-Gaullist who openly flirted with hard-core right-wingers and allegedly made anti-Semitic remarks in public.

Supporters of Barre still make the feeble defence that he was a lightning rod for the most popular and populist views of the far right. Without him, the argument runs, Lyons would have long been established as a fiefdom of the Front National. This much is probably true, even if Barre's remarks and views are inexcusable. Throughout the late 1990s, the Front National was steadily advancing towards a substantial majority in Lyons at local and national elections, and had targeted the city as its strategic capital, away from 'cosmopolitan' Paris.

Lyons' links to the far right in French politics, however, run much deeper than the Front National. Most notoriously, throughout the 1980s and 1990s, the Université Jean Moulin (known as Lyon 3) – named after the Resistance hero captured by Klaus Barbie in Lyons, and intended as the city's flagship of republican values – was rocked by a series of scandals.

The first of these came at the height of the Barbie trial, when it was revealed that the university was also the home of some of France's most powerful and influential *négationnistes* (Holocaust deniers), who were deeply embedded in both the faculty and the student body. By 1984 I was studying Lettres Modernes at Lyon 3. It was there that I began to understand the true nastiness of the city's right-wing culture. I had started my studies in the French Department of Manchester University and was a reasonably typical product of the *NME*-reading, Smiths-fan leftist culture of the day. Lyon 3 was like a trip through the looking glass; here it was the norm to be ultra right wing, even to the point of expressing open contempt for blacks, Arabs and Jews, who were hardly visible in the student body. I was stunned.

This ugly strain of Lyonnais culture could be traced back to the late 1970s, when Robert Faurisson, Lyon 3's Professor of Literary Theory, had declared the Holocaust a 'myth' and a 'hoax'. In his wake came a trail of even more sinister fanatics and nutters, writing theses to disprove the gas chambers or to defend Hitler. By the 1990s, Lyons and its university were known as the 'world capital of negationism' and a national disgrace. This was like having David Irving and his acolytes in charge of Manchester University.

The scandals came to a head in 2001 when the Minister for Education, Jack Lang, commissioned an official inquiry into

Lyon 3, led by Henri Rousso, the respected veteran historian of Vichy. Rousso's report, published in 2004, was political dynamite.[6] Among other things, it revealed that Bruno Gollnisch, who had been Jean-Marie Le Pen's number two in the Front National since 2005, a leading figure in the European Parliament, and Professor of Japanese, was at the centre of the 'negationist cancer' at the university. Gollnisch's public response to the Rousso report was to denounce the inquiry as a politically motivated fraud.

In January 2007, partly as a punishment for this statement, Gollnisch was fined 55,000 euros and given a three-month prison sentence under the 1990 Loi Gayssot, which makes Holocaust denial a crime in France. Gollnisch was also suspended from the university. On his return to the campus, Jewish and left-wing groups tried to bar his way to a classroom; fighting then broke out on campus between Front National thugs, Gollnisch's minders, police, university security staff and left-wingers. Incidentally, in the wake of these events Gollnisch was described as a 'good servant of Lyons' by the mayor, Raymond Barre.

Despite the trials and the suspensions, the politics of Lyons continue to be a mess. The most recent political drama to engulf the city has been the sacking of Alain Morvan, the rector of Lyons' Academy (the equivalent of the local Department of Education), who opposed the building of Islamic schools and mosques. Morvan, it is said, was being rooted out by Nicolas Sarkozy's government as an attack on the right-wing caucus that rules the city. This has been a cause for mild celebration in Paris and much grumbling in Lyons.

But the real danger of the right-wing underground culture in Lyons is that it stands in such sharp contrast to the multiracial composition of its population. It is likely to be the dominant factor in the political life of the city for several generations to come. For this reason, despite the recent claims of urban renewal, the Arab youth of Lyons still see themselves at war with the state, their anger and frustration exacerbated by the sense that they are not being listened to. Even deeper is the feeling that they don't matter, that they don't properly exist. They feel annihilated – 'We are less than nothing to the Lyonnais,' I was told by a male teenager in les Minguettes. 'That's why we always need to fight back.'

Bad Feelings

Thirty-odd years on from my first trip, I returned to Vaulx-en-Velin in 2012. Although the transport system is much improved since the 1980s, to get there still takes the best part of an hour on the bus from the centre of Lyons.

The racial divisions between central Lyons and the *cités* are most marked at the bus stop near to La Part-Dieu, the main railway station. The bus-goers are almost all North African or black. There are housewives and some moustachioed old guys in flat caps. But the travellers are mainly young, boys and girls in a variety of hip-hop gear – a culture that was in its infancy thirty years ago. They come to hang out in the huge shopping mall, now one of the largest in Europe. Thirty years ago, this place barely existed, at least not on this scale.

The municipal authorities in Lyons are immensely proud of La Part-Dieu, which has connections to Turin and Geneva, the Alps and the South of France. It is a hideous place, all the more so because it is so at odds with the noble architecture of central Lyons. You also suspect that it serves a more sinister purpose. Like the Gare du Nord in Paris, it is a frontier zone between the suburbs and the 'civilized' centre of town. Some of the young people I spoke to later in les Minguettes told me that they sometimes went into central Lyons, but that there was no real point other than to pick a fight occasionally with *les souchards*. Otherwise, central Lyons was boring. It was enough for the young *banlieusards* to hang out in the shopping mall of La Part-Dieu, which, with its McDonald's,

Nike and Apple stores, was as near to America as they would ever get.

After fifty minutes of steadily climbing out of Lyons, there is still not much to suggest urban warfare when the bus arrives in Vaulx-en-Velin. Even on a bleak, rainy afternoon in December, there is little visible poverty – the streets are in good order and quite clean. Opposite the main square is a new police station, which looms larger than it probably should and is obviously busy. But most people are friendly and well-dressed and going about their business. This is nothing like the poverty I have seen outside Europe and in the most frightening parts of American cities.

None the less this is a strange and disturbed place. The bad feeling starts fifteen minutes into the journey as the bus moves away from the nineteenth-century buildings which define all French cities, and in some ways constitute the core of French urban identity. Quite quickly, you are surrounded by high-rise buildings, often spread out in irregular patterns and interspersed with small parks and walkways. When they were originally designed, these estates were conceived in a spirit of utopian optimism. They were built during or shortly after the *trente glorieuses*, the 'thirty glorious years' after the Second World War when France moved forward, away from its past – which had led to the disaster of 1940 – into a new world of consumerist capitalism. These buildings were the incarnation of this modernity – they represented a new way of living where nobody need be unhappy ever again.

The architects and engineers who built these places, and even the politicians who commissioned them, were mostly acting in good faith. Nobody deliberately intended to make blueprints for misery and exclusion. But that is what happened. The big problem for the French authorities now is that these blueprints have been rolled out across France.

In all French towns and cities with a significant immigrant population, there has been a singular failure of vision and imagination around the issue of the *banlieues*. The problem is both simple and complex. It is simple in that the people who live there are angry and unhappy. It is complex in the sense that these people do not necessarily live in tangible, material poverty but rather in a kind of spiritual poverty. This is because they do not belong here. No one does. This is the secret truth of the *banlieues* of Lyons and its replicas across France.

Vaulx-en-Velin, like nearly all French *banlieues*, has the queasy artificiality of a science-fiction set. This is unsurprising, given that it was designed and built when the French embraced a particular version of modernism which looked to the space race, Soviet as well as American, as a model for design. Vaulx-en-Velin feels weird, out of date and unreal; a stage-set from a forgotten 1960s B-movie.

At a bus stop next to le Mas du Taureau, one of the most notorious *cités*, I commented to a group of young North Africans that, for all its bad reputation, this place didn't look too bad to me. 'This place can make you sick,' Rashid replies. 'But it's hard to say why. It just feels bad. It's got a bad atmosphere.' These lads had been involved in trouble, most recently in 2010, when a pack of several thousand from the *banlieues* invaded the centre of Lyons for a riot. 'It was supposed to be a demonstration, but really it was just a big fight,' they told me. 'And that's why it was good.'

All of their families have lived here for several generations and none of them wants to leave. They described to me the strictly structured society, with its 'caïds' (chiefs) and '*grands frères*' (big brothers), who ensured security and order. This was not anarchy but its opposite.

They were all united, however, in their hatred of Lyons. 'I don't feel safe there,' one said, and the others agreed. Lyons is not really ever a dangerous place. But it is emotionally intense, claustrophobic even – the heart of all that is most Catholic, most French, in the most extreme sense. It is clear why it would make these boys, all of them tough and no strangers to a fight, uneasy. Better to stay safe, stay on the outside, where you belong.

This is the real problem of these *banlieues*: thirty years on from the first riots here, this place still doesn't feel like Lyons. Mostly, it doesn't even feel like France.

3

A Soldier for God

It is hard to describe exactly what happens when a whole country goes into shock. On Monday 19 March 2012, the most visible signs of trauma in Paris were armed soldiers in shopping malls and railway stations, bomb alerts on the metro and, despite the sunny weather, far fewer customers than usual at the *café terrasses*. More telling still was the subdued atmosphere everywhere in the city. Certainly by the time of the evening rush hour there was a distinct sense that everybody wanted to get home to safety and watch the evening news on television.

The reason for all of this was news of the murder of a thirty-year-old man and three small children at a Jewish school just outside Toulouse. That morning, as Rabbi Jonathan Sandler was dropping off his two boys, aged five and three, at the Ozar HaTorah school at about 8 a.m., all three were shot dead by an armed man on a Yamaha TMax scooter. Other teachers and pupils thought at first that the noise of the shots was fireworks. But as they approached they saw a terrible scene unfold. The gunman had seized an eight year-old child, Miriam Monsonego, the eight-year-old daughter of the school's director. She was being pulled back by her hair. The gunman then blasted a bullet through her temple. This scene was captured by security cameras at the school. Understandably, very few people have seen this footage. For most of France, imagining the image – even just knowing that it existed – was more than enough.

At first there were theories about a rogue soldier or a neo-Nazi psychopath on the loose. These theories were given credence by the fact that the previous week two French soldiers of North African origin had been killed in the same region by someone using the same weapon and techniques. But then events took another turn for the worse. At 1 a.m. on Wednesday 21 March, an editor at the French news channel France 24, Ebba Kalondo, was just about to pack up for the night when she received a call from a phone box in Toulouse from somebody who claimed responsibility for the murders. She heard a young man, 'apparently in his twenties, very calm, who spoke impeccable French, placing a great weight on his words'.

He went on to give details of all the murders which only the killer could have known. He said that he was linked to al-Qaeda, and that his aim was to protest against the French law banning the veil and to take revenge on the French army for its presence in Afghanistan and on the Israelis for the killing of Palestinian children. He said he was proud of his actions; that he had bought his weapons in France and that he would 'go to prison with his head held high, or die with a smile on his face'. He declared that he 'wanted to bring France to its knees'.

Within two hours the French police had traced the caller – Mohamed Merah – to a flat in a building at 17 rue du Sergent-Vigné in Côte Pavée, a suburb twenty minutes from the centre of Toulouse. It turned out that Merah was not only the owner of the Yamaha scooter but was also heavily armed. After an initial attempt to break into the apartment building, special police units settled down for a siege. Over the next few hours Merah claimed to have filmed the killings at the Jewish school and given the tapes to his 'brothers' to distribute on the Internet. He said he would trigger assaults in Lyons, Marseilles and Paris.

On Thursday morning Merah again confronted the police as

they made another assault on the building. He was wearing a bulletproof vest and carrying a Colt 45 when he was shot dead with a bullet to the brain by a sniper.

It was only then that the full complexity of the story began to take shape. As *Le Monde* described it, from this point on, the murders were no longer '*un fait divers*' (a mere news story) but '*un fait politique*' (a political fact). This much had already been anticipated by President Nicolas Sarkozy, who had gone straight to Toulouse on Tuesday afternoon in his traditional role of 'protector' of the French nation. Other politicians (with the notable exception of Marine Le Pen, on the far right) publicly undertook not to make political capital out of the killings. But once Merah's identity was made known, neutrality became impossible.

Mohamed Merah was not simply an Islamist killer. He was also a French national with an Algerian background. The young Algerians of France have been targeted in recent times by Ayman al-Zawahiri, now leader of al-Qaeda. He has declared that France is ready for radicalization, or, as he puts it, 'awakening'. Indeed, Zawahiri (who speaks French) reserves a special hatred for France, which he blames for a series of criminal acts in the Middle East, from Napoleon's invasion of Egypt in 1798 to providing Israel with a nuclear reactor. Most important of all, in the French context, Zawahiri has identified North Africa, and Algeria in particular, as ready for 'liberation' in the 'long war' against France.[1]

The day after the death of Mohamed Merah, I made my way to the Barbès district of Paris. This is a tiny, overcrowded space, largely Muslim and Algerian, which provides a neat lesson in French colonial history. I wanted to speak to people here and see for myself the emotional response to the events of a terrible week. As I stepped down off the iron staircase of the metro during Friday prayers, the area was its usual chaotic self. This part of Paris may have the highest concentration of Muslims in the city, but it is hardly noted for its piety. Instead, as you walk away from the station, you plunge into packs of Arab lads flogging *trabendo* – Algerian slang for contraband goods, mainly cigarettes but also wristwatches, dope and cheap alcohol. Young Arabs and Africans are slouching on benches, smoking weed, gossiping, leering at girls.

In a bar at the far end of the rue des Poissonniers, I ordered a drink and asked the barman what people round here thought of the events in Toulouse on Thursday. '*Parle pas français*,' he said. But then a large black guy, a Muslim from Senegal, said to me, 'He can speak French, he just doesn't want to.' He then went on – his name was Malik – to say that people here were as shocked as anyone in France.

Further down the road, outside the mosque in the rue Myrha, I chatted to a few lads in hip-hop gear, slightly younger than Merah. They identified themselves as Algerians and Muslims and seemed ready to talk. So, what did they think of the killings in Toulouse? They laughed, partly embarrassed and partly out of bravado. Then one of them began to speak. 'That guy was bad,' he told me. 'He didn't give a fuck. But so what?'

Did that justify what happened? 'Who knows?' he said. 'Who knows anything? Maybe everything was a set-up to provoke the Muslims . . . We're Muslims. We hear stuff. France is our enemy.' So why live here? 'France is easy. No one is hungry. In Algeria you could starve to death. And that's because of the French.' Did they admire Merah? 'Fuck knows. He was just a guy who wanted to fight the enemy. He wanted to be a soldier.'

Later, I spoke to an elderly Jewish businessman in the next street. He would not give me his name but told me that he had been in Barbès for over thirty years, one of the few surviving Jewish businesses in the area. His family was from Fez in Morocco and he spoke fluent Arabic. 'Most of my customers are Muslims and we have a good relationship,' he said, 'and some people have told me that they thought it was bad what happened in Toulouse. But I know it is a façade – that collectively they feel differently about Jews and Palestine. The worst time I have known is during the last intifada [starting in 2000] when they boycotted all Jews in Paris. But now I think this is worse. On the surface, everything is the same today. But I cannot forget the image of a bullet in the brain of a child. That guy, that Muslim, he was just like a Nazi. He was a Nazi.'

The day before the killings in Toulouse was the fiftieth anniversary of the end of the Algerian war, perhaps the most important moment in the post-war history of France. In truth, half a century on, there is little to celebrate on either side. More than one observer has noted that Merah's murderous actions all seem to have been determined by an internal logic related to collective memories of the Algerian war – constructed almost like a bizarre memorial, or anti-memorial, to the past. For example, Merah's murder of North African soldiers in the French army echoed the slaughter of the *harkis* fifty years ago. *Harkis* were Algerians who had fought on the French side during the Algerian War of Independence. It is also a contemporary word and very much alive in the *banlieues* these days – there is no greater insult.

The killing of Jews in France also has deep historical resonances. Pogroms in France date back to the eleventh century. Jews have always divided the nation, from the Dreyfus affair to guilt over French complicity in the Holocaust. To be French and to be a Jew is a double crime in the mind of an Islamist such as Merah. More to the point, in colonial Algeria, Jews enjoyed special favoured status under the same French law that excluded Muslims from citizenship. For this reason, Algerian Muslims saw Jews as traitors who had taken the country by stealth.

Even Merah's method of execution – tearing around a city on a scooter with a gun – seemed to pay homage to the tactics of the Algerian Nationalist death squads at the height of the so-called

Battle of Algiers in the 1950s. But beyond the symbolism, there is a wider strategic meaning to Merah's actions. It does not matter very much whether he was or was not an al-Qaeda operative or, as has been alleged, close to the radical Salafist Forsane Alizza (Knights of Pride), a Toulouse-based group that was banned by the hard-line Minister of the Interior, Claude Guéant, in January 2012. With his actions, Merah had taken to the next level the al-Qaeda strategy of moving operations away from Pakistan and on to a new front, deeper into North Africa and France.

This shift in al-Qaeda thinking had been developed partly to take advantage of the anticipated political chaos in the wake of the Arab Spring, and partly because – as Zawahiri argued – this was the moment to take revenge. It is no accident that Zawahiri's threats were followed by a resurgence in activities of al-Qaeda au Maghreb Islamique, or AQMI (al-Qaeda in the Islamic Maghreb), the North African wing of the movement which has its base in Algeria and Mali. The French security forces fear that AQMI will soon begin to operate on French soil.

In the days after the killing, Mohamed Merah was described in the French press and by politicians as a '*un loser*', a narcissist, a lone wolf, a one-off. Everybody knew that this was not true. Indeed, what no one wanted to say out loud is that although he may have been a loser, he was far from being alone.

A week or so on from the horror of Toulouse, the sense of shock in France had given way to an all-too-familiar nightmare – the memory of Algeria.

French politics almost returned to normal, but there was also an understanding that many of the critical issues on all sides had been derailed: Sarkozy was forced to debate security with the Front National leader, Marine Le Pen, when really he wanted to talk about the economy; the leader of the Parti Socialiste, François Hollande, and others on the left were barricaded into an uncomfortable silence, unwilling to speak on behalf of the *banlieue* and unable to blame the government for this latest act of terror.

In the meantime, Merah's elder brother Abdelkader was taken into custody in Fresnes prison, just south of Paris, where he said that he was 'very proud' of Mohamed and was proclaimed by some of his fellow prisoners as a hero. In Algeria, the father of Mohamed Merah called for his son to be buried there. He also publicly declared that 'France killed' his son, that his death 'must be avenged' and that 'France will pay'.[2]

The Call of Duty

The journey that led Mohamed Merah to commit mass murder followed a pattern that was by now very familiar to experts in counter-terrorism and security. He was brought up in a poor part of Toulouse by a single mother, in an atmosphere of racism and hatred towards France and French people. The family had its origins in Algeria and was frequently visited by relatives from the home country, who brought with them fresh anger towards France, fuelled by the conflict in Algeria in the 1990s and the rise of radical Islam there.

Merah himself displayed little interest in Islam as a youngster but had a reputation for a quick temper and violence. He first served a prison sentence at the age of nineteen for robbery, but had been known to the police since his mid-teens for driving offences, bag-snatching and other acts of delinquency. In 2010 the French intelligence services began to track his visits to Pakistan and Afghanistan, trying to work out whether he had any links to the Forsane Alizza group.

In 2008 Merah tried to hang himself in prison. The subsequent psychiatric report described him as a 'narcissist', not just because of his slicked-back hair and fastidious attention to his appearance, but because there was a deeper disturbance of his sense of self: this was a classic profile of the delinquent or criminal whose identity is threatened with annihilation and seeks to remake a new identity for himself in a disordered world. By now Merah had already been radicalized by the Islamists he had met in prison. Turning himself into a 'jihadi superhero' was only a short step away.

One of Merah's brothers, Abdelghani, has published a book in France called *Mon Frère, ce terroriste*, in which, for obvious reasons, he disowns Merah and distances himself from his actions. He also paints a portrait of a wildly dysfunctional family – their mother, Zoulika, has no control over her sons; their father, a drug dealer, is almost totally absent, either in prison or away in Algeria.

As a child Merah was a fan of horror movies – he was particularly keen on a film from the 1980s called *Monstre de lande* (entitled *Rawhead Rex* in English), in which a demon escapes from his underground lair to terrorize the Irish countryside. As a teenager Merah was addicted to the video game *Call of Duty*, whose selling point is that 'there is a soldier in us all'. He also enjoyed clubbing, girls and cars.

None of this makes a killer or a terrorist; indeed it might well be said that such interests are all part of the standard twenty-first-century leisure portfolio of young people in Europe. The toxicity in Merah's background came from his family links to radical Islam, the extremism encountered in prison and then during his trips to Afghanistan and Pakistan, which his family covered up as visits home to Algeria. He later went to Cairo, developed contacts in Syria, and all of a sudden felt himself to be important, to be needed: he was a soldier for Islam.

Alongside this journey was a catalogue of hurt and betrayal. In 2008, the same year that he had tried to kill himself, he was turned down by the French army. He tried again to join the French Foreign Legion in 2010 but he left the training centre before he could be properly evaluated. He clearly needed to fight for one side or the other – video games could never be enough to fulfil this desire. At this point it's easy to see how a young man like Merah finds comfort in a friendly Salafist, who says he knows what it is to be betrayed, and who has the answer to all society's problems. The 'return' to Islam is also a return to the 'authentic self' that has been wiped out by colonialism and the degraded state of Western society.

In the days and weeks before the first murder, Merah prepared with military precision. In Geneva, he bought the GoPro video camera which he would use to film the killings. He emptied his bank accounts to buy weapons and a scooter. He left and abandoned his wife, a young Algerian from Toulouse whom he had married only months before, in December 2011. He talked constantly of martyrdom and death. He told his mother that she would soon be proud of him. He had already elevated himself above this world.

According to Abdelghani Merah, Mohamed had entered this 'operational phase' as a soldier for Allah in early 2011, on his return from Afghanistan, probably on the orders of senior figures he had met there. Abdelghani noted that Mohamed talked with more venom than usual about the Jews and the French, and how they would meet justice. He didn't get angry anymore, but spoke with an icy sense of certainty. He planned criminal activities – more robberies – but he now justified them with religious ideology: he invoked the principle of *ghanima*, the 'spoils of war', allowed by the Koran as the booty that could be taken from the conquered infidels. This was the pure logic of holy war.

As noted above, the immediate reaction in the French government and media after the killings was to disassociate Merah from anti-Semitism and Islam. The issues were immigration, unemployment, psychiatric problems. But this was not how Merah's death was celebrated in Toulouse or indeed in Algeria. At his wake in Toulouse, Abdelghani reported in his book, Merah's mother was told by neighbours and friends that she should be weeping with pride and joy and not with grief. There are dark rumours, believed by senior police officers, that Merah did not act alone; worse still, that, as with the killing of Ilan Halimi, many people in his *quartier* knew what was happening at the height of the terror, but simply did not dare to speak.

In the aftermath of the funeral, Merah's father further fuelled public anger in France by declaring that his son was murdered by the French state. He found two female lawyers to take on the case: an Algerian called Zahia Mokhtari, who was alleged to have close links with terrorist groups in Algeria, and a Frenchwoman, Isabelle Coutant-Peyre, who was the wife of the Venezuelan terrorist Carlos the Jackal and who had defended Youssef Fofana, the leader of the Barbarians; at his trial she had smilingly admitted to the court that he was 'proud' to have tortured Ilan Halimi. The lawyers wanted to argue that Merah should be buried on Algerian soil, and sought to defend him as the victim of a conspiracy organized by the French security forces. There was no court case, but this version of events has now, inevitably, taken on its own momentum in Islamist circles.

On the other side of the Mediterranean, Merah was hailed in some quarters as a saintly warrior. This was not, of course, the official reaction: the affair was a ghastly embarrassment for the Algerian government, which was slowly and carefully trying to rebuild political and business relationships with France after the carnage of the 1990s. The Algerians cited 'security reasons' for refusing the family's request that Merah should be buried in Medea, near Algiers. Their fears were well founded: Merah's name was now frequently invoked by Islamists in Algiers as a model soldier and martyr, and a funeral in Algiers would almost certainly have provoked violence between the Algerian security forces and radicals.

Many ordinary Algerians wanted to pass the affair off as an internal French matter and did not want to be contaminated by association. There was much loud anger in the press at the way the murders were linked to Merah's Algerian origins; for many, this was pure racism. There were also murmurings about the timing of the affair – so close to the French elections and a handy way of stirring anti-immigrant, anti-Islamic emotions in France.

But this none of this stopped Merah from becoming a hero in the radical mosques of Algeria. Leading the praise was Ali Belhadj, the fiery and charismatic preacher and leader of the Front Islamique du Salut (the Islamic Salvation Front, or FIS) in Algeria in the 1990s, who had led the war against the Algerian government. Belhadj blamed Sarkozy for not allowing Merah to be buried in Algeria, calling him a 'despicable man' and arguing that Merah was not a 'heretic' but should be buried in a Muslim cemetery. Prayers should be said for him.

In front of a medium-sized crowd in one of the mosques of the working-class district of Bab-el-Oued, another man (he said he was a lawyer with dual French and Algerian nationality) went one step further. He said that Merah was not wrong in what he done, invoking the 'scholarly principle': 'You kill our women, we kill your women. You kill our children, we kill your children.' Merah was in fact a 'lion' and Sarkozy was 'a pig, a Jew'. The man cursed the French people: 'May Allah freeze the blood in their veins!' He then went on to tear up his French passport to cries of 'Allahu Akbar'.

What is most astonishing about this scene (easily found on YouTube) is that these men are neither monsters nor madmen. Those who speak are fluent, articulate and coherent. Their audience is a perfectly respectful and restrained group of believers. The problem is that they believe something monstrous – that Mohamed Merah was justified by God to murder innocents.

This provides a grim counterpoint to much of the wishful thinking that went on in the West during the Arab Spring. The belief was that the Arab people would seize the historic moment and finally establish themselves in history on the side of freedom and democracy. The model was 1989, when the Berlin Wall came down and all the grand narratives of history,

of Left and Right, culminated in a global hegemony. The wars
of the 1990s in Bosnia and the wreckage of the Yugoslavian
state soon indicated that this was an illusion. More importantly,
the massacre of 9/11 in New York revealed this as a specifically
Western illusion.

Like the United States, France is a country built on an idea:
the universal values of the Rights of Man. The challenge which
is being made to the French Republic by the foot-soldiers in
the French intifada demonstrates that this is only one belief
system among many others alive in the twenty-first century. To
understand how this way of thinking really worked, I realized
some years ago that I needed to get nearer to the belief systems
which oppose the Republic, to get inside them.

On a bright autumn morning in 2009, I took a bus to the
airport of Roissy in northern Paris. And then warily, wired with
coffee and apprehension, I boarded a plane to Algeria.

Part Two

ALGERIA,
PRISONERS OF LOVE

4

The Walls of Algiers

Like most first-time visitors, most of what I thought I knew about Algeria had been learned in the cinema. This obviously included the 1937 French gangster classic *Pépé Le Moko*, but also its American remake of 1938, starring Charles Boyer and Hedy Lamarr, called simply *Algiers* – as if the name of the city were enough to conjure up the strange mysteries of the place. *Algiers* was also the model for the classic *Casablanca*, in which Humphrey Bogart incarnates the laconic, existential hero, trapped in an Oriental wilderness. I loved, too, Gillo Pontecorvo's *La Bataille d'Alger*, which told the story of the Algerian War of Independence as a gripping and heroic epic. More recently, the 2010 film *Hors-la-loi* (*Outside the Law*) set the stories of three Algerian brothers against the background of the war against the French from 1954 to 1962. It had a mixed reception – although it was thrilling and breathless, it was also firmly in the older French tradition which glamorized the country and its violent ways.

However, one of the best films set in Algeria in recent years is not about war, politics or terrorism; it is a sophisticated, bitter-sweet comedy called *Délice Paloma*, which stars the Algiers-born actress and singer Biyouna as an ageing prostitute who runs a variety of scams in the city. Witty, fast-paced and sexy, with a scabrous view of the Algiers underground scene, this film has more in common with the work of Pedro Almodóvar than with Gillo Pontecorvo's movie.

But although it is a comedy, *Délice Paloma* is laced with sadness. The most powerful scene is at the end, as Madame Aldjéria sits outside a seedy nightclub, swigging bottles of beer with a male friend, a pimp, both of them ruminating on life's disappointments. She recalls her time in prison, all the working girls she has met who had been kicked out of France, Spain, Italy, even Iran and Egypt. 'But Madame Aldjéria,' says her companion, 'do you know anywhere in the world that likes Algerians?'

'Of course not', she replies. 'It's like that song by Clo-Clo, "*Le mal aimé*" [the unloved] – we are always the *mal-aimés*'. This is a poignant and arresting moment of cross-cultural traffic. Of course, with their French cultural heritage, Algerians know of and identify with the schmaltzy French singer Clo-Clo (the nickname of 1970s *variété* singer Claude François). But the real point, as Madame Aldjéria confesses with a sigh, is that these days the French, and the wider world, seem to know little of Algeria, and care even less. The scene ends with the old whore throwing beer bottles at a passing taxi before staggering off into the night.

This seems an apt metaphor for the rage that Algerians often feel towards the world in general and France in particular. At the mid-point of the twentieth century, the Algerian War of Independence, fought by Algerian Nationalists against the occupying French authorities, held the attention of the world. It lasted nearly a decade and was the most vicious of all the wars of decolonization, with no quarter given on either side, and its outcome – it was argued at the time – would determine the rest of world history. It was a Frenchman, the economist Alfred Sauvy, who coined the term 'Third World' in 1952 to describe the countries that refused to align themselves, as they emerged from colonial government, with either side in the Cold War.[1]

Like the Third Estate during the French Revolution, they would claim their own place in the world. Throughout the 1960s, this *tiers-mondisme*, as it was called, became a safe haven for French intellectuals who felt stifled by the constraints of classical Marxism. Algeria, they believed, would lead the way.

But this is not what happened. The Algeria that emerged from the war and from French rule was poor and psychologically damaged. Instead of following a policy of Third World leadership, the country sought to heal itself with a 'return to its sources'. This meant the Arabization of culture, accompanied by a resurgence of Islam as the arbiter of the non-European values of the new Algeria. Western intellectuals slowly deserted Algeria as a cause and the country quietly slipped into the role of being a backwater in the Arab world and elsewhere.

History returned with a vengeance in 1992 when the army took control of the country in the wake of elections which had apparently been won by the Front Islamique du Salut. The FIS had vowed to lead Algeria into an Islamic revolution on the Iranian model; this was clearly unacceptable to Western governments and the oilmen in the south of the country, and to the stagnating but still toxic remnants of the government who had led Algeria to independence. When the results of the elections were effectively cancelled by the government, the hardmen of the FIS took to the mountains. Ordinary people blamed the French, once again, for stifling their voices, and the Second Algerian Civil War – this time between the Algerian government and dissident Islamists – began.

Nobody knows how many people died in the following decade, although sensible estimates are never much short of 200,000. Nobody knows how much of the violence was orchestrated by the government to terrify the population into giving them support. But a flavour of the viciousness of the violence is given not by the figures but by the details. These include, for example, a primary school teacher who was raped outside her humble classroom in a village outside Oran. She was then beheaded in front of her class, all of whom were under the age of ten, and her severed head was placed on the desk at the front of the class 'as a warning'. This is not warfare but psychosis.[2]

How to explain this? The supreme theoretician of the Algerian War of Independence is Frantz Fanon, a psychiatrist from Martinique who detested French colonialism and worked for the Algerian side until his death in 1961. According to Fanon, colonialism was a form of psychic violence which destroyed the identity of the colonized. As a response, Fanon advocated total rejection of European civilization, by which he meant the creation of a new culture, defined by force of arms if necessary. He called this the will to be a nigger.[3]

Fanon was right about the devastating psychological effects of colonialism, even if the means of resistance he advocated are arguably just as destructive. The origins of the Algerian trauma, however, are unusual in that there has been a long history of complicity and intimacy between France and Algeria. This is not the straightforward binary relationship between colonizer and colonized; the question of Algerian identity, for Muslim and non-Muslim, has always been fraught with double binds and contradictions.

These tensions are the defining feature of the work of Albert Camus, who is undoubtedly the most famous writer to have been born on Algerian soil and whose life and career were shaped by his experiences there. It is no accident that his greatest book, *L'Etranger*, a classic account of the alienated mind, is set in Algeria in the late 1930s, and that its central motif is the pointless shooting of an Arab by its icy narrator, Meursault. In one of the most chilling scenes, Meursault is thrown into a prison cell packed with Muslims. One of them asks him what he has done. 'I killed an Arab,' he says.

Camus' depiction of Algiers and Algeria was as strong an influence on my understanding of these places as the films I had watched. As I teenager I read *L'Etranger*, and then his memoirs and essays; like most readers who approach Algeria through the prism of Camus, I remember being puzzled by this place which, as he described it, was so French that it might have been in France, but was also so remote, foreign and out of reach.

To some extent this is because the Algeria Camus describes is only partly a Muslim country. He sees Algeria as an idealized pan-Mediterranean civilization. In his autobiographical writings on Algiers and on the Roman ruins at Tipasa, he describes a pagan place where classical values were still alive and visible in the harsh but beautiful sun-drenched landscape. This is the key to Camus' philosophy of the Absurd, which is often associated with the Existentialism of Jean-Paul Sartre, but is really a more nuanced evocation of older, sterner moral choices about life and death. In Camus' Algeria, God does not exist; life is an endless series of moral choices which must be taken by individuals on their own, with no metaphysical comfort or advice, and with little or no possibility of knowing they ever made the absolutely correct choice.

It is easy to see how Camus' philosophy appealed to the generation of French leftist intellectuals who fought in the Second World War, a period when Occupied France was shrouded in moral ambiguity as well as in the military grip of the Germans. Camus' philosophy was less effective, however, in the post-war period, as Algerian nationalism began to assert itself against France, modelling itself on the values of the French Resistance. Camus was sympathetic to the cause of Muslim rights. However, like most European *algériens* on the Left, Camus spoke no Arabic and had little patience with religion, including Islam. Most importantly, throughout the 1950s, as the violence between the French authorities and Algerian Nationalists intensified, Camus found himself endlessly compromised. His intentions were always noble, but by the time of his death in a car crash in 1960, he acknowledged that he no longer recognized the country of his birth.

During the 1990s it became all but impossible to visit Algeria. By then reading Camus as a way-in to this Algeria was simply a waste of time. This was a country dominated by terror. Algerian Muslims were regularly massacred by Islamist and other unknown forces. Foreigners were declared enemies by the Islamists and targeted for execution. The government could not be trusted either. The only non-Algerians who braved the country were hardened war reporters like Robert Fisk, who described hiding his face behind a newspaper when travelling by car in Algiers and staying no more than four minutes in a street or a shop – the minimum time, he reckoned, for kidnappers to spot a European. For Algerians and Europeans in Algiers in the mid-1990s – formerly the most cosmopolitan of cities, just an hour's flight or so away from the French mainland – kidnap and murder could be only a matter of minutes away.

By the time I arrived in Algiers in October 2009, the city I found was not like this. The ceasefire and amnesty had been in place for several years and you no longer had to hide your identity as a European. As recently as 2007, however, there had been a wave of deadly bombings and assassinations and the city was still tense. On the drive from the airport, I passed no fewer than six police or military checkpoints, all manned by heavily armed men. It was getting dark and Algiers was emptying for the night. During the long nightmare of the 1990s, nobody had dared to be out of doors after dark and the habit still remained.

As we drove against the rush-hour traffic towards my hotel in the centre, you could see that, like Marseilles, Naples, Barcelona or Beirut, this was one of the great Mediterranean cities. In the dusk I could still make out the pine forests of the surrounding

hills and the magnificent dark-blue sweep of the bay. Unlike any
of her sister cities, however, with maybe the exception of Gaza,
Algiers went into lockdown at the first shadows of evening.

Over the next few days I crawled all over the city, walking
the boulevards, climbing steep streets and staring out at the
sea from the heights. I spoke to everyone I could – teachers,
shopkeepers, students, journalists, political activists. They were
all remarkably frank and impatient to tell their stories to an
outsider. Their suffering during the years of Islamist terror had
been incalculable. An elegant university lecturer, a specialist in
Marxism and feminism, told me how she went to classes at the
university every day, driving past the headless corpses which were
regularly tied to the gates of the Institute. A journalist recalled
the vicious paranoia of everyday life in Algiers in the 1990s, and
how strangers, bearded young men, would hiss at him and make
a throat-slitting gesture as he walked down the street. A young
female student who had grown up in the so-called 'Triangle of
Death' – the villages and suburbs controlled by terrorists just
outside Algiers – recounted a childhood memory of washing
other people's blood off her feet, having waded through the
sodden streets of her village after a massacre.

Despite the horror stories, my exhilaration at first overcame
my fears. I had waited a long time to be here. Over the past
two decades I had worked and travelled extensively in the
sister countries of Morocco and Tunisia. All the time I had
been dreaming of visiting Algeria, seeing Algiers: the capital of
French North Africa.

Most of all, I wanted to see the Casbah, the old Ottoman city
which runs from the hills of Algiers down to the sea. I found
that the Casbah is a rotting slum. Its narrow, ancient streets stink
of sewage. There are gaping holes left by unfinished renovation
projects or where unloved houses have shattered and collapsed
from neglect. Many of the inhabitants mutter that the authorities
would like to see the complete destruction of the Casbah, which

they consider a haven for criminals and terrorists. There is talk, too, of property speculators who want to build hotels and shops on prime real estate. Still, this is one of the most iconic and historically significant spaces in North Africa.

Walking down through Algiers from the Casbah is an eerie experience. This is not because of the usual clichés about Arab or Ottoman cities – that they are 'timeless', or 'medieval'. These are meaningless European notions of chronology, urban order and modernity, which have been grafted on to the living reality of twenty-first-century Muslim life. Rather, the uncanny feeling you get during a first visit to Algiers is classically Freudian: the dream-like sense that, without knowing it, you have been here before. This is partly because of the myriad films, books and paintings that have made Algiers probably the most-known unvisited capital in the world. It is also because walking through Algiers is like walking through the wreckage of a recently abandoned civilization, whose citizens have just departed in a hurry, leaving behind their most personal possessions, which you immediately recognize.

As you go down to the packed streets leading towards Place des Martyrs, the ruins of the French city begin to reveal themselves. Past the Turkish-style mosque, where the city widens towards the sea, the arcades, passages and streets are constructed with the geometric precision to be found in any French town. The centre of gravity of the French city was here, between the rue d'Isly (now rue Ben-M'Hidi) and rue Michelet (now rue Didouche-Mourad).

The streets may now be named after heroes of the war against France, but Algiers feels as purely French here as Paris, Lyons or Bordeaux. This much is revealed in the details – the signs, the street-lamps, the carefully constructed squares, the blue-shuttered balconies, the old tram tracks and the cobbled paving stones. At the dead centre of the city, on the boulevard Khemisti, is the Jardin de l'Horloge, a compact garden terrace which looks out directly on to the harbour, and where the monument to the French dead who gave their lives for *l'Algérie française* has been covered up. I loved the fact that, as in Venice or down by the port in Marseilles, passing ships seem so near that you could walk on to them.

This is the cityscape which had been lodged deep in my cultural memory, from paintings, books and films. It is the place I already knew from *Pépé le Moko*. Now, I visited all the main sites in the film and found that, in one form or another, they were all still there.

The film begins when Pépé, a Parisian gangster played by Jean Gabin, on the run from the Parisian police, holes up in Algiers in the Casbah. Pépé falls in love with Gaby, a young Parisian tourist, who fills him with longing for the Paris he has abandoned. In the closing scene of the film, he risks capture by the police by leaving the Casbah and running down to the French city and the port, down to the ship where Gaby has embarked to return to France. He is arrested and led away. In a final gesture of love for Gaby (and the Paris she represents), he calls out to her, pushing against the steel gates that bar his way. She cannot hear him. In frustration, Pépé takes out a penknife and stabs himself in the heart. The scene closes with a shot of Pépé's corpse stretched on the gates that have kept him in Algeria and cut him off from the ship, which sets sail for France. The drama of this moment is heightened by the backdrop of the French city and the Casbah – two worlds locked for ever in mutual antagonism.

Were it not for this antagonism, Algiers would be called a '*lieu de mémoire*' (place of memory) by contemporary French historians who subscribe to a theory of history that deciphers historical meaning from geographical sites as well as books and archives. From this point of view, the landscape of France, from the châteaux of the Loire to the battlefields of the First World War, can be read by the historian as a complete text, a text which has been memorialized and made legible to the present.

The trauma of Algerian history cannot yet be classified in this way. As I entered the city for the first time, I noticed that the bay is dominated by the Monument aux Martyrs, a brutal concrete sculpture on one of the heights of Algiers. It is shaped – surely an accident? – like a huge gallows. It is meant to commemorate those Algerians who gave their lives for independence. In fact the ugliness of the Monument aux Martyrs is terrifying. But this is why it is such a suitable emblem for a city, and a country, haunted by past and present fears. Algiers today is a site of impossible mourning for both the French and the Algerians.

It is now over seventy years since Pépé killed himself at the harbour gates in the film. But in the twenty-first century, for the present generation of young Algerians who cannot get visas to leave the unemployment and poverty of a city that feels like an open prison, the sea remains impassable. As I stood by the harbour gates – they were now raw and fragile with rust – I reflected that it has been this way since the first battle between France and Algeria nearly two hundred years ago.

5

Conquest

In the thin, grey dawn of 14 June 1830, in the sheltered bay of Sidi-Ferruch, some twenty-five kilometres from Algiers, a handful of French soldiers climbed out of the small flotilla of landing boats which had brought them to the coast and began to wade ashore.

The sea was shallow, warm and still, and there was just enough light to make out the Torre Chica, a white fortified tower which had been used in previous raids by Spanish forces. Walking through the waves at waist-height, holding their guns above their heads, fearful of waking the inhabitants of the town, the small band of soldiers made silently for this tower; once captured, it would provide cover for the rest of the invading French army as it swarmed inland to take Algiers over the coming days. To their surprise, the troops found that the tower was not properly defended and it was secured without a fight. A white flag was hoisted and the signal to manoeuvre was sent back to the waiting French fleet, which had dropped anchor in the bay the day before. The regiments on ship and in the landing craft quickly exploded into action, charging through the water with their bayonets held aloft, crying '*Vive le roi!*' and competing to be the first infantrymen to step on to African soil. (This honour apparently went to a young Jewish officer from

Alsace called Max Cerfberr.) In a blaze of noise and smoke, the French invasion of Algeria had begun.

For these soldiers, the experience of coming ashore on a new and unknown continent must have been like landing on another planet. They had no idea what to expect of the natives, but they had prepared for violence. Instead, they found the town was all but deserted. A group of Bedouins was spotted fleeing the city wall, no doubt to report the French landing, but otherwise the atmosphere was distinctly strange.

A civilian eyewitness to the landing described the initial mood of the troops as 'humiliated' and the town as 'sinister and frightening', with some officers sensing a trap. Later in the day, there was some real fighting as a small force of defenders emerged from the bushes where they had been hiding in order to surprise the French. The French lost some fifty men in the firefight, but the Arabs were disorganized and there were too few of them to offer any convincing resistance. Those who were not killed immediately melted away into the countryside. This lifted the spirits of the troops and by nightfall they were exultant, exploring and plundering the town of Sidi-Ferruch in search of trophies.[1]

This army of 34,000 men was the largest fighting force assembled by the French since the Napoleonic Wars. It had been formed with the express ambition to enact the greatest, most historic event of modern times. The landing on the African beach was perfectly choreographed against a blaze of noise, colour and smoke from the ships in the harbour. Cannons thundered and Congreve rockets screamed and hissed overhead as the troops moved ashore in formation.

But although this was a brilliant spectacle, it was hardly a great victory. The Congreve rockets were a good example of how meaningless the operation was as a feat of arms. They were a military innovation that the French had borrowed from the British and were acclaimed as the cutting edge of military technology, with a range of 2,000 metres. But they made only small holes in the stone houses, and the town was mainly empty anyway, save for the sick, the very young and the old.

The so-called battle of Sidi-Ferruch had been carefully stage-managed a long time before by the authorities in distant Paris. French spies in Algeria (originally sent there by Napoleon) had chosen the spot for landing and had informed military planners in Paris that, as long as the expeditionary force was large, a victory was a foregone conclusion. Members of Parisian high society had sailed on pleasure ships from Marseilles to watch the bombardment, which had been planned as an extravagant *fête galante* – a fashionable form of amusement popular with the sophisticated French élite in the late eighteenth and early nineteenth centuries. It usually combined a theatrical display and an garden party and was at its most refined in the grounds of the Palace of Versailles, where dramatic lighting heightened the unreal and poetic atmosphere. The show on the beaches of Sidi-Ferruch had both a political and an aesthetic significance: it was a demonstration of technological might which would reveal to the world the overwhelming superiority of French civilization.[2]

Among the audience for this spectacle was a certain Captain Mansell from the British Navy, who had seen action in Algiers when the British bombarded the city in 1816.[3] He watched the battle wrapped in the cape of a French officer, and it was he who had advised the French that the bay of Sidi-Ferruch was not only a sheltered landing place but a natural theatre.

So, this is how the first invasion of an Arab country by a European power since the Crusades began: as an elegant entertainment and fireworks display. The Arab corpses that lay strewn in the streets and along the coast were no more than incidental colour to the Parisian spectators watching the slaughter through opera glasses from the deck of their cruise ships.

★

The rest of the invasion was not quite so straightforward. French infantry met resistance and really did have to fight as they moved towards Algiers. At Staouéli, halfway between Sidi-Ferruch and the city, the French encountered a force of 7,000 Ottoman troops sent from Constantine and Oran, led by Ibrahim Agha, renowned as one of the toughest commanders under the Dey's jurisdiction.

Until the French invasion, Algiers had been legendary throughout the Ottoman Empire for its distinguished history of resistance against European conquerors. This tradition dated back to a challenge made by the Spanish who, exultant at their successful expulsion of the Moors in 1492, sought to extend their victory across the Mediterranean, with Algiers as one of the prizes. The Muslims of Algiers called upon the Ottomans for help, which came in the form of two brothers, Aru and Khair ed-Din Barbarossa, from the island of Djerba off Tunisia. The Barbarossa brothers became notorious in European minds as 'pirates', but they fought off the Spanish and were astute political and military commanders who effectively fixed Algiers as the front line between Catholic Spain and the Ottoman Empire.

From 1529 the Dey of Algiers paid money to Constantinople for the sultan's protection against the Spanish. Along the coastline the sultan also encouraged the lucrative business of piracy, which enraged European governments and sometimes brought violent revenge raining down upon Algiers. The Ottomans were happy to tolerate this as long the money flowed eastwards.

Deeper inland, Ottoman troops controlled roads and passes throughout the territory of Algeria, which was divided into three regions: Constantine, Mascara and Titteri. The Ottomans struggled to maintain power over the tribes who inhabited these regions and developed traditions of privilege and patronage, playing one tribe off against one another to maintain a political balance. They particularly favoured the Sufi brotherhoods, which existed outside the tribal structures but held great sway over tribal leaders. These Sufi orders were devoted to the contemplation of the mystical life within Islam. As such they had great prestige and political power. The Ottomans cultivated fragile alliances with the Sufis, providing them with mosques and tombs in return for the enforcement of taxes. There was still, however, frequent armed conflict between the central authorities and the Sufis as well as the tribes. These conflicts grew in intensity as the Ottoman dominion over Algeria began to crumble in the nineteenth century.[4]

By the time of the French invasion of 1830, the government of Algiers was under severe threat from a wide-ranging revolt among the Sufi orders in all the regions of Algeria. The tactic of the Dey was not to take on the French at Sidi-Ferruch, which had been mined, but to ambush them further inland. But the Dey's troops were already disheartened by their unpaid salaries and lacked any real political loyalty to their leader.

They soon melted away when they came into contact with the French artillery and the grizzled infantry, many of whom were battle-hardened diehards from Napoleon's Great Army. The tactics of the Dey's army were naïve, relying on a heroic cavalry charge into French ranks, where they met bayonets, gunpowder and certain death. This much is shown in a famous painting by Jean-Baptiste-Prudent Carbillet, which depicts the Ottoman cavalry in bloody disarray among the disciplined ranks of French soldiers. This was not just mere propaganda but a military fact.

'Dancing on a Volcano'

France's pretext for launching this massive invasion was an insult delivered three years previously to the French consul, Pierre Deval, by the Dey of Algiers (or El-Djezair as the city was then known). The story went that the insolent Dey had swiped at the consul with a fly-whisk when he demanded excessive interest on a French loan made to the Regency of Algiers. In reality, the French had never had any intention of coming to terms with the Dey. The background to this incident was that by 1830 the French had established a highly profitable trading post at Bône, which they had fortified heavily. The Dey's income from privateering had been severely reduced by European naval power and he could not afford to let the French carry on trading. He declared that no French cannon could remain on Algerian soil and that the French could enjoy no commercial privileges. According to the British consul who was a witness to the final interview with the Dey, the French consul had provoked the Dey by saying things 'of a very gross and irritating nature'. The Dey reported to the Ottomans that the consul had insulted Islam and 'your majesty, the Protector of the World'. When the consul refused to pay an earlier debt to two Algerian Jews for the delivery of wheat to France, and the Dey lashed out.

The so-called 'fly-whisk attack' quickly became a *cause célèbre* in France. The popular press in Paris, egged on by monarchists and other right-wingers, was alive with fury. The nationalistic *Gazette de France* harangued its readers with the shame of this event and declared that national honour was now at stake over Algiers. These articles were often illustrated by etchings which depicted the Dey as a swarthy, bearded thug threatening the mannerly, civilized European with open fury. The French public bayed for revenge.

The press also raised the spectre of British expansion, arguing that if action was not taken it was obvious that Algiers would fall to the dreaded British Navy. The British had in fact launched an attack on Algiers in 1816, led by Lord Exmouth, in order to demand an end to piracy and the practice of slavery, and the return of ransom money for some 3,000 Christian slaves held in Algiers. A small fleet bombarded Algiers for a day and a night before the Dey capitulated. The action was, however, only a partial success and it was not long before the traditional slave trade resumed in Algiers. The French, who had refused to join with Exmouth in the action, although they, too, publicly deplored piracy, watched and learned from the battle (most notably, they observed that the stone houses of the Casbah could not be destroyed by cannon fire and that to take Algiers they would need a huge land force).

On the eve of the French invasion, in May 1830, Edward Blaquière, an English Hellenist and friend of Lord Byron, published an article which analysed the severe dangers facing the French in Algeria. He described the North African coast as similar to that of India, comparing the Turks who ruled over the territory with the British, who governed a population of 100 million in India. However, unlike the British in India, who thrived on the disunity of the peoples they conquered, the French would find conquest an impossible task,[5] because all of the tribes and races of 'Algeria' were in fact united by religion. The French invasion, he insisted, would only bind them together in anger. The real question, he states, was not whether the French could take Algiers – this was obviously the case – but what would they do when they got there? They would, of course, attract the 'jealousy' of the European powers, including Great Britain. Most dangerously, they would be facing a holy war launched from the deep interior of the country.

Blaquière's thesis was easily dismissed in Paris as Anglo-Saxon propaganda. But there were those in France who were equally aware of the dangers. Indeed, the invasion of Algeria was publicly and loudly opposed in the National Assembly by politicians of the Left and Right. Crucially, both sides argued that it was a distraction from the pursuit of French policy in Europe, and that the government was ignoring the threat of nascent German nationalism ('I would gladly rather exchange Algiers for the most wretched hole on the Rhine,' argued one deputy). This was an argument that would resurface time and again throughout the nineteenth century, as the French military found itself at war in Algeria until 1848, and thereafter committed to difficult and expensive policing missions, while the Germans extended the threat westwards, ultimately towards Paris itself.

However, in 1830, the mood was celebratory. At a great ball held for the King of Naples in Paris on the night before the fleet set sail, revellers drank and danced until dawn. Late into the night, the Comte de Savandy commented in a witty but prescient aside to the Duc d'Orléans, who would in a few short months become King Louis-Philippe, 'This is a truly Neapolitan *fête*, Sire, for we are indeed dancing upon a volcano.'[6]

The French expeditionary force to Algeria reflected Charles X's messianic ambitions. Modelled on the massive fleet that Napoleon had sent to Egypt in 1798, it consisted of 153 armed frigates, 450 merchant ships and 37,000 armed men. As the fleet prepared to leave, the atmosphere on shore was busy and excitable. A dream of untold riches had been inspired by the partial success of Napoleon's campaign in Egypt, which had triggered a vogue in Paris for all things Oriental, from rugs, carpets and furnishings to jewellery and hashish. Algeria itself had become source of much fantasy in France. Jean–Toussaint Merle, a Parisian theatre director, who was travelling with the armada for his own amusement, was caught up in the fever to plunder North Africa. 'To Algiers!' he wrote in his journal, waiting on shore for the ships to leave. 'This cry is all one hears from all ranks in the taverns, hotels and brothels on shore. It's a new Crusade. Surely this is how the Romans must have once cried – to Carthage!'[7]

On New Year's Day 1830, Alexander Tulin, the British vice-consul to Algiers, noted languidly in his diary that 'nothing particular has happened'. Everything changed in March, however, when he noted with rising alarm, 'By the arrival yesterday of a small Spanish vessel from Alicante, positive information has been received that the French fleet are preparing an expedition against Algiers.'[8] By the end of that month, British ships had arrived in Algiers to evacuate Spanish, Danish, English and American diplomatic families to Malta or Minorca. The Algerians, left to themselves, watched and waited.

The French fleet left Toulon on 25 May and stopped briefly at Palma. It was first sighted off the North African coast on 3 June. On the ships, the naval and military officers were outnumbered by map-makers, engineers, architects, professors, artists, archaeologists, businessmen and a host of expert linguists, who were mastering not only Arabic and Turkish but also the Berber dialects of Kabylia and the Tuareg languages of the desert. Some of these adventurers had been commissioned by the French government, while others were acting as private entrepreneurs. They all talked up the treasures awaiting them in Algiers. They sent ahead pamphlets translated into as many languages as they could muster. The rhetoric was that the French were bringing democracy to a troubled land:

> *We French, your friends, are leaving for Algiers. We are going to drive out your tyrants, the Turks who persecute you, who steal your goods, and never cease menacing your lives . . . our presence on your territory is not to make war on you but only on the person of your pasha. Abandon your pasha: follow our advice. It is good advice and can only make you happy.*[9]

In Algiers, the Dey read this propaganda with despair. He was well aware of the massive preparations that the French were making for the onslaught upon his capital. As they set sail from Toulon he reported to the captain of an English frigate, 'with true Oriental apathy', that 'God was Great, and the sea uncertain and dangerous', praying for a hurricane to destroy the French fleet. No such act of God would deliver him.

On 5 July 1830 the Comte de Bourmont, the supreme military commander of the French forces, marched into the city of Algiers to the sound of a marching band playing the

William Tell Overture. He immediately pronounced the 'Treaty of the Capture of Algiers', which was signed by the humiliated Dey. The Comte de Bourmont then declared that 'at ten in the morning precisely, French troops will enter the Casbah and henceforth all strongholds and ports in the territory will be under French law'. In France the 'Fall of Algiers' was described in the press and by elated politicians of all hues as a great triumph. The French stock markets fell briefly, as the bankers feared an exodus of money towards a potentially doomed foreign adventure, but they recovered quickly when it became clear that Algeria was now irrevocably under French control.

6

The Secret World of the 'Algerines'

During the first days of the occupation of Algeria, in a fever of curiosity and impatience, Jean-Toussaint Merle explored the military encampments along the coast. As a literary man, Merle was eager to describe the fateful moment of history. He found that the mood was exultant – even the humblest infantryman felt privileged to be taking part in such an historic adventure, restoring France to its rightful place as the leading power in the world, while enjoying the climate, food and thrill of a new and exotic land.

After a few days talking to generals and drinking with the troops, Merle braved the summer heat and walked from the French military headquarters near Staouéli along the old Roman road that led to the undefended city of Algiers. Finally, after some fifteen kilometres that covered him in sweat and dust, he entered the Casbah by the northern edge of Bab el-Jedid. There Merle was amazed by the riotous scenes – he came across drunken soldiers gorging on fruit and sweetmeats, the cackling laughter of prostitutes, 'a flock of Jewish merchants' pillaging shops and market stalls, cowed and sullen Turks and Arabs. There was no sign of military discipline: French troops of all ranks looted palaces and bazaars, slept off the drink in the streets, raped respectable women in full view, desecrated mosques and defiled cemeteries. All of this took place, he wrote, 'in a whirlwind of smoke and noise so loud that you could not hear a single voice'. In the midst of this chaos, as he fought off fatigue and wandered the labyrinth, half dazed and awestruck by the confusion, Merle stumbled on one of the great scenes of nineteenth-century history. This was the spectacle of the Dey of Algiers leaving his palace in the company of his generals, his harem and twenty black slaves weighed down with great trunks filled with jewels, carpets and crystals.

The Dey's palace overlooked the Casbah from the heights of the city. It had been one of the first military targets of the French and, although still intact, was battered with bullet holes – they are still there to this day – and wreathed in smoke. Merle described the Dey as silent and impassive amidst the confusion, patiently making his way on a white horse through the wreckage of his court. In a final gesture of rage and defiance, the Dey had refused to meet the French ambassador. Merle commented, with surprise, that the Dey did not look humiliated or ashamed, but 'dignified, noble ... a slight twitching of the eyebrows at the joyous scenes around him, which he watched with contempt'.[1]

As the Dey left his palace and the Casbah for the last time a whole world was lost for ever. This was the secret civilization of Algiers under the Ottomans – a complex and deeply nuanced society that was mostly unknown to or misunderstood by Europeans.

Although Algiers was a mystery to Westerners, there were a good number of descriptions by Europeans of life in the city before the French invasion. These included diplomatic and military reports and also first-hand accounts of life in 'captivity' by those held hostage by pirates (the most famous of these was, of course, Miguel de Cervantes, who was in Algiers for five years in the 1570s).

One of the most unwittingly insightful accounts was written by an Italian poet, Filippo Pananti, who was captured by Algerian pirates off the coast of Sardinia in 1813. When he finally returned to his native Tuscany in 1817, Pananti wrote up his adventures as a slave and exile in Algiers in a book called *Narrative of a Residence in Algiers*. This was immediately published in English, French and Italian, and became a kind of minor bestseller, with its overheated accounts of Oriental laziness, cruelty and sex. Pananti intended his book as propaganda for the European conquest of Algiers and indeed all of the 'Barbary states', on the grounds that they were a menace to the safety of European shipping. He denounced his captors as savages and primitives who opposed all civilized, European values. For this reason alone, they deserved to be conquered and subjugated.

He began his story in typically lurid fashion by describing the bloody, severed heads of Christians impaled on spikes outside the Dey's palace, the 'barbarous pomp and horrid majesty of the court', the 'terrifying and repulsive Dey'; the region, he wrote, was 'governed by monsters who vie with each other in the bitterest hatred towards Christianity and Civilization'. Pananti described the Casbah as oppressive and threatening – he could not stop himself from feeling 'a secret horror in walking the dark and filthy streets of this shocking city', where he was 'at every instant liable to insult, chains and assassination'. The morality of such a place was summed up, Pananti said, in an old Muslim proverb (which he may well have invented): 'We glory in discord, agitation and blood!'

Despite his protestations of suffering and horror, the truth was that Pananti was technically a slave for only a few days, before being released at the demand of the British consul. And, although he had lost most of his possessions to his captors, his exile thereafter was relatively painless. He occupied a privileged position as a man of letters stranded abroad, and spent most of his time lodging with European friends near the British consulate and trying to buy enough books to build 'a tolerable library' – no easy task but, according to Pananti, not impossible in 'barbarous' Algiers. As the weeks and months passed, the city Pananti discovered was in fact a homely and relatively well-ordered capital – far from the anarchic pirate city of European legend.

The stability of Algiers owed a great deal to the strict social stratification of the city. As Pananti described it, the 'Algerine' world was constructed upon a hierarchical caste system headed by the Turks and then, in descending order, Moors (Algerian Arabs), 'Chiloulis', Bedouins, Berbers, Negroes and Jews – the 'seven races of Algiers'. These races all spoke different languages but could communicate with each other and with Europeans by using the so-called 'lingua franca' – the language of the Franks – a pidgin dialect which borrowed words from all southern European languages and bore no real relation to French (this dialect is the origin of 'Arancia' – a mixture of Arabic, Berber, French and Spanish, which is still widely used across the Maghreb).[2]

The Turks formed a political and financial élite who, on Pananti's account, were vain and cruel, and tacitly hated by the 'Moors' over whom they ruled. Marriage between Turks and Moors was discouraged but did occur. The offspring were called 'Chiloulis' and held an ambiguous position in society – they were objects of suspicion among the Turks and often worked as accountants and agents for private houses, scorning the public world of politics or the military.

The Moors enjoyed a culturally superior position over all other classes and races as the native inhabitants of the territory. Next in line were the 'Renegadoes' – a small group of European converts to Islam and a life of piracy. The Renegadoes were the stuff of legend back in Europe, where little was known about their lives but it was rumoured that they lived in the greatest luxury. In reality, although they enjoyed all the privileges of the Ottoman state – including a wife and salary for serving as a soldier – they were distrusted, and actively despised by both Turks and Moors. The Bedouins, as described by Pananti, were arrogant and aloof and, true to their origins in the desert, held city life in contempt. But they had also 'a natural goodness of heart'. They claimed to speak the purest Arabic and, in their savage nobility, were unafraid to appear in the city half-naked.

The city also had its outsiders and underclasses. The Berbers of Kabylia were described as the 'poorest and most filthy' as well as 'jealous, discontented and rebellious'. In contrast, the black Africans, nearly all slaves, were nearly always 'mild . . . and of a natural gaiety'. Lowest of all ranks of society were the Jews, who were forced to walk barefoot when passing a mosque, forbidden to drink from a well if a Muslim was present, and forced to carry out all public executions. Their wives were often violated in their own houses, in full view of the family. It was forbidden for a Jew to raise his hand against a Muslim even in self-defence. The few Christians in the city suffered no such insults.

In line with the prevailing European view of the 'Oriental', Pananti described the principal passion of the true 'Algerine', whether Turk, Moor, Berber or Jew, as 'the gratification of a sensual appetite . . . in a sea of voluptuousness and debauchery'. What this meant was that Pananti, like all Europeans in Islamic territories, was thrilled by the notion of polygamy, without necessarily understanding its historical roots or the complex economic contracts that it entailed. He was unashamedly enthralled by the 'savage glory' of the harem and dancing girls, whom he described as 'prostitutes' but by far 'the most agreeable spectacle in Algiers', always 'accompanied by the most significant smiles and ogles'. The other great pleasures of the Algerines were drinking coffee and sitting chatting with friends in the *kioscos* (little shops) of the Casbah, where they smoked opium or *khaf*, the locally grown cannabis.

The Algiers that Pananti lived in had changed little in the

centuries under Ottoman rule. Essentially, it was divided between the élite hill, or mountain (*al-jabal*), which was the fiefdom of the Turkish ruling classes, and the lower part of the city (*al-wati*), which stretched down to Bab-el-Oued and the sea. As you descended the hill, the population became more socially and racially mixed, and there were mosques, taverns and churches as you approached the docks. This was the site of the Jewish quarter, where some 5,000 Jews lived as well as a contingent of Italians and Spaniards. Next to it was the 'quarter of the Franks', the base for some hundred or so European traders and diplomats. Just outside the city walls were shelters for the *Barraniya* (outsiders) – poor temporary labourers from the Sahara or Anatolia.

As a man of the Left and a stern advocate of democracy, Pananti was initially sceptical about the importance of religion in the carefully structured life of the Algerines. But slowly he began to profess a grudging admiration for the 'free city of Algiers' and the 'perfect impartiality' of the legal system, which was entirely based on the Koran. Pananti noticed that theft was rare and travel in any part of the territory was always safe. The law was applied with rigour and had its own internal logic: in punishment, Europeans were always strangled, Jews were burnt and Muslims beheaded.[3]

Despite its reputation in European eyes as a den of anarchy and crime, Algiers was a fully functioning political entity with a well-ordered class system. This had been the case since 1529, when the Ottoman Regency had blended the tribal territories of Algeria into a single region, with its own borders and financial and judicial legitimacy.

Interestingly, the relationship between France and Algeria can also be traced back to this era. The French had kept a permanent consul in Algiers from 1536 onwards, when Francis I, the shrewdest of French kings, thought it prudent to stay on good terms with the Ottoman Empire. In the next hundred years or so, there were a few efforts to launch military expeditions against Algiers, mainly to punish its rulers for piracy, but the city was largely regarded as unconquerable, or at least not worth the effort required.

Still, the territory had enough impact on the French imagination for Bernard le Bouyer de Fontenelle, a member of the Académie Française and key figure in the nascent Enlightenment, to name the territory as '*Algérie*' and its people as '*algériens*' in his *Entretiens sur la pluralité des mondes* of 1686. Fontenelle's intention was innocent enough; his reference was, in the spirit of the age, a pseudo-scientific attempt to name the area from a transliteration of the Arabic *Al-Djaza'ir* (the Islands), referring to the cluster of islands which lay off the coast of Algiers. A century and a half later, the French authorities used the term *Algérie* to name and define the territory they had conquered by 1839.[4]

7

New America

Landing on the African continent and conquering Algiers was the easy part for the French military. From then on, the war was never that simple. The 'Fall of Algiers' in 1830 may have looked to the world like a brilliant victory, but the French were confused about what to do next. Algeria is a huge country and even the most organized armies had found it impossible to control the movements and supply lines of the native inhabitants, who not only knew the terrain but knew how to turn it to their advantage. This would be the defining fact of the military struggle during the 130 years of French occupation. Yet when they planned their invasion, the French had no idea of these real dangers.

The situation was further confused by the turmoil and shifting political sands in Paris. Even as the 'Fall of Algiers' was announced, Charles X was succeeded as monarch by Louis-Philippe, the last king of France and an Orléanist. Louis-Philippe had not instigated this war and privately complained about the burden he had inherited. Publicly, he was forced to pursue the Algerian adventure with as much vigour as possible, mainly because he could not afford to lose face in Paris or be seen to be conceding ground to the English, who had been observing all French manoeuvres with predatory eyes from the outset. For the time being, now that the party was over, Parisians themselves were largely indifferent to the project.

The new reality facing Louis-Philippe was that a strategy had to be developed on the ground. Politicians and military commanders were arguing about whether the occupation should be 'total' or 'partial'. These policy divisions in turn determined the local response to the 'natives' – should they be driven out of the territory, on the model of the native Americans, or co-opted and assimilated into the political structures of the French Republic? Either way, the invasion of Algeria triggered a frenzied land grab, as Europeans poured first into Algiers and then into the outlying areas. They bought out shops, farms and other properties at rock-bottom prices or, in many cases, simply took them by force of arms.

In 1834, under Louis-Philippe's guiding hand, France officially annexed the occupied territories as a colony. This meant that the area was under the jurisdiction of a governor-general, Bertrand Clauzel, who reported directly to the Minister of War in Paris. This is when the term 'European' came to have legal status. At the same time three million Muslim inhabitants were not given French citizenship but were placed under the '*régime du sabre*' (the régime of the sword) – effectively a permanent state of martial law. This marked a key political turning point: Algeria had become a legal possession of France and it was now more costly and dangerous to withdraw from Algeria than to remain.[1]

The pressure for martial law came from the Europeans, both French and non-French, who had established themselves in the country before the formal annexation had been ordered but who were unofficially protected by the French military from the Muslims, whose homes and businesses were being stolen. Effectively, the Europeans were calling for force of arms to protect them from the local people.

This disgraceful state of affairs became official French policy in 1835 when Governor-General Clauzel set up a company to take over agricultural land. Clauzel fantasized about building 'a new America', with cotton plantations in the Mitidja plain served by a workforce of 'natives' and administered by French officials.[2] Clauzel invested his own money in these plans and speculated profitably, expanding the French zone of occupation at bayonet point. This colonization of the countryside and the ousting of the Muslims who had lived there for centuries was the single biggest factor in the destruction of traditional society, creating a displaced population of several hundred thousand Muslims who, within the space of a few short years, lost the ties of religion, birth and language that held them together as a community.

The divisions deepened as settlers arrived en masse from the European mainland to work in Algeria. One of the dilemmas facing the nascent French authorities was how to regulate the settlement of this 'empty land'. France itself was not particularly over-populated at this period and the areas with a tradition of emigration, such as Auvergne or Brittany, sent their sons and daughters to Paris as a first port of call, so the first *colons* (colonists) were mainly non-French – they were most often low-paid urban workers or peasant farmers from the poor southern areas of Corsica, Sardinia, Sicily, Catalonia, Murcia, Almería and Malta.[3] There were also criminals and political dissidents, deported from France in the same way that Britain sent its convicts to Australia.

Most of the *colons* came driven by poverty in their own countries and rumours of wages ten times higher than Europe in the 'new America'. When they got to Algeria, they settled at first in the coastal towns and cities, before fanning out into the hinterland, where they aggressively drove native Algerians off their land. They proved impossible to regulate or police. French bureaucratic frustration is evident in a law passed in Algiers in 1831, which forbade captains of visiting ships to allow any passengers to disembark without a passport. But this was a futile gesture as the new Algeria was beginning to take shape.

French Justice

Within a few years of 1830, the Turkish language disappeared, while French, Spanish, Italian, Corsican, Catalan and Maltese were all superimposed on the local dialects of the Arabs and Berbers. This massive cultural shift reflected the efficiency and speed with which Algeria changed course; it was now effectively conquered by Europeans on all fronts.

The first 'European Algerians' quickly developed a tough frontiersman mentality. During an extended stay in Algiers during the late 1830s, the Swiss artist Adolphe Otth noted in his journal that nearly all crimes in Algiers, from robbery to murder, were committed by 'undesirable Christians that the galleys and prisons of Europe have vomited up upon this country since its conquest by the French'.

The worst crimes were mostly committed in the countryside, a long way beyond French attempts to impose judicial order on the anarchy they had unleashed with the conquest. French justice was arbitrary, at best, and at times actively sadistic. One of the most notorious examples of this was a revenge attack by the French in 1832 on a tribe called the Ouffia, on the grounds that they had committed a robbery against a local sheikh loyal to the French. The order to put the whole tribe to the sword was given by the Duc de Rovigo – a former police commander under Napoleon and now an elderly figure known for his cruel severity – while he was at a dinner party, gambling and drinking. The mission was ruthlessly carried out by the Foreign Legion and the Chasseurs d'Afrique, a new regiment made up of European and Muslim soldiers, who were becoming notorious as the most efficient 'Arab-killers' in the French army.

The tribe, numbering a hundred or so men, women and children, were taken by surprise in their encampment in the

Maison-Carrée, an old Turkish fort on a small hill outlying Algiers. A contemporary described the scene as 'old men waiting for the death blow, women crying for mercy, children who did not know what was to befall them'.[4] The soldiers returned to their camp, caked in blood and with the gory heads of the Ouffia on lances and bayonets. They drank and sang their way through the night. In the morning, bloodied earrings or a bracelet still attached to a severed wrist were on sale at the open market at rue Bab Azoun.

Such casual slaughter was clearly meant to spread terror and terrify the population into submission. Instead it stoked a slow-burning hatred of the French and all Europeans among the native Algerians. The Ouffia were revenged within a few weeks of the original atrocity when the Foreign Legion were ambushed near the site of the crime and all killed without mercy. The bodies were beheaded and mutilated – an act meant to dishonour the enemy.

'The Algerian Cromwell'

It was not enough for the Algerians simply to oppose the French with isolated acts of vengeance. At first the resistance was fragmented, led by individual tribes who took up arms in response to a particular crime in their territory (such as the killing of the Ouffia). But any concerted response needed a military command with a political mind. This came eventually in the form of a marabout (a Muslim holy man) and great warrior who would lead the Algerian resistance through the 1830s and the 1840s, and indeed at one stage almost drove the French back into the sea.

This leader was a quietly spoken young man called Abd el-Kader, who was brought to power by a wave of popular acclaim in the Mascara region in 1837. Famous throughout the various territories for his piety, his poverty and his melancholy disposition, he had witnessed the French invasion and their crimes with rising horror and finally decided that no Muslim could watch this suffering and continue to serve God. He was a charismatic speaker and this clear statement of intent became a watchword among the rival tribes throughout Algeria, bringing former enemies together for a political and religious cause.[5]

Most importantly for his political prestige, Abd el-Kader had been prophesied as a sultan by a dervish in Mecca when he made his first pilgrimage to the holy city. He knew the power of gestures and symbols among his people and how to manipulate them for propaganda. Above all, he understood how to act like a prophet: it was therefore with a single gold coin in his pocket and wearing a ragged, torn burnous that Abd el-Kader walked purposefully into the Palace of the Dey in Mascara on the day of his election as leader and declared a 'holy war' on the French nation.

In Paris, no less a man than the great philosopher of democracy, Alexis de Tocqueville, would later hail Abd el-Kader as the 'Algerian Cromwell'. This was not too far from the truth: one of Abd el-Kader's great achievements was to fuse religion and Algerian patriotism into a single force. He denounced the Turks as corrupt and weak and heralded a new Algerian nation, led by Algerians themselves.

In simple terms, Abd el-Kader was a fine soldier and a brilliant military tactician. He ran an intelligent and sophisticated campaign and had spies at work in Paris, following debates in the Chamber of Deputies and assessing the popular mood. At one stage Abd el-Kader was in correspondence with Léon Roches, a former French ambassador and spy, who was under orders to establish a ceasefire. But Abd el-Kader had other operatives in place who told him how unpopular the war in Algeria was and, based on this knowledge, he fought hard to drive the French into brokering a peace. He began his war by launching lightning raids against all French interests in the territory. His soldiers constituted a regular army of some 75,000 men.

They attacked French forts, trading posts and *colon* settlements, making it impossible for the French to govern outside the larger towns and cities. The strength of Abd el-Kader's hand at this stage was such that it forced the French into an uncharacteristic compromise: at the Treaty of Tafna in 1837, Abd el-Kader was grudgingly recognized by the French authorities as the sovereign leader of two-thirds of Algeria.

The treaty did not last, partly because the borders were badly defined, but, more importantly, the *colons'* lust for land could not be denied, even by the 'Commander of Faithful', as Abd el-Kader was known to the Muslim population. Despite his military prowess, Abd el-Kader was a poor policeman, and ordinary Algerian Muslims all too often found themselves driven from their farms and villages by armed *colons*, tacitly aided and abetted by the French military. Muslim anger soon became a wave of righteous violence – but attacking and killing isolated packs of *colons* was not a military campaign and only exacerbated French frustration with this difficult and murderous mission.

'Exterminate Them to the Last Man!'

By 1838 Louis-Philippe's exasperation with Algeria was at breaking-point. Despite the brokered peace, the newspapers in Paris reported massacres and attacks on *colons* and the king was criticized as a weak and gluttonous bourgeois with no under-standing of the fact that French honour was at stake across the Mediterranean. In his impatience, Louis-Philippe had declared that all methods of winning the war were justified. 'What does it matter,' he famously announced, 'if a hundred million shots are fired in Africa. Europe does not hear them.'

In 1840 Marshal Thomas-Robert Bugeaud was appointed as military commander in Algeria. Bugeaud was the right man for the job. French historians have exalted Bugeaud as the strong man who had the stomach for a fight and made the French colonial project a reality. Initially, however, Bugeaud had misgivings about the Algerian project, describing it as a useless possession that France would find hard to lose. But having committed himself to his command in 1841, he declared that total conquest could only be achieved by total war. Bugeaud executed a scorched-earth policy of no mercy and maximum cruelty, strangling the Algerian resistance wherever he found it. 'The aim is not to hunt down Arabs,' he announced to his generals. 'That is simply a waste of time. Instead, we must stop the Arabs from sowing, making a harvest or pasture. We must burn down their crops everywhere, and exterminate them to the last man!'[6]

He revamped the army's tactics: instead of marching long columns of infantry deep into the hinterland where they were easy targets for ambushes and snipers, he broke the regiments into small groups which, copying Abd el-Kader's own strategy, could surprise and harry the enemy, punching them out of position at will. With every fresh success, ordinary French soldiers became harder and more brutal. Louis-Philippe was delighted, assuming that this was the way to win the war as well as the hearts and minds of his sceptical domestic audience in Paris.

The Parisian public was in fact deeply shocked by the methods of the French army. Parisians were even less inclined to sympathize with their own government when they learned that the general with responsibility for such massacres was Bugeaud, the so-called 'butcher' responsible for the massacres in the rue Transnonain in Paris in 1834. These were carried out by soldiers who were searching the streets for insurgents during the popular uprising of April 1834. A shot was fired towards a captain in Bugeaud's brigade; in swift revenge the soldiers marched into the nearest building on the rue Transnonain and bayoneted to death twelve of the occupants, including women and children. Another twenty civilians were seriously wounded. The event was grimly commemorated in a painting by Honoré Daumier, a work of realist propaganda produced in horror at the events, which depicts a dead man whose body is slumped over a dead baby. The painting caused a sensation at the time, for political as well as aesthetic reasons, but it did stop the rise of Bugeaud and his increasingly cruel methods.

In Algeria Bugeaud promoted a new genocidal tactic, *les enfumades* (smoking-out), which led to the death of tens of thousands of Algerians who had never even heard of France until the French army arrived on their land. The first *enfumade* was ordered by a General Cavaignac, whose men had pursued a group of Arab fighters, as well as women and children, into mountain caves. Cavaignac ordered his men to wall up the caves and set fires at the entrances. After a day or so, as people died of asphyxiation and bodies began to pile up, the fighters emerged to ask for pardon. Cavaignac refused and continued with his plan to turn the area into 'a vast cemetery'.

Bugeaud was impressed with this tactic and exhorted his commanders to use it whenever they could. 'If any of these rascals retreat to their caves,' he said, 'you must imitate Cavaignac and smoke them out like foxes.' In 1845 Bugeaud's own men killed almost a thousand Algerian men, women and children of the Ouled Riah tribe by lighting fires at the entrances to the caves where they lived and letting them choke to death.

By this time, the Muslim state under the leadership of Abd el-Kader was in a state of near-collapse. The French now had 108,000 troops on Algerian soil. Bugeaud's overall strategy had been to fuse the colonial mission with his military aims. As the army and the colonial authorities converged, the Muslim state began to melt away as more 'native' farms, villages and towns were arbitrarily seized and their inhabitants displaced for ever.

Abd el-Kader's initial strategy had been to lure the French deep into the interior, where they would be isolated and overstretched. 'You will die with disease in our mountains, and those whom sickness will not carry off, my horsemen will send with their bullets.' However, this strategy was undermined by the ferocity of the violence which Bugeaud unleashed on the Arab armies. The French destroyed everything in their path in pursuit of their quarry, burning farms, driving cattle away, destroying crops and massacring women and children. The suffering became unbearable and many tribes and villages found the price of their holy war too high. Slowly, as the rural economy died, open support for Abd el-Kader declined and the Algerian leader began to lose the taxes from these farmers that were vital to support his campaign. In their anger, many poor Algerians threatened violence against Abd el-Kader and his soldiers as they travelled across the territory.

The wives and families of Abd el-Kader's armies were protected in a *zimala*, a huge encampment, whose location was kept secret – such was the prize it represented to the French army – until it was betrayed by a spy. The French launched a vicious onslaught on the innocents who lived there. The troops moved silently among the civilian population, stabbing and shooting at will, the corpses of the dead heaped up inside the bloodied tents.

The massacre frightened and angered Abd el-Kader's soldiers, who wondered what kind of moral criminal they were fighting. Most importantly, it started to break their morale. Soldiers deserted, fearing for the safety of their families more than they dreaded the anger of their commander or God. As his army began to disintegrate, Abd el-Kader retreated to the Moroccan border, near Oudja, and called upon the Moroccan sultan for military aid. This was in vain, and in 1846 Abd el-Kader was forced to surrender his armies and authority to the forces of Bugeaud. He negotiated an honourable exile to the Middle East (in fact to Damascus, where it is claimed he helped save the lives of several hundred Frenchmen during one of the periodic insurrections in the Syrian capital). In France Abd el-Kader was recognized as a noble and worthy opponent, but the reality was that the Algeria he tried to defend was lost.

In contrast, Bugeaud, the cold-blooded killer whose fanaticism gained him the total subjugation of the Arabs, was honoured with the title of the Duc d'Isly after his victory over Abd el-Kader at the Battle of Isly. In 1840 he had been made governor-general of Algeria, which meant that from this point Algeria would be wholly French territory. With this one brutal gesture, the French nation dispossessed all future generations of their land, their history and their heritage.

As a final insult, in 1852 Bugeaud was honoured with a statue and the Place Marshal Thomas-Robert Bugeaud in the centre of Algiers was named after him. This was a celebration of the governor-general whose 'pacification' of Algeria consisted of a systematic campaign of massacre and genocide.

In 1966, four years after Algerian independence, the elegant square was renamed Place Abd el-Kader. Lined by colonnades and palm trees, it is the focus for celebrating great football victories. In the 1840s Abd el-Kader had almost brought France, a great European nation, to its knees. Now, astride his horse, on a tall, modernist concrete plinth, he waves his sword defiantly at the blank sky as traffic chaos swirls around him and young Algerians hang out at the Quick Restaurant, a Belgian fast-food chain which has been here since 2007. Bugeaud's statue has long since been returned to France, but in Algeria his name still persists, bowdlerized in dialectal Arabic as 'Al-Bujea': a bogeyman who still haunts the dreams and nightmares of small children.

8

The French Kingdom of the Arabs

Every time I visit the Denon wing of the Louvre, I am dazzled and confused by two of the masterpieces on show, which share so much technically – the soft, flowing shapes and deep colours – and yet which seem to be so far apart. The first is the great work by Eugène Delacroix, *Liberté guidant le peuple*. Painted in the autumn of 1830 and exhibited at the Salon of May 1831, this is the great painting of revolution, as the armed and bare-breasted 'Liberty' clambers over the wreckage and corpses of history to lead the French people into the future. The second, *Les Femmes d'Alger dans leur appartement*, painted only a few years later, in 1834, after Delacroix's visit to North Africa, is intimate, erotic, passive. Here we see three women and their servant lounging indolently in an opulent interior room.

In both paintings Delacroix is responding to his instincts as an artist – that much is clear in the mastery of technique and theme. It's harder, however, to see what this juxtaposition tells us about French history: on the one hand, in *Liberté guidant le people*, we have the war-like spirit of Freedom incarnate as a woman, changing history. And in the second painting we have Muslim women as soft, domesticated creatures. The paintings show two sides of French civilization. In the first we are instructed to admire the urge towards 'freedom' at all costs.

The second is more ambiguous. It demonstrates a fascination with the secret and exotic world of Muslim women in Algiers. But Delacroix's eye is also that of the outsider, the explorer of hidden lands: for all its fine colour and composition, it is worth remembering that, in every sense, the painter had penetrated a secret and closed world. In the Muslim world, this painting still represents the gaze of a conqueror over a conquered people – a stark contradiction to the freedom-loving idealism of *Liberté guidant le people*.

'The Oriental Style'

Delacroix was among the first visitors who came to North Africa in 1832, as part of a French diplomatic mission to Morocco to pacify the sultan, who was nervous about French intentions in that country in the wake of the conquest of Algeria. The mission returned to France via Algiers. At this stage the occupation was still fragile and the 'Algerian question' was a subject which divided politicians and the public back in France. Delacroix himself was sympathetic, at least on an aesthetic level, to those who argued that the French should leave Algeria and that the destruction of the Arab city was a crime. 'Since 1832 it seemed to be the task of Europeans to destroy in Algiers, and wherever they like the layout and ornament of Moorish houses,' he complained in his journal.

As an artist, Delacroix was intoxicated by the light and land-scapes he found in Africa and filled over seven notebooks with sketches and drawings. He was also captivated by the interiors of the houses of the Casbah, the closeted intimacy which hinted, at least in the artist's imagination, at a secret world of sensual delight. *Les Femmes d'Alger* was the most famous product of his visit. When it was exhibited in Paris in 1834 – as Abd el-Kader was launching his first jihad against the French – it caused an immediate sensation. Critics admired its strength of com-position, the richness of the surfaces and the eroticized posture of the women. More than this, it revealed the deep splendour of Algeria to a generation of well-heeled Parisians, always in pursuit of a new fashion. The fact that the women in the painting were actually French models did not diminish its impact. The painting was immediately bought by Louis-Philippe, heightening both its prestige and its fashionable subject.

Les Femmes d'Alger has often been attacked as a work loaded with cultural and political significance. Specifically, the inviting and submissive nature of the women has been described as a metaphor for the way in which the French saw their future colonial project – in other words Algerians, and by extension Algeria, were represented as asking to be raped. This was not a reading that occurred to critics in the 1830s. Instead, the painting unleashed a vogue for the Orient. The French began to fall deeply and irrevocably in love with Algeria – a process which was arguably more dangerous for the native Algerians than being at war – and in Delacroix's footsteps came a constant stream of artists, poets and travellers, who wrote home to describe the timeless marvels that they found there.

Once the war against Abd el-Kader ended, resistance to the French occupation took the form of a slow-burning insurgency which was controlled quite easily by the tens of thousands of French troops now committed to Algeria. This meant that the newest visitors to Algeria were mainly tourists. Most of them stayed longest in Algiers, with occasional forays to the other coastal cities of Annaba in the East and Oran in the West. The most daring adventurers accompanied the occupying military on expeditions to the mountains, and reported back on the savage beauty of the countryside and the people.

The literary pilgrims to Algeria in the mid-nineteenth century included such diverse figures as Alexandre Dumas, Eugène Fromentin, Théophile Gautier. Even Gustave Flaubert passed through Algeria in 1857 en route to the exotic Ottoman world of Tunis, which he wanted to explore as research for his historical novel *Salammbô*, set during the Punic Wars. Flaubert was in pursuit of a violent and exotic Orient and was unimpressed by Algeria. In his travel log he described the country as a disappointment and denounced it in a gouty and bad-tempered mood as too French. Algeria was, he wrote, 'the bodyguard of the west' and had 'a strong odour of absinthe and the barracks'. Unlike Flaubert, however, most visitors to Algeria were delighted by the place: the landscape was savage and stunning; the light and fauna had a sublime quality which immediately possessed the imagination; the people were seen as noble primitives from an ancient world; and the cities and towns had the dream-like quality of belonging to another civilization, indeed another era. All of these qualities spoke directly to a succession of artists and writers who had the Romantic urge to celebrate the transcendent in exotic scenarios and for whom Algeria was both muse and inspiration. For them a journey through Algeria was a journey into the exotic, a fusion of the past and the future which was a world away from the banality of contemporary Europe.[1]

This enchantment quickly made an impression on all aspects of French cultural life, from poetry to interior design. The poet Victor Hugo, one of the most famous and influential men in France, led the way by having a whole room in his apartment on rue de la Tour-d'Auvergne decorated in the 'Oriental' style. The most fashionable cafés followed suit: these included such chic watering holes as the Grand Colbert on rue Vivienne, the Café des Moresques on the boulevard des Italiens and the Closerie des Lilas on the boulevard Saint-Michel, which were all decorated in the 'Moorish manner'.

From now on every self-respecting bourgeois apartment in Paris, Lyons or Marseilles would not be complete without adornments from the East – carpets, vases and perfumes. The fashion even made its mark on the street furniture of Paris and other great French cities: Arabesque doorways and intricate carvings now adorned the entrances to otherwise banal buildings, such as the façade of the apartments at 28 rue de Richelieu or the Bains Deligny public baths – a meeting place for *le tout-Paris*. One of the most popular drinks of the period was Picon, a bitter aperitif made from oranges and caramel (and often, incomprehensibly, added to beer). This was invented by Gaetan Picon while serving in the French army in Algeria in 1837, and was advertised in Paris with images of sultry women lounging under orange trees, in the style of Delacroix's *Femmes d'Alger*. Even the cancan – the wildly sexualized dance craze which was now sweeping through Paris music halls – was said to be based on a 'savage rite' of Algerian origin.

France's passion for Orientalism was matched on the political front, in the aftermath of the war with Abd el-Kader, by administrations in Algiers that explicitly sought to accommodate 'the Arab Kingdom' within the French Empire. The French authorities in Algeria at this point were often led by Arabists, sophisticated intellectuals with an enthusiasm for Arab language and culture, and a distinct sympathy towards the people they had conquered, which allowed them to sidestep the terrors of the Algerian project. This refined form of Orientalism and cult of the 'noble primitive' was both a fashion and a political gesture of dandified contempt for the dull and severe verities of Europe.

The Emperor of the Arabs

Among those who were caught up in this passion was Napoleon III, who came to power in 1848 with the stated purpose of extending the French Empire, and therefore French greatness, across the world. In 1852 Napoleon welcomed the exiled Abd el-Kader to Paris, where he was greeted with all the ceremony appropriate to a head of state, a great war leader and a worthy adversary of the French army.[2]

This was, of course, pure propaganda. In front of an emotional crowd at the Opéra, at a performance of Rossini's *Mosè in Egitto*,

Napoleon III hailed Abd el-Kader as the '*Vercingétorix algérien*', a reference to the great leader of the Gaulish nation who had capitulated to Caesar but held a place in French folklore as a symbol of a poetic, primitive past. The crowd, roused by the sight of the noble defeated enemy in their midst, broke into spontaneous applause. The event was recorded on the front page of the popular journal *L'Illustration* under the headline: 'Abd el-Kader is the lion at all our public entertainments!'

In fact, Abd el-Kader had no interest in Parisian culture and as a young man had actively despised music as a frivolous, anti-Islamic activity. He had come to Paris to negotiate his future, while Napoleon III had brought him there to impress the Algerian adventure upon the French imagination. By comparing him to Vercingetorix, Napoleon was able to suggest that France's mission in Algeria was a modern version of the Roman Empire. More subtly, by associating the Arab general with the Gaulish past, he reduced the mysterious Other to a legend familiar to ordinary French people. The separateness and strangeness of the Arab world was thus assimilated into French cultural memory. Napoleon's public display of magnanimity was in fact a shrewd manoeuvre.

Abd el-Kader was paraded throughout Paris during the autumn of 1852. He cut a melancholy figure as he traipsed to the cathedral of Notre-Dame and the churches of the Madeleine and Saint-Louis des Invalides, ostensibly to demonstrate the tolerance of Islam. Photographs of the period portray him as a sullen, brooding presence. Napoleon's plan was to flatter Abd el-Kader into feeling political sympathy towards France, with the aim of establishing him as diplomat who could lobby for French interests within the Ottoman Empire. It was on these terms that Abd el-Kader negotiated his status as an exile in Damascus.

On his first visit to Algeria in 1865 Napoleon admired the toughness and tenacity of the Arabs and, partly inspired by his encounters with Abd el-Kader, began to construct an elaborate fantasy of Algeria as the 'French Kingdom of the Arabs', where native Algerians and the French shared equal status as citizens of the French nation. He declared that he was opposed to what had happened in America, where the native population had been exterminated by military force, and instead exalted in the most poetic terms the rich contribution Arabs would henceforth make to French culture. 'Algeria is not a colony but an Arab kingdom,' he declared. 'And I am as much emperor of the Arabs as of the French!'[3]

Such high-minded ideals were not, however, shared by the European settlers who came to establish complete control over the local culture and countryside. Napoleon III was regarded as a dangerous clown by these tough-minded *colons*, who emphasized their distance from and indifference to Paris by making sure that all legislation concerning ownership of land and property was ratified in Algeria, and to their advantage. There were inevitably clashes with the Arab sympathizers who ran the local administration, but, with the army on their side (this was the legacy of Bugeaud's command), the colonizers always got their way.

Napoleon exacerbated tensions by introducing the *sénatus-consulte* of 1865, a clumsy piece of legislation which deepened the religious divisions between the Muslim and European populations. In a misguided gesture towards recognizing and preserving Arab traditions, Algerian Muslims gained the right to be governed by Islamic law rather than the French Civil Code in non-criminal cases. They could apply for French nationality, but only if they renounced the right to be governed by Islamic law – effectively an act of apostasy, which meant abandoning the social structures of family and community. No Muslim could seriously contemplate this betrayal, so the result of the legislation was to make native Algerians subjects rather than citizens in their own country. Muslims had no vote and therefore no control or stake in the society in which they lived.

Their disempowered status would be the main trigger for revolt from now on.

The European settlers in Algeria were largely content with this state of affairs but still resented what they saw as high-handed and badly thought-out interference from Paris. They were often right, in that Napoleon III was really a fantasist who had no idea of the realities on the ground in North Africa. He was equally despised by the political élite in Paris (he was famously described as a 'cretin' with the features of 'a melancholy parrot' by a leading figure of the day). However, he was not to be underestimated. Far from being a clown, he was a Machiavellian adventurer driven by an over-inflated sense of his own destiny. This was to be his undoing. His dreams for Algeria came to a sticky end with the humiliating French defeat at the hands of the Prussians at the Battle of Sedan in 1870. The Second Empire over which he had presided crumbled, to be replaced by the much harder realities of famine and insurrection before the restoration of the Third Republic.

9

Latin Africa

In Algeria, the defeat of Abd el-Kader had been seen by Muslims as a punishment sent to them from God. While the French tightened their grip on the country, another call for a jihad came from a tribal leader called El-Mohkrani, who was incensed by the granting of French citizenship to Jews in 1870. The call was met by 8,000 Muslims, who launched a revolt in the mountains of Kabylia. But the revolt was badly thought out and was quickly crushed.

The French military response was merciless: women, children and old people were slaughtered wholesale as villages and farms were razed to the ground. In the wake of this French victory, Arabic was declared a foreign language and Koranic schools and pilgrimages to Mecca were closely watched in an effort to isolate Algeria from the rest of the Muslim world. The extreme violence of the French army and the visible contempt of *colons* for Algerian Muslims made it inevitable, however, that Muslims looked to Fez, Tunis and Cairo as their centres of cultural, political and moral gravity, not to Paris, Lyons or Marseilles.

By now, Algerian towns of any size were home to significant populations of French *colons*, as wells as other southern Europeans from Malta, Spain or Italy. They started to redesign the towns and settlements in their own image, replacing the complex structures of the old Arab cities with gridiron streets, statues and piazzas. This legacy is most clearly visible in towns such as Constantine and Oran, which have a distinctly Spanish flavour, reflecting the large numbers of Spaniards who settled there.

During this period, the term '*mission civilisatrice*' entered the French language, and by the end of the nineteenth century, it had passed into common usage as a justification for French military activity in Algeria. The background to this ideological development was an address to the French Parliament in 1882 by the republican politician and journalist Jules Ferry. He famously asserted: 'We must believe that if Providence deigned to confer upon us a mission by making us masters of the earth, this mission consists not of attempting an impossible fusion of races but of simply spreading or awakening among the other races the superior notions of which we are the guardians.'

Two years later Ferry added: 'The superior races have a right to dominate the inferior races, to civilize them.' Essentially, this 'civilizing mission' was driven by a belief in the superiority of Western philosophy, religion and culture and the need – almost a religious duty – to bring this to other more barbarous and backward lands. It was also partly a mission against Islam in the pursuit of modernity. In his inaugural speech at the Collège de France in 1862, Ernest Renan, philosopher, historian and an admirer of Darwin, had spoken for many of his contemporaries when he declared that 'Islam is the complete negation of Europe ... Islam is contempt for science, the suppression of civil society; it is the shocking simplicity of the Semitic mind.'[1]

Paris in Africa

The *mission civilisatrice* took its most visible and direct form in the centre of Algiers, which was gradually reconstructed as a mini-Paris on the Mediterranean. An army officer described Algiers in 1830 as a 'dazzling whiteness' made up of 'narrow and torturous streets where two mules could not pass side by side', but after the conquest the military systematically drove straight lines through the labyrinth of the Arab city, for reasons of surveillance and control, blasting through streets and alleyways which had stood for centuries.[2] The army engineers made detailed maps of the 'Moorish houses' and, where they could not be destroyed, they constructed avenues and boulevards around them, encircling the native houses with balconies and balustrades. Most shocking to the local population was the arrogance of militant Christianity on the march; even the venerable mosque of Djemaa el-Kebir, at the very heart of Algiers, was converted into a cathedral and the crescent on its minaret replaced by a cross.

The French command took over all the houses that had belonged to the Ottoman military élite, seizing palaces and mansions. Below the Casbah, the army installed a 'Museum-Library' in the Dar Mustapha Pasha mansion, and a series of military headquarters leading to Place d'Armes. The highest-ranking officers took over the mansions on the heights overlooking the city. At the lower levels, many buildings were rebuilt to face on to the new, wider streets, with arcades and entirely new façades. Contemporary observers noted with approval the development of this pleasing new 'Mediterranean' style.

For the French, there was both a political and aesthetic rationale for cutting through the apparent confusion of the old city. Firstly, European architecture was held to be both modern and democratic, as opposed to the perverse, anti-civilizing aesthetic which had previously prevailed. In 1784 Montesquieu, one of the great political philosophers of the Enlightenment, had described the typical Oriental mansion as a flawed political model: 'In despotic states,' he wrote, 'each house is a separate empire.' Secondly, the streets had to be straightened and widened to accommodate the traffic which would flow through the new capitalist city that Algiers was about to become. For both reasons, the old world had to be destroyed. Ironically, this process would soon be replicated in the streets of Paris, as Baron Haussmann began his vast project of remodelling the city in the 1850s, employing many of the architects and engineers who had learned their techniques and their trade in Algiers.

Like the new Paris designed by Haussmann, Algiers was conceived of as a spectacular city, a showpiece of French military and commercial might. One of the fashionable entertainments for visiting Parisians in the 1830s and 1840s was to travel over the wide bay of Algiers in a hot-air balloon, peering down through opera glasses at the city which was being built below. It was in every sense a panorama of European modernity in motion.

As part of the vision for a new, modern Algiers, the main artery on the waterfront, rue Militaire, was planned in 1837 as both a promenade and a gateway to the sea. It was finally finished in 1866, when it was named boulevard de l'Impératrice, in honour of the visit of Empress Eugénie and Napoleon III to Algiers the same year. It was an especially prestigious and skilful feat of engineering because a series of classical arches, which looked like a Roman aqueduct, were constructed to bridge the change in level between the boulevard and the slope of the hill. The ramps, all in white, which rise above the harbour and make such a dramatic visual impact on the waterfront, took another eight years to complete. This is the most famous view of Algiers from the sea and gave the city its nickname of Alger-la-Blanche (Algiers the White).

The architecture of the lower part of Algiers is a triumph of French urban planning, but it also contains a specifically political meaning: the straight lines of the French city enclose and dominate the Casbah, imprisoning its inhabitants in the displaced Ottoman past. In 1845 Théophile Gautier wrote that the Casbah should be preserved 'in all its Original Barbary', while the Europeans should stay in the lower part, close to the harbour, because of their taste for 'large streets and commercial movement'. He complained that the modern French city was both vulgar and ugly, and that the Casbah was beautiful because it was dishevelled, half in ruins and belonged to an ancient, non-European past. To his mind, trying to remodel the Casbah on European lines was no less than vandalism.

Intriguingly, this foreshadowed the complaints that artists and writers made about what they saw as Baron Haussmann's destruction of Old Paris. In the Romantic imagination at least, this was a world of labyrinths, alleyways, secret passages and a mysterious, unknowable people called the 'working class'. Haussmann's new, spectacular Paris of wide boulevards, arcades, department stores and open squares was declared vulgar, commercial and inhuman by a generation of artists, writers and intellectuals who longed for the stinking, fetid but poetic streets of 'le Vieux Paris'. This mood was best caught by the poet Charles Baudelaire (a disciple of Gautier) who, in his 'Tableaux Parisiens', included in the 1861 edition of Les Fleurs du Mal, wrote of drunks, murderers, beggar-girls, whores and thieves who belonged to an older, more vivid and fervid city. However, as in Algiers, this reading confused the facts of history with nostalgia. The greatest danger of nineteenth-century French Orientalism was that, while it wished to be sympathetic to Algerian culture, it froze the everyday life of the Casbah in an imagined past, a fresco of 'timeless' or 'medieval' scenes which reduced real life to folklore.

By the end of the nineteenth century Algerians under the French occupation were prisoners in two senses. The first was that they lived under the control of the French government and military authorities and, as Muslims, had no political status in their own country. This was made worse by a law of 1881, the Code de l'Indigénat (the Native Code), which forbade Muslims from making 'anti-French' remarks about the Third Republic or behaving in an insolent manner towards a colonial official.

The second form of imprisonment was less visible but no less damaging: the tendency of Orientalist artists and writers to describe Algerians as colourful and exotic natives, creatures from a mysterious but primitive world which was somehow not quite real.

'Long Live Us!'

By the end of the nineteenth century, the *colons* had a firm grasp on the political administration in Algeria. Although the central authority was nominally still Paris, in reality most of the day-to-day affairs of Algeria, in the cities, towns and even the most remote villages, were run by the *colons*, who developed a network of Muslims whom they believed were friendly to their cause, or who could at least be bribed. These functionaries were known as 'cadis' and they had enormous power over a mainly illiterate Muslim population. The cadis acted in the interests of the *colons*, but they also served their own private causes, dividing up territory in an arbitrary fashion or demanding high illegal taxes on crops and land.

As the *colons* consolidated their political power, they also began to develop a cultural identity of their own, nothing to do with metropolitan France or with Paris. The *colons* cultivated their own slang, songs and jokes. A distinct dialect developed, *le Français de l'Afrique du Nord* (North African French), which was grammatically and lexically separate from the language of metropolitan France, *le Français natural* (Natural French). More informally, North African French was known in Algiers as *pataouète*, a word derived from the Catalan *el patuet*. First used by Catalan speakers, mainly from the Balearic Islands, who settled around Oran in the late nineteenth century, *pataouète* soon became a generic term for the French used by all Europeans in Algeria, which included borrowed words from Arabic, Italian and Maltese, and southern French regionalisms.

The accent was harsh and nasal and the vocabulary drawn from the realities of everyday life: the police, brothels, money and fighting. It included words like *barouffa* (a brawl or scrap), *coulo* (homosexual), *balek* (Get out of the way), *boujadi* (a fool, or sometimes a drunk). The speakers of *pataouète* also loved homely proverbs which had a entirely local meaning; for example, *anisette*, a potent and fragrant aperitif considered the best in the Mediterranean by all true French Algerians, was 'swigged down as sweetly as the piss of the Baby Jesus'. The drinking of *anisette* was accompanied by *kémia* – a snack of snails, squid or fried bread, which were staples of the raucous bars of the lower Casbah and around the docks.[3]

The cuisine developed into another badge of a unique French-Algerian identity, using local produce and borrowing freely from Arabic and Turkish dishes. So, alongside the southern European staples of bouillabaisse and paella, the *colons* also used spices, mutton, almonds and fruit such as figs and melons to produce a hearty, hybrid cuisine. Visiting Parisians turned their noses up at its lack of refinement and tended to regard genuine Arab dishes (couscous or tagine) as barbaric. None the less, the French Algerians celebrated their culture with pride. By the time Algeria gained its independence in 1962, they had come to be known as 'pieds noirs' (black feet), allegedly from the fact that the settlers in the cities wore smart black shoes, unlike the Muslims.

The emblem of French Algerian culture was the fictional character Cagayous, a picaresque rogue invented by the writer 'Musette' (the pseudonym of a certain Auguste Robinet, an outwardly respectable pied-noir civil servant). Cagayous appeared in a series of illustrated stories in the popular journals *La Revue Algérienne* and *Turco*, in the 1880s, and soon became a hero to a community of readers across the social spectrum; his adventures were then published in serial form between 1896 and 1920.

Most of the stories involved Cagayous in some kind of brawl or scam with his gang of hooligan pals in the Bab-el-Oued quarter. He spoke nothing but fluent *pataouète*, one of the reasons why he was so loved by his readers, and was fond of drink, whores and fighting. In one story, Cagayous went to Paris to visit the Exposition Universelle and was asked by passers-by who heard his strange accent whether he was French; he famously responded in the ungrammatical syntax of the Casbah: '*Algériens nous sommes . . . et que?*' ('We is Algerians . . . and whatcha gonna do about it?') This riposte would become the famous battle cry of future generations of French Algerians who rejected the political and cultural niceties of France.[4]

In Catalan or Occitan, *cagayous* means 'wheezy-chested'. However, all of Cagayous' readers could easily make the connection that the first part of his name was clearly related to the Spanish *cagar* (to shit); less certain was whether the second part, *yous*, was related to *youpin*, an insulting French term for 'Jew', which is usually translated as 'yid'.

What is beyond doubt is that, like most of his readers, Cagayous was unrelentingly anti-Semitic, and this was a large part of his appeal. At the end of the nineteenth century, 'Jew hatred' was at its height in France, too, among those of all political persuasions (indeed, many deputies were elected to the National Assembly purely on the grounds of their anti-Semitic views). The country was then both traumatized and divided over the Dreyfus affair, the drama which unfolded in 1894 when an unsigned letter, containing French military secrets and apparently on its way to the German military attaché in Paris, was intercepted by French intelligence. The letter was attributed to Captain Alfred Dreyfus, whose only mistake was to be Jewish.

In Algeria, the Dreyfus affair had a specific resonance, given the pervasive anti-Semitism among the *colons* and the Muslim population. This hatred had been sharpened by the Crémieux Decree of 1870, which gave Algerian Jews French citizenship. This apparently progressive move, engineered by Minister of Justice Adolphe Crémieux, a well-meaning Catholic, had the effect of deepening the divisions between Jews and Muslims, who were denied citizenship and remained colonial subjects. The Muslims also blamed the Jews for supporting the original colonial project – most probably, it was argued, for commercial reasons.

The Europeans hated the Jews with, if anything, more viciousness than the Muslims. This hatred was an essential ingredient in the formation of a national character among the *colons*; the most disparate races were united in their contempt for the Jew: the non-European bloodsucker and betrayer of France. The deputy for Algiers in the 1890s was Edouard Drumont, the leading anti-Semitic ideologue of the day and the author of the bestselling tract *La France Juive* (*Jewish France*), which made a racial opposition between 'Aryans' and 'Jews', accusing Jews of polluting and weakening the French national character, yet taking control of the economy. In Algiers Drumont was the inspiration for a new version of the 'Marseillaise', which was loudly sung by the welcoming crowds at the port when Drumont arrived in April 1898. In this version, the familiar verse which begins '*Aux armes, citoyens . . .*' is replaced by:

> *Français de France d'Algérie,*
> *Serrons les poings et terrassons deux fléaux,*
> *Les youpins et les francs-maçons*
> *A bas les fourbes et les traîtres*
> *Crachons dans les gueules des juifs*
> *Nous les connaissons à leur pif*
> *Ces salauds qui parlent en maîtres.*

> Frenchmen of France of Algeria
> Clench your fists and smash two vermin among us
> The yids and the freemasons
> Down with frauds and traitors
> Spit in the faces of Jews
> We know them by their big noses
> These bastards who speak like masters.[5]

This was a view shared by the mayor of Algiers, Max Régis (who was actually of Italian origin), with the added twist that Régis also claimed independence from France, which was degenerate, weak and Jew-ridden. Régis was elected to the Algiers city council, partly because of his unremitting hatred of the Jews, which he proved by whipping up hatred with every speech and systematically organizing pogroms. In January 1898 two Jews were killed and hundreds more threatened, humiliated or beaten up.

The fictional world of Cagayous reflected these events. The story *Cagayous anti-juif* presents him as an enthusiastic supporter of Drumont and Régis; with his band of mates, and with even more enthusiasm, 'the greatest of the Casbah' takes part in anti-Jewish riots in Bab-el-Oued, exclaiming, 'Down with Jews! Smash them all! A good hiding is what they all need!' However, there is a strange moment in this tale when Cagayous watches the lynching of two poor Jews. One is killed, and the second is near death, being battered by a crowd who 'are stronger than a herd of wild bulls'. At this gory spectacle Cagayous is moved to an uncharacteristic moment of pity. 'Killing two poor Jews, that's not good,' he says. The reader draws back at the next sentence: 'Throw them all into the sea, that's what should happen,' he continues. 'Or if you threw them all into a big box and sealed it up, I'd happily seal it up myself so none is left breathing.' What Cagayous actually objects to is homicide, whereas he has no qualms about genocide.

This view can still be found today, in a slightly mutated form, on the streets of Algiers, where the mainly Muslim population celebrates Cagayous as part of their own history and folklore. Anti-Semitism is still very much alive in the streets of Bab-el-Oued, although there are no more pieds noirs. 'All for Cagayous,' wrote a journalist in the newspaper *El Watan* in 2005, in a piece celebrating Cagayous as 'anti-everything'; 'Long live us!'[6]

The Blood of Races

By the end of the nineteenth century, the *colon* had constructed an image of himself as a rugged and fearless soul who, far from bringing the French civilizing mission to a savage land, was in fact making a new nation. However, although this 'nation' was clearly a living political entity, defined and united in its antagonism towards France and in its collective hatred of Jews and contempt for Muslims, it also needed an ideology, or at least a mythology.

The father of this movement was the novelist Louis Bertrand, who spent nine years in Algeria from 1891 to 1900. Bertrand was born in the Meuse in north-eastern France and enjoyed a brilliant academic career which finally took him to Algiers as Professor of Rhetoric at the university. At this stage he was tall and slim, cultivated a long, elegant moustache, and posed as a dramatic, Romantic figure, clearly possessed of great intellectual charisma as well as a surefooted style as an aesthete. He was a political conservative, eventually veering even further to the Right in the footsteps of his hero and mentor Maurice Barrès, who was a key influence on Bertrand's ideas and theories. (Many years later, Bertrand – obese and wheezing with emphysema – was elected to Barrès' seat in the Académie Française, but on taking the seat was accused of betraying his father-figure with a lukewarm eulogy.)

In Algeria, Bertrand dreamt of a 'Latin Africa'. The *colons* who were settling there might seem rough and hardy and uncultured, but in his novels and essays Bertrand celebrated them as the heirs to Roman and Greek civilization, which was now being reclaimed from the 'decadent' Arab usurpers.

In his memoirs he wrote: 'I believe I introduced into novelistic literature the notion of a wholly contemporary Latin Africa, which no one had deigned to see before I pushed aside the Islamic and pseudo-Arab decor which fascinated superficial viewers and showed, behind these sham appearances, a living

Africa barely distinguishable from the other Latin countries of the Mediterranean. The rest is only death and decrepitude, and all Africans who wish to live modern life – whoever they are – will have to enter into the framework of this new Africa.'[7] Bertrand's novels set in Algeria were minor bestsellers in their day. This was partly because they were entertaining fables of an imagined Mediterranean ideal. They also fed an appetite in the popular imagination for tales of a tougher, more vital world beyond the softness of Europe. To this extent, they function as colonial propaganda almost incidentally, much like the tales of the Old West which were beginning to circulate in the United States at the same time.

Rafael, the hero of Bertrand's first Algerian novel, *Le Sang des Races* (*The Blood of Races*), is a carter of Spanish descent who spends his time brawling, boozing and whoring in the streets of Bab-el-Oued, before finally settling down as a farmer and married man. He makes his way in a society made up a variety of European races. Interestingly, Bertrand denounces those French writers who have come to Algiers in search of local colour or the 'exotic' – usually located in Arab or Berber culture. Instead, he insists on the everyday reality of the life of the *colons* as the true portrait of Algeria.

Using Zola's panoramic technique of describing the crowd, Bertrand evokes the streets of Algiers: 'There were men present from every nation ... The most peaceful Northerners kept themselves apart: they were almost all Alsatian immigrants or Badois from the Black Forest ... Near the Spaniards, there were whole tables of Neapolitans, and Majorcans, very much at ease and speaking like people at home. The Maltese [...] stroked their heavy Victor-Emmanuel moustaches. Many had gold earrings. At bottom, however, the others despised them because of their mixed blood and their resemblance to the Moors and Jews.' The hatred of Arabs is matched by the hatred of Jews. In a central scene, Rafael enthusiastically joins in as a crowd throws stones at two Jews crossing the street dressed in the European style. 'Kill them all!' the crowd chants. 'They're disguised as us!'

Sex is a fundamental part of Bertrand's Mediterranean fantasy. When Rafael settles down into his life on the land, he does so with 'the joy of conquest ... his veins more ardent than the sun'.[8] In Bertrand's *Les Nuits d'Alger*, written towards the end of his life, nearly all of the chapters are set in the parts of the upper Casbah known for prostitution, in streets which are visibly disintegrating as they come into contact with Europeans. The union between the European adventurer and the prostitute is, however, no casual moment of exploitation, but rather an honourable, even heroic, act on the part of the European. Bertrand wrote: 'The prostitutes took me back to the most distant age of Africa, to the ritual prostitution of the temples, when the sexual act was a deeply serious thing, a religious act, when love was a terrible ill and when the act of reproduction helped the fertility of the earth and the germination of seeds.'

This scene reveals the real ideological content of Bertrand's work. As a follower of Barrès, Bertrand hated the idea of the French Republic and wished to replace it with the 'nation'. Essentially, Barrès' political theories were based on the notion that the French nation was a product of the family, the village and the region, and was subservient to them. Barrès opposed the democratic values of liberty, equality and fraternity because they were abstract concepts, with no connection to the soil of France and therefore to its people. Barrès argued instead for an ethnic nationalism, which defined Frenchness as a multiplicity of local forces, in direct opposition to the controlling central power of Paris. Unsurprisingly, he called for the return of Alsace-Lorraine on the grounds that it was a lost province of the national patrimony.

Bertrand took this theory and applied it to Algeria, which he described as a lost Latin land which was now being reclaimed by the French. He justified his ideas by arguing that the Arab invaders of the seventh century were merely occupying what had once been Roman territory. He saw the evidence for this in the plentiful ruins around Algiers and the main cities, and even in the indigenous Berber people, whom he claimed were proto-Europeans rather than Arabs.[9] It was perhaps also no coincidence that, as Paris was rebuilt by Baron Haussmann in the mid-nineteenth century, architects and engineers had uncovered the remains of the Roman city of Lutetia. For writers and historians of the Right and Left, this proved not only the antique and noble past of the French race, but also legitimized its mission to bring Latin civilization to the world.

More than this, for Bertrand, Algeria was a territory in which Frenchmen, weakened by the degeneracy of democratic government, could rediscover the strength, ardour and martial spirit which were the true glories of the French nation before the catastrophe of the Revolution of 1789 swept them away. Little wonder that in 1936 Bertrand praised the Nuremberg rallies and wished that he could see them in France, and devoted pages to praising the neo-classical architecture of Mussolini's Italy.

Bertrand is thus revealed as that most toxic combination: a French patriot and a fascist sympathizer. He died in 1941, before the Nazi occupation gave shelter to a whole generation of right-wing intellectuals who thought in this way. But it was enough that in less than a decade in Algeria, Bertrand had defined a mythology of the colonial experience that reinforced the most severe political decisions taken by Paris about Algeria. These would eventually and inevitably lead to bloodshed.

There was, of course, no sense of this unfolding tragedy in Paris or Algiers. Rather, the French were proud that they had proved themselves the supreme force for civilization, through marshalling together technology, industry and, above all, the French flair for creative artistry. This is what the French meant by progress and modernity, and what they had achieved with the reinvention of Paris in the mid-nineteenth century as the glittering capital of the world. They celebrated it with the construction of the Eiffel Tower, the supreme symbol of power and strength, for the Great Exhibition of 1889. At the exhibition, mosques and souks were constructed along the rue du Caire, to allow visitors to 'travel' from one world to another, from the glories of the West to the fantasy regions of North Africa.

The same trick was repeated to even greater effect in the Great Exhibition of 1900: there was belly dancing in cafés where you could smoke *nargilehs*, and whole streets in the 7th arrondissement were turned over to recreating the exotic, sensual, passive East that the French had conquered and made their own. In this stage set, the North African world of Islam was dramatized as a world of savage cruelty, sexual pleasure and infinite riches. All of this was so much entertainment for the Parisian audience, who thrilled, swooned, and then moved on to new tricks and pleasures.

10

Awakenings

In Algeria the twentieth century began quietly, with no sense of the storms to come. Yet there were already dangerous under-currents at work in this unstable and unfixed world. Around the turn of the century, most Algerian Muslims were caught between despair, anger and frustration at what had happened to their land. Waves of migration had transformed the country from an essentially rural backwater into an economic powerhouse. Resentment against the *colons* was fierce and widespread, but there was no real nationalism or Nationalist movement.

One of the stumbling blocks for Muslims was that, for most of them, there was no such country as 'Algeria'. Until the invasion of 1830, the territory, according to the French, had been nothing more than an unruly wilderness of warring clans and tribes. Although this was not entirely accurate, it was true that even by the end of the nineteenth century, most Muslims did not describe themselves as 'Algerian' but defined themselves as belonging to a family or a local region, or to the wider world of the Muslim umma.

There are two words in contemporary Arabic which can be translated as 'nationalism'. The first is *qawmiyya*, from *qawm*, meaning 'tribe' or 'race', and this is often taken to mean a kind of pan-Arab nationalism without reference to a specific country.

The second is *wataniyya*, from *watan* (homeland, or nation), which refers to a precise region. The shift between these two poles was often blurred and ambiguous in Algeria, but when the two did come together later in the century, they did so with devastating effect.[1]

None the less, after decades of humiliation, by the beginning of the twentieth century there were the first stirrings of a sense of pride in these twin identities. This was cultivated first of all by looking to the East, to the journals and newspapers of Cairo or Istanbul, where young intellectuals were beginning to assert a new sense of self in the face of Western colonialism. For Muslims in Algeria, turning to the East was natural, since it was also the home of the purifying force of original Islam. In 1908, when the French introduced compulsory conscription, several hundred leading Algerian intellectuals migrated to other Muslim countries in protest. The Italo-Turkish war of 1911–12 gave the Algerians new hope, as they prayed for a Turkish victory over the Europeans and dreamt of *nahda* – the rebirth of Islam. In the years before the First World War, this renewed sense of community was commonly expressed in the mosques in the prayers for a Mahdi – the 'messenger of God' who would also be *moual es-sa'a*, 'the master of the hour', capable of delivering Algerian Muslims into freedom. But for all their prayers, no one in the Muslim nation knew how this might happen.[2]

These nascent hopes were soon in ruins after the outbreak of the First World War. Suddenly, the intellectual and cultural traffic between Algeria and the rest of the Arab world came to a halt, with the introduction of passports and travel restrictions. Most importantly, the disintegrating Ottoman Empire was split into two by the conflict between the European colonial powers. The Germans cultivated Turkey as an ally, providing money, troops, advisors and equipment in return for an Ottoman declaration of war. The Turks agreed to this alliance because they believed that the Germans were the only European power that could stop further encroachment into Ottoman territory by Britain, France or Russia. The Germans also persuaded the Turkish authorities to call for a jihad against Britain and France – a potentially devastating move, given the millions of Muslims in French and British colonies.

The call was never answered. But the already fragile links with the Ottoman Empire which had underpinned Algerian Muslims' sense of self were now broken, and at the same time the old trading patterns with the East were wrecked by the new realities of war. Most devastating of all was that Muslims in Algeria now had to look to France for employment and for military protection that they didn't want. All of a sudden those who had looked to the East were forced to look to the North, a place which few Muslim had ever visited but which they all knew to be a spiritually barren and hostile territory.

'Algerians' and the Great War

With the war came the first wave of Algerian immigration to France, as 120,000 Muslims were forced to come to France to replace the domestic labour force lost to the trenches. For most of them, this was their first encounter with 'Western civilization' and it came as a profound shock. The Muslims found that the world of their 'masters' was a harsh and brutal place. They encountered not only ignorance and racism, but also exploitative working practices and class hatred. In Algeria, the pieds noirs and the Muslims were not friends, but they were bound together in a society that both sides understood. In France, the Algerian Muslims were cast adrift in every sense.

In a parallel shift, one of the consequences of the war was that it brought together the pied-noir community in a new way. Until 1914, most pieds noirs had rarely or never visited France, a country which existed in their minds only as a distant and abstract concept. Although the notion of France as the motherland was always a useful rallying point for all pieds noirs, the reality was that Paris and its politicians were all too often seen in Algeria as meddling bureaucrats with no direct knowledge of the harshness and the beauties of 'Latin Africa'. To this extent, Algiers and Paris were usually locked in combat over the everyday politics of taxes and legislation.

From 1914 onwards, several hundred thousand pieds noirs were conscripted into the French army. On French soil they naturally found a sense of solidarity and common destiny – Corsican, Maltese, Spanish, Italian and French pieds noirs were now bound together in a single identity. In the conflict 22,000 pieds noirs were killed. One of them was Lucien Camus, a poor farmer of Spanish origin from the region around Oran. Lucien was the father of Albert Camus, who belonged to the generation of French Algerians who, when they felt that France was about to betray them by granting Algeria its independence, 'returned to this blood sacrifice and asked that France repay them this debt'. This view was not shared by Camus, but he was 'Algerian' enough to understand it.[3]

During the war, a few Muslims discovered Socialist politics and began to think of their return to their homeland of Algeria in terms of reform or even revolution. These ideas were underscored by the events of the Russian Revolution in 1917 and Woodrow Wilson's declaration in 1918 of peoples' right to self-determination. They were one of the roots of the nascent Nationalist movement in Algeria after the war.

Many more Algerian Muslims, suffering in exile, found comfort in Islam. German propaganda disseminated among Muslim soldiers in the French army sought to take advantage of this instinct. The propaganda campaign was informed by a young intellectual, Shayk Salih Al-Sharif, who fervently believed that the Germans would free the Algerians from the French. Al-Sharif was born in Tunis around 1880 to an Algerian family known for their devout religiosity and hatred of the French. He began his career as an Islamic scholar and took an interest in the debates emerging from Cairo and Istanbul on reforming Islam. Essentially, Al-Sharif was opposed to modernity and the Egyptian and Turkish modernizers who were trying to separate Islam from politics. He took a hard-line position against the possibility of secular democracy in Islamic lands.

In the run-up to the war, from 1902 onwards, Al-Sharif undertook a complicated and shadowy itinerary which took him from Istanbul, where he worked for Turkish Intelligence agencies, to Berlin, where he represented the Turkish Minister of War and was soon asked to draft pamphlets in Arabic against the French. The Germans treated him as an honoured guest and he enjoyed swaggering around at meetings and parties, always dressed in traditional clothes, hobnobbing with the leading German figures of the day, the men who dreamt of the destruction of the French and British Empires.

Al-Sharif was by now known to the French authorities for texts he had published in Tunis and Algiers. In these he loudly supported the caliph's call for jihad. In an essay entitled 'A Declaration on the Machinations of the French against Islam and its Caliph', which was secretly distributed in Algiers at the beginning of the conflict, he called for Muslims not to betray their religion and to fight the 'unbeliever' wherever he could be found (mainly France). He also wrote a longer, historical text, 'An Account of the Savagery of France in the Lands of Tunisia and Algeria and an Appeal to Aid', which described how France had ignored international law and had done exactly as it pleased in Algeria and Tunisia. These arguments, in reduced form, were dropped on the trenches by German aircraft, in the hope of encouraging Muslim soldiers to desert.

There were also rumours among North African Muslims that the German emperor, Wilhelm II, aware of the spiritual emptiness of the West, had converted to Islam, and might even be wreaking holy justice on the French as the Mahdi, the 'master of the hour'. Wilhelm was renamed El Haj Giyum (from the

French 'Guillaume') and songs were sung in his honour. One of these, popular on the battle-front, was:

> *Russia is dead*
> *Germany has stripped her bones*
> *France takes mourning and weeps*
> *Hail, Giyum,*
> *Who rises in an aeroplane does battle with the stars*[4]

Al-Sharif himself also believed in propaganda by deed. As the conflict intensified, he toured the German prisoner-of-war camps, seeking out Muslim prisoners, making sure that their religious needs were met, and reassuring them that the final victory of Islam was at hand. This was also the message that he preached in the trenches, where – presumably to the bafflement of French, German and Muslim troops alike – he appeared in the full costume of an Arab knight, declaiming in classical Arabic and reading from the Koran.

Al-Sharif was clearly not a Nationalist in strict terms. Rather, he was a virulent anti-modernist to whom 'nationalism' was part of the modernity he hated. He was calling for revolt in Algeria to save Islam, but in the early twentieth century even the most faithful Muslims did not see that this could be a political reality in a world defined by the economic and military might of the colonial powers. After the catastrophe of the First World War, the countries of Europe and America held the reins of power, slicing up and scattering the remains of the Ottoman world at will. This was not just the end of a civilization; it was the end of the unity of the Muslim world. Those who wanted to resist the Europeans needed new weapons, a new set of ideas.

11

Enemy States

In 1930 the French celebrated one hundred years of conquest. There was a series of commemorative festivals across Algeria and France that year and again in Paris in 1931, at what would be the last Great Exhibition. Algeria was now an integral part of France and the Muslims were grateful, so the French argued, for the benefits of peace and civilization.

At the opening of the Great Exhibition in May 1931, Paul Raynaud, Minister for the Colonies, declared, 'colonization is necessary, for it is in the nature of things that peoples who have arrived at a superior level of evolution lean down towards those who are at a lower level in order to help them up'. The Italian Minister for State put it in slightly less sophisticated terms when he described the French Empire as part of the 'Homeric odyssey of the white race, which, having reached into every corner of the world, has transformed and continues to transform the barbarian continents into civilized regions'. The Catholic Church joined in: a certain Cardinal Verdier praised the 'powerful colonizing genius of our dear France', while his colleague Monsignor Durand of Oran added, 'Let God fold all of those from beyond the sea and natives of Algeria into the flag of France, which is so dear to Christ!'[1]

Resistance to the French took many forms. One of the less

overtly political ways of challenging the French authorities was through football, which had been popular in Algeria since the early 1920s. The sport allowed young Muslims to come together in a collective identity that was otherwise denied them, and matches against *colons* permitted direct physical contact (which was probably why they often ended with brawls on the pitch). The North African Championship of 1927 helped to unify and organize the sport.

For the young Muslim players and supporters, football was a way of subverting the French state and of organizing collective activity out of view of the authorities. The name of the Mouloudia Club, founded in the Casbah in 1921, for example, was taken from Mouloud, the festival celebrating the birth of Mohammed, while their team colours were the red and green of Islam. Naturally, the authorities were suspicious that these teams might be a front for Nationalist activities. In 1928 a new law declared that every team in Algeria must have at least three European players (this was increased to five in 1935). It was possible, however, to circumvent this rule by fielding 'naturalized' Muslims, or simply saying that Europeans were just not good enough.

The first real organized resistance to colonialism was, however, founded in religion. The years after the First World War saw an Islamic revival in Algeria as Muslim soldiers returning from the front line in Europe found comfort in their faith. The wider Muslim population in Algeria was also now learning from the dismal realities of the European war that their colonial masters were not all-powerful and unbeatable.

In 1931 Shayk Ben Badis founded the Ulema, a political movement which began to articulate these perceptions of colonial weakness and desire for a homeland into a kind of religious and cultural faith. In spiritual terms, Ben Badis' faith closely resembled the Wahhabi form of Islam, which was a powerful force in the deserts of Saudi Arabia: he scorned saints and superstition and advocated Islam as an active rather as a passive faith. So Muslims were told to be no longer 'the domestic animals of colonialism'. His political credo was enshrined in the statement: 'Islam is my religion, Arabic is my language, Algeria is my country. Independence is a natural right for every people on earth.'[2]

The Islamic revival in Algeria which began in the 1920s was also driven by charismatic Egyptian intellectuals such as Muhammad Rashid Rida, who argued against colonialism and made the case that Islam was not a quaint museum piece but a living component of the modern world.

In 1933 the French colonial authorities banned the Islamic reformers from preaching in the mosques of Algiers and Constantine, preferring the more traditional and politically naïve forms of Islam. The inevitable result was growing anger among the Muslim masses. In 1936 the mood was caught in the words of Shayk Ben Badis, who declared: 'this Algerian nation is not France, cannot be France, and does not want to be France . . . [but] has its culture, its traditions and its characteristics, good or bad, like every other nation of the earth.'

The first wave of modernist ideas in politics came from the Young Algerians, a group founded in 1907. Its members were intellectuals from the Muslim upper middle classes who spoke French as well as being fluent in the Arabic of the Koran. Taking their cue from the Young Turks – the movement of radicals which did so much to modernize Turkish society in the early twentieth century – they argued for 'integration' between the Muslim and French populations and saw no contradiction in these dual identities. The Young Algerians were unashamedly élitist and demanded preferential treatment for '*les évolués*' – the more 'evolved' elements in Muslim society who accepted that modernity in its European form was an unshakeable and powerful force. On this premise they argued for reform and indeed were successful in extending the vote to more (though not all) Muslims.

In the wake of the First World War, the Young Algerians were led by Khalid ibn Hashir, the intellectual and hard-headed grandson of Abd el-Kader. Emir Khalid, as he was called by his supporters, pressed hard for changes in legislation and won several important victories and concessions from the French government, which still saw Algiers as a fundamentally unstable city, but which wanted to reward the Muslim population for the sacrifice of those who had died in the trenches. Emir Khalid retired to Damascus in 1923, exhausted by the struggle, but his legacy was the abolition of travel restrictions on Muslims, equal pay for government employees and the abolition of the *Code de l'Indigénat*.

These were also the demands made in the 1930s by Ferhat Abbas, who, following the Young Algerians, sought an 'integrationist' model which would give the French-speaking élite among the Muslim population parity with French citizens. The question of Islam was separate from the political agenda pursued by Abbas, who – at least at first – believed that the French insistence on the secular state meant that religion was an individual, not an ethnic, issue. In other words, to be an Algerian Muslim was an act of choice, like being a French Protestant or Catholic, but all rights were equal and guaranteed in the Republic. On these grounds, Abbas argued that Algerian Muslims could not be denied their rights as citizens.[3]

But such reforms were still a long way from any real challenge to French colonial authority in Algeria. This came in 1927 from a group called Etoile Nord-Africaine (the ENA, or North African Star). This was originally a loose coalition of factions which came together in Paris to support and defend the rights of North African workers in France. Their inspiration was the French Communist Party, which taught many of its first members the language of anti-colonialism and human rights. In 1927 the leader of the ENA, Ahmed Messali Hadj

– a charismatic speaker and shrewd political operator – called for the overthrow of French rule in Algeria and a declaration of sovereign independence. Even more provocatively, he also called for freedom of the press, universal suffrage and the return of all stolen lands to their original, Muslim owners.

His speech exploded like a bomb planted at the heart of the French political system. All parties, of Left and Right, condemned Messali Hadj and, unsurprisingly, the ENA was made illegal in 1929. This forced Messali Hadj underground, but he did not disappear. Instead, learning the language of liberation from such mentors as the Lebanese ideologue Shakib Arslan, he moved further away from Marxism, necessarily limited as a European world view, and began developing a clearer idea of what it meant to Algerian and a Nationalist. By 1934, still operating in clandestine form, the ENA's newspaper had a readership of 43,000 in France and Algeria.

Initially, Messali Hadj saw no contradiction between Islam and Socialism. He was, however, disappointed at the indifference or even contempt of his European Socialist peers towards Islam and consequently began to drive his party towards a more explicitly Nationalist position. In the 1930s, after a spell in a French prison, he returned to Algeria, and in 1937 he founded the Parti du Peuple Algérien (Party of the Algerian People), which agitated for an uprising among the Algerian working class. Although he espoused class-based politics, for Messali Hadj the Algerian working class meant Muslims.

On 14 July 1937, during a parade of the French Communist Party, Messali Hadj was the first person to carry the Algerian flag through the streets of Algiers. The flag had been designed by his French wife in the colours of Islam, with the crescent as its emblem. Carrying it on 14 July, the national day of celebration of the French Republic, was a provocative gesture that immediately identified all Muslims as true Algerians and non-Muslims as French. This division had already been given a sharp edge by the French authorities' opposition to the strengthening ties between Algerian Muslims and the Arab world, a dangerous coming together of *qawmiyya* and *wataniyya*.[4]

Algerianists and Parisians

All of the currents for reform in Algeria – integrationist, Nationalist or Islamic – were opposed with equal ferocity by the *colons*, who had built a nation in their own image. The fantasy of 'French Algeria' explored in the novels of Louis Bertrand had been made real in architecture, town planning, military power and the sheer number of settlers who now ran the big cities, traded in the ports and swarmed across the countryside and the mountains. For them, by the early twentieth century, Paris was as much an enemy as the Muslims.

This growing French Algerian nationalism was expressed in the 'Algerianist' literature which discarded French identity altogether for a new Mediterranean civilization. The term 'Algerianist' was coined by the *algérois* writer Jean Pomier in the founding issue of his journal *Afrique* in 1921. In the journal's manifesto Pomier called for a future 'Franco–Berber race' which 'would be of French language and civilization'.

This was not the 'Latin Africa' of Louis Bertrand, although Bertrand was the acknowledged father of the movement. Rather, the 'Algerianists' imagined a mixed race of Mediterraneans, including the Berbers as the 'original Africans', who, forged by the hardships of living on African soil, would produce a new generation of virile, self-reliant French Algerians. One of the leading lights of the Algerianist cause was 'Robert Randau', whose real name was Robert Arnaud and who been a colonial official in the Upper Volta (now Burkina Faso). By the time of his death in 1950, Randau had published over twenty novels, many of which described the life he found in Algeria. Randau never explicitly called for a separate French Algerian state, but, like many settlers, he dreamt of an autonomy which would effectively have made French Algeria a 'state within a state'. He expressed this in one of his first novels in 1907: 'We are those who want Algeria to have complete administrative and financial autonomy, who advocate racial fusion, and who believe that the union of interests is the precursor to the union of hearts.'

This 'racial fusion' is, however, firmly within limits defined by Europeans. In *Cassard le berbère*, Randau tells the tale of Jean Cassard, a settler who fought in the First World War at the head of a unit of Berber troops drawn from his estate. What he admires about the Berbers is that their vigour and brutality, which are missing in feminized and weakened Europeans on the mainland. Cassard's neighbour says of the Berbers: 'They are filthier than pigs, but they don't fight progress! Sure, four million of them and one million French Algerians, that'll make a country! And we'll be through with the bullshit they send us from Paris.' Randau's view was that the new country would be built by Africanizing the Europeans as well Europeanizing Africans.

As a young man Albert Camus was influenced by the Algerianist movement, even if he did not agree with the political views of its members. For Camus, to be an Algerianist was to speak French as one's mother tongue, but to belong to a Mediterranean world which saw Paris as a dark, distant, entirely separate place. Even when he had become famous in Paris, Camus always described himself as an 'Algerian writer'. Camus celebrated this Mediterranean world in his meditations among the Roman ruins at Tipasa, some seventy kilometres outside Algiers. In his 1938 essay *Noces à Tipasa*, dedicated to rediscovering the ancient classical memories of Algeria, Camus evoked the pagan, sensual world which he saw reflected in the vital, physical life on the sun-soaked shores of North Africa. Camus' most Algerianist work, however, was the *Le Premier homme* (*The First Man*), the unfinished manuscript that he was working on when he was killed in a car crash in 1960. In this semi-autobiographical text which draws on his childhood in the working-class district of Belcourt in Algiers and his quest for a missing father, Camus reminisces about his upbringing with tenderness. He recalls the houses at the foot of the Casbah where the 'homes smelled of spices and poverty', and the 'obstacle course of Arab peddlers' stands bearing helter-skelter displays of peanuts, dried salted chick-peas, lupin seeds, barley sugar coated in loud colours, and sticky sourballs . . . Arab fritters dripping with oil and honey, a swarm of children and flies attracted by the same sweets.'[5]

The Arabs of Algiers are more present in this work than in any other of Camus' books set in Algeria; it is the European child, who has lost his father in a European war, who feels displaced and an outsider. 'The Mediterranean separates two worlds in me,' he wrote. By 1960 terrorist bombs were a regular occurrence in Paris and Algiers, and Camus could not feel at home in either city.

In 2013 I asked his daughter, Catherine Camus, who was a small child at the time, whether she had any recollection of her father's anguish. We were sitting in the back room of Camus' house in Lourmarin in south-eastern France, surrounded by his books and papers, original editions of the journal *Combat* and his letters. 'We did not understand what was happening,' she said. 'But we knew that when Papa came back from Algeria he was always sad.' Catherine looked exactly like her father – the determined jawline and saturnine eyes. The house was full of dogs. 'My father loved all animals, especially dogs,' she told me. It was one of his habits to find stray dogs and give them away to friends and neighbours. After the family was forced to leave Algeria and moved to Lourmarin, Catherine missed North Africa. When she later fell ill, her father promised that if she got better he would get her a donkey sent over from Algeria. He was as good as his word and Catherine's childhood companion was an old donkey from Philippeville. She still referred to the town as 'Philippeville', rather than Skikda, its new Arab name.[6]

Slowly, through the 1920s and 1930s, Paris was beginning to wake up to the fact that 'French Algeria' was not necessarily driven by French interests. This was a volatile state of affairs, not only because of the Muslims' violent resentment but also because the *colons* were now presenting a direct threat to the authority of Paris.

Liberals in Paris favoured an 'integrationist' solution, but were blocked by the *colons*, who dismissed all attempts to advance the Muslim cause as betrayal. In Algeria, the *colons* had control over the business world and the armed forces, and had powerful supporters in the National Assembly. This was the basic framework for what would soon become not so much a colony as an enemy of metropolitan France.

In 1936 the Front Populaire (Popular Front) swept to power in Paris. This coalition of Communists, Socialists and other forces on the Left, led by the Socialist Léon Blum, had come together as a response to the rising tide of right-wing leagues and political parties. When the Front Populaire took office, everything changed in France more or less overnight. A maximum working week of forty hours and paid holidays were introduced for the first time in the history of Europe. Folk memories of the Front Populaire usually conjure up images of cycling trips to the countryside, expeditions by train to the sea, huge soccer crowds, Sunday picnics with wine and flirting, and, above all, a long-sought-after sense of dignity for the working population. There were new products, such as suntan lotion by l'Oréal or the fizzy drink Orangina, which brought what had been luxuries to the masses. Paris was declared a workers' paradise on a par with Moscow.

It was, of course, no more than an illusion. As inflation and depressed wages began to bite, the workers' demands soon created real hardships for the workers themselves. The right-wing press, ever alert to the 'Red Terror' in Paris, began publishing cartoons of workers raping rich old ladies in the name of their 'rights'. Fear returned as the dominant leitmotiv of everyday life. Anti-Semitism was rampant. It was rumoured that Léon Blum, a Jew and a vociferous supporter of Dreyfus, was planning to wreck France and take refuge with his co-conspirators, the deadly and hypocritical English. The gutter press was alive with the wildest allegations, which no one dared refute or challenge in case the attacks became worse. The press also regularly carried dire predictions of a devastating future war which would destroy France once and for all.

In Algeria, the Front Populaire government was welcomed as a potential ally by the integrationists led by Ferhat Abbas and by the Nationalists led by Messali Hadj. However, it was also met by deep suspicion, which soon became hatred, among the working-class settlers, who feared any move towards political power for the Muslims. None the less, Blum was determined to resolve the 'Algerian Question' by drawing Muslims into French citizenship.

To this end, in the wake of a congress held in Algiers in 1936, the Blum government announced the 'Viollette Plan' (named after its author, Minister of State Maurice Viollette), which would immediately extend French citizenship with full political equality to certain members of the Muslim élite, including university graduates, elected officials, army officers and professionals – some 25,000 Muslims, with numbers growing every year. Predictably, these proposals were vehemently opposed by the *colons*, who feared a Muslim majority in elections. Messali Hadj disdainfully dismissed the plan as 'an instrument of colonialism'. (This statement led the Front Populaire to ban Messali Hadj's Etoile Nord-Africaine, only for it re-emerge in 1937 as the Parti du Peuple Algérien, or PPA – the Algerian People's Party.) The Viollette Plan was also rejected in Paris by the politicians of both the Right and the Left who had a vested, usually commercial, interests in French Algeria.[7]

By 1939, as France lurched towards the catastrophe of the Second World War, there was no longer any middle ground in Algeria. The stage was set for a conflict which would engulf France in the post-war period, and, like the Nazi occupation, would threaten the very existence of the French state.

12

Switching Sides

The Second World War was both a shock and a trauma to all sides in Algeria. Most terrifying of all was the Fall of France in 1940. No one had seen this coming or prepared for what might happen next. In one fell swoop the settlers lost the nation that gave them political legitimacy. The hopes of Algerian Muslims had already been dashed by the failure of the Blum–Viollette Plan, and they clearly expected little from an aggressive Germany whose main aim seemed to be to take over as much of the French Empire at it could: the Germans, too, were Europeans, and they too were Imperialists. On the other hand, Muslims took note of the fact that the French, who had dominated their lives for so long, were no longer invulnerable.

The *colons* were terrified that the Fall of France might mean the break-up of the colonial administration. They were relieved when, on June 25 1940, it was announced that Germany would preserve the integrity of the French Empire. Straight away, the majority of *colons* threw themselves behind the Vichy government of Marshal Pétain. No German soldiers were stationed in Algeria and it was easy for the *colons* to believe that Vichy meant a return to order in France and the possibility of organizing a military retaliation against Germany. In Algeria it was possible to be pro-Vichy and anti-German.

The French government's delegate in Algeria was General Weygand, who was a patriotic soldier and, it was understood, fiercely anti-German. After the British attack on the French fleet at Mers-el-Kebir in July 1940, the French army in Algeria was increased to 120,000 men, incorporating different races, which was larger than the French army on the mainland and gave rise to the fantasy that Weygand was planning to save France from Algeria.

Weygand was removed from his post in 1941 under German pressure on the French authorities (he had opposed German encroachments on Algerian soil). Although the Vichy government immediately lost prestige among the *colons*, Pétainism remained alive as a political credo. Above all, many of the *colons* admired Pétain for his call for a 'National Revolution' – a return to the land, family and patriotism as the central values of Frenchness, which was what many French Algerians had been arguing for all along. The southern European population of Algeria – Spaniards, Sardinians, Maltese – whose sympathy during the Spanish Civil War had been with General Franco, saw Pétain playing the same role in France. In the cafés of Bab-el-Oued, over glasses of beer and *anisette*, the received wisdom was that Pétain was a crafty fox who had outwitted Hitler; 'The old man's got the better of Adolf!' was a common refrain.[1]

There was also a small minority of Algerian Muslims who supported the Vichy government, partly because they found Pétain's emphasis on authority reassuring and partly because they were hoping for political concessions. Both the *colons* and the Algerian Muslims were happy to accept the anti-Jewish laws that the Pétain government so shamefully and swiftly put into place. On 7 October 1940, when anti-Semitism had been legally ratified by Vichy, the Minister of the Interior repealed the Crémieux Decree, which had given Jews in Algeria the right to French citizenship. Most *colons* were delighted to carry out the anti-Semitic policies of Vichy and did so with an enthusiasm that occasionally shocked the German authorities in France; in Algiers, however, anti-Semitism had long been a casual fact of daily life.

At the beginning of the war, most Algerian Muslims had pledged their allegiance to France, despite misgivings. They mainly saw the conflict as the unfinished business of the First World War, and even the most radical Nationalists preferred to deal with the French government rather than with an even more alien foreign power. Their view changed when the Vichy régime came to power. Although some Muslims were elected to its Conseil National, most of them opposed the government, not because it was clearly morally and politically vicious, but because it was evident that Vichy had no interest in the Nationalist ambitions of Algerian Muslims. Pétain's government appealed to Messali Hadj to collaborate, with the promise of future concessions. He refused on the grounds that he was in favour of an independent Algerian nation and not a colony. In March 1941 he was sentenced to sixteen years of hard labour. Algerian Muslims saw this as yet another savage betrayal.

Arabs and Americans

The authority of the Vichy government and the triumphalism of the settlers were, however, short-lived. In 1942 Algeria fell to British and American troops as part of Operation Torch, the mass Allied landings in North Africa which would prove to be a turning point of the war and the launch pad for the Allied assault on southern Europe. The Allies landed at Sidi-Ferruch, as the French had over a century earlier. The troops disembarked in the shadow of the Stars and Stripes and brought with them military armour and organization which impressed the Algerian Nationalists, who watched impassively as the Vichy régime mounted a disjointed if sometimes murderous resistance. The British and American troops were pinned down on the beach for several hours by sniper fire, and commanders feared the arrival of German paratroopers in support of the French. When Marshal Pétain heard the news in Vichy, he told the American consul: 'France and her honour are at stake. We are attacked. We shall defend ourselves. This is the order I am giving.'

Operation Torch was politically challenging. Although there were no Germans in French North Africa, it was not clear how much resistance the Vichy troops would put up. The American consul in Algiers, Robert Daniel Murphy, reported that the mood in the city was anti-German and that resistance would be minimal. He also made secret contact with senior French officials in Algiers who confirmed this view. But the Americans were also vehemently opposed to General de Gaulle and his Free French forces, who had already infiltrated Chad, Congo and Cameroon, and wanted to avoid installing him in power in Algeria at all costs. Instead they made friends with hard-line right-wingers, some of them members of the monarchist Action Française.

To make matters even more complicated, the Americans and British had initially been reluctant to take part in Operation Torch, favouring a single Second Front with a big push into occupied Europe. The Soviet Union made the argument that an assault in North Africa would take the pressure off its own hard-pressed troops and divert the German forces towards the south, trapping the German army in Egypt and preparing the ground for the assault on northern Europe. Churchill was finally persuaded that North Africa was the 'soft underbelly' of Europe, and convinced Roosevelt in turn. However, the British role in the operation was reduced so as not to antagonize Vichy France, which had been hostile to Britain ever since the sinking of the French fleet at Mers-el-Kebir in 1940. Operation Torch was constructed as a simultaneous amphibious landing, with the Allied forces seizing the ports and airports of Casablanca, Oran and Algiers. By the evening of 8 November 1942, after firefights with Vichy troops in the suburbs and in the main squares of Algiers, the city was under the control of the Allies.

The invasion of Algiers was none the less a tense affair. Originally the Americans had wanted to place Henri Giraud, a conservative, anti-German anti-Gaullist in power. Giraud, however, missed his rendezvous with the American submarine that was to pick him up in southern France and was stranded in Gibraltar as the landings took place. The Americans suspected that this was a ploy and that Giraud was waiting to see what happened in Algiers and wanted no responsibility for having French blood on his hands.

As the American warships prepared to land in Algiers, it became known that the pro-Pétain Admiral François Darlan was in Algiers, visiting his son, who was ill with polio. Darlan, who until two months earlier had been commander of the Vichy forces, seized control of the situation and declared to the population of Algiers that the Americans would never dare to enter the city. When they did, he called in the Luftwaffe (who never came) and ordered the Vichy troops to fight back; 1,356 Frenchman and 456 Allied troops were killed before Darlan ordered a ceasefire.

Darlan was a vain and ambitious man, who was quickly persuaded by the Americans to sign an accord giving him control over North Africa. The British were unhappy with this – Darlan was a clear collaborationist – but they were not quite as furious as Pétain himself, whose power started ebbing away as the Germans invaded the 'Free Zone' of France in response to the American victory in Algeria.

Darlan did not last long in power: he was shot in dead on Christmas Eve 1942 by Fernand Bonnier de la Chapelle, allegedly a monarchist and a member of the French Resistance. In turn, Bonnier was mysteriously shot on Boxing Day. Algiers buzzed with rumours and conspiracy theories. Chief among them was the story that this was a plot by the British Secret Service to stage a coup d'état in Algiers. Whatever the intrigue, the Americans could now install their chosen candidate – General Giraud, who had finally arrived in Algiers to take command.

On the ground, the Allied invasion of North Africa was the first time that Anglo-American cultures had properly been engaged in this part of the world. For the ordinary soldiers, the military operation in Algiers was their introduction to the reality of the Arab world.

Although the Americans saw the Maghreb through the prism of French colonial politics, it was also – as it had been for the French before them – the source of fantasy as an exotic, intriguing and sexualized world of its own. Hollywood had recently picked up on the popular taste for tales from this newly discovered Oriental playground. In 1938 the film *Algiers*, an Americanized version of *Pépé Le Moko*, starring Charles Boyer and Hedy Lamarr, had given cinema-goers a glimpse of the lurid life of the Casbah. This was followed in 1942 by *The Road to Morocco*, a musical comedy with Bob Hope and Bing Crosby, and by *Casablanca*, both of which were released to take advantage of the newsworthiness of Operation Torch.

American soldiers inevitably tended to see this first meeting with the Arab world in terms of Hollywood images and what they knew of 'native American' cultures. In the pages of the *New Yorker*, A. J. Liebling recorded the views of a soldier called Bill Phelps from Twenty-Nine Palms, California. Phelps observed of the dry and dusty landscape: 'This is exactly the way it is back home, except that back home we don't got no Ayrabs.'

As the Allies settled in for the occupation, ordinary soldiers came into closer contact with the Muslim population, but it tended to be limited to touts and street traders. In the official US Army newspaper, 'the Arab' was referred to as an amusing sub-species, servile but essentially harmless; there was no insight into the anger of the colonized population, who were portrayed as a weak and emasculated race:

If the Arab was often a pest and pretty generally a nuisance, he nevertheless was indispensable. He shined our shoes, sold us oranges, delivered eggs to our front lines right through enemy fire, and continually reminded us what blessings we had in the form of chewing gum, chocolate and cigarettes. Above all he provided the American soldier with plenty of jokes . . . Actually the Arab was a spectator in last winter's grim business. You can chalk that spectator attitude up to history, of which he has seen quite a lot. He used to be a fighting man himself but that was a long time ago, when the zeal of the Prophet Mohammed's followers expressed itself in a continuous brandishing of the sword. Since that time he has learned to wage his campaigns with oranges, eggs, dates, almonds and shoeshine boxes rather than with hand grenades and howitzers. The North African Arab hasn't been intimately mixed up in a first-class war for centuries now, having been by and large content to let the other races do the squabbling . . . It's a fair assumption that he has developed by this time what could be called a neutral attitude.[2]

The Anglo-American fantasy of the 'Orient' also included sex. But this, too, was a disappointment. Sergeant Len Scott had sailed from Liverpool to Algiers on board SS *Duchess of Richmond* with over 6,000 infantrymen. He recorded his initial amazement at the beauty of Algiers, the stench of the city, their first encounters with 'natives', and the unalluring reality of the fabled veiled women of the Orient:

It was on my twenty-ninth birthday that I saw Algiers. How beautiful it looked in the clear, hard sunlight, the white buildings stretching around a bay, buildings separated by groves of cypress and palm. How surprised were most of us at its unlooked-for size and outward splendour . . . Western architecture for the most part, with a few minarets as Islamic exclamation-marks. All that day we stood off from the shore until the white walls turned bluish and the lengthening shadows crept across the city. We docked at last but not until the following morning did we make physical contact with Africa – on Friday 13 November! That floating white purity when seen far off, became a nasal offence. We [. . .] admired the view – the sea on one side and the Kasbah on the other . . . a higgledy-piggledy heap of white buildings and grim little alleys climbing up a hill. Figures moved on the flat roofs – Arab women washing their linen. Picturesque, but if the wind were blowing from that direction we did not linger.

The Kasbah was out of bounds [off-limits] to all military personnel. Legends circulated – maybe more than legends – about soldiers who had tried to 'chat up' Arab women and whose bodies, when discovered, lacked certain organs. The ordinary British soldier had a half-contemptuous, half-amused attitude towards the 'natives'. We were unaware that 'Arabs' were sometimes Berbers.

The veiled women aroused little erotic interest. Most of those appearing in public were obviously so old and fat that the veil was a kindness. 'I'll get one for my old woman when I get home,' was a common remark.[3]

Algerian Muslims, in contrast, greeted their new conquerors with curiosity and also the hope that they might lead them to freedom from the French. In the days before the landings at Sidi-Ferruch, Ferhat Abbas had made several visits to Consul Robert Murphy, seeking reassurance that the invasion would be the prelude to Algerian independence. Murphy could never give such an assurance, but the dream of freedom persisted.

Algerians noted, however, the racial segregation among the US forces. The contradiction between the American claim to bring freedom and the fact of racism had long been reported in the *Chicago Defender*, the most influential Afro-American newspaper in the United States. The landings in North Africa were celebrated in the columns of the *Defender* as a return to the homeland. One cartoon showed Hitler fleeing across the desert pursued by a black soldier in US army uniform, a barefoot African wearing a fez and an Arab wielding a scimitar. There was a kind of truth at work here: from now on Algeria was the base for Allied troops to fight the desert war in Tunisia. But the notion that this was a multiracial coalition against European racism, incarnate in Nazism, was no more than a fantasy, and would soon be revealed as such by events.[4]

In 1942 the European population of Algeria, somewhat grudgingly, switched sides. Giraud was a conservative and popular with the *colons*, who saw him as continuing the old order. He spoke Arabic and also had an admiration and affection for Islam and the 'natives'. Combined with his visceral anti-Semitism, this made him reluctant to change the anti-Jewish laws established under the Vichy régime. It was only in 1943, as de Gaulle began to establish his authority, that the Crémieux Decree was reinstated and Algerian Jews regained their French citizenship. In the meantime, the Muslims were encouraged to join the Allied forces, which they did with unbridled enthusiasm, believing the Americans would soon be their liberators. On 15 August 1944 several hundred thousand Algerian Muslims landed on the beaches of Normandy. Under the flag of the United States, they fought and died for the French nation – a country that most of them had never seen and where they had no status as citizens.

As part of his strategy to reclaim all the French territories that had been under the control of Vichy, General Charles de Gaulle, leader of the Free French forces, visited Algeria in 1943. He saw straight away the dangers of an angry and mutinous native population and set up a commission for Muslim reforms. The commission promised that French citizenship would be given to tens of thousands of Muslims at the end of the war in recognition of their sacrifices for France, the Mother Nation. The *colons* reacted angrily, arguing that de Gaulle was abandoning them. But he went even further, promising two-fifths Muslim representation in local assemblies and governing authorities.

By 1943 this was already too late. Betrayed by Paris, Vichy and ultimately America, the veteran Nationalist and liberal reformer Ferhat Abbas had hardened his position and demanded a completely new status for his country. He joined forces with Messali Hadj and together they drew up a manifesto for a New Algeria. Their demands were unequivocal: they both wanted an autonomous republic with the same status as any other nation in the world. There was to be no negotiation.

> *At the end of hostilities, Algeria will be set up as an Algerian state endowed with its own constitution, which will be elaborated by an Algerian constituent assembly, elected by universal suffrage by all the inhabitants of Algeria.*[5]

This was obviously unacceptable both to the *colons* and to Paris. There was to be no more dialogue between the Algerian Nationalists and the French. Having only recently been released from prison, Messali Hadj found himself deported to Brazzaville in the Congo. Meanwhile, Ferhat Abbas continued to organize for a future Algeria free of the French.

The end of the war also brought famine to Algeria. There had been bad harvests in 1944 and 1945, exacerbated by the deprivations of wartime. In the winter and spring of 1945, thousands of hungry peasants swarmed into the towns and villages, desperate for food and shelter. They congregated around soup kitchens set up by supporters of Abbas and Hadj. Along with the soup, the Nationalists ladled out propaganda: the French were deliberately starving the Muslims, the French would never give up Algeria, the Americans were traitors, freedom would never come. The atmosphere in Algiers was heavy with the promise of violence, which soon turned into real killing on both sides. The future of France would come to be determined by events in Algiers, but for the time being most Parisians cared very little about events so far away, until the betrayals in Algeria found their violent echo in the streets of Paris.

The catastrophe began in 1945 with a vague report of a massacre in Sétif, in the Constantine area of Algeria. Sétif was then not much more than an obscure market town set on a bleak and treeless plain. In the words of Harold Macmillan, who had passed through in 1943 in his capacity as the Minister Resident in North Africa, it was 'a town of no great interest'.[6]

On 8 May 1945, at around 8 o'clock in the morning, a crowd of some 10,000 Muslims from Sétif and the surrounding villages started gathering. The German High Command had finally surrendered the night before, heralding the VE Day celebrations in Europe. The demonstrations in Sétif began quietly enough, with a flurry of British, French and Russian flags on parade. There were placards in French with slogans such as 'Free Messali!', 'We want to be your equals!', 'Down with colonialism!', but this was nothing that the police had not seen before. Sétif had long been an occasional base for Algerian Nationalists, and anti-French sentiment was a staple of daily life here. The marchers had been granted permission to parade as long there were no anti-French slogans, and no flag other than the French or those of the Allied nations was allowed. The police tolerated the singing of the Nationalist anthem, '*Min Dijbalina*' ('From our Mountains'), which accompanied the first marchers.

Then, around 8.45 a.m., the mood – tense but unthreatening – suddenly changed as Aissa Cheraga, a young Muslim, unveiled the Algerian flag at the head of the parade. When the marchers reached the Café de France in the centre of town, a police commissar called Olivieri tried to seize the flag. Scuffles broke out, punches were thrown and Olivieri was knocked to the ground.

There were gunshots from the police and from the crowd, and then a twenty-six-year-old Muslim, Bouzid Saal, staggered out of the parade, dripping with blood, clutching an Algerian flag, and fell to the floor, shot dead.

Rage and panic now overwhelmed the marchers and the Europeans who had gathered to watch or police the parade. The crowd of Muslims drew guns, staves and knives, and with the cry *'N'katlou ennessara'* ('Kill the Europeans!') launched themselves at passers-by and the police. The riot went on through the afternoon and by early evening had spread to the neighbouring town of Guelma.

The riot sparked a general uprising in which over a hundred Europeans were killed in five days of fighting. The Muslims across the region were ferocious – it was if the rage of over a hundred years was now being unleashed in this paroxysm of violence. This was the Europeans' worst nightmare, as even trusted servants and employees turned against their masters in a bloody festival of unexpiated guilt, shame and terror. Many of the Europeans had their throats slit and were horribly mutilated. Men were castrated, genitals stuffed down their throats and women were raped. Even moderates from the Communist and Socialist parties had their hands chopped off. The local religious leaders had called it a jihad and declared that it was a religious duty of all Muslims to kill all unbelievers – 'Kill them all!'

It was bad luck, but no coincidence, that this uprising started on VE Day. In Paris, understandably, all news from abroad was lost in a seemingly endless swirl of dancing, drinking, kisses and celebrations. Very few people were aware of what was happening in Algeria, which was technically a part of France. No Paris newspaper thought it necessary to send a correspondent there. De Gaulle himself shrugged off the events 'as a beginning of insurrection, occurring in the Constantinois, [...] snuffed out by Governor-General Chataigneau.'[7]

This 'snuffing-out' was merciless. Over the next few weeks nearly 6,000 Muslims were slaughtered by the French army, who wished to show 'a strong hand' (and possibly avenge recent humiliation by the Germans). The French troops were aided by American forces, who helped 'evacuate' Europeans from sensitive areas before allowing the French soldiers free rein. Radio Cairo reported that more than 45,000 were killed – a figure which was then taken as a fact by Algerian Nationalists. The insurrection finally came to an end on 22 March 1946. The army then organized public spectacles during which local Muslim men were forced at gunpoint to prostrate themselves before a French flag and declare, 'I am a dog and Ferhat Abbas is a dog.'

For Algerians, the massacre at Sétif revealed the true face of 'French Algeria'. In France Albert Camus was one of the few to raise his voice in protest, writing in the journal *Combat* on 22 May 1945: 'The Arab people exist and they have the same right to the democratic principles that we claim for ourselves.'[8] He argued that this was a crisis and not an isolated incident, and that the Arab was not inferior to the European simply 'because of the condition he lives in'. He recognized that from now on nothing could ever be the same again between Europeans and Muslims. The poet and journalist Kateb Yacine, recalling the massacre as an adult, wrote:

> *My sense of humanity was affronted. I was sixteen years old.*
> *The shock which I felt at the pitiless butchery that caused the*
> *deaths of thousands of Muslims, I have never forgotten. From*
> *that moment on my nationalism took definite form.*[9]

In the wake of Sétif, the *colons* were in an even stronger position of power. This did not make them any more generous when it came to reforming the status of Muslims. Instead, they pursued a policy of control, containment and coercion. Crucially, with the tacit backing of the government in metropolitan France, the *colons* did their best to ensure that they held the majority vote on all matters. Their tactics included electoral fraud and corruption at all levels. Meanwhile, many Algerian Nationalists who had seen their leaders humiliated and their people massacred, went underground. The thirst for revenge was more powerful than ever, but this was also the time to watch, wait, arm and train.

For the time being, the conflict in Algeria was limited mainly to skirmishes between French forces and the rival Nationalist forces of the Parti du Peuple Algérien (PPA) and the new and more potent Front de Libération Nationale (FLN). During the late 1940s and early 1950s Nationalists moved between Paris, Algiers and Cairo, studying the currents of pan-Arab nationalism in Egypt and gauging the mood of the Left and of people across France. They concluded that a war against French Algeria, and probably also against France, was the only solution to their suffering, and began to plan their opening moves. The explosion would surely come. It was now only a matter of time.

13

The Reconquest

The mountain range of the Aurès Massif is a dramatic and beautiful region which cuts across the north-eastern edge of Algeria. The winters are long and bleak and the land is then mainly covered in snow. The summers reveal lush, green valleys, rich with apples, walnuts and honey. As you move further south, from the city of Constantine to the towns and villages around Batna and Biskra, the temperature seems to rise with every kilometre, signalling that this mountainous area is also the end of the Mediterranean world of Algeria and the passageway to the Sahara.

The people who live in these mountains are known as the Chaoui, and this is also the name of their language, which is a dialect of Berber. They have been here for over 4,000 years. The women outline their eyes with kohl, tattoo their faces and refuse to wear the veil. Both men and women work the fields. The Chaoui are known to other Algerians for their indifference to the city life of Algiers or Constantine, and, above all for their defiance of all conquerors – Roman, Arab or French. The mountains are steep and rocky and the area seems empty. But this is not the case; the Chaoui, used to harsh conditions, live in isolated settlements across the region, often high in the mountains. They are protected by the terrain and

158 Algeria, Prisoners of Love

any approaching army is easily spotted from the high peaks. The landscape has much more in common with the mountainous regions of Afghanistan or Pakistan than with the urban civilization of the Mediterranean coastline.

This is why, in 1954, this territory was chosen by the armed Nationalists of the Front de Libération Nationale as 'the principal revolutionary stronghold' of Algeria. For operational purposes, the FLN divided Algeria into six *wilayas* – an Arabic term meaning an area under government or military control. It was their stated aim to bring 'the war home to France', and in doing so to make Paris the 'seventh *wilaya*'. The war would be launched and driven, however, from the Aurès Massif, which the FLN designated as the 'first *wilaya*'.

By the early 1950s, most of the European population of the Aurès – some 60,000 settlers – lived either around the garrison at Batna or in the small town of Arris. Very few were able to make a living by farming or could settle in the parched, mountainous land. Both of these towns were connected to the rest of Algeria by tiny, winding roads that were easily made impassable by bad weather or bandits. There were regular threats to the safety of the settlers and occasional violent clashes. Despite this, the region was under the protection of a single French administrator and a handful of gendarmes. Vulnerable to attack, most European settlers lived with a siege mentality. This was a frontier zone, a long way in every sense from Oran or Algiers. In late October 1954 the French authorities received another warning from an unnamed terrorist group that any Europeans on their own in the Aurès were targets, so they issued a statement calling all Europeans back to the main towns. Most were schoolteachers, often working in remote villages with high ideals of bringing literacy to the rural poor.

By this time of year the first cold winds of winter were already forcing shepherds down from the high peaks. On 1 November, which was Toussaint, or All Saints' Day, the morning dawned bright and clear, auguring well for the public holiday. At around 7 a.m., in the dusty open space that passed for a village square in Tlefel, a remote village deep in the Aurès, Djemal Hachimi was revving the engine of the clapped-out Citroën bus belonging to his brother, which he regularly drove over the mountains from Biskra to the neighbouring town of Arris. Among the country people making the long trip were two schoolteachers setting out on a holiday: a young couple, Guy and Jeanine Monnerot, aged twenty-three and twenty-one.

The Monnerots had only just got married and had only been in Algeria for a matter of weeks. They had come to the Aurès Mountains to teach local children. They were both Arabophile, bookish, and left-wing in their views. The Chaoui in the village where they lived and taught had accepted the couple with friendship and sympathy. As the couple got on the rickety bus, the news had not yet arrived in Tlefel that Europeans were to get out of the region.

The bus was soon making slow and steady progress through the tight gorge of Tighanimine – the road is very narrow and surrounded by steep, rocky cliffs, and the soil here is blood red. Once you are in the gorge, there is no way out; it is the perfect place for an ambush. Not far from the entrance there is a plaque commemorating the Third Augustan Legion, which came here in AD 2 to crush a revolt. Now, high in the hills, a group of thirty-five armed men, all FLN militants, were waiting for the arrival of the bus. They had been there since 3 a.m., having been given orders to halt any traffic in the gorge and kill any French soldiers or Algerians faithful to the French. They knew that Hadj Sadok, a local caïd, or chief, who had been a captain in the French army and was loyal to the French, was on board.

The bus driver, Djemal Hachimi, was a supporter of the FLN and had been told the day before to expect a roadblock of stones and boulders at the seventy-nine-kilometre signpost. As he approached, he noticed nervously that there was no more than a scattering of stones, barely enough to justify stopping. None the less, he brought the bus to a sudden, stuttering halt, throwing sleeping passengers into the aisle. As he did so a shot was fired and the bus was suddenly surrounded by fifteen armed men, wearing leather jackets and khaki trousers.

Hadj Sadok was dragged off the bus. He was confronted by Sbaihi Mohammed, the leader of the commando unit. Hadj Sadok had been sent the declaration of independence by the FLN the day before and had screwed it up and thrown it away. Sbaihi Mohammed addressed him directly: 'Are you with us or against us?' Hadj Sadok shouted defiantly that he had no respect for bandits. He then turned to get back on the bus.

Hadj Sadok was shot dead on the spot. In total thirty-five bullets were fired at his body – by the armed men on the ground and also by snipers positioned on the cliff. In full view of the terrified passengers, who were crouching on the floor of the bus, many of them weeping in fear and horror, his body was then thrown on to the front seats and Hachimi was ordered to drive on to Arris.

At that point one of the snipers higher up the cliff spotted the two young Europeans, who were trying to make themselves as inconspicuous as possible. Sbaihi Mohammed ordered Hachimi to bring out the Europeans. As they stepped off the bus, the two young people were cut down by a hail of bullets. Guy Monnerot was shot in the chest, Jeanine in the left thigh. On Sbaihi's orders the bus started up again, the FLN dispersed and the young couple were left to bleed to death in this empty wilderness.

Guy Monnerot died slowly and in great pain. His wife, in agony beside him and unable to move from her wounds, watched his life fade away and waited to die herself in a pool of her own blood. This was how the Algerian War of Independence began.

Jeanine's life was saved by Jean Servier, an ethnologist who had taken command of Arris as news of the shootings came through.

He heard about the dying French couple from the traumatized passengers who arrived in Arris with the bloodied corpse of Hadj Sadok. He set out with an armed patrol and brought Jeanine back to the town; from there she was taken in a helicopter to Constantine.

The murder of Guy Monnerot provoked disgust and anger among French settlers and Muslims alike, but no one yet talked of war – the FLN were unknown and officially this was still a native mutiny – and the news made little impact in the French press. *Le Monde* gave the events two columns under the headline 'Several Killed in Algeria'. *L'Express* attacked Messali Hadj and his 'subversive schemes', designed to promote the Arab League and the pan-Arab nationalism that had its capital in Cairo. The French public greeted this with a distinct lack of interest – the recent deaths of Henri Matisse and Colette, and the awarding of the Nobel Prize to Ernest Hemingway all earned more news space.

This was an historic moment, yet, like most historic moments, it did not seem so at the time. Even now, the memory of 1 November 1954 is confused in the French and Algerian imagination. The FLN wanted to prove itself as a well-organized and ruthless fighting force. It was crucial that the Algerian population understood this and afforded them respect. They wanted to demonstrate their superiority over other Nationalist groups – that the FLN alone could bring the Algerian nation to independence. At this point the FLN was still a shaky coalition of Nationalist groups and paramilitary forces, who were mostly known for being at war with each other. Most Algerian Muslims remained unconvinced. The killing of the French teacher disgusted the majority, who read about the attack in the newspapers. or heard the news on radios in cafés; they wanted no part in such squalid brutality. The unit that committed the murder was later punished by the FLN for breaking its order that no European civilians should be killed.

The murders were the first in a wave of seventy attacks launched by the FLN as a declaration of war on the French state. The day later became known as '*Toussaint Rouge*' (Bloody All Saints' Day). The date had been chosen partly for its symbolic value – it celebrated the struggles of early Christian martyrs – although it was never clear whether the FLN identified with the martyrs or the persecutors. The FLN had also calculated that security would be more lax during the holiday.[1]

Other attacks took place across Algeria that day against police stations, military installations and public utilities, including a cork warehouse and a gas works in Algiers. They were clumsy and amateurish affairs, and the masses stubbornly refused to rise. None the less, the FLN had announced itself to France and the world. Their objective was stated boldly on broadcasts from Radio Cairo: 'restoration of the Algerian state – sovereign, democratic and social – within the framework of the principles of Islam'. Their methods included 'every means until the realization of our goal'.

Over fifty years later, this initial act of the Algerian Revolution can be still a source of guilt and recrimination. When the film-maker Malek Bensmail returned to Aurès in 2008 to make a documentary about the memories of 1954, he captured on camera the veterans of the war arguing among themselves, claiming the murder was an accident or that they had been provoked. Nobody had wanted to kill the schoolteachers, but they should not have been there, they were armed, or they were spies. The unit in Aurès had broken the order of the FLN high command that no European civilians should be injured during the launch of the National Revolution. Once the damage was done, the FLN were portrayed in the French Algerian press as thugs and killers. '*Toussaint Rouge*' was murder, and it brought shame on the revolution.

When Bensmail asked the young people about the events at Tighanimine, they were bitter about the past and the present.

This is still a wretchedly poor region and the future for young people is a choice between emigration and endless poverty. They were indifferent to the monument to the revolution that had been placed there in 2008. None of them knew what the revolution had been for – their prospects in this impoverished region were probably worse than those of their grandfathers. Some of them did not know who they had been fighting. 'Who were the settlers?' a teacher asks a student in one revealing scene. The student is genuinely puzzled. 'People from far away,' he says. 'They came here to kill Algerians. They were Americans.'[2]

'Ici, c'est la France!'

For most of those who fought in the Algerian War of Independence, France was a distant and unknowable place, but they had a straightforward choice between tolerating being made to feel a stranger in your own country or fighting the occupying enemy. In the days after *Toussaint Rouge*, Arabic graffiti appeared everywhere in Algiers. The slogan was soon translated into French and sent a chill through all French Algerians: '*La Valise ou le Cercueil!*' (The Suitcase or the Coffin!).

But even the FLN could not argue that *Toussaint Rouge* was a success. In their attacks across Algeria, nothing had gone quite to plan, which only confirmed in the minds of many Muslims that the Nationalists were big on talk but short on organization. Worst of all, in Oran the raid on a police station had left eight FLN militants dead, while the weapons promised from Morocco never arrived. Many Muslims described the night as a *bavure*, a police 'cock-up'.

Toussaint Rouge left the French government in no doubt about the dangers of what was happening in North Africa. In the past twelve months, both Morocco and Tunisia had begun the journey towards independence from France. To the French, Algeria was different: it had ceased to be a colony in the nineteenth century and had become an integral part of France – as French as Alsace-Lorraine, Provence or Brittany, and to be defended with due vigour. On 12 November 1954, President Pierre Mendès-France made a combative speech to the National Assembly:

> *One does not compromise when it comes to defending the internal peace of the nation, the unity and the integrity of the Republic. The Algerian departments are part of the French Republic ... Between them and metropolitan France there can be no conceivable secession ... Ici, c'est la France!*[3]

Mendès-France was supported by the Minister of the Interior, François Mitterrand, later to become president of France, who also declared: 'Algeria is France. And who among you, mesdames, messieurs, would not hesitate to employ every means to preserve France?' In late October Mitterrand had already been to Algeria on a brief visit to establish his presence. In a canny political manoeuvre, he now ordered in the crack divisions of the CRS (Compagnies Républicaines de Sécurité) riot police from Paris, thereby treating the violence as a police matter and not a military one.

In Algeria, however, the revolt confirmed everything that the settlers claimed they already knew about the volatile and potentially evil Muslims in their midst. Opinion was divided over whether this was tribal uprising, common in the French colonies of sub-Saharan Africa, and ultimately meaningless, or whether this was terrorism sponsored and organized by Cairo. Either way, the response was, as usual, a swift and stern assault on any Muslim suspected of involvement or sympathy with the rebels. The governor-general described the situation to Paris as 'disturbing but not dramatic', and military and police operations soon filled the jails. The main target were the Nationalist followers of Messali Hadj, who was initially furious when he heard of the revolt – he had been badly wrong-footed by the FLN – but soon let it be known that he had in fact orchestrated the events. The police arrested everyone they could, including an innocent pharmacist who had written to *Alger républicain* to complain about the heavy-handed police action. Meanwhile the settlers declared loudly that they had known for a long time that this would happen and started to blame Paris for being soft on the Muslims. 'The evil is spreading', declared François Quilici, the deputy for Oran. 'French peace in Algeria is ruined. Weakness always encourages new adventures.'[4]

In Paris and Algiers no one was ready to believe that France had now entered into a new war. Certainly no one suspected that what would happen in Algeria over the next few years would be every bit as brutal and murderous as the darkest moments of the Second World War, or that France's international prestige would be damaged beyond repair in its empire and beyond. Yet the events of 1 November 1954 were to be the catalyst for a complex triangular conflict which pitted Muslim against Muslim and the French Algerians against the population of mainland France. Within this triangle, shadowy terrorist and espionage groups launched 'black operations' to subvert one side or another.

The war passed through three main stages. In 1954 the FLN was desperately fighting to survive, killing Muslims who did not support them, terrorizing them with mutilation and assassination. The FLN was based mainly in Algiers but had influence throughout the country in cells drawn from the ranks of other Nationalist groups. Their main targets were '*béni-oui-oui*' (yes-men), Muslim supporters of the French. The FLN had to assert itself as the sole Nationalist authority and ordered all Nationalist parties to rally to its cause. Ferhat Abbas went over to them almost immediately but Messali Hadj refused to concede any ground and launched the Mouvement National Algérien (the MNA) as a direct rival to the FLN.

The second phase, the 'Battle of Algiers', lasted from January 1956 to May 1957. A series of terrorist attacks by the FLN provoked the French government to send in the army, led by General Massu. The French president was Guy Mollet, a Socialist and a veteran of the French Resistance. An honourable man who saw events in Algeria through the prism of the 1930s, he was determined not to sell out the settlers in the way that the Czechs had been sold out to Hitler in 1938. He also began secret talks with the FLN. The government view was that this was now a battle between French universalism and Arab nationalism. Massu crushed the FLN in Algiers with merciless efficiency, but his ruthless methods angered world opinion.

The third phase was heralded by the fall of the Mollet government in 1959 and the eventual collapse of the Fourth Republic. Fearing that they would be betrayed, European settlers rioted in Algiers, lynching Muslims in the street and smashing the heads of Muslim women and children with iron bars. The crisis brought Charles de Gaulle out of retirement to take control of what suddenly looked like a potential civil war in Algeria and France. He proposed a truce with the FLN, but when this was rejected, he set about defeating them with maximum force.

'No Pity, No Quarter!'

From its opening moments, the defining and most shocking feature of this war was the extreme violence on both sides. The FLN slit throats, decapitated bodies and mutilated genitalia; the French razed whole villages and practised torture as a systematic weapon of war. This violence could not simply be explained by politics alone.

The background to the war had been the lies of the settlers regarding citizenship for Muslims, which was promised but never came, and the corrupt French electoral system. The elections of 1948 and 1951 had been fraudulent, and even moderate Algerian Muslims felt angry at being cheated by such open contempt for their rights. Muslim veterans of the Second World War returned to Algeria to find that they were third-class citizens of the country that they had been fighting for. The massacres and the massive bombardments which followed the uprising at Sétif showed that while the French claimed to defend democracy and freedom in Europe, they were not prepared to allow such ideals to flourish in Africa. It was out of the bitterness and frustration of these experiences that the FLN was born – bringing together those Nationalists who no longer believed that France would ever make concessions and convincing them that the only way forward was independence achieved by an 'unlimited revolution'. By the 1950s, the birth rate in Algeria meant that Algerian Muslims outnumbered the French by three to one; if this population could be mobilized, they argued, Algeria would be free.

So the first phase of the 'unlimited revolution' began with the FLN's terror campaign against any Muslim suspected of collusion or sympathy with the French. This was not new in anti-colonial wars. The FLN openly took inspiration from the Vietnamese nationalist leader Ho Chi Minh, whose strategy for getting rid of the French in Vietnam was stated thus: 'For every nine of us killed, we will kill one – in the end you will leave.' Ho Chi Minh began his campaign by killing 25,000 Vietnamese villagers whom he deemed sympathetic to the colonizers. Like the Vietnamese Communists, the FLN knew that they could never outgun the French in military terms. Their aim, therefore, was to create a climate of fear and insecurity which would make it impossible for the French to stay. The FLN's violence was, however, a new form of viciousness. It was not enough to kill. They sought to murder in the most grisly and dramatic manner so as to drill fear deep into the Muslim imagination.

The first victims during the winter of 1954 were all soft targets – country policemen, local caïds faithful to the French, or anybody working for the settlers as servants or in trade. The

FLN wanted to destroy the settler economy based on wine and so decreed a ban on all Muslims drinking alcohol or smoking. The penalty for the first offence was to have the lips or nose sliced off; the second offence was punished by throat-slitting. This is associated with the killing of sheep and is seen as a profound humiliation in the Algerian imagination. The other forms of killing included dismemberment – cutting off legs, arms and genitals and stuffing them into the mouth of the victim. Rows of severed heads were regularly found neatly lined up at the roadside. As the death toll rose through the spring of 1955, living in rural Algeria took the form of a strange and disturbing dream.

In the main cities, much to the anger of the FLN, life for the settlers went on as normal. It was almost as if *Toussaint Rouge* had never happened. In the West this was the era of rock'n'roll and the consumerist culture emerging from the United States – a new form of modernity which promised freedom and excitement to young people across the world. The children of the settlers in Algeria embraced this new culture with the same enthusiasm, but there was also awareness that their society might not be as stable as others.

The big American film of 1955 was *Blackboard Jungle*, which depicted rebellious teenagers and featured 'Rock Around the Clock' by Bill Haley and his Comets. In the United States and Britain teenagers slashed cinema seats and rioted at screenings as they asserted their independent identity. France and French Algeria were not immune to the shock waves of these cultural shifts, but they were set against the background of the violence in Algeria. The French rocker Eddy Mitchell sang of 'young guys who set the night on fire, then set off for Algiers, Algeria'. Young French Algerians embraced the new fashions and music. Cafés such as Le Milk Bar or Otomatic installed juke boxes and had space for young people to dance, chat and flirt. But as the violence in the countryside spiralled and the FLN grew stronger in the cities, the fragility of these symptoms of Western modernity was soon exposed.

'Much Meat'

The first major turning point of the 'war' took place on 20 August 1955 in Philippeville, a coastal town in the north-east of Algeria. These days Philippeville is known as Skikda and is a large and relatively prosperous port, with a marina, steep streets and a view of the Mediterranean. Its present-day air of busy calm is, however, an illusion. This is a place of terrible memories for Algerians and Europeans alike.

The twentieth was a day of searing, almost unbearable temperatures. Even in the early morning, the town could only be seen through a haze which made everything – the buildings, the streets, the people – seem hallucinatory. This eerie atmosphere pervaded the suburbs of the city, where around eleven o'clock thousands of Muslims gathered, answering the call of the FLN to resist the French in an uprising.[5]

During the days leading up to the mutiny, observers noticed that strange things were happening. Taxis were no longer at their ranks. Muslims were flooding into the region, semi-hidden in garages, cellars and gardens. Bakeries and food stores were emptied as families stocked up to prepare for the hard days to come. The French secret services were watching and waiting. One Arab grocer informed them that he usually sold a sack of flour every two days; now he was selling two tonnes every day and being paid in cash. A local pharmacist reported to police that Arabs unknown to him had been buying huge amounts of bandages. The French secret services reckoned that there were maybe 3,000 or 4,000 militants hiding in the hills and forests around Philippeville. They were mainly country people, bringing women and children with them. The local European population was being slowly surrounded.

On the appointed day, the Muslim crowds, armed with sickles, pitchforks, knives, axes and sticks, were loosely organized by armed FLN militants in khaki uniforms or red turbans, carrying guns and rifles. There was high tension in the air. Philippeville had seen mass violence before: in 1942, Senegalese riflemen under French command had shot dead thirty Muslim civilians in the old quarter of the town, before intervention by American troops had brought the killing to a halt. Now, in the broiling sun, the crowds were alive with rumours that Americans were again on the way to help the Muslims, that Egypt was sending gunboats. As the militants advanced towards the city, women and children moved through the crowd – the excited talk was of divine justice and holy war.

The scene in the centre of Philippeville was a typically French summer weekend – the *café terrasses* were packed with locals and holidaymakers, drinking wine and pastis, chatting up girls, planning an afternoon on the beautiful beaches along the Gulf of Stora. Nobody heard the first gunshot as the Muslim crowd entered the edges of the town, but as soon as the Muslims reached the main street there was total panic.

The militants advanced in lines, six abreast, waving the Algerian flag and singing the battle hymn of the PPA as they headed for the rue Clemenceau and the church of Saint-Coeur-de-Marie. The cry went up from the terrasses and cafés: 'The Arabs are here! Get off the streets!' This was a normal enough response to the spectacle of an angry mass protest. But this was not to be a demonstration: it was a massacre.

The Muslims were under orders to attack all Europeans – civilians, women, children – who stood in their path. This was the new policy of the local FLN commanders, Youssef Zighout and Lakhdar Ben Tobbal. They had declared total war on the French. The date had been chosen to mark the second anniversary of the exile of the Sultan of Morocco – organized by the French because of his opposition to the French protectorate. The aim was to bring Algeria on to the world stage and awaken the sympathy of all those countries in Asia and Africa which were freeing themselves of the colonial yoke. Zighout had announced to his followers: 'To colonialism's policy of collective repression we must reply with collective reprisals against the Europeans, military and civil, who are all united behind the crimes committed on our people. For them, there will be no pity, no quarter!'[6]

There was pandemonium in the streets of Philippeville as the FLN columns attacked and killed at random. Grenades were thrown into cafés, tables overturned, motorists dragged from cars – Europeans were slashed with knives and razors, heads split by axes and sickles. There was a euphoric frenzy to all of this – Muslim women were ululating, giving a terrible, sinister soundtrack to an orgy of slaughter. As the blood flowed, the crowd grew ever more cruel. When French paratroopers arrived on the scene, they were shocked by what they found. One soldier recorded his disgust in a diary:

> *Bodies literally strewed the town. The Arab children, wild with enthusiasm – to them it was a great holiday – rushed about yelling among the grown-ups. They finished off the dying. In one alley we found two of them kicking an old woman's head. Yes, kicking it in! We had to kill them on the spot: they were crazed . . .*[7]

These scenes were repeated across the district of Constantine, in twenty-six towns or villages. The worst of the horror took place in the hamlet of Aïn Abid and in El-Halia, a mining town near Philippeville. These were places where the Muslim majority had a long tradition of living and working in friendly intimacy with Europeans. When the paratroopers arrived in El-Halia, they found the streets stained red with fresh blood. Women had had their throats ripped out and their stomachs slashed with hooks. Babies had been thrown against walls, their heads smashed open so that brains spilled out. Men had been ambushed in their cars returning home from the mines. In Aïn Abid a family called Mell had all been slaughtered, dismembered and disembowelled. A five-day-old baby had been knifed to death and then carefully placed back in the dead mother's open womb.

One of the most terrifying aspects of the violence in Philippeville was the way in which Muslims had turned on their former friends and neighbours with such fratricidal savagery. One survivor of El-Halia was Marie-Jeanne Pusceddu, who was born in Philippeville and lived there all her life. She was seventeen in 1955 and had been married a few weeks before the massacre. She recalled that on the night before the killing, as she returned home from her honeymoon, a taxi driver, well known to the family, had told the couple: 'There will be a *fête* tomorrow. There will be much meat!' Marie-Jeanne was puzzled at this as she knew all of the Muslim festivals and none of them was due. She thought the man was joking.[8]

The next day, as the family was sitting down to lunch shortly after midday, she heard ululations and gunshots from the street. The door crashed open, hacked into by an axe, and the same taxi driver launched himself at the family, armed with a rifle. Marie-Jeanne was shot in the thigh but managed to escape, hiding for sixteen hours, drenched in blood, in the laundry room of the house. Her mother was shot in the chest, as were her sister, younger brother and sister-in-law. Their bodies were mutilated – fingers, ears and lips chopped off. There was indeed 'much meat'.

The Arab Mentality

Europeans were shocked by the nature of the violence as well as by its scale. Forgetting the fact that French history consisted of a series of bloody insurrections, intellectuals, police and colonial administrators agreed that there had to be a 'scientific' explanation for this. In Algiers, in the late nineteenth century, an entire school of psychiatry had been established to explain this kind of violence. More specifically, psychiatrists sought to make a link between Islam and what they called the 'Arab mentality'.

This school of thought can be traced back to the racial theories of the nineteenth century, and also to the writings of a certain Dr Boigey, who, while travelling in Algeria, produced a 'psychological study of Islam'. Boigey's theories were based on a crude form of Darwinism, which defined Europeans as the product of a 'civilization' that keeps them active and inclined to progress. According to Boigey, Arabs are essentially indolent, mainly because of the warm climate but also because they have been degraded by their worship of 'a brilliant impostor known as Mahomet'. Islam, Boigey declared, is a 'mental pathology'. The symptoms of this 'neuropathic state' include sexual perversion (masturbation and homosexuality), fatalism, delusional melancholy, an obsession with words ('Allah, Allah'), and, worst of all, auditory hallucinations that provoke sudden and extreme spasmodic violence.[9]

Boigey's theories were not always accepted by his peers, but they helped to foster a view among French psychiatrists of Islam as unknowable or unreal. This was often allied to an anthropological conception of the Arab as having a primitive or pre-logical mentality. The Arab was, of course, not a true primitive – this was to be found in sub-Saharan Africa – but the 'Arab mentality' was a form of 'mystical causality'. Islam was therefore not a form of religion but really a form of magic. What is perhaps most surprising is that these 'psycho-anthropological' theories had persisted in Algeria in the minds of respected doctors until the 1950s. In the pages of the French Algerian press, the massacres at Philippeville were thus explained by the innate savage instinct of the Muslim.

It is true that in the days leading up to the massacres, many of the killers of Philippeville and El-Halia had worked themselves into a murderous ecstasy – praying, smoking *khaf* (the local form of cannabis) and singing. Angry, humiliated and stoned, the crowd lost all contact with pity or remorse. But this state of mind was not inspired by Islam, nor was it unique to the 'Arab mentality'. From the French Revolution to Philippeville, all rioting mobs have in common the same sense of transgression – in the moment of mass violence, the individual ego is lost in the exhilaration of combat and the sense of unlimited freedom. By the time the mob arrived in the streets of Philippeville, it was already a killing machine, and the violence was deeply symbolic. Throat-slitting was the traditional way of killing a goat or sheep and so a way of dehumanizing the victim. Similarly, cutting off lips and nose defiled the seat of man's honour (*nif* is the dialectal Arabic term for this notion). The scenes were grotesque but they had a meaning: they encoded both a primal rage and a howl for justice.

When Governor-General Jacques Soustelle arrived in the area he was appalled at the scenes. He visited the hospitals and attended the funerals. A total of 123 people had been killed during the FLN attacks. At the cemeteries, crowds of relatives trampled on and destroyed the flowers sent from the governor-general's office in Algiers and railed in despair at how they had been abandoned. Soustelle was essentially a liberal Gaullist, but the scenes in Philippeville hardened him and he now determined to crush the FLN by whatever means necessary. This was a war between civilization and barbarism, and the French military were now suddenly at the front line of the conflict.

This was also the view of Paul Aussaresses, a captain in the Special Operations Unit in Algeria. Aussaresses was then thirty-five years old and had had a distinguished career in the French Resistance and in Indochina. He arrived in Philippeville in May 1955 with the mission to monitor and prevent FLN attacks. He quickly learned that the local police were more effective than the military at this task because the police were experts at torture.[10]

As a military man, this was the first time that Aussaresses had met such practices and he was initially repelled. But the massacres changed his mind. The FLN had to be destroyed, and if this meant that the suffering of a prisoner — usually already a convicted terrorist — could save the lives of hundreds or thousands of settlers, then there was no more discussion. With the aid and expertise of the police, Aussaresses began to torture prisoners, using physical beatings, rape and suspension by the wrists and ankles. These practices were officially illegal but were tolerated throughout the territory.

For Algerian Muslims, a police interrogation became synonymous with being tortured — '*musclé*', as the French soldiers termed it. The practices soon became more refined in their cruelty: one of the most effective was to lower a victim into a bathtub of dirty water, with a policeman or soldier pushing his head under; when the victim was about to drown, he was taken out and battered to a pulp. More deadly was the practice of making the victim sit on a broken bottle, with a torturer pushing the victim down, at first gently and then with increasing pressure from the shoulders. This would leave a victim in agony for months, if he did not die from a perforated intestine. All victims and torturers agreed that the most excruciating part of the process was the anticipation and the fear. Young French recruits, new to the army and to Algiers, were themselves often traumatized, shaking and vomiting at the smells and the cries.

In the field, Aussaresses ordered his soldiers to shoot suspected rebels at will. In practice, this meant every Muslim they came across. Within weeks, the death toll among Muslims had risen to 12,000, according to FLN estimates. Certainly eyewitness accounts and recorded footage show the French army and police shooting unarmed victims in the stomach and face, taking back the land with a harsh indifference to the killing. The French authorities disputed the FLN figures but conceded that 1,273 Muslim were probably killed.

By 1955, there was no longer any common ground left between Muslims and Europeans across the territory. In the weeks before the massacre at Philippeville, Albert Camus had written two articles in the left-leaning journal *L'Express* on the subject of terrorism and repression. He argued that since the elections in recent years had been falsified, the Muslims lived with 'no future and in humiliation'. He did not excuse terror as a weapon of war, but he did understand that, as he put it, 'In Algeria, as elsewhere, terrorism can be explained by a lack of hope.' Even at this late stage, Camus hoped for a compromise solution in Algeria, which would allow settlers and Muslims to return to the relatively peaceful existence that Camus had known in Algeria in the 1930s.

However, the nature of the violence in Philippeville changed everything. The poet Jean Amrouche, like Camus a child of Algeria, wrote that Camus' idealism and liberalism were finished: 'The evil is too profound. No agreement is possible between the natives and the French of Algeria. I no longer believe in French Algeria.'[11] After Philippeville, the French and Algerian communities waited for Camus to speak, to propose a way out of the impasse, but he was now exhausted. 'My days are poisoned,' he wrote to a friend. 'But Arabs and Frenchmen must find a way to live together.' However, he was doubtful whether this would happen. 'Algeria is not France,' he wrote in *L'Express* in 1957. 'It isn't even Algeria, it is that unknown land which a cloud of blood hides.'[12]

In 1956 Camus had decided to visit Algeria himself. He hoped to begin a dialogue between the warring sides, even perhaps to help orchestrate a truce. At a series of public meetings he tried to engage his audience with the idea of 'humanizing the war' – advocating that the FLN abandon terrorism against civilians. However, he had severely underestimated the climate of hate. He was denounced by the FLN for referring to the 'Arabs', not the 'Algerians'. By the end of his stay, he was receiving death threats and was told he was a kidnapping target. FLN supporters tried to infiltrate his final meetings. Behind the scenes, Camus was actively campaigning to have the death penalty lifted from Algerian militants in prison.

At his final talk, in a hall near the Place du Gouvernement, thousands of French Algerians gathered outside the lecture theatre to chant 'Death to Camus!' His audience were visibly moved by his plea that all men should be free 'not to employ or submit to terror'. He met with Jacques Soustelle, who admired Camus' argument for a truce but did not see how it could work.

As Catherine Camus had recalled, the writer returned to Paris in deep despair. He described the situation in Algeria as a 'Munich of the left-wing', meaning that the French Left was making compromises with a political force, the FLN, which had no stake in the universal values of the Left. The French Left was indeed generally sympathetic to the Algerian cause, and many intellectuals took the view that the only proper response was to actively participate in the struggle. Most notably, the philosophy teacher Francis Jeanson, an intimate of Jean-Paul Sartre, organized a support network for the FLN in Paris, which led to his arrest and trial in 1960. A campaign organized by Sartre himself resulted in the famous 'Manifesto of 121', a petition against the Algerian war signed by prominent intellectuals. The wider argument ran that the French in Algeria were now acting like the Nazis had done ten years earlier in France. As allegations of torture and murder perpetrated by the French army became widely known and were corroborated, it was hard even for moderates to justify the war in Algeria. Brigitte Bardot, then the sexy avatar of post-war freedoms in France, was one of those who spoke out, saying, 'I refuse to live in a Nazi country!'[13]

Camus, however, was almost alone among his contemporaries in understanding that the revolution that the FLN craved was not modelled on the Enlightenment ideals of the French Revolution but on something else altogether: a return to the

'Islamic empire', a religious totality which Camus could no more embrace than Communism or Nazism. He told his old teacher, Jean Grenier, that the Muslims 'are making insane demands for an independent Algerian government, where the French will be considered as foreigners unless they want to convert to Islam. War is inevitable.'[14]

This was, of course, exactly what the FLN wanted. The mass-acres at Philippeville marked a great victory for the FLN – they were a spectacular form of terror with a worldwide impact. At the national level, the FLN had also now achieved their aim of dividing and militarizing the whole of Algerian society. Documentary footage of the period shows settler children in military fatigues toting guns. Innocent Muslims, including women and children, were frequently attacked for no reason in the street: all of them were now seen as suspects and enemies. No war had been officially declared by the French in Algeria, but terror had become the main fact of everyday life.

14

Capitals of Madness

The outbreaks of violence in Algeria coincided with fresh waves of immigration in Paris. Most of these new arrivals were North African. Between 1947 and 1953, the official figures note that 740,000 immigrants reached Paris from Algeria alone. The real figure, of course, was probably much higher than this.

At first they settled in parts of central Paris already known to the North Africans who had arrived in the 1920s and 1930s – Place Maubert, rue des Anglais, Les Halles, or the suburbs of Clichy and Gennevilliers (where there was an established community of Moroccans). This pre-war generation had long been the object of suspicion and the target of police surveillance; a special brigade was set up in 1925 by the Prefect of Police, Jean Chiappe, to control the North African population. This brigade had its headquarters at 6 rue Lecomte in the 17th arrondissement. It was dissolved in the wake of the Liberation – its staff of ex-colonials had been suspiciously close to the Gestapo and the Vichy government.

North Africans in Paris were quick to realize that many of the promises of racial toleration made after the Liberation were never going to be met or had already been broken. 'When we got to Paris it was dirty and dark,' I was told by Karim Dellal, who had been part of the post-war wave of immigration and was now in his eighties and living in Barbès. 'We didn't mind that, although we missed the sun. But worst of all, we did not feel free. Algiers had plenty of police, but it felt like home. Here, we were being watched and it did not feel like home.'

The immigrants encountered prejudice on a daily basis and, like the Jews before them, they began to cluster together around the city, as much for their own security as anything else. They organized politically in groups which were immediately banned. In 1952 Messali Hadj had been condemned to house arrest in Paris. At the same time, to drive home the dangerous nature of these immigrants, Parisians were reminded in the press that Algerian Nationalists such as Abderrhamane Yacine, Si Djilani and Mohamed el-Maadi had collaborated with the Germans. There were public complaints on the Left and the Right about the hygiene of these foreigners, the incompatibility of Islam and 'European civilization' and, most commonly, the North African propensity for violent crime.[1]

Like Karim Dellal, many of the newly arrived immigrants found that life in Paris was in fact more dangerous and strictly controlled than under colonial rule at home. The great fear of the Parisian police was the spread of pan-Arab nationalism, which was then incarnate in the charismatic figure of President Nasser of Egypt. Radical pan-Arab publications were constantly launched, only to be shut down. By the early 1950s, tension was clearly rising on the streets, taking the form of regular and popular Arab demonstrations, which often erupted into violence. On 14 July 1953 a group of Algerian militants, members of the Mouvement pour la Triomphe des Libertés Democratiques (MTLD), the successor and rival to the PPA, were shot dead by police as they demonstrated alongside some 4,000 Nationalists at Place de la Nation, demanding the freedom of its leader Messali Hadj.

As an act of solidarity, more than 20,000 Arabs of all nationalities gathered at the Cirque d'Hiver a few weeks later to mourn their dead. The Prefect of Police, Maurice Papon (who had been involved in the deportation of the Jews at the Vél d'Hiv), immediately set up a special unit, the Brigade des Aggressions et Violences (BAV), specifically to deal with 'the Algerian problem'. This was the moment when colonial tensions really started to be imported into the streets of the capital.

The task of the police was made even more complicated by the turf war which was being fought in the streets of the 13th, 15th and 18th arrondissements between the FLN and other rival Nationalists. There were also regular shoot-outs in the 19th arrondissement in the rues Petit and Meaux between the FLN and the MTLD or PPA. Maurice Papon was to rely on inside information from native Algerians for intelligence, but most of the time the police were pleased to let the rival Algerian factions fight it out between themselves. The newspaper *L'Aurore* noted in 1957 that the area of La Goutte d'Or, nicknamed the 'Medina of Paris', was effectively a no-go area for Europeans and a place where FLN and MTLD militants flaunted machine guns in broad daylight. Most dangerous of all were the rues de la Charbonnière, de Chartres, Myrha and Stephenson in northern Paris, a step away from Barbès metro station; these were parts of Paris where 'the police did not dare to tread'.

At the same time, the French authorities in Paris and Algiers refused to believe that the Algerians could arm and organize themselves effectively; they assumed there had to be a guiding hand reaching out from either Cairo or Moscow. This was a fatal error of judgement. It revealed the extent to which they misunderstood the land that they claimed to control and, more crucially, how blind they were to the growing tide of anger in Algeria which finally triggered the shift from radical dissent to war, from anger with the colonial administration to full-blown conflict.

In October 1956 the French committed a grave tactical error, when a French air-force jet threatened a plane carrying the FLN leader Ahmed Ben Bella and four of his colleagues from Rabat to Tunis, forcing it to land. The idea was to arrest the leadership of the 'revolution' and break its spirit, but this action only forced the hitherto 'domestic' problem of French Algeria into the full glare of world opinion, including that of the United Nations. Ben Bella and his comrades disappeared into a French prison. FLN commanders in Algiers agreed that the way forward was to focus their violence on the urban centres, forcing the French military away from the guerrilla warfare in the countryside and provoking the kind of chaos that results from random attacks on the heart of the metropolis. The most important target for revolutionary justice was, of course, Algiers, and the nerve centre of the operation was the Casbah.

The Battle of Algiers

In the first months of 1956, the FLN had been in a weakened position. Under the direct orders of François Mitterrand, the army in Algeria had effectively taken over the justice system and began a series of executions of FLN prisoners, using the traditional method of the guillotine. These took place in Barberousse prison, a white-walled fortress which stands at the summit of the Casbah. The few prisoners who ever left the prison reported that it was stiflingly hot, overcrowded, dirty and frightening. The corridors resounded with the cries of prisoners in agony, calling to God to take them into heaven. The beheadings took place just before dawn. This was when the Casbah fell silent and held its breath until the killing was finished. Then women would break out in ululations and men and children shouted for vengeance. The image of the guillotine was the purest emblem of the cruelty of the colonial machine in action.

On 19 June, under fierce pressure from *colon* public opinion, two FLN members, Zabane and Ferradj, were executed on the same day. The inhabitants of the Casbah could take no more.

Ferradj was blind and crippled – the object of particular pity and compassion – and the FLN leadership vowed to take revenge. This was not just driven by anger. The Muslim population needed to see that the FLN was not standing by impotently.[2]

That same day, the FLN issued a communiqué which instructed all members to 'kill any European between the ages of eighteen and forty-four. But no women, no children, no old people.' The slaughter started straight away. Led by Saadi Yacef, armed groups of FLN militants roamed the city, shooting at random. In the first week of the terror, forty-nine people were shot. Until then, Algiers had been relatively immune to the kind of indiscriminate massacres that had taken place across the rest of the country. It had been possible for Europeans to go dancing, swim, play tennis, socialize in the cafés and live the everyday life of a French city. This all now came to an abrupt and violent end.

The European community blamed the police and the military for not taking firm enough action against the '*bicots*' or '*bougnoules*' ('niggers'). On 10 August a small group of Europeans, who called themselves La Main Rouge (the Red Hand) and had Fascist sympathies, set off a bomb in a house on the rue de Thèbes in the heart of the Casbah. They claimed that the building housed an FLN cell and complained that they were doing the police's work for them. Three neighbouring houses collapsed. Seventy Muslims were killed. No Europeans were ever arrested. This was the beginning of the struggle for control of the city's population that would later be called the 'Battle of Algiers'.

The population of the Casbah responded by arming themselves with knives, axes, guns, whatever they could find, intent on tearing down the hill of the Casbah and killing all they could in the wild frenzy of grief. This was exactly what the FLN leadership did not want.

'Until the massacre of the rue de Thèbes, we only committed

actions in Algiers in response to massive arrests or executions,' said Saadi Yacef. 'But now we had no choice: we were mad with rage and everyone wanted to come down from the Casbah to avenge the dead. I had trouble, great trouble, trying to stop them, calling them from the balconies, telling them to avoid a bloodbath. I shouted, "The FLN will avenge you!".'[3] Yacef knew full well that the inhabitants would have been met with a hail of bullets from the army, who were waiting for this to happen. So the FLN persuaded them to hold back. Instead, an even more terrible revenge was plotted by Yacef and his fellow militants.

On the morning of 30 September 1956, three young female militants from the FLN, Zohra Drif, Djamila Bouhired and Samia Lakhdari, were called to a meeting with Yacef in one of the safe houses he used in the Casbah. They were each given a small bomb, weighing no more than a kilogramme, and ordered to plant them in the Milk Bar on Place Bugeaud, the Caféteria on rue Michelet and the nearby Air France terminal. The appointed time was 6.30 p.m. as the offices were emptying and the streets and *café terrasses* were packed with students and workers lingering in the early autumn sunshine.

At first the girls recoiled from the task. Yacef quietly but forcefully reminded them of the bloodied and broken bodies of the children killed in the rue de Thèbes. They took off their veils, put on make-up and light cotton dresses or slacks and set off for their destinations, flirting past the checkpoint to gain entry to the European world that no Muslim could normally enter. The Milk Bar was a popular place for families to relax after a day on the beach, while the Caféteria was always busy with students and young people, a good place to dance and pick up members of the opposite sex. As she left the Caféteria, Samia Lakhdari had to fend off the advances of an insistent young man who wanted to dance a mambo with her.

The Air France bomb failed to go off due to a broken timer. The other bombs killed three people, with dozens more slashed by the shards of glass from the plate-glass windows that were shattered by the explosions. Blinded, and deafened by the noise of the bomb, the young customers of the cafés, some of them adolescents or children, staggered into the streets in mute agony, their skin cut to ribbons, the pavement soaked in dark-red blood.[4]

All of European Algiers was now gripped by rage and terror. Throughout the months of October and November, schools were closed. If Europeans were followed down the street by a Muslim – man, woman or child – they now slowed to let them pass for fear of an assault. European men armed themselves with automatic pistols, ready to kill any Muslim who threatened them. For the FLN this was great success – Algiers, the capital, was dominated by a nerve-jangling state of anxiety. The tension broke on December 28 when Mayor Froger, a conservative who supported the 'petits colons' and advocated a strong hand against the Arabs, was shot dead on his doorstep. The killer, who later become notorious as a hero of the FLN, was Ali la Pointe, a petty criminal from the Casbah who had become Yacef's second in command. At Froger's funeral a week later, a bomb exploded in the cemetery and would have killed hundreds of mourners if the cortège had not arrived late. Europeans now took to the streets with any weapons at hand and attacked the first Muslims they saw. Veiled women had their heads staved in with iron bars; children had their limbs ripped apart.

The governor-general, Robert Lacoste, a Socialist and by nature well disposed to the Muslims, had now reached a new crisis. On 7 January 1957 he met with General Salan and General Jacques Massu, newly arrived in Algeria from Suez and leader of the 10th Para Division, one of the most feared and respected forces in the French army. Lacoste complained that he could no longer properly police the city. He proposed giving Massu full responsibility for maintaining order. As Massu accepted his mission, Lacoste did not realize what he done: he had fully militarized what had been a police operation, thereby tacitly accepting the FLN's declaration of war. And in doing so, he effectively set in train the events that would lead to the end of the Fourth Republic.

Massu's strategy was straightforward and effective. Algiers was divided into zones, with a regiment responsible within each zone for house-to-house searches, policing the security cordons between zones, taking lists of names and making arrests. Muslim areas were placed under searchlights and put behind barbed wire. On 28 January, the FLN declared a general strike, aiming to bring the Algerian crisis to the attention of the United Nations debates scheduled for that date.

At first the FLN seemed to have achieved another great victory over the French; on the evening of 27 January, all the shops in the Muslim quarters were shut down, as were all the cafés. Nothing moved on the streets. It was the same the next day, until Massu ordered his troops to break the strike by any means necessary. This included forcibly opening the steel shutters of shops, forcing angry shop owners to come out and mind the stock, or rounding up workers and bussing them into factories under threat of jail if they didn't comply. No one wanted to end up in the dreaded Barberousse prison. Within days, the strike collapsed and the United Nations paid scant attention to an obscure rebellion in a North African territory.

Massu pursued his quarry hard. Algiers was now under complete military control. The bombings went on but the FLN were being systematically torn apart and its leaders arrested. The number of attacks gradually fell and by summer 1957 Europeans could confidently return to the beach, cafés and restaurants. The Paratroopers were heroes and the 'Battle of Algiers' was over.

★

But although the French military had won a major battle, it soon became clear that they were going to lose the war. The main reason was that the French commanders in Algeria had not applied the first rule of counter-insurgency: to gain the support of the population rather than control of the territory. Most importantly, the Battle of Algiers had been won by the systematic use of torture, wiping out any last vestige of French moral authority in Algeria.

In the military's hands torture became politicized. It was not simply about beating up the 'natives', as it had been for the colonial police, but also about extracting information. Torture was no longer just about control; it was a weapon of war, which was already well established in the armoury of the French Empire elsewhere in the world. There were reports that torture was used by the French in Indochina in the 1930s and the 1950s, in Madagascar, Tunisia and Morocco, most often by the police. As in other colonial empires, including the British Empire, torture was used as a demonstration of the contempt that the Europeans felt for the sub-human colonized subject.

In Algeria, torture often took spectacular, even artistic forms. A popular technique of General Bigeard, aimed at terrorizing the whole Muslim population, was to throw FLN prisoners into the port of Algiers from military helicopters, with their feet bound in concrete. These murders were watched with glacial horror by the civilian population, Muslim and European. The bodies were washed up on the beaches, bloated and wrecked. The *algérois* – the French population of Algiers, who prided themselves on their sharp wit – called them '*Crévettes à la Bigeard*' (Bigeard-style prawns).

Another French torture technique was the *gégène* – a piece of military electronic equipment which could be fastened to the human body – normally to the penis – and delivered a powerful shock but which left no physical trace. 'This was nothing serious,' said Massu, the commander who introduced

it and occasionally used it on himself to test it efficacy. 'They
are just electrodes.' The journalist Henri Alleg, a Jew suspected
of Muslim sympathies, was tortured with these devices. He
described it as 'a flash of lightning, a great pain in all my body,
images of fire; spasms of excruciating agony'.[5] Other techniques
involved water torture – hoses in mouths, half-drownings in
baths of salt water, pressure hoses in rectums; bottles thrust into
the vaginas of Muslim women. Worst of all could be the cries
of fellow victims. Alleg recalled a terrified elderly Muslim who
shouted, '*Vive la France!*' to appease his tormentors between
beatings. Alleg described his prison as 'a school of perversion for
the French nation'.

In 1958 Alleg published an account of his experiences in a
book called *La Question*. The title referred not only to the act
of verbal interrogation but also to the euphemism for torture in
pre-revolutionary France. At first the book seemed to slip under
the net of the authorities in Algiers and Paris – despite the graphic
descriptions of Alleg's month at the hands of French torturers,
it was neither censored nor refuted by the government or the
military. Indeed, at this stage the victors of the Battle of Algiers
were boasting in garrisons and barracks about their severity in
the face of human suffering, while the high command, aware
that torture was a well-known tactic, justified its use, claiming
that it saved the lives of Europeans and Muslims alike. One
piece of propaganda was the story that extremist settlers had
planned to firebomb the Casbah and then roll barrels of flaming
kerosene through its streets, endangering the lives of its 70,000
inhabitants. This was no doubt a fantasy, but one bred in the
febrile atmosphere of a city where everyone knew someone
who had been tortured.[6]

Alleg's book was finally banned in France and Algeria at the
end of 1958, only to become an underground bestseller. It also
split French society into two camps: those who argued that the
Battle of Algiers had to be won, and could not have been won

without the use of torture, and those who argued that the use of torture made Frenchmen no better than the Nazis. This opinion was first developed in Liberal-Left circles but soon became an accepted mainstream view – no French patriot, Right or Left, could use such a vicious weapon in defence of the Republic. The loudest and most influential voice in the debate was that of Jean-Paul Sartre, who argued, in a 1958 article for *L'Express* entitled 'A Victory', that Alleg's book had great implications for the future of the French nation. This article was censored but, like Alleg's book, it circulated clandestinely, making a deep impact on the French imagination.

Those on the Left who defended French Algeria argued that Algeria was not only French territory conquered by force of arms, but that it embodied the universal values of the Republic: liberty, equality and fraternity. This was the real meaning of the 'civilizing mission' in Algeria – to bring European democracy and democratic values to all men and women, especially those who were still enslaved by Islam. The reality, however, was that most Algerians were not citizens of France, and for many French Algerians, who believed that the Muslims did not understand the law but only brute violence, they were not even properly human. There were racist notions that Algerian Muslims, bred on the dour plains of North Africa, had a higher tolerance for pain than Europeans, and that they expected violence, even welcomed it as a necessary constraint on their savage nature. A police report from 1961 noted casually that 'most French citizens think it is really quite normal to strike a North African'. As a result of this belief system, torture had been a long-established fact of life for Algerian Muslims.

As he patrolled the wards of psychiatric institutions in Blida and Algiers during the 1950s, Frantz Fanon was struck by the way that neurosis and trauma took physical forms.[7] Unsurprisingly, the psychiatric wards of the hospitals in Algiers were full and reporting more cases of trauma than ever before. Most of the patients were Muslims. The symptoms included anorexia, pins-and-needles, stomach pains, aching legs, a fear of electrical equipment, of even turning on a light or touching a telephone. Sexual impotence was a common symptom among men, often allied with murderous aggression or suicidal thoughts. One former FLN militant despairingly wanted to destroy himself because his wife 'had tasted the French'. She had been raped and told him about it, and therefore she could not be forgiven. For their part, the Algerian women whom Fanon met suffered depression after childbirth, delusions of persecution (a fear of being bled to death or 'vampirized' was common) and high levels of anxiety.

Fanon also treated the torturers, many of whom were suffering breakdowns under the intolerable burden of the grim tasks that they performed. Most psychiatrists, including Fanon himself, usually considered this a form of 'war neurosis', but Fanon also noted a distinction between guilt and horror and 'radical sadism'. One of his patients, for example, was a policeman who suffered nightmares and had started beating up his children and wife. He had no intention of giving up being a torturer, but he wanted Fanon to 'help him torture Algerian patriots, without having a guilty conscience, without behavioural problems, in serenity'. This, Fanon recorded in his notes, was the product of a total, closed system – colonialism – which needed no justification beyond itself. It was the mentality and morality of the Nazi death camps.

Other torturers were less robust. Fanon treated a twenty-year-old conscript who was woken at night by the remembered screams of his victims. He claimed he was able to register the pain of those under torture as a musician reads a score, hearing the intensity of the violation in the pitch of the screams. The young man broke down after a chance meeting with a victim in Fanon's garden. The victim was found later, trying to kill himself with an overdose.

This fatal encounter – a painful recognition of the agony suffered on both sides of the conflict – was a metaphor for the psychotic state of French Algeria and for the experience of life on the streets of its town and cities. Again it was Albert Camus, reflecting on the trauma of life in Algiers, the 'capital of madness', who took a clear-sighted view of the political meaning of this condition. He explicitly condemned torture, not only as an ineffective weapon that only created more rebels in its wake, but also as the moral degradation of the torturer, and the power he represents. There was no way of turning back or recovering from this position. 'It is better to suffer certain injustices than to commit them,' he wrote. 'Such fine deeds would lead to the demoralization of France and the loss of Algeria.'[8] Tragically for the settlers, Camus' nuanced observation would soon become a prophecy.

15

De Gaulle and the French Civil War

May 1958 was fervid and crackling with tension in both Paris and Algiers. On 9 May came news of the assassination of three French soldiers by the FLN. This event galvanized the pieds noirs to new heights of vengeful rhetoric against Muslims. The military itself was at breaking point, more ready than ever to turn against its political masters in Paris and take matters into its own hands. The high command despatched a telegram to the Chief of Staff in Paris, urging the government not to 'abandon' Algeria and betray the soldiers who had made such a sacrifice. This communiqué also contained a threat: no one could predict the actions the army might commit in 'outrage' or 'despair'. If the army were to intervene directly in French politics, this would be the first time that it done so since the 18th Brumaire, the coup d'état of 1799 when Napoleon seized control of the French Directory.

On 13 May a ceremony for the dead soldiers was to be held at the Monument des Morts, the grim memorial in the gardens in the centre of Algiers. Behind the memorial stood a bust of Marianne and the great white building of the Gouvernement-général – the symbolic seat of all French power in Algeria.

The ceremony was due to start at 6 p.m. In the hours leading up to the event, the streets of Algiers were packed with pieds noirs, many of them poor farmers from the interior. They had come not to support the French government but to show how much they hated its policies of appeasement towards the Muslims, and to display the power that they held as the true owners of *Algérie française*. Their cars buzzed around the city streets, sounding their horns to the slogan '*AL-GER-IE FRAN-ÇAISE!*' After the laying of the wreath, the tall, wiry figure of the hard-line student leader Pierre Lagaillarde, wearing a military uniform and flanked by four tough-looking *harki* minders, leapt up and called the mob to attack the Gouvernement-général. Regular French troops stood back as the mob surged forward, knocking over the bust of Marianne on the way. Lagaillarde was next seen on the balcony, presiding over the anarchy that he had unleashed. For a few days, this building held the world's attention as it waited for the next French Revolution.[1]

Paris was also watching, nervously and in confusion. To most Parisian eyes, the seizing of the Gouvernement-général, with its smashed windows and scattered papers and documents, ominously resembled the sacking of the Hôtel de Ville in Paris by the Communards in 1870. The right-wing *Le Figaro* wrote drily of 'Dramatic events' in Algiers. The headlines of the Communist newspaper *L'Humanité* warned of a Fascist coup. There were also shaky memories of the riots in Paris in 1934, the last time that a mob had nearly seized power in France.

By 27 May 1958 there was a brief but very real threat of civil war in France; the conflict between those who wanted to keep Algeria 'French' and those who favoured Independence was heightened when General Salan ordered his troopers from Algiers to Corsica, a short distance from the mainland. This was no longer just about Algeria but about whether France could maintain its integrity: the 'state of France' itself was at stake. Parisians, fearing the revenge of the army in Algeria, watched the skies for incoming aircraft, the prelude to a coup d'état. The writer Simone de Beauvoir, companion of Sartre, recorded in her diary that she had dreams of a python dropping on her from the sky.[2]

The real aim of Salan's manoeuvre, however, was to force the hand of Charles de Gaulle, who was drawn out of retirement, acclaimed as the hero of the 'Great Nation' and, in January 1959, given a mandate to establish a Fifth Republic.

Within a month de Gaulle flew to Algiers, where he was welcomed with delirious enthusiasm by crowds who saw him as the saviour of French Algeria. In a speech delivered to the packed streets of central Algiers, he famously declared, '*Je vous ai compris!*' ('I have understood you!'). Most French Algerians went wild at this statement, believing it to be an expression of solidarity. In fact, it was anything but, and de Gaulle was already planning the end of war, which would mean compromise and ultimately the independence of Algeria.

In the meantime, through the summer of 1958, France itself was the target of a concerted terrorist assault by the FLN. In August and September alone, there were 181 attacks on buildings and assassination attempts on 242 people. These attacks happened all over France – a train was derailed at Cagnes-sur-Mer; police headquarters came under fire in Lyons; bombs were placed in boats in Marseilles – but Paris was the main target. The FLN were unafraid to break cover and shoot policemen and politicians in the heart of the city. There were notable exchanges of fire in Avenue Friedland, Place de l'Etoile and the rue de Rivoli. A bomb was found and defused in the ladies' lavatory on the upper level of the Eiffel Tower.

Parisians lived through this with a mixture of anger and cynicism. The Communist Left denounced the FLN's actions. The police worked harder than ever to track down all Algerians in the city as suspects. The cruel mood of the moment is captured by the writer Janet Flanner, Paris correspondent for the *New Yorker*, who described an Algerian who had been stabbed (no one knows by whom), dying in a pool of blood outside the chic

Brasserie Lipp, all of this observed by a nearby flower vendor 'shuffling in the gore and offering his faded bouquets for sale, as if it were a scene from a Surrealist picture'.[3]

De Gaulle's first proposed solution was an honourable peace and reform of the constitution to give universal suffrage and two-thirds Algerian Muslim representation in Paris. The wounded response of the FLN was to set up a provisional government in Tunis, led by Ferhat Abbas. The FLN also began to mobilize in Morocco and Tunisia, taking advantage of the fluid borders to train paramilitary units who were receiving Chinese and Russian weaponry.

Throughout 1958 and 1959, de Gaulle made frequent appearances on French television and radio, declaring 'auto-determination' as the solution in Algeria. In truth, de Gaulle was frustrated: his vision of post-war France was as a nuclear power and world leader, a counterbalance to Anglo-American hegemony and Soviet imperialism. To his inner circle, he was visibly irritated at being pinned down in a messy and brutal war which only harmed France's international prestige. Still, in public he did his best to hold together the loyalty of the army, the quarrelling factions in Algiers and Paris and, most troubling of all, the murderous extremists among the settlers, many of whom understood the FLN's refusal to compromise as a statement of intent: this was a deadly fight to the finish.

By 1960 the French army was convinced that it had won the war. They cited as proof the 'pacified' areas of the countryside around Oran, where civilian vehicles could move freely without military escort. Some members of the FLN also started to believe the French propaganda and broke ranks to begin negotiations with de Gaulle. These were a failure, but the beginning of a hope for peace on both sides.

Peace, however, was precisely what the extremist settlers did not want. The anger of the pieds noir erupted into violence in

January 1960. Convinced that de Gaulle was about to betray them, the various factions of hard-core settlers came together to defy the French military authorities, then under the command of General Maurice Challe. The insurrection began on 23 January, a Sunday evening. At around 6 p.m. the demonstrators gathered in Bab-el-Oued and started moving towards the centre of the city, intending to confront the police and the government. The demonstrators were armed and were buzzing with the ambition to '*se payer un gendarme*' (kill a cop). As the police moved down towards Bab-el-Oued to block the demonstration, shots seemed to come out of nowhere. Home-made bombs were lobbed at the gendarmes from balconies, and petrol bombs rolled towards them in the street. On the fifth floor of a smart building a woman in a dressing gown was spotted, shooting at the police randomly with a revolver. Wounded policemen who crawled into stairwells were mercilessly despatched by the pied noir youths who had been waiting for them.

As the violence escalated, and dead bodies were to be seen on the boulevard Laferrière, General Challe declared Algiers to be under a state of siege. Barricades went up around the centre of Algiers: this was the '*semaine des barricades*' (Week of the Barricades).

There was a strangely festive atmosphere to the rebellion – the whole of pied-noir Algiers came down into the streets to talk, argue and drink (much alcohol was dispensed by the barmen of the Saint-Georges and Aletti hotels). But for all the bonhomie, this was a fatal moment: the first time in the conflict Frenchmen had fired upon and killed each other. There were dark memories of the Second World War and the Commune of 1870. Some insurgents noted that there were no Muslims on the streets, although occasionally the slogan '*AL-GE-RIE AR-ABE!*' could be heard chanted from the depths of the Casbah, a parody of the slogan of the pieds noirs.

There was a great deal of confusion. This was expressed in

the dying words of an Algiers policeman: 'For two years I've been fighting against the Fellagha [the FLN]. Now I'm dying at the hands of those who cry *Algérie Française*. I don't understand ...'[4] Among those who did indeed cry '*Algérie Française*' was Jean-Marie Le Pen, the future leader of the Front National from the 1970s onwards, who was then an aspiring politician. Le Pen argued that the barricades should be extended to Paris.

De Gaulle was furious and refused to acknowledge the insurgents' demands. Eventually, on 29 January 1960, he gave a masterly and unbending speech, describing the insurrection as 'stab in the back for France' and denouncing the rebels as 'liars and conspirators'. The rebellion faded away as most of its leaders were imprisoned or went underground. In his speech, de Gaulle had also made it clear that the independence of Algeria would be the choice of Algerians. This, of course, only hardened the will of the pieds noirs.

Later that year, the leaders who remained free began to organize themselves in Algiers and Oran into a group which called itself Front de l'Algérie Française (FAF) and included political veterans such as Jacques Soustelle and military men, notably General Jouhaud and General Salan. The FAF declared de Gaulle a traitor to French Algeria. When he visited Algeria that year, the FAF launched a series of assassination attempts. The organization was swiftly banned by the French authorities, only to be replaced by the Organisation Armée Secrète (OAS), probably founded in Madrid. Led by the now exiled Salan, it vowed to bring French Algeria to war with France.

The Knife Edge

The OAS very nearly achieved its aims. In the early hours of 22 April 1961, the 1st Foreign Parachute Regiment announced that it had seized control of government and military facilities in Algiers, taking the local army and civil commanders captive. General Maurice Challe had come out of retirement and flown to Algiers to lead the putsch, declaring himself sole authority in Algeria and the Sahara. De Gaulle was stunned that Challe, who had stood firm against the rioters during the 'Week of the Barricades', should take the lead in this way. The military and civilians in Algeria and France watched with bated breath. Crucially, the army in France declared its loyalty to de Gaulle and the putsch collapsed before it had begun. But it was yet another dangerous moment for France.

The failure of the putsch did not mean that the war was over. Instead, the Algerian conflict was transformed into a triangular configuration, with the FLN against the French and the OAS, and the OAS at war with the French security forces. In Algiers, the OAS had set up an élite death squad, drawn from the prisons, the criminal underworld and rogue military men, which they called DELTA. The death squad targeted not just Muslims but leftist Europeans and the more liberal elements in the police. They took their cue from the Afrikaners who supported apartheid, and the Zionist group Haganah. More precisely, they admired Haganah – a Jewish paramilitary force which took on both the British forces in Palestine and the Arab population – for taking the fight to the enemy. DELTA terrorists regularly and casually gunned down innocent Muslims in the streets of Algiers, which – like all other Algerian cities – was under curfew and where only killers on both sides moved around at night.

The violence intensified in Algiers through the winter and spring of 1962. Many of the OAS gunmen were no more than boys – teenagers who had been given weapons by senior figures in the organization and ordered to kill as many Muslims as they could. These youthful assassins loafed around the city or the beach in the daytime and then prowled the Muslim quarters when darkness fell. In the morning the streets were often littered with Muslim corpses. By the summer of 1962, the OAS had formulated a scorched-earth policy, which culminated in attacks on the town hall of Oran, setting oil refineries alight and burning the University Library in Algiers to the ground.

In Paris, both DELTA and other operatives of the OAS now singled out left-leaning intellectuals who were sympathetic to the Algerian cause. For the next two years the crack of plastic explosives echoed around the Left Bank, as the campaign intensified. The effect of the OAS's campaign was largely counter-productive: Parisians could not tolerate terror on their home ground and were sickened by the attack on the pharmacy on the Champs-Elysées or the bombing of newspaper offices.

The Parisian police responded by cracking down harder on the city's Algerian population. Disastrously, on 5 October 1961 Maurice Papon imposed a curfew on all 'French Muslims of North-African appearance'. Any Algerian on the streets after 8.30 p.m. was now considered a suspect by the law. Posters appeared across the city with the warning: 'Algerian worker! Do you think that these killings will make your life better? They will only make it worse!' This police propaganda was made all the more offensive by addressing its immigrant readership with the 'tu' form, a vocabulary for children, servants and animals.

This policy had terrible consequences. On 17 October tens of thousands of Algerians gathered in the centre of the city to demonstrate for peace and independence. They were mainly poor people, most of them flooding into the city on foot from the suburbs. The police response was harsh, and in a terrible echo of the evacuation of Jews to the Vél d'Hiv, Papon organized police trucks and wagons to take away demonstrators to the Stade de Coubertin, the Palais des Sports and the Château de Vincennes, where they were savagely beaten up. On the pont de Neuilly a skirmish between demonstrators and police became a riot. Heavily armed police charged into the crowd, killing two and wounding many more. The police then began to kill Algerians, throwing their bodies into the Seine.

This conflict was later dignified with the name 'the Battle

for Paris', but it was really just another massacre in a long line of Parisian mass-murders. Papon's priority was to cover up all evidence of police wrongdoing. The morning after the demonstration, a small group of Communist militants – all Europeans – led by the writer Arthur Adamov and the actor Jean-Marie Binoche set out to paint the slogan 'This is where we kill Algerians!' on the bridge, before retreating back to the Old Navy bar on the boulevard Saint-Germain. The slogan was quickly wiped away, but the police could not destroy all the evidence of the killings. The bloated corpses of Algerians were regularly found by ordinary Parisians over the coming weeks and months.

'Paris was weird, much weirder than I thought it would be,' I was told by the English artist Harold Chapman, now a distinguished photographer but then a young student come to Paris for a taste of bohemia. 'There were police and soldiers everywhere. It was not free at all; it was a very tense place. Worst of all was the sense that something bad was happening but you couldn't be sure what it was. October 1961 was like a hazy nightmare in Paris. The hatred of Arabs was very clear among the police – they were cracking heads all over the place.'[5]

There was more to come. On 7 February 1962 a bomb aimed at Jean-Paul Sartre's apartment on the rue Bonaparte went off by mistake on the wrong floor of his building, injuring a four-year-old girl who had been playing with her dolls. Her disfigured features, cut by shards of glass and splinters of hot metal, appeared on the front pages of all the French newspapers. The editorial of *Le Figaro* spoke for the nation when it declared: 'France wants no more of this!'[6]

Against police orders, a demonstration against the OAS was hastily organized for the next day, attracting Parisians from all walks of life. It far exceeded the numbers that the police could properly handle. Inevitably, the crowd began to spin out of control around the Bastille and boulevard Beaumarchais. The police responded the only way they knew how –indiscriminately clubbing demonstrators, throwing marble-topped café tables and iron tree guards at the terrorized crowd. A group of demonstrators who tried to shelter in the Charonne metro station were pursued by police, beaten up, crushed against metal railings and their broken bodies tossed on to the tracks. There were eight dead, including a postal worker, an apprentice and a railway worker. Their funerals on 18 February were attended by over half a million people. This was the biggest public demonstration since the violent anti-government riots of 1934. No French government could allow the Algerian war to spill over any further or spread any deeper into French life.

Bitter Victory

In December 1961 both sides had met in the small village of Les Rousses, high up in the Jura mountains of Switzerland, less than a kilometre from the French border and a short drive to Geneva. The location was chosen to allow the FLN delegates to sleep in neutral Switzerland and because it was out of the sight and beyond the range of the OAS or nosy journalists. The talks were fractious at first and, from the French point of view, it was almost impossible to see a way forward. The Algerians refused to make any concessions to the French team, and the senior French diplomat, Louise Joxe, reported despairingly to de Gaulle that even French surrender was not enough for these Algerian hardmen. They wanted to humiliate France in revenge for the shame of colonization. The French complained that this was the politics of anger rather than international diplomacy.

On the very last day of the talks at Les Rousses, two French warplanes made a mortar and machine-gun attack on an FLN base near Oujda, a Moroccan town near the Algerian border. This was not an official military operation but a wildcat strike by two civilians, one of whom was avenging his brother's death at the hands of the FLN. The raid was a squalid affair – the base was not a military installation but a refugee camp. The casualties included a wounded man who was shot on the operating table along with the nurses who were tending him.

And then, suddenly, on 18 March 1962, there was a break-through: at the neighbouring spa town of Evian, the French and the Algerians agreed to a ceasefire. A referendum on Algerian independence was put to the French and Algerian electorates, who both voted overwhelmingly to set Algeria free. On 3 July, Algeria was made formally independent.

But the end of the war did not mean the end of the killing. The OAS maintained their policy of aggression, and the death toll in Algiers averaged between twenty and thirty murders per day. In response to the ceasefire, the OAS patrolled the city, ripping down the posters which showed smiling European and Muslim children beneath the rubric 'Peace in Algeria. For our children.' They declared the French army an enemy and a target, and banned all Muslims from entering European quarters on pain of death. The headquarters of the OAS was the working-class pied-noir district of Bab-el-Oued. This is where the OAS committed its greatest acts of sedition so far, which included, on 23 March, gunning down a truck-load of French conscripts, new to the army and Algeria, who found themselves surrounded by a baying crowd of pieds noirs as they tried to pass through the narrow streets of the area. OAS gunmen smilingly responded to the taunts of the mob, killing seven of the conscripts and leaving eleven more critically injured, left to die alone, trembling with fear and pain in the street.

In a fury, the French commander-in-chief, General Ailleret, launched an all-out assault on Bab-el-Oued, aiming to eradicate the OAS once and for all. The area was sealed off – the district contained some 60,000 inhabitants – and a tank and artillery battery strafed the old buildings and streets for the next three days. During this period, the ordinary inhabitants of the area were caught between the French army in the European city and the FLN in the Casbah.

On 24 March the pieds noirs again took to the streets to demonstrate against the shelling. They broke through the cordon around Bab-el-Oued and poured into the city, towards the Grande Poste and the rue d'Isly. Here they met a roadblock – held by one of the few French regiments which still had a majority of Algerian Muslims in its ranks. These troops were mainly young country lads, who had performed well in the field but now, for their first time in Algiers, were faced with an angry mob of several hundred thousand. The inevitable happened: a shot was fired from a balcony and the scene descended into bloody anarchy. The crowd stampeded: men and women were trampled underfoot. Meanwhile the nervous troops shot at random into the wall of angry faces, killing forty-six and injuring hundreds more. When the shooting stopped, the elegant streets of modern Algiers were littered with the wounded and the dead.

The final weeks of March 1962 saw the OAS at the height of its power and influence, but it would also turn out to be the beginning of its decline. The pied-noir population was angered by the double betrayal that Algerian Muslims and mainland France had inflicted upon them and they wanted vengeance if nothing else. Elegant bourgeois ladies were captured on newsreels around the world, interviewed by reporters to whom they barked, 'This is to the death, monsieur.'[7] But as youths in black leather jackets drove around the cities, now shooting in the daytime at will, Europeans were already beginning to leave Algeria. They knew that they were outnumbered nine to one and feared that, abandoned by the French in the wake of the ceasefire, they would be slaughtered. On street corners Muslims sold cheap suitcases – a provocative gesture which made real the threat in the FLN slogan, 'The suitcase or the coffin!' – and did a roaring trade. The OAS had no strategy to counter this tide, other than trying to provoke the FLN into revenge attacks.

In the event, the FLN militants held their nerve and their discipline. The situation became more volatile as the ranks of the FLN were swelled by so-called '*marsiens*' – Muslims who had remained non-committal throughout the war but who in March (*mars* in French), when they saw the tide of history turning, threw their lot in with the Nationalists. They were motivated partly by an instinct for self-preservation and partly by the greedy anticipation of claiming property and land as the chaotic exodus of the Europeans began. Against FLN orders, many *marsiens* committed atrocities as a desperate way of declaring their new-found allegiance.

The FLN leaders struggled hard to control these new elements but this was all but impossible in the febrile days leading up to the declaration of independence. The final act of violence in the war occurred in Oran on 5 July. As the FLN moved in to take control from the French troops, a mob of Muslims tore through the centre of the town, waving Algerian flags and lashing out at all Europeans – men, women and children – with indiscriminate fury. Shots were fired at motorists. The promenade on boulevard du Front de Mer was soon littered with dead bodies. A woman who came out on to her balcony to see what was happening was shot dead. The fighting grew in intensity as the afternoon wore on – a European was hung from a meat hook outside the Rex Cinema. The Muslims slit throats, nearly tearing the heads off cadavers in the process. The panic-stricken French made for the offices of *L'Echo d'Oran* or the French garrison by the port. French troops watched all of this, unable to intervene under the terms of the Evian ceasefire.

The French government had guessed that some 100,000 pieds noirs would leave Algeria during the first year after the handover of power. By the first weeks of August 1962, over 350,000 had abandoned houses and businesses, making for the docks of Algiers or Oran and a boat to Europe. A million more would follow them, one of the greatest mass migrations in history.

In the streets of Bab-el-Oued, pieds noirs destroyed everything they could not bring with them. Only two suitcases were permitted per person. They left behind the paraphernalia of everyday life – family photos, ornaments and mementoes, furniture and crockery. All was smashed or burned so that 'they' – the Algerian Muslims – could not complete the act of dispossession. The scenes down by the port were pathetic and heartbreaking. Most of the pieds noirs were as poor as, or poorer than, the Muslims. Old people and children had known no other country, no other life, than Algeria. With meagre belongings and little money they were leaving for a country that, as they saw it, had betrayed them and now forced them into a permanent exile.

16

An Experimental Nation

The new government of Algeria flew into the city of Algiers on 3 July 1962. They arrived in a Tunis Air Caravelle, making the short trip from the Tunisian capital in a few hours and landing at Algiers airport mid-morning. When the FLN had started the war, they could not have hoped that victory would be so swift and overwhelming. More to the point, having prepared for conflict for so long, they had really no idea how to manage peace or – most crucially – how to make a nation out of the wreckage of war.

The cortège of limousines bringing the FLN home was received in delirious triumph as it drove slowly from the airport to the centre of the city. The streets were lined with children wearing military uniforms and carrying wooden rifles, imitating the Mujahideen, the legendary warriors who had brought them freedom. Older Algerians waved the green and white flag and chanted '*Yaya Djezair!*' (Long live Algeria!).

When the new president of Free Algeria appeared on the balcony of the Town Hall, however, it came as a shock to many in the crowd. They had been expecting either Mohammed Khider or Ahmed Ben Bella, both of whom were legends to this generation of Algerians: 'historic chiefs' who had dreamed of and fought for liberty. Instead, the crowd was confronted by Ben Youssef Ben Khedda, a strategist rather than a soldier, who was unknown to many Algerians. They feared that their heroes had been usurped and that the revolution was being hijacked in front of their eyes. They were not reassured by Ben Khedda's dour speech, railing against 'the military dictatorship some of whom are dreaming of personal power, the ambitious, the adventurers, fascists of all stripes'. Many in the crowd were confused at this stern warning on what was to be supposed to be a joyful day of national liberation.

There was also a threat of yet more war in Ben Khedda's speech, as he invoked the potential danger of Houari Boumédienne, a daring FLN commander, with his 'army of the border', a division of hardened fighters who preferred to watch events from their base on the Tunisian border. Boumédienne had his eyes on power. As Ben Khedda greeted the crowds in Algiers, he knew that the possibility of civil war was very near.

As the celebrations continued over three days, the situation appeared to be sliding into civil unrest, and on 5 July Ben Khedda ordered everyone on the street back to work on pain of arrest. The reality, which all the FLN chiefs had now grasped, was that the new nation was about to be born in a mixture of hope and bloody confusion.

'The New Havana'

In the first instance, the hope was that Algeria would become a beacon of freedom in the post-colonial world, especially in Africa. For this reason, several thousand French Algerians with left-wing beliefs opted to stay on in independent Algeria, with the dream of building a new Socialist republic, free of the baggage of European history and ideology. The optimism radiated across the Mediterranean and over the next few years other Europeans, mainly French left-wingers – teachers, journalists, doctors – flocked to the new Socialist paradise. These utopian dreamers were nicknamed '*pieds rouges*' (red feet) in an ironic homage to their French background. They took the revolution in Cuba as their model and called Algiers the 'new Havana' – a city halfway between a revolutionary playground and a laboratory for new ideas about freedom.

However, nothing could have been further from the reality of Algeria in the course of the 1960s. The early part of the decade was defined by a power struggle between Ben Bella and Boumédienne. Ben Bella was voted into power in September 1962, but only after a month of anarchy and vicious in-fighting between FLN factions. Ben Khedda had by now withdrawn from the conflict. Ben Bella's hold on power, however, was always fragile and in June 1965 he was arrested by Boumédienne, who replaced him as president, bringing with him the hard men of the military. When Boumédienne's tanks took key strategic points in the city to enforce the coup d'état, the citizens of Algiers assumed that this was just another set piece for the Gillo Pontecorvo film, *The Battle of Algiers*, which was then being filmed. They only realized later that the course of their history had yet again been determined by arms.

Boumédienne was tough and paranoid and had more in common with a South American right-wing dictator than with a leader of a liberation struggle. The *pieds rouges* were soon obvious objects of suspicion and many of them found themselves in prison and were tortured as 'spies', 'infiltrators' and 'subversives'.

Traitors and Collaborators

The defining moment in Algeria's first decade as a free nation, however, was a series of events as disgusting and bloody as any massacre during the war.[1] This was the mass killing of the pro-French Muslims who, in the summer of 1962, had been abandoned by the French as the exodus of the pieds noirs became a stampede.

The pro-French Muslims were known by the Arabic term *harki*, a word derived from *haraka*, meaning 'movement', which,

Left & Below
A riot at the Gare du Nord.
'Fuck France!'

Above
'Fuck the police' graffiti in Paris

Jean Gabin playing a
Parisian gangster on the
run in Algiers in Julien
Duvivier's 1937 film
Pépé le Moko

Below
The conquest of Algiers

Portrait of Abd El-Kader

Below
Eugene Delacroix's
Les Femmes d'Alger (1834)

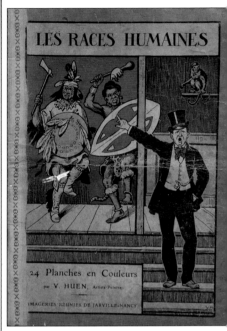

Above Left & Right
Posters representing the French
colonial world

Left
The Algiers street urchin Cagayous

Street fighting in Algiers, 'the Capital of Madness'

General Charles de Gaulle, being greeted in Algiers as the saviour of the French
in Algeria in 1958

Above
'Here we drown Algerians': graffiti marks
the spot of the massacre in Paris on
17 October 1961

Left
'France will bring freely to Morocco
Civilisation, Wealth and Peace'

Mohamed Choukri. 'The Prince of Exile in Tangier'

Sarkozy and Ben Ali, the best of friends?

Above
The fall of Ben Ali

Left
Fresnes prison: a photograph of the cells circa 1910 and the building as it looks today

in Arabic military parlance, was commonly used to conceal small groups of guerrillas from external enemies. During the war, the term *harki* was applied to the groups of auxiliary troops formed by the French army to provide police and military cover at a local level, defending towns, villages and tribes against the FLN. By 1962 they numbered some 26,000 men who played a variety of roles, from local policemen to conscript troops in the field. The *harkis* were mainly peasants themselves and were often motivated by a determination to defend land and family against the FLN; they had no real interest in politics and certainly not the politics of national liberation.

In the summer of 1962, the *harkis* became the focus for anger and revenge for the victorious Nationalists and those fellow-travellers who now wanted to show their commitment to the new Algeria in blood. Terrible stories began to come out of Algeria of crucifixions, eyes gouged out and castrations. 'Tahar' from Palestro, who worked for the French security services, described watching two comrades being hung from the nose in a village square. The FLN charged the villagers 500 francs for the pleasure of whipping the men with canes. The whipping lasted for four or five hours, continuing even after the victims had died. Apparently the village women took a particular delight in the task. 'Tahar' managed to sneak out of the village and was rescued by a passing French army patrol.[2]

However, the first betrayal of the *harkis* was committed by the French. As the peace deal was being settled, leaders of various *harki* factions grew increasingly nervous and began to lobby the French government for reassurances that their safety could be ensured, either by military protection or by 'repatriation'. The French government did not want either of these. On 16 May Louis Joxe, the French Minister of State, issued an order which secretly prohibited the transportation of *harkis* back to France. The French wanted to observe the principles of the peace agreement and, perhaps more obliquely, to avoid the OAS and the *harkis* joining forces to cause trouble on French soil.

When the policy became known, it sent the signal that France did not care about those who had fought for its honour. The point was that they were not French. De Gaulle was clear on this matter: the *harkis* were 'toys of history' rather than integral elements of the French army. When a Muslim deputy, whose family had been killed by the FLN, put it to the general that his community would suffer in independent Algeria, de Gaulle responded icily: 'Yes. You will suffer.'

And suffer they did. A mere 15,000 *harkis* made it to France, where they were treated as pariahs, herded together and left to rot in camps outside the big French cities. These were wretched places, sometimes out beyond the suburbs, in the countryside or in forest clearings. The idea was that they would be protected from possible FLN reprisals, but in fact the French authorities were happy to hide them away and forget that they were there. Their lives in these camps were worse than they had been at home – assimilation and even the most menial work was out of their reach.

The fate of those left behind in Algeria was, however, truly terrible. Acting under the terms of the peace agreement, the French soldiers were often obliged to disarm their former comrades. They were then abandoned in a climate of frenzied bloodlust, which echoed the '*épuration sauvage*' (wild purification) of 1945 in newly liberated France, when most suspected collaborators were lynched, murdered and mutilated in revenge for their treachery. In Algeria, the *harkis* were systematically rounded up and sent to work in labour camps or on pointless projects in the desert. In both instances they died of starvation and disease. Even more horrible were the individual acts of retribution which merged into a wave of violence that swept across newly independent Algeria. Whole families were massacred. Former soldiers were ordered to dig their own graves and swallow their decorations before being shot. Torture, being dragged behind trucks, and castration were all commonplace. One frequent act of sadism was to burn the victim alive, feeding the cooked flesh to dogs.

The fate of the *harkis* is still very much an issue in Algeria and France. In the 1970s the *harkis* were out in the camps, forgotten by their former masters. There were occasional riots in protest at the miserable conditions, but there was no official recognition of their status or their difficulties. The policy was to keep them separate from the 'good Algerians' who were arriving in massive numbers to work in France. It was only in 2001 that Jacques Chirac began the healing process when he declared 25 September a day of official homage to the *harkis*; a plaque was placed in the Cour des Invalides – the tomb of Napoleon and seat of all French military triumph – honouring the '*harkis* and other supplementary formations of the French army'. Since then the French government has sought to make reparations, in response to fierce campaigning by *harki* families. In 2007 Nicolas Sarkozy met an official delegation at the Elysée, although he still refused officially to acknowledge the 'responsibility of France in the abandonment and massacre of the *harkis*'. Finally, in April 2012, Sarkozy acknowledged French responsibility for the 'abandonment' of the *harkis*, opening a memorial in the now derelict camp of Rivesaltes near Perpignan.

However, in Algeria *harkis* are still denied access to higher education and exiled *harkis* cannot be buried on Algerian soil. On an official visit to France in 2000, the Algerian president Abdelaziz Bouteflika said on French television that the *harkis* were 'as bad as Nazis and their collaborators'.[3] And in the Algerian community in France, the word *harki* remains loaded with poison. During the infamous France–Algeria football match at the Stade de France in September 2001, the Algerian supporters taunted the French superstar Zinédine Zidane, who is of Algerian origin, with cries of 'Zidane-harki'. As riots broke up the match, Zidane left the pitch in tears. When I interviewed him a few years later in Madrid, he described the match as the worst moment in his footballing career. The rumour persists in the *banlieues* of Marseilles and Paris that Zidane's father was a *harki*. When I put this to him, he flinched visibly before denying that it was true.[4]

Arabization

The twin pillars of Boumédienne's Algeria were the military and Islam, with financial backing from the USSR and China, who both saw Algeria as a strategic ally against the West. The key posts in his government were held by military men, either former commanders in the FLN or the so-called Déserteurs de l'Armée Française. These were officers who had been trained and promoted by the French and come late to the War of Independence, spending most of the war outside Algeria. Under Boumédienne they promoted themselves to posts they would never have achieved in France and began to construct the new Algeria as a rigid hierarchy, strictly enforced by the security services, the much feared Sécurité Militaire (SM), which were famous for high-profile assassinations of renegade FLN figures and others thought to have misunderstood the revolution. Boumédienne's government was also populist – he won great prestige in the streets by sending Algerian military units to Palestine during the Six Day War and made much of breaking off diplomatic relations with the United States in the name of pan-Arab unity. The average Algerian admired Boumédienne's '*redjla*' – a term which roughly translates as 'toughness' – in defying the West.[5]

The most significant development under Boumédienne's régime was his encouragement of a resurgence of Islamic values. He called this 'a return to the sources' of Algerian culture, positioning Islam against French or European values as a new step forward in the liberation struggle. This resurgence went hand-in-hand with the aggressive promulgation of Arabic as the first language of Algeria, displacing French. This was a complex issue. Algerian Arabic is a dialect which is spoken with massive regional differences. For this reason, even the most hard-line revolutionaries found French the most effective *lingua franca* of the country. What is more, Egyptian Arabic, which arrived with a wave of Islamic teachers from Egypt, was incomprehensible to many Algerian Arabic speakers, while classical Arabic was as remote or distant as Latin.

The Egyptian teachers brought with them a new ideology which was not then known as 'Islamism' or 'political Islam', but which was already at work as a subversive force against the kind of pan-Arab nationalism that had inspired the FLN until now. The most militant Islamist group in Algeria during this period was a religious association called al-Qiyam (Values), established by a group of clerics in 1953 in imitation of the Muslim Brotherhood. Founded in 1928 in Egypt by Hassan el-Banna, the Muslim Brotherhood believed that Islam had to reclaim the political dimension which had been lost with the collapse of the Ottoman Empire. They opposed Arab Nationalism with the slogan: 'The Koran is our constitution!' Islam was a complete and total system and there was no need to look to Europe for any other model – Marxist, Socialist or Nationalist. During the 1930s this had become a mass movement in Egypt, attracting the lower middle classes, who had only recently become literate and who defended their faith as 'Islamic modernity'.

In Algeria in the 1960s, the ideas of the Muslim Brotherhood had a clear appeal for Muslims who sought a way of opposing colonial structures and were suspicious of Western ideas being imported into Islamic territory. The most influential figure during this period was Sayyid Qutb, who emerged as the intellectual leader of the Muslim Brothers, who were brutally suppressed in Egypt under the régime of General Nasser. Qutb's key argument against Arab Nationalists – including the FLN – was that they were leading the Islamic nations back to *Jahiliya*

– a state of ignorance and barbarity which predated Islam. The ultimate sanction against those who are *kufr* (impious) is *takfir*, which means the unbeliever is left outside the law and therefore condemned to death: according to the holy formula, 'his blood is his forfeit'. Although Qutb died in one of Nasser's prisons in 1966 before he could fully define these terms, this ideology is what justifies most contemporary Islamist terrorism.

It was also the logic that defined the core beliefs of al-Qiyam, setting it against the FLN government in Algeria, which it regularly attacked as irreligious and anti-Muslim. In one famous example, Djamila Bouhired, one of the FLN's heroines of the Battle of Algiers and a symbol of the new Algeria, was reported to have got off a plane without a veil during an official visit to Kuwait. This was held up by al-Qiyam as a clear example of the FLN's scorn for true Muslim values. When Qutb died in prison in Egypt, al-Qiyam protested vehemently to Boumédienne's government that no Algerian could tolerate this. In 1967, the government banned gambling and the sale of alcohol to Muslims. It was an initial concession, and the first step towards a wider Islamist radicalization of society.

Radical Chic

Algeria's first decade as a free nation ended with a massive political statement by Boumédienne, who wanted to situate the new Algeria as the leader of an African renaissance, and make Algiers the global capital of Third World-ism. In 1969 Algiers hosted the first ever Pan-African Cultural Festival, set up by the Organization of African Unity, a loosely Marxist anti-colonial coalition. He invited delegates from all parts of the world that were at war, literally or metaphorically, with the West. These included representatives from North Vietnam, Cuba, Chile, Mexico and Palestine. One of Boumédienne's most notorious guests was the American Black Panther Eldridge Cleaver, then on the run from the police but filmed wandering nonchalantly through the Casbah by the photographer William Klein, who made a documentary about the festival.

Prior to his arrival in Algeria, Cleaver had been arrested in Oakland for attempted murder, having led a group of Black Panthers in a shoot-out with local police. He jumped bail, made his way to Cuba and then to Algiers, where the Algerian government welcomed him with open arms. Cleaver was a provocative symbol, a way of tweaking the nose of the Americans as well as announcing Algeria's radical anti-Western credentials to the world. Cleaver was paid a stipend by the North Vietnamese and housed in a villa, said to be a haven for American black 'revolutionaries' returning to Africa as well as a safe house for deserters from the US military. Among those who visited Cleaver in Algiers was Timothy Leary, the guru of the psychedelic revolution, who had also been busted out of jail and smuggled over from America.

Despite his venerated status in exile, it was not long before Cleaver returned to his criminal past. Most of the 'revolutionaries' who made it to Algeria turned out to be accomplished gangsters. Cleaver was soon running rackets himself and left the country pursued by Algerian secret police, who suspected him of killing his wife's lover. But in 1969 the images of Cleaver in Algiers – which made it on to the cover of *Life* magazine – proclaimed Algeria as the cool capital of the Afro-American revolution.

Other visitors to the Pan-African festival included Miriam Makeba, the South African singer and anti-apartheid militant. One the highlights was the free jazz sax player Archie Shepp jamming with Tuareg musicians and, in a virtuoso performance, breaking down the harmonic structures of Western music and rediscovering the atonal source of jazz in the music of Mother Africa. In his opening speech, Boumédienne had made it clear that the festival was not just a 'distraction' but the 'revolution taking place in everyday life'. The art and music of Shepp and Makeba, and the presence of the Panthers, captured the excitement of this historical moment, as well as heralding a new dawn where art and politics dissolved into each other. For many of those who attended the festival, it was as if the promise of freedom in the revolts of May '68 was now being made real in Algeria.[6]

At the same time as Western fantasies of freedom were being played out in Algeria, Islam was on the rise. Until independence, Islam in Algeria was reasonably relaxed and multi-denominational. The Sunni school of Maliki Islam, which had been the religion of Islamic Spain, existed alongside the schools of Hanifi and Ibadite Islam. These schools all take the Holy Koran as their primary source but adapt it and co-exist with local customs, which meant that the cult of local saints and regional variants were all tolerated. Boumédienne wanted to make this the official state version of Islam; it was what he really meant by 'a return to the source'.

To the fledgling Islamist movements, this was a betrayal of the Algerian revolution. Boumédienne's sympathy for Socialism on the Cuban model and Third World politics in general was also detested by the various underground Islamist groups growing in popularity and strength in the early 1970s. Although al-Qiyam was banned in 1970, Abdellatif Soltani, one of its most charismatic figures, became a kind of folk hero in Algeria, as he persistently escaped capture by the police (usually by slipping over the border into Morocco) and went on to preach and publish texts which described Boumédienne's government as anti-Islamic and therefore anti-Algerian.[7]

The first manifesto of the Algerian Islamist movement was published by Soltani in exile in Morocco in 1974 under the title *Al-Mazdaqiya Hiya Asl Al-Ishtiraqiya* (*Mazdaquism is the Source of Socialism*). This was a full-frontal assault on the FLN's attempt to marry Islam and Socialism. For Soltani, this was nothing short of atheism – only the word of God could determine the values and laws of Muslims. The title is a reference to the Mazdaq Persians, a sect from the pre-Islamic age who practised an early form of Communism. The FLN were like the Mazdaqs, atheists who sought to infect the purity of Islam with foreign ideas, just as earlier Muslim scholars had misguidedly tried to introduce Greek philosophy into the Muslims' religion. For Hachem Tidjani, who picked up Soltani's mantle as the fiercest critic of the Algerian state, the FLN was no more nor less than 'the party of Satan'.

17

The Algerian Intifada

In Algiers on the morning of 5 October 1988, groups of young men began to gather in the districts of Bab-el-Oued, El Biar and Belcourt. Most of them were local, but there was also a sizeable contingent of country lads, who spoke with a different accent from the *algérois*. They had no leaders and belonged to no organization but were coming together with one single aim: to march into the centre of the city to show how much they hated the government. Some of them carried stones, sticks, machetes or iron bars, knowing that the police or the army would give them no quarter. As they set off many of them drew scarves over their faces, partly in imitation of the rioters from the French *banlieues* they had seen on television, and partly in homage to the young Palestinians they had seen taking on the Israeli army – and in their minds the whole world – in the Palestinian intifada, which had been declared some twelve months earlier.[1]

This was a generation which had known nothing but poverty and boredom. Since the late 1970s the Algerian economy had been in free fall. As the population grew larger and younger, the government – now led by President Chadli, who had come into power on the death of Boumédienne in 1978 – had imposed austerity measures which had made unemployment the defining fact of life for Algerian youth in the 1980s. Emigration was an impossible dream if you had no money or connections. Everybody knew that Algeria was rich, thanks to the oilfields, and nobody believed the government when it said that the hike in oil prices meant that the cost of bread and sugar had to rise. But no one knew exactly where the money went; people speculated that it went to a corrupt government and its cronies, known as '*le pouvoir*' (the Power).

The packs of young men arrived by bus, taxi or on foot, and by mid-morning had converged on the city centre, coming together at the head of the rue Didouche Mourad, the long, elegant spiralling street that takes you down to the heart of Algiers and the Grande Poste. The authorities had known that trouble was coming, but they did not know what form it would take. Tensions had been rising across Algeria for months – that summer, in the Aurès, women from peasant families had led street protests against water rationing. The local police had openly clubbed them down and then thrown them into jail. In Annaba, in early September, striking workers had deliberately wrecked hundreds of refrigerators on their way to be exported to Tunisia. 'Why should we make them, when we can't afford to buy them or even buy any food to put in them?' said one striking militant.

On 4 October the word had gone out that there was to be a general strike in Algiers. The big joke was that it was hard to strike when you were chronically unemployed. Still, the message was passed on by word of mouth and on tatty Xeroxed pamphlets, which would land you a beating and a prison sentence if the police caught you with one.

The violence started as soon as the first wave of young men began to march down the rue Didouche Mourad. None of what happened had been planned, but for the protesters the very sight of shop fronts, advertising hoardings, travel agencies, fashionable arcades and cafés – all mean and wretched by First World standards – was too much to stop the anger rising to their throats. These were the most visible emblems of what *le pouvoir* had stolen from the people, things which no one else could dream of touching or possessing. 'The President is Killing our Youth!' and 'Young People Stand Up!' the battle cries went up. The anger made everyone fearless – they threw themselves on to the bonnets of police cars and threatened the small groups of armed police, who did not know what to do.

The city was suddenly wide open to these angry young rioters and they did not hesitate to rip it apart. Windows were smashed, cars torched and, within an hour or so, as the marchers hit the Grande Poste, the centre of Algiers was in flames. The targets included the Blue Note nightclub (known for its prostitutes as much as for its Western music) and the shopping centre at Riad El-Feth. This was a grim, concrete 1970s-style mall which was supposed to be a celebration Algerian modernity; for this reason it was built alongside the monument to the martyrs for independence on the heights above the city (when I visited it was mostly empty, bleak and smelling slightly of damp). As fire and smoke wreathed the lower floors, on a nearby government building a cynic had replaced the Algerian flag with an empty couscous sack. It was a forlorn image which perfectly captured the mood that had propelled the uprising in the first place.

Over the next few days, these scenes were replicated in towns and cities across Algeria. The enemy was President Chadli. In the ten years since he had come to power, Chadli had presided over a country which had lost its way: the FLN government had ossified into a decadent and pampered élite which let its own people starve; the liberators of the Algerians had become their jailers. Special hatred was reserved for Chadli's wife Halima, who – according to popular folklore – had cut his balls off. The events of October 1988 were a very male affair, characterized by roaming gangs of young men eager for a fight. They made up songs and rhymes in Arabic which endlessly made Chadli out to be a queer, a eunuch or a thief, or all three at once.

Afters days of chaos in Algeria, the army's response was vicious. Chadli declared a state of siege – something which had not happened even during the worst moments of the War of Independence. All civilian authorities were placed under military control. The army was unleashed. Organized death squads patrolled the streets and fired at will into crowds, at individuals, into mosques. The death toll rose by the hour. There were fresh reports of torture. At the same time, staple foods which had been unavailable – oil, flour, semolina – suddenly reappeared in the shops. For nearly everyone, this only confirmed the wicked duplicity of the government.

The demonstrations continued. After Friday prayers on 7 October, a group of about 8,000 believers, chanting 'Islamic Republic' and 'God is Great', took on the police in the streets of Belcourt. These were not the angry street kids who had started the rebellion, but fighters led by known Islamic radicals: the first public sight of Islamists organizing against the authorities on the streets of Algeria.

On Monday 10 October, as public anger rose to a crescendo, a march of 20,000 people orchestrated by the Islamist imam Ali Behdadj marched down to the sea front, where they were met by military blockades. The Islamists flung insults at the soldiers – many of whom were semi-literate peasants – calling them worse than Jews or Zionists. Shots were fired, then there was tear gas. By now 500 people had been killed during the revolt. This stand-off between Islamists and the military was the turning point when a political crisis gathered the deadly momentum that would take Algeria to civil war.

'Everything is Broken'

This moment had been a long time coming. For the previous decade Chadli had played a dangerous game with the rising tide of Islamists in Algeria. On the one hand, he wanted to show Algeria off to the world as a modern, dynamic nation, but he also courted the Islamists, partly because he needed their political support and partly as a way of controlling so-called 'street Islam' – a concoction of superstition, magic, notions of the evil eye and other folklore. This was obviously a threat to official state Islam, and allying himself with the Islamists was a way of bringing it under some kind of jurisdiction.

The essential flaw in this strategy, however, was that Islamist ideology was at odds with the easy-going forms of Islam indigenous to Algeria. Much Islamist thought and practice was based on Wahhabism, a puritanical import from Saudi Arabia that was opposed to all forms of Western modernity, from dancing and drinking to gender rights, consumerist culture and democracy. Wahhabism was a movement on the move; its clerics talked about the necessity for the rebirth of Islam as the supreme religion in the 'post-millennial age' (by which they meant the collapse of the West). Wahhabism is indeed a chiliastic version of Islam – a religion in which believers scorn the world as it is and prepare for the world to come. As such, it is the perfect theological underpinning of the 'political' Islam of Sayyid Qutb and the Muslim Brothers, whose mission is to rid the world of *Jahiliya* (barbarity) in the 'Lands of Islam'.

One of the more absurd confrontations between the Islamist movement and Western values took place at the El Bey University in Constantine in 1985. At the annual Islamic Book Fair, the organizers set up an exhibition on Punks and New Romantics to terrify Algerian youth with the dangers of bisexuality and drugs. Most of the images were taken from French pop magazines and were pinned up alongside texts that warned of the chilling and degrading effects of listening to music made by homosexuals. The featured artists included, predictably, Boy George, David Bowie, Soft Cell and the Thompson Twins. A special hatred was reserved, however, for Marilyn, the one-hit wonder and junkie pal of Boy George. His photo – not so much androgynous as quite feminine and sexy – deeply troubled young Algerian males, whose macho stance was compromised by this 'man-woman'.[2]

The contempt for Western pop music, at least in this softened form, was not solely due to Islamist objections. Most young people in Algeria in the 1980s were not Islamists, but were simply disaffected, trapped in a city and a country that felt like a prison. The false promises of Western pop music, from Michael Jackson down, belonged to the 'chi-chis', the gilded youth of Algeria who had some family or political connection to le pouvoir, and who flaunted their wealth and privilege with their fast cars, fashionable clothes and international travel. Most galling of all for ordinary Algerian young men, the chi-chis (nicknamed for their posh and effete way of speaking) had access to Europeanized girls who offered glamour and easy sex.

During this period, the streets of downtown Algiers were also thronged in the daytime by so-called 'hittistes'. These were young men, usually with university qualifications, who spent most of the day propped up against a wall (hit, in colloquial Arabic), smoking, chatting, hustling. The hittistes had their own subculture – they spoke in a slang made up of French, Spanish and Arabic words, engaged in low-level criminality, dealing in drugs or trabendo (contraband goods), smoking hash and drinking zombreto, a potentially lethal cocktail of fruit juice and illegal industrial alcohol.[3] Their code was summed up in the word zaguet, meaning 'everything is broken'. They measured out their lives in what was forbidden, or, in Algerian Arabic, la yadzouz. The hittistes hated the chi-chis and went out of their way to rob them or insult them, a small way of getting back at le pouvoir.

These rebels also had their own music. This was 'raï music' (the slang word raï means 'argument' or 'opinion'), which had its origins in Oran in the 1930s. It was traditionally made by chebs (from shabab, meaning 'young'), who sang about social or political issues, rather than by the *sheikhs* (meaning 'old'), who sang about love or religion. By the 1980s, *raï* was a fully fledged underground movement with its own heroes, such as Cheb Hasni or Cheb Khaled, who toured a circuit of clubs, selling home-made cassettes and attacking the government in their songs. It was the Algerian equivalent of rap, reggae or punk, given an extra edge by the politics and the raucous, hard electric sound of the music.

The football terraces were one of the few public spaces for expressing anti-government feeling. The supporters of teams in Algiers, Oran and Constantine took their cue from Spanish football and the rivalries between Madrid and Barcelona – the Catalan team was the model of a team expressing contempt for the ruling state. Violence was inevitable and frequent between the poor young men who followed football, but it was also easily contained by the heavy-handed and well-armed police force; for now, at least, neither music nor football were considered seriously subversive by *le pouvoir*.[4]

However, beyond the streets, terraces and the illegal drinking clubs where *zombreto* and *raï* came together, the forces were gathering which, within a few short years, would see Algeria brought to its knees and bring North African terrorism back to the streets of Paris in the mid-1990s.

From the outside, this swift fall from grace seemed incomprehensible. Despite the chaos of the 1980s, until the riots of 1988 Algeria had been the strong leader of the Non-Aligned Movement, whose global authority and status had helped bring back the US hostages from Iran in 1981. With its prestige then high in the West and the Third World, Algeria was the only country which could have accomplished this diplomatic feat. Algeria's influence in the Arab world, and indeed in the post-colonial world, came from the fact that independence had been forged in a revolutionary movement – a mixture of Islam,

Socialism and, most potently, Fanonism. This was the political philosophy derived from Frantz Fanon, which had made the quest for 'authenticity' the defining feature of the state. By the 1980s, as the FLN stagnated and decayed, Fanonism, like its corollary in the Soviet Union, had become a justification for privileging national identity over ethnic identity, the collective over the individual. This was, of course, legitimized by the recent revolutionary past and enforced with violence if necessary.

The breaking point for the Algerian government came in 1992. There had been a brief period of reform and political openness in 1989, when Chadli had allowed multi-party elections for the first time. Throughout North Africa and the Middle East, Algeria suddenly became the focus for optimism as parties were formed from across the political spectrum, from Feminists to Islamists.

Among the new parties, one emerged that had the popular support to threaten the government. This was the Front Islamique du Salut (FIS), a hard-line Islamist party led by two men: Abassi Madani, a veteran of the War of Independence, with a PhD from the University of London, and Ali Benhadj, a teacher in Bab-el-Oued who had been a key figure in the revolt of 1988. The stance of the FIS was to replace 'popular sovereignty with divine sovereignty'. All of sudden, as support for the FIS grew and they accelerated towards power, the hard-fought-for Republic of Algeria stood poised to dissolve into an Iranian-style theocracy.

Support for the FIS came from the poorest in society, who were sickened by the corruption they saw around them: the most literal form of *al-Jahiliya* (pagan barbarity). They believed Algeria to be cursed, because the people did not follow religion. The answer was simple and preached in mosques across the nation – the FIS would deliver Algeria back to the Algerians and its religious mission. Most powerfully and convincingly, the FIS argued that parliamentary democracy had been invented by the French to confuse Muslims and make them deviate from the true path of righteousness. They were prepared to take part in democratic elections, but only to destroy the concept of democracy itself.

The FIS were violently anti-French. In their rhetoric, the French were crusaders, sometimes Jews, but always waging war against Islam. The French fought this war not just with arms but with culture. On the one hand, this took the form of Algerian writers and journalists expressing themselves in French – the heroic author Kateb Yacine was a particular hate figure for the FIS. On the other hand, the FIS also hated the French pop culture that was imported into Algeria on satellite television; they railed against game shows, advertising and soft porn as the work of Satan and the French. Most of all, the FIS targeted women who wore Western fashions and make-up, who read books and had careers: this, they argued, was how the French would seduce and weaken the Algerian male.

Unsurprisingly, the FIS attracted precisely the bored, angry and repressed young men who had no access to Western pleasures anyway. As followers of the FIS, they imagined themselves as warriors for Islam, taking on the forces of the French and the Zionists, terms which were now applied to anybody in Algeria who was not an Islamist and a follower of the FIS. The most popular figure was Ali Benhadj, who had the stern charisma of the true fanatic, and whose language, fiery and imperious, spoke directly to the young men who wanted to go into battle for Allah. From the outset, Benhadj evoked armed struggle as the way forward: 'We do not underestimate the value of arms,' he said in 1991; 'the impious *pouvoir* and the miscreants do not deserve to be killed with bullets, for during the war of liberation one cut the throats of the traitors, one did not shoot them.'[5]

The FIS cause was further bolstered by the Gulf War of 1990–91. Officially, Algeria supported the anti-Iraq coalition, but on the streets Saddam Hussein was an anti-Western superhero, defying the forces of Imperialism and Zionism. The FIS described the Algerian army as a eunuch and the government as apostates. Soon all Algerians who did not support the FIS were denounced as apostates and as such became targets for execution.

It was against this background that the Algerian government lurched uneasily into elections in 1991. An announcement was made on 15 October that there would be two rounds of voting – in December 1991 and January 1992. The stakes could not have been higher. In the months leading up to the election, the FLN was weak and growing weaker, while the mainstream opposition party, the FFS (Front des Forces Socialistes), was increasingly despised by pious Muslims as the voice of the Francophone middle class. Meanwhile, the FIS argued that to vote against them was to vote against God.

This rapidly deteriorating situation was alarming to the army, who began to envisage Algeria as a fully fledged Islamic state – effectively Iran on the Mediterranean. The fears of middle-class Algerians were fuelled by constant intimidation from the FIS: wherever they could, they forced women to wear veils, banned music, and launched a wholescale assault on the nature of everyday life in Algeria.

In an attempt to decapitate the FIS, the army arrested Benhadj and Madani on 30 June 1991, on the grounds that they were plotting to bring down the Algerian state. This much was true – the policy of the FIS was to use democratic methods to bring down democracy. The problem was that under *le pouvoir* the concept of democracy had been degraded, as the morale of most Algerian people, especially the unemployed youth and impoverished working classes, ebbed away. As more and more young men were locked up, the country seemed more than ever like a prison camp rather than an independent nation.

The arrest of Benhadj and Madani only increased the prevailing bitterness. Young men began to make for the hills, where they started to train as an organized resistance force. Between boredom and poverty on the one hand, and armed struggle on the other, the choice was clear. By the end of the summer, the mountains of Zbarbar to the south-east of Algiers were dense with fledgling armed groups and known cynically to the *algérois* as 'Zbarbaristan'.[6]

If anything, Benhadj became even more influential in prison. His tracts were smuggled out and distributed in their tens of thousands, the voice of a real martyr and hero. At a massive FIS demonstration on 1 November in the Place des Martyrs, a Koran was held aloft on a chair to show that only God could occupy the space of president. In a PR master stroke, Benhadj's five-year-old son addressed the crowd. As soon as he became visible, the crowd was transported by a wave of religious emotion and the child's voice was drowned out by cries of 'God is Great!'

During this period the atmosphere in Algiers for non-Islamist Algerians was tense and occasionally terrifying. The un-employed young men who had found their vocation in the FIS now dressed differently – they did not wear modern 'Western' clothes, nor traditional Algerian outfits, but adopted the 'Afghan look': short trousers, tidy beards, Pakistani-style headgear. They intimidated the middle classes, who were now identified by their European-style clothes, by making throat-cutting gestures and a hissing sound. Journalists, schoolteachers, ordinary businessmen – none of them rich or properly corrupt like *le pouvoir* – were the 'near enemy', who had already been sentenced to death. The elections, in the Islamists' imagination, would provide the mandate to carry out the executions.

In the event, the FIS won a stunning victory in the first round on 1 December 1991. The figures were overwhelming – they took 188 of the 231 seats. There were 199 seats to be won in the second round; if the FIS repeated the performance, they would hold a clear two-thirds majority in parliament.

The non-Islamist population of Algeria now began to under-
stand the nightmare that was unfolding in front of them. On
3 January 1992, 300,000 people took to the streets chanting
'Neither police state, nor Islamic state, but a democratic state!'
By this time, the army generals had already taken their decision.
On 11 January, four days before the scheduled elections,
President Chadli publicly resigned on television. Power was
transferred to the Haut Conseil de Sécurité (HCE), the High
Security Council – a coalition of senior politicians and military
men. The head of the HCE was named as Mohammed Boudiaf,
one of the great leaders of the uprising of 1954, who was cajoled
back to Algeria from his retirement in Morocco by senior
generals. Effectively, the army had now taken power and the
next Algerian civil war had begun.

18

The New War with France

The immediate response in the region to the army takeover of the Algerian government was relief. In Libya Colonel Gaddafi welcomed the move, while President Mubarak in Egypt warned the international community to stay out of the fray. Closer to home, President Ben Ali of Tunisia fulsomely approved of the new regime; the Tunisian newspaper *Al-Sabah*, a propaganda mouthpiece for Ben Ali, described the manoeuvre as 'a last-minute change of direction by a train heading for the abyss'.[1] All of these governments raised the spectre of Islamism to justify their hold on power, and made it clear that this was a game that the Western powers could neither control nor understand.

The coup d'état had, however, a special resonance in France, which now had a population of some three million Muslims of Algerian origin. Opinion was divided in this community about how to respond. Algerians who were frequent visitors to the country reported back on the fear and panic that had gripped the nation; although many older Algerians in France privately despaired of the corruption of *le pouvoir*, they did not want an Islamist state. A younger, harsher generation in the *banlieues* of Paris, Lyons, Marseilles and other major cities listened keenly to imams who had recently arrived from Algeria and who declared that they would die for the FIS as martyrs. The French government continued to give visas to key members of the FIS, both hard-line and more moderate elements, with the rationale that this allowed the French secret services to infiltrate and monitor Islamist traffic between France and Algeria. The reality was that the FIS was now gaining a foothold in mainland France, where in most mosques they claimed the war against the generals was also a war against the West, against *Jahiliya* – the barbarity which they could see every day on the streets of French cities, which was both an insult and a humiliation to the true Muslim.

The French government, aware of the sensitivities among the Muslim population, watched events in Algeria nervously but said little. François Mitterrand encouraged ordinary Algerians to 'take up the threads of democratic life' as soon as they could, but this didn't really mean anything. The ambiguous nature of the official French response was compounded by the fact that one of the leading figures in the new government was Sheikh Tedjin Haddam, rector of the Paris mosque and perceived by most radicals to be a tame, Frenchified Muslim. In the meantime, the French set about restructuring Algeria's 25 billion dollars of debt, effectively underwriting the new government. Within two months the money had been so badly handled (or stolen) that food prices again began to rise beyond the reach of even middle-class Algerians.

The French were furious that the money, which was meant to provide social stability, had been so easily squandered. So, too, was Boudiaf, an honest broker who saw his role as returning dignity to the revolution he had fought for. Boudiaf immediately announced a high-level anti-corruption campaign – beginning with the arrest of a senior general and the liberalization of the oil and gas sectors, which provided most of Algeria's wealth. This, however, was to effectively write and sign his own death warrant, as dark forces in Algeria now began to awaken, concerned above all with preserving a deeply entrenched system of bribes and state theft.

*

To this day nobody knows who organized the killing of Boudiaf. The simple facts are that shortly after 9.30 a.m. on 29 June 1992, Boudiaf began to address an audience in a conference hall in Annaba and at the very moment when he used the word 'Islam', a grenade was thrown behind him, exploding with a loud crack; within seconds, in a blast of gunfire, Boudiaf was shot, his body slumped over a table as he lay dying. The audience cowered on the floor, taking cover where they could. A terrified silence hung in the air for almost a minute. All of this was broadcast live on television to a stunned nation.[2]

The official line was that the killer was a deranged Islamist who had acted alone but whose actions showed how much the nation needed a strong government. He was named as Lembarek Boumaarifi, a middle-ranking army officer who had been part of Boudiaf's security force. He confessed on national television, claiming that he was acting on his own conscience. Nobody was convinced. For one thing, as the newspapers pointed out, there were glaring lapses in security around Boudiaf that morning which made the murder appear to have been quite carefully choreographed. Most tellingly, the armed guards around Boudiaf failed to act when the shooting started and were outside the conference hall. They did not react to the shooting, even as Lembarek Boumaarifi was fleeing the scene. A senior officer did, however, manage to shoot and wound the only policeman who had pursued Boumaarifi. Even more sinister was the fact that there were no other ministers at an important conference where there would have normally been representation at the senior level.

Straight away journalists began to speculate about whether the killing had been organized within the government. Their suspicions were compounded by the fact that there was no autopsy on Boudiaf's body. At the funeral at Al-Elia, hundreds of Islamists gathered at the gates, chanting anti-government slogans and proclaiming the greatness of God. Everybody talked about how 'they', *le pouvoir*, had killed him. Boudiaf had been the last hope of a corrupt and broken nation, which now splintered visibly into Islamist and pro-government factions. Many middle-class and professional Algerians started to plan a life abroad as the shadow of civil war loomed large over the towns and cities. In the run-down areas, particularly in Algiers, young men began to gather and plan revenge on the state which hated them. Their leaders were in jail, but this did not stop them arguing and plotting. The next move was to retreat into the purity of the mountains – like the Prophet – away from the impious life of the plains. They did this in the summer of 1992, moving in small, disciplined groups to begin weapons training.

The first shot of the new war against France was fired on 26 August at Houari Boumédienne airport in Algiers. This was one of the busiest days of the year for the airport, when thousands of Algerians were packing up after their summer holidays and returning to France. In the morning the airport authorities received several calls warning of a bomb; the last was received at 10 a.m. Fifteen minutes later, as a hundred or so passengers were making for the airport terminal, a huge bomb exploded, ripping through the building. Ten people were killed and 128 people injured. Over the mess of dismembered corpses, witnesses called for the death of whoever had done this.

The problem was that nobody really knew who had planted the bomb. The Algerian government, now under the presidency of General Liamine Zéroual, immediately blamed Islamist factions, as did many ordinary Algerians. In the event some fifty-five Islamists were found guilty of involvement. Privately, however, the French intelligence services wondered about the incongruities of the case – the botched warnings, the lack of official response – and, most importantly, the bigger political game that the bombing served. Put simply, it was cautiously and discreetly argued in some diplomatic quarters that the bombing at Algiers airport was the excuse the government needed to move into a new, more repressive phase in the war against the Islamists.

One of the problems that the government faced was that the Islamist movement was by now not a single organization with a straightforward command structure. By driving the FIS underground, they had unwittingly caused it to break up into small, agile groups which had no formal connection to each other and so were almost impossible to monitor and police. However, this fragmented 'army' comprised some 22,000 men: a real and visible threat to the state – a state made up of 'monkeys, Jews and Crusaders', in the language of Islamist doctrine.

Action Heroes

The Islamist groups came together under a French name, the Groupe Islamiste Armé (GIA). It had no central committee but instead operated as a matrix of autonomous units, each with its own lethal speciality, such as placing car bombs, or murdering journalists, university teachers or government officials. However, the GIA was unified by a guiding theory: that the dream of an Islamic state was under threat from the Hizb Franca, the Party of France. In Islamist doctrine, these were the new *harkis* or pieds noirs: the Francophone Algerian élite who spoke the language of democracy but whose goal was to colonize the 'real' Muslim Algeria with European ideas and values.

The defining feature of the GIA's war was its ultra-violent methods. The terrorists did not simply kill people but turned the murders into a form of performance or ritual. As in the original War of Independence, throats were slit and heads cut off. But now spectacular refinements were introduced: often the victim's tongue was cut off and tied around a severed head (this was in homage to a technique employed by Colombian drug cartels); heads were also impaled on poles at crossroads and along the roadside, where trees and bushes were draped in entrails as a grotesque and chilling decoration. Policemen were welcomed home by the sight of their wife's head hanging from a pole by its hair. The carnage carried a message: Algerians who did not fight for the Islamist cause were non-Muslims and deserved to die.[3]

There was also a cruel logic which impelled the Islamists ever deeper into the spiral of extreme violence. It was partly driven by the social background of the young men who joined the GIA – they were the unemployed and dispossessed inhabitants of the backstreets and *banlieues* of the big cities. Like the fighting on the football terraces, which had been the first act of defiance for many of these young men, competitive rivalry with other gangs rather than organized revenge against the government motivated them. As such, each group within the GIA sought to outdo its rivals in how far they were prepared to go in 'killing Devils' in the name of God.

The GIA fighters often identified themselves with action heroes such as Jackie Chan, Bruce Lee, Arnold Schwarzenegger or Sly Stallone, and in the big cities sported fashionable jeans, slicked-back hair and an insolent manner in the face of authority. Some became the stuff of legend, with nicknames to match their ruthlessness; in Algiers these included Lyes '*l'égorgeur*' (the throat-cutter) or 'Flicha' (the arrow), so-called for his elegant swiftness in killing cops and whose name soon became a terrace chant. But murder was not just fashionable: the very act of killing also induced a sense of ecstasy and purification as powerful as any drug. These men were warriors who had absolute righteousness on their side in their battle with the forces of evil. And the most evil force of all was the French.[4]

It was inevitable that the violence should reach France. This much had been presaged by regular attacks on French citizens in Algeria. No less significant was the way the French language had become a divisive weapon which split Algerian society: as the stand-off between the Islamists and the government became more tense, the choice of which language you used on the street in Algeria – Arabic, Berber or French – could be an act of life or death.

The first attempt to attack the French mainland began on 24 December 1994. At Algiers airport four armed GIA men, disguised as cleaners, managed to sneak on to an Air France airbus destined for Orly. There were 240 passengers on board, forty of whom were French citizens. The hijackers began by collecting passports and then shot three passengers – an Algerian policeman, a Vietnamese diplomat and the cook from the French Embassy – to show they meant business. They demanded that the FIS leaders be released from house arrest.

Their plan was to fly to France and crash the plane into the Eiffel Tower, but for the next two days the plane remained on the runway in Algiers as the French and Algerian governments sought a way out of the stand-off. Initially, the Algerians refused any offer of military assistance from the French, but eventually, as the tension mounted, they gave in and allowed the plane to be flown to Marseilles. After a day of frustrating negotiations, the French Special Forces launched an assault on the cockpit and at the rear of the plane, shooting the GIA gunmen dead in minutes.

The violence came to Paris in July 1995, when Abdelbaki Sahraoui was killed in the rue Myrha. Sahraoui was in his eighties, a fluent French speaker, the imam of the local mosque and a founding member of the FIS. He had been in Paris since 1991 and travelled regularly to London to meet members of the FIS in exile. At around 6.30 p.m. on 11 July, two men walked into the mosque and began praying. After prayers they asked to speak to Sahraoui. They met in a small office at the back. Within a few minutes, one of them had taken a rifle out of a bag and shot Sahraoui dead. The mosque was normally under the watchful eye of the French intelligence services, but today they were strangely absent. A friend of Sahraoui tried to stop the men leaving the mosque but was shot dead in turn. The killers ran out on to the street, where they hijacked a car at gunpoint, before abandoning it a few kilometres up the road.

With Sahraoui's assassination, the French secret services had lost a vital link to the FIS high command. Most intelligent observers blamed the GIA, who no longer heeded their elders, and who had been condemned by Sahraoui for their excesses. In London, at the notorious Finsbury mosque, Abu Hamza proudly declared, 'We killed him because he was a democrat.' In Paris, the faithful at the rue Myrha blamed the murder on the Algerian secret services. The political consequences were what really mattered, however: Sahraoui had been the guarantor that the war would not come to France; his killing was a declaration that this was now precisely what would happen next. In Algiers, Paris and London, the GIA distributed tracts which showed the Eiffel Tower in flames. They now began actively to seek recruits among the Algerian population of France, sending willing volunteers to train in Afghanistan.

Parisians' fears deepened on the discovery of two bomb factories in the same district of Paris. Then, just two weeks after Sahraoui's death, on 25 July, a bomb exploded at the Saint-Michel metro station in the heart of the Latin Quarter of Paris. The bomb went off at the height of the rush hour on the RER line, the train which connects the suburbs to the city. Ten people were killed and fifty-seven injured. On the evening news that night, the French nation was confronted with images of bodies being carried across the familiar *café terrasses* of one of the most popular tourist spots in the world.[5]

The bombing at Saint-Michel was followed three weeks later by a bomb at the Arc de Triomphe. This time seventeen people were injured. By now there were troops on the streets and the fear was clearly visible on the faces of ordinary Parisians on the metro and in other public places. Nor was this a good time to be North African in Paris. For those who remembered the last Algerian war, Muslims were once again the enemy. 'I am not a racist normally, but in the summer of 1995 I hated the Arab faces that I saw, even people I had known for years,' I was told by one Parisian, a respectable left-leaning teacher. The sense of unreality was heightened by a bizarre note which had been sent to the French ambassador in Algiers, calling on President Jacques Chirac to convert to Islam, signed by the alleged head of the GIA.

On the surface, it seemed that the GIA's strategy was to export the Algerian war to French soil so that the French people would quickly tire of terror and put pressure on the government to sever its close links with *le pouvoir* in Algeria.[6] This strategy was a total failure; if anything, the French were at pains to reinforce *le pouvoir* as a counterweight to the rise of Islamist influence in France. Another more nuanced theory was that the GIA had been infiltrated by the Algerian secret services, who organized the terror campaign in France to secure even more robust French support for the Algerian government. None of this has ever been proved. In any case, these strategies would not have concerned the foot soldiers of the terrorist groups in France, who fought out of rage and despair.

Orphans

On 27 September 1995 a group of mushroom pickers in Malval, a small wood on the hills above Lyons, reported seeing a wanted man. His name was Khaled Kelkal and he had been identified as the mastermind behind all the terrorist attacks that summer, including the murder of Sahraoui. His image – a startlingly accurate police drawing which captured angular, angry features – had been distributed all over France.

The police tried to apprehend him and were met by gunfire from Karim Koussa, Kelkal's friend and accomplice. Kelkal slipped away, only to be tracked down two days later by police in the suburb of Vaugneray, just outside Lyons. His pursuit and capture were filmed by a crew from the TV channel France 2, and the killing was shown on prime-time news the following day. The police claimed that, although Kelkal had already been shot in the legs, he aimed his weapon at them. France's entire population was able to listen to a senior police officer who instructed his men to shoot, saying, 'Finish him off! Finish him off!'[7]

Kelkal immediately became a hero in the *banlieues* across France. This was not just because he had defied the police and the French state, but also because of his life story. He had been born in Algeria but came to France as a child, to the suburb of Vaulx-en-Velin. In 1984, at the age of thirteen, he had watched and joined in the first riots and 'rodeos' – learning that the police could be taken on and defeated on his home ground. He was clever and attended a good school, La Martinière Monplaisir de Lyon, but he soon drifted. Kelkal was partly influenced by his elder brother Nouredine (who would eventually serve a nine-year prison sentence for armed robbery), and felt alienated from his mainly white peers. He was a classic example of what young North Africans in the *banlieues* called a *gris* (literally a 'grey'), meaning an immigrant who is caught between two cultures and is neither black nor white.

By the age of eighteen, Kelkal was serving time in prison for robbery. He was befriended by an Algerian cellmate called 'Khélif', an Islamist who had escaped prison in Algeria, only to find himself locked up in France. Khélif's mission was to recruit young Algerians to the Islamist cause, promising them that this would allow them to find their true selves. The next step was to act on this discovery, fighting against France and its proxy in Algeria. Kelkal listened to all of this, began to study the Koran and Arabic (which he never quite mastered). On his release Kelkal returned to Vaulx-en-Velin a fully fledged radical; in his local mosque he made contact with a certain Ali Touchent, a hard-core Islamist who soon had Kelkal delivering guns and money on trips to Algeria. Kelkal felt that he had found meaning in his life, as well as excitement and glory. It was not long before Touchent convinced him of the need for military action in France.

By chance, Kelkal gave an interview in 1992 to a German sociologist, Dietmar Loch, who was writing his doctoral thesis on the youth of the French *banlieues*. In this interview Kelkal came across as an intelligent, sensitive, articulate and reflective young man. He was anguished about his place in French society. 'There's no place for me here,' he said to Loch. He could only feel at home in Vaulx-en-Velin; the world outside – the city centre of Lyons – was a foreign country from which he was excluded on grounds of his class and race. 'In the *banlieue* we are separated from France by a wall, an enormous wall.'[8]

Loch concluded that Kelkal's bitterness came from disappointment: he sought dignity and recognition in French society but, at a crucial point in his adolescence, he felt rejected. Crime, prison and then Islam were the negative reflection of this society and the only context in which he could feel 'at home'. By 1995, there was a whole generation of young men who felt like Kelkal on both sides of the Mediterranean, in Algeria and France.

19

Mysteries and Martyrs

The monastery at Tibhirine was founded in 1938 in the heart of a wild and mountainous region called Médéa, some ninety kilometres south of Algiers. Like other missions in North Africa, it had been established not with the purpose of bringing Christianity to the native population – the Vatican had long recognized that this was more or less impossible in Islamic North Africa – but rather as a place for meditation, reflection and spiritual study. The surrounding area, harsh and beautiful in equal measure, provided a suitable environment for leading the monastic life, close to nature and far from civilization.

The presence of the monks at Tibhirine had never been a source of controversy in the area: the local people admired them for their simplicity and piety, their fluent Arabic and knowledge of Islam, and they valued the medical expertise which they brought to this remote region. It was, however, the monks' misfortune that this area was one of the strongholds of the GIA. This became clear in 1993, when twelve Catholic workers from Croatia had their throats cut in the vicinity of the monastery. The monks were then visited by the local chief of the GIA, a thug with a reputation for having killed 145 people, who asked for money and medicine. The monks refused to comply, but from now on they knew that their lives were in severe danger.

They had seen the fear on the faces of the country people and villagers, the tense convoys of motor vehicles which braved the so-called 'triangle of death' – the arc between Algiers and Médéa. They had seen buses and cars set alight and had first-hand experience of the brutality of local GIA bosses, who took it in turns to swagger into the monastery and demand some favour or other. Still, they voted to stay. This was not simply because they were exceptionally courageous, but because they saw it as their Christian duty never to back down in the face of evil. To capitulate would be to undo every act of charity they had ever performed.

As the winter of 1996 gave way to an early spring and the violence in Algeria escalated, the risk to the monks was growing every day. Between 1994 and 1996, nineteen Christians in religious orders were killed by Islamist factions. Djamel Zitouni had declared that it was the duty of every Muslim to 'cleanse' the country of Christians and Jews, who were plotting to undermine Islam. On 26 March the monks held a meeting of Lien de Paix, a group devoted to finding links between Islam and Christianity. On the following night, they were visited by the GIA.

The first they knew of this was when windows were smashed and the telephone wires cut. Twenty armed men then strolled into the monastery, casually pointing their guns at the monks they came across. They ransacked the building for medicines, cameras and anything else they could use. Seven of the monks were forced into stolen taxis, which were driven into the mountains, and then the group continued the journey on mules deeper into the wilderness.[1]

The kidnapped monks were held for fifty-six days. On 18 April the GIA issued a communiqué asking for the release of Abdelhak Layada, one of its founders. Two days later a cassette tape of the monks talking was delivered to the French Embassy in Algiers. There were no negotiations. On 23 April the GIA issued another communiqué which declared simply: 'We have cut the monks' throats.' Their severed heads were found on 31 May. Their bodies were never recovered.

This was the largest whole-scale massacre of French nationals since the violence had begun in 1992, and the few French citizens left in Algeria began to fear more intensely for their safety. The French public, shaken by events, watched the televised scenes of the funeral Mass for the monks at Notre Dame d'Afrique in Algiers, where thousands of Algerians filed past the coffins to pay their respects. As the coffins were lowered for burial, one Algerian soldier cried out in Arabic: 'These men loved God and Algeria more than any of us.' On Pentecost Sunday a Mass was held at Notre-Dame in Paris; as part of the ceremony, the Archbishop of Paris snuffed out seven candles which had been brought from Tibhirine. And bells rang out across France.

Behind the rituals and spectacle of death and mourning, there were mysteries, however. The Catholic Church had been seeking a way to negotiate with the GIA during the crisis, but complained they had found their efforts inexplicably hampered by the French Embassy in Algiers. Some elements in the French intelligence services suspected collusion between the Algerian secret services and the GIA. The strategic value of this bloodbath, however, was never quite clear. French intelligence suspected that the kidnapping might have been intended to undermine the Algerian government and reinforce the power of the army. The FIS in exile claimed that the kidnapping was organized by Algerian Special Forces to raise tensions between Paris and Algiers and to teach the French to stay out of the internal politics of Algeria.

The French foreign minister, Hervé de Charette, went to Algeria on 31 July for an official visit, aiming to build bridges between Algiers and Paris. As part of his mission, Charette met the Bishop of Oran, Pierre Claverie, a pied noir whose family had been in Algeria for four generations and who was an outspoken critic of the secrecy, lies and murder which had engulfed Algeria. Not long after the minister's departure, the bishop (who had no doubt shared his views with Charette) was killed by a car bomb. The Algerian government condemned the killing and blamed Islamist insurgents. Other observers noted that there were no known armed groups in operation in Oran, and that this was a carefully planned, sophisticated operation well beyond the expertise of the known Islamist gangs.

Something like the truth about the killing of the monks emerged much later in the French newspaper *Libération* in 2002, which published the testimony of a former Algerian intelligence officer, Abdelkader Tigha, who had been involved in infiltrating armed groups of Islamists. The story was that the monks had been kidnapped by the GIA, led by Djamel Zitouni, who had taken them to his base in the caves at Tala Acha. The government had wanted revenge on the monks because they were alleged to have given medical aid to 'terrorists' from the GIA. So, up to a point, the kidnapping was under the direct control of the Algerian secret services. However, Zitouni had fallen out with a rival GIA group, independent of the secret services, who had demanded that he hand over the monks. Zitouni himself was conveniently killed in an attempt to seize back the monks, who were then clumsily killed by the GIA.

By 1996 nobody had a clear sense of what was really happening in Algeria. This was true of the French government, who, through diplomacy and intelligence work, were being lured deeper into a conflict they had no control over and which they did not really understand. As winter turned to spring, Algeria was caught in a terrible vortex of violence, which seemed as unstoppable as it was insane. President Zéroual was determined to hold on to power at all costs in the elections which were scheduled for June 1997. In the run-up to the elections, horror was piled upon horror, with massacres reported in villages across the country. Foreign reporters could not easily gain access to these areas and relied on the government for information, which, they realized, was all too often disinformation. Rumours abounded that the government was behind some if not all of the massacres, implementing a classic, deadly strategy to terrify Algerians into turning away from the Islamists.

Perhaps the most grotesque event of all was the massacre in September 1997 at Bentalha, a small town on the Mitidja plain, some twenty kilometres south of Algiers. At around 11.30 p.m. on 22 September, around a hundred men entered the town, some wearing military uniform, others wearing tunics, carrying knives and axes. They banged on doors, shouting that they were the military and ordering the inhabitants to open up. If the villagers didn't respond, they blew up the doors with TNT or hacked them open with axes.

The men had a list of names, but they killed everyone they came across. It was a dark night: space and time were suspended in an orgy of murder. The killers seemed to revel in the balletic drama of their tasks – mutilating the corpses, wiring them with explosives, throwing babies into ovens. 'We are coming,' they hissed in the blackened streets. 'We will cut all of your throats. It is our duty.'

The killing went on for six hours. Before dawn broke, the drivers of the trucks which had brought the men to the town sounded the horns as a signal to leave. The murderers made their way to the edges of Bentalha, using children to carry the loot, hacking them to death when the job was done. The night's work left four hundred dead. What shocked the journalists who arrived later that day, driven there by the government to witness Islamist terror at first hand, was the sheer scale of the butchery. The town was a slaughterhouse, the streets running with blood and everywhere stinking of shit and death.

Who did this? The government blamed 'evil terrorists', but none of the Algerian or foreign journalists on the ground were able to find definitive evidence that this was the work of the GIA or any other armed group. In any case, Bentalha was known to be home to many families who were sympathetic to the GIA. The government's description of who had done what and why was unclear.

In 2000 Nesroullah Yous, a native of Bentalha who moved to Paris after the attack, published a book called *Qui a tué à Bentalha? (Who killed at Bentalha?)*. Yous described how men silently made their way into the town through the outlying alleys, some of them wearing combat fatigues and others dressed in *kachabia*, the Afghan-style clothes worn by Islamists. Some wore hoods or beards and they spoke in the accent of Eastern Algeria. They were armed with automatic rifles.

Men and women sought safety and refuge together. A group gathered in Yous' house and began to fortify the walls and doors, throwing home-made firebombs at the killers. They held out as long as they could but were eventually overcome. Yous found himself at the centre of the carnage:

> *Those who didn't want to follow the criminals were executed with axe blows or were thrown to the ground to have their throats cut. Suddenly I saw one of the killers tear a child from his mother. The woman tried to hold the child but he hit her with a machete. He took the child by the foot and, making a half turn, smashed its head against a concrete pillar. The others followed suit, gripped with a frenetic laughter.*[2]

There were rumours that the killers took cocaine and other drugs before setting out to do their work. This explains the viciousness, the laughter and the terrible theatricality of these actions.

Yous, like other victims and journalists, asked why the massacre had been allowed to happen only a few hundred kilometres from a military base. Why did searchlights seem to light the way for the attackers? How did they have such good local knowledge? How was it that the local militia who normally guarded the town had been called away on the orders of the local chief of police? The accumulated details in Yous' account were compelling: if this was not prima facie evidence of government collusion, it was still a case to answer. *Le pouvoir*, then as now, remained silent on the matter. Ordinary Algerians, whatever their political views, now felt as if they were surrounded by demons on all sides.

20

Family Secrets

Something, anything, had to be done to show that France at least cared about what happened in Algeria and about its own Algerian Muslim population. The problem was that it was impossible to take any kind of responsible position when events in Algeria were so mysterious and frightening.

The French prime minister in 1997 was Lionel Jospin, a committed humanitarian of the Left. He was also an intellectual who remembered the Algerian War of Independence, and the divisions it had created in French society. He took the Algerian question very seriously, but he did not know what to do. In an interview on French television he admitted as much: 'The difficulty is that we do not have much idea of what is going on in Algeria. We are confronted with a fanatical and violent opposition fighting against a régime which itself has recourse to violence and the power of the state. We have to be careful.'

A 'day of solidarity' with Algeria was organized in France on 10 November, with various French celebrities showing their support, including the actors Gérard Depardieu, Isabelle Huppert and other showbiz luminaries. However, they did not know who or what they were showing solidarity with. For their part, the Algerian government remained icily silent. The

Algerian press thundered against the patronizing French and their paternalism. The killing went on.

In June 1998 the French football team won the World Cup for the first time ever, a victory for the so-called 'Rainbow team' – a squad composed of players of French nationality from all parts of the French-speaking world. Aside from the inevitable criticism of hard-line right-wingers such as Jean-Marie Le Pen, the leader of the Front National, the victory was also seen as a triumph for a newly tolerant, multicultural France. At the heart of the winning team was Zinédine Zidane, then probably the best player in the world and a Frenchman of Algerian origin. On the night of the victory, the Champs-Elysées was awash with champagne and celebratory songs: over the crowds huge screens showed the image of Zidane under the rubric 'Zidane président'. In the days to come much of the French press and media would celebrate this as the great healing moment of reconciliation between Algeria and France.

This was mostly wishful thinking. In Algeria, the French win was celebrated by most of the population as Zidane's victory. This was also true in the French banlieues, where many young Algerians had ambiguous feelings about Zidane: on the one hand he was a role model whose wealth, fame, talent and good looks were to be aspired to; on the other hand, he was an object of suspicion, a tame Arab in the service of the hated French Republic. In reality, Zidane was a much tougher, streetwise character than his carefully cultivated public image allowed. On the surface he was gentle, self-effacing and modest; in the dressing room and on the training pitch, I was told by Aimé Jacquet, the manager of the French team, he swore, fought and spat, and was quick to take offence at racist banter. Jacquet had been a conscript in Algeria during the War of Independence. 'Zidane was a hard nut,' he told me. 'He had to be to gain the respect of the others, which he always did with his football and his mind.'[1]

In the summer of 1998 there was also the feeling that violence in Algeria could not get any worse and that some kind of normality would soon be re-established. The year had begun with still more massacres, but these had diminished in intensity and scale by the summer, with the military claiming that it now had the upper hand over the Islamists. Exhausted by the past few years, President Zéroual stepped down in September 1998. This was met by surprise and cynicism. One of the most common chants at football matches that autumn was a refrain attacking the government that went: 'If the country was stable for one hour/ We would escape on a merchant ship/ We would escape from Zéroual's face/ I would call myself Michel/ And spend the night at the Eiffel Tower!'[2]

In April 1999 Abdelaziz Bouteflika became president of Algeria. Bouteflika may have been physically unassuming – bald, jowly and already in late middle age – but he had a pedigree that could be traced back to the heroic days of the War of Independence. He was also untainted by any direct link to the dark era of the 1990s. He appeared to be honest and blamed the chaos of the past decade on the cancelled elections of 1992. His own election was dubious, but at home and abroad Algerians placed their faith in his promise to reconnect with the young generation, to bring peace and reconciliation 'to extinguish the fire'.

Bouteflika's first aim was for Algeria to lose its pariah status and to return to the world stage. He courted the Americans and the British but most of all the French, whom he saw as the surest guarantors of stability in the new Algeria. He visited France in 2000, where he was honoured by a dinner at the Hôtel de Ville in Paris and private meetings at the Elysée with President Jacques Chirac. He visited key sites such as Verdun, where he recalled the 180,000 Muslims who gave their lives for France in the two World Wars. The major theme of his visit was Franco-Algerian reconciliation. This was partly to signal to

Algerians at home that all wars were now over, and partly to reassure French companies that the Algerian economy would soon be open for business again. The tacit message was that the War of Independence had really been a kind of fratricide, and it was now time to restore normal family relations.

In his rhetoric Bouteflika also acknowledged Christianity and Judaism as part of Algeria's national heritage and identity. He called Saint Augustine one of the fathers of the Algerian nation and hailed Monsignor Duval, one of the archbishops of Algiers, as a 'true Algerian'. He praised the Algerian Jewish community in France and declared that Jewish history also belonged to Algerian history. These were brave statements, usually made in addresses to Algerian university students or business leaders but which also had an impact on the international stage, where the Bouteflika régime branded itself as intellectually open and serious about the process of healing. At home, however, there was a policy of official amnesia – the line was that the 1990s had been a battle between demented fanatics and a noble and enlightened government. Nobody in Algeria who had lived through the traumas at first hand believed this.

Most damaging to Bouteflika's cause was a book published in 2001 called *La Sale Guerre* (*The Dirty War*) by Habib Souaïdia, an ex-lieutenant in the Algerian Special Forces. The book was a bestseller in France and was discussed all over the world. It was lurid and full of mistakes, but it provided enough substantial evidence to show that the war of the 1990s had been fought by an unscrupulous military that routinely employed torture, massacre and rape. In Algeria Souaïdia was attacked in the press as a traitor and an enemy of Algeria, a thief and the son of a *harki*, who had sold his story to the French to revenge himself upon his country. In retaliation, in an interview on French television, Souaïdia called the Algerian leadership 'deserters from the French army who led the country towards anarchy'.

In Algiers it was decided that Souaïdia's statement could not go unchallenged or unpunished. In April 2001 Khaled Nezzar, a general who had been a key figure through the 1990s, gave an interview to *Le Figaro Magazine* in which he refuted all of the most serious accusations made in *La Sale Guerre*. On the back of this, the general announced that he was coming to France to promote his own memoirs. On 25 April Nezzar flew to Paris and gave a press conference at the Centre Culturel Algérien in Paris. He appeared in public for a matter of minutes before he was taken back to the airport and returned to Algiers. A few hours earlier, as soon as he landed on French soil, an Algerian family resident in France had launched a civil lawsuit against him, accusing him of 'torture, inhuman and cruel treatment'. Neither the French nor the Algerian authorities wanted this legal embarrassment, and so Nezzar found himself back on Algerian soil in the early hours of 26 April.

The affair did not end there. In July 2002, Nezzar issued a writ for libel against Souaïdia. Although Nezzar was defended by respected figures such as the novelist Rachid Boujedra, he lost his case. But he had not yet lost the argument. In the twelve months since his unseemly flight from Paris, the events of 11 September 2001 completely transformed perceptions of the complex political map of North Africa and the Middle East. Nezzar now cleverly argued that the evils in Algeria in the 1990s could only be properly understood through the prism of 9/11 and the 'War on Terror'. By 2003 the Bouteflika régime was confident enough of support from the Bush Administration to declare that it had 'won' the war against the Islamists.

Since then, Bouteflika has been caught between cultivating the French as his closest international ally and appeasing the angry generation at home. He is also unafraid to attack France in public – he did so in a speech in 2005 at a rally to mark the fifty years since the Sétif massacre, where once again France was cast as the genocidal monster responsible for all of Algeria's ills and agonies.

'Pray for Us and the Muslims'
I visited Algiers most recently in the summer of 2011. Throughout the spring, rumours had been reaching Paris that Algiers was again preparing for radical change, possibly even revolution. French television showed scenes of young men confronting the police – and meeting less resistance than usual. I spoke to intelligence and diplomatic sources in Paris and they told me that, although the police were not 'cracking heads' in the way they had done in the 1990s, the government had the situation under control. They assured me that there was no possibility of the kind of uprising that had just happened in Tunisia and Egypt.

None the less, I found the atmosphere in Bab-el-Oued to be crackling with violence. Police in paramilitary gear lined up outside the mosques after prayers, threatening and driving worshippers back down into the city, away from a stand-off. Some of the worshippers were ex-FIS members or retired 'terrorists' who had taken advantage of the amnesty. But the FIS men were older now too. They were being replaced by a younger generation who did not wear beards or robes, but hoodies, scarves and replica football shirts (Liverpool FC and Olympique de Marseille were the most popular). They looked like their brothers and cousins in the *banlieues* of Lyons, Marseilles or Paris. They jeered at the police but shied away from real physical contact. The anger was real, however.

'You cannot believe how it is to live here,' I was told by 'Ali', my driver for this trip. 'Everything is an illusion.' Ali had a very black sense of humour; he revelled in revealing what he called the 'mysteries of Algiers' – all the spots in and around the city where bad things happened and the government said nothing had happened. Here a massacre, here a beheading, here a famous kidnapping – all off the map. One of the most disturbing aspects of this visit was the way everyone lied systematically. Every night from my hotel balcony, drinking duty-free vodka,

I watched gunships floating out in the harbour, heading for the southern part of the city, the 'triangle of death'. When I told the hotel staff what I had seen, they said, smiling, 'Fiesta!' They didn't even believe their own lies.

During this trip, I climbed the hill to Notre Dame d'Afrique. This church is visible practically everywhere in Algiers, but on all my journeys to Algeria I had never got round to visiting it. During the 1990s there was a permanent police presence here, and the priests were under twenty-four-hour police protection. Now I found the atmosphere relatively relaxed. It was a bright, sunny day and the esplanade around the church was thronged with families, picnicking, enjoying the views (which are some of the best in Algiers), kids playing football. The terrace overlooks the district of Bologhine, where there is the football stadium (sometimes still known by it colonial name of Saint-Eugène) and the Christian and Jewish cemetery. The seafront houses look like a small town from Brittany or Normandy which has been grafted on to a Mediterranean vista.

Inside the church there was a handful of elderly pieds noirs at prayer. I talked to a few. They told me that this was still their home and that they prayed for peace, which they hoped for but never expected to see. In the foyer of the church, where we talked, you could buy DVDs of *Des hommes et des dieux* (*Of Gods and Men*), the powerful film which documents the massacre of the monks at Tibhirine. This was not meant for tourism, I was told by a middle-aged French lady who was looking after the church, but as a warning. The film carries a powerful Christian message of sacrifice and redemption. The church itself is dominated by the rubric over the altar, 'Pray for us and the Muslims', which dates from 1858, when the church was built.

Outside in the sunshine, I chatted to the families and kids at play. I asked them if they had ever been inside the church. They all shook their heads and said something about Satan. I asked one boy, aged about ten, wearing a Chelsea shirt, kicking a ball, if he knew what the building was. '*Eh bien, oui,*' he said in perfectly accented Mediterranean French that could have come from Marseilles, '*ça c'est la mosqueé des Roumis. Mais il n'y plus de Roumis.*' ('Oh, yeah. That's the mosque of the Romans. But there aren't any more Romans.')

After this encounter I walked back into the town, skirting through the Casbah, down into the heart of Bab-el-Oued, heading for the seafront. I had become quite familiar with this part of the city. Most of all I liked it when you started to smell and glimpse the sea, as if at the end of an alley or passageway. The overall effect is a chiaroscuro, an endless play of light and dark. This seems to be an accidentally poetic motif for Franco-Algerian history but the effect is quite deliberate. The French architects who designed this part of the city wanted to rival Paris as an urban spectacle. To do so, they built Algiers with arch-theatricality, opening the city to the sea and the sunlight. The streets here are also stairways, punctuated by small squares and arcades. This is dream architecture, all quite beautiful and now spookily in ruins.

In today's Algiers, the French may have left, but France is still the enemy. Yet it also represents the Promised Land. By day, the streets of downtown Algiers are still thronged with *hittistes*, who dream of France but have no chance of getting the visas they need to get there. The visits by Chirac (in 2003) and then Sarkozy (in 2007) were met by crowds chanting, 'Give us our visas!' For the young men of Algiers, France remains as far away and as unknowable as America.

And so they hate the place and its people – nothing hurts more than unrequited love. It can literally drive you mad. This is why what has happened in Algeria is best understood in the language of psychoanalysis. Frantz Fanon, the psychiatrist, uses the term 'motherless rage' to describe the psychosis in Algeria. This was, he says, the direct result of the unique status of Algeria – an integral part of France not just a colony – which gave the relationship between the French and the Algerians its strange intimacy. The loss of Algeria, it follows, was less like losing a dependent colony than like the sudden death of a family member. The bereavement continues to affect colonizer and colonized.

The Algerians who have made it in France can find the atmosphere strange and unfriendly when they come back to their homeland. The DJ and rapper Sinik, from Seine Saint-Denis, came to Algeria in the summer of 2008 and swore that he would never come again: he was met by heckling crowds and general indifference. For a whole generation, so-called democracy has made Algeria feel like a prison. They don't need to be taunted by those who have escaped.

No one knows exactly when the last 'war for liberation' ended. It is true that the rate of killing has slowed down, but nobody feels free. So far, the prediction made by my intelligence and diplomatic sources that there would be no Algerian revolution in the wake of the Arab Spring has proved to be correct. But the shockwaves from neighbouring countries continue to be felt across Algeria. The tension hangs in the air, waiting to be transformed once more into an electric storm.

Part Three

IN MOROCCO

21

Queer Tangier

I was just about to order a drink when a Moroccan man lurched over towards my side of the counter and tried to punch me in the face. This was in Dean's Bar, a tiny hole-in-the-wall place in the Ville Nouvelle of Tangier. It was late afternoon and for this guy – mid thirties and heavily built – a long day of booze was now starting to kick in. His friends pulled the drunk back and then pushed him into a seat in a corner of the room, glassy-eyed and still swearing at me.

It is against the law in Morocco for Muslims to drink, although there is a strong heavy-drinking culture among Moroccans in all of the cities. The main streets of Tangier and Casablanca in particular are littered with bars, which are usually former cafés from the period of the French and Spanish protectorates, hidden from public view by drapes or blacked-out windows. Everybody can pretend that they don't exist. Another way of sustaining this lie is for the police to arrest any Moroccan who looks even mildly drunk in the street. This pleases the Islamists, who can say that Islamic law is being upheld in Morocco, while allowing the government to get on with the job of policing the bars, which serve up cheap alcohol and low-grade prostitution to a mixed clientele of office clerks, manual workers and the unemployed.

My attacker's friends were trying to make him look respectable enough to avoid a beating or jail on his way home. I was the only non-Moroccan in the place. Nobody apologized or offered me a drink. On the face of it, this incident was unremarkable. The bars of Morocco are generally rough places where hard drinking often ends in violence. Foreigners rarely enter this world, preferring the hotel bars and nightclubs that cater for Western customers with credit cards. So it was not unusual for a European like me to be cold-shouldered or even insulted in a place like this. But this man was angry for a very precise reason. He thought I was French.

Towards the end of 1955, as the war in Algeria was catching fire, Morocco was cynically granted independence by the French, in a straightforward calculation to avoid fighting on two fronts. The move was against the wishes of the settlers, who argued for armed resistance and were reassured by the then resident-general, Boyer de la Tour, that the Moroccan king, Mohammed V, would never return to the throne. However, on 6 November Mohammed V flew from exile in Madagascar to Paris, where he informed the foreign minister, Antoine Pinay, that he was now ready to form a government in Morocco. This was not a negotiation on the part of the Moroccan sovereign but a clear statement of intent. Given the imminent slide into chaos in Algeria, the French could not afford to stand in his way.

Ten days later the king flew to Morocco, where he was welcomed by the native Moroccans as a martyr and hero. Millions went onto the streets in a delirious ecstasy, not quite believing that this had finally happened, that the invincible French had handed back the country so swiftly and with so little bloodshed. They attributed magical or semi-divine powers to the king. This was against Islamic teaching, but Morocco was also built on deep layers of superstition and sorcery, and many people found it possible to see religion and magic as part of the same universe.

On a practical level, the French abrogated the Treaty of Fez, which had established the original protectorate in 1912, while the Spanish, unwilling to fight over a territory which was useless to them, conceded control of the northern region. The only exception was Tangier, which was strategically important to all of the Western powers and so was maintained as an International Zone under the control of the French, British and Spanish.

The signing of the Tangier Protocol in October 1956 was effectively the beginning of a Moroccan civil war, which would linger on for several decades. From now on it was a nation divided between the north and the south. The people of northern Morocco, with Tangier as their capital, felt betrayed by the French, who had brought violence to the streets and then given the territory away. They also felt anger at the French-speaking Moroccans who founded a ruling élite in Casablanca and Rabat in the south, abandoning Tangier to poverty and predatory foreigners. Moroccans believed that Tangier was an integral part of the nation and they watched with horror as its international status – which meant no taxes and a weak and corrupt police system – attracted exiles, misfits, sexual outsiders and gangsters from the entire world.

This complex political scenario was largely unknown to or ignored by the most famous names who came here from the English-speaking world. These included the writers Paul Bowles, William Burroughs, Truman Capote and Tennessee Williams, who thought that they had come to the 'end of the world', for what seemed to be freely available gay sex, easily procured drugs and the sense that the apparently loose moral culture was the very opposite of the uptight America they wanted to leave behind. The truth, however, was that they had no real sense of the political reality of Tangier or of Morocco, at war with itself as it sought to disentangle itself from European influence.

William Burroughs certainly understood very little of the violence around him, which frequently erupted in the streets or markets in the 1950s. He delighted in its apparently random and meaningless nature. It gave him a feeling he called the 'Jihad Jitters' and he fantasized about joining in the riots he watched from a distance. 'The possibility of a riot is like a tonic, like ozone in the air,' he wrote in a letter to a friend. 'The chaos in Morocco is beautiful.' Burroughs gleefully imagined 'the all-out massacre of everybody by everybody else'.[1]

In another letter Burroughs counselled a friend to torch Arabs with gasoline if he ever found himself in the face of an approaching mob. This image recurs in the closing pages of *Naked Lunch*, the sinister hallucinatory novel composed in Tangier (renamed as 'Interzone'), which would make Burroughs world-famous as a founding father of the 1960s counter-culture in the West. Burroughs writes: 'Coming over a hill of rusty iron we meet a group of Natives . . . flat two-dimension faces of scavenger fish . . . Throw the gasoline on them and light it . . . QUICK . . . white flash . . . mangled insect screams.' This was written in 1956, after a short trip to Libya and Algeria, when Burroughs declared himself, with no obvious sense of irony, as 'definitely pro-French'.[2]

Meanwhile the real history of Morocco was being made during this period by Moroccans themselves. One of the powerful intellects in Moroccan politics was Allal Al-Fassi, a charismatic Islamist intellectual and Nationalist who had spent the decade before independence in exile in Cairo. Tangier was the first city he visited on his return to Morocco and he denounced it as a city which brought shame on the whole country. He gave a speech there which made a direct challenge to the authority of the king, arguing for the unification of all Moroccan territory. This was not just a political argument but also a religious one. Al-Fassi belonged to the Salafist tradition in Morocco, which saw the nation as part of the wider family of the Islamic world and as such a sacred space. He was suspicious of democracy and what he perceived to be the 'modern' aspects of Moroccan life, such as 'European' theories of Socialism and secular government.

He had supported the return of the king as the necessary prelude to a free Moroccan nation, but thereafter maintained a difficult, grudging and aggressive relationship with the monarchy. To this extent, Al-Fassi laid the ground for future Islamist groups in Morocco, which defined the monarchy as too secular, and the country as a whole too much in thrall to French or other Western models of development. Al-Fassi was a cultured man who was not afraid to engage with Western culture (he was said to be a keen reader and an admirer of Paul Bowles, especially liking *The Spider's House*, set in Al-Fassi's native Fez during the time of an uprising against the French). The arguments of these first Islamists found a willing audience in the majority of ordinary Moroccans, whose expectations had been raised to an impossibly high level by independence and the *baraka* – the semi-divine aura of the king.

King Hassan II, who ruled Morocco from 1963 to 1999, hated Tangier. This was mainly because it was full of foreigners in search of drugs and sex. He declared the city a bastion of un-Islamic values, and there were periodic police raids on 'immoral persons', but the foreigners tended to be too rich and too powerful to be driven out of the city.

For many Moroccans, Tangier is still an apostate city, a place that is so spiritually corrupt that it opposes God himself. This corruption takes its most visible form in the Casino at the beach of Malabata, an imposing white skyscraper, allegedly owned by Saudis, which dominates the bay of Tangier. It is surrounded by armed guards and said to be the meeting-place of Middle-Eastern playboys, arms dealers, drug warlords and politicians, who indulge in expensive prostitutes and other Western pleasures.

The Casino stands diametrically opposed to the Medina – the poorest and holiest part of the city – and can be seen from most points in Tangier. Even the most moderate Muslims regard this as an insult. The Tanjawis also complain that it is always the Casino which goes into lock-down and is guarded by armed police during periods of tension and the mostly unreported riots that still occasionally rip through the city. The Casino is the source of much fantasy among Moroccans, who tell stories of orgies fuelled by drink and drugs organized for the Saudis and other Gulf Arabs who are the main clients. In one lurid tale circulating in the cafés of the Medina, a Tanjawi prostitute is supposed to have returned from an orgy minus one of her breasts: it had been carved up and eaten by a rich Kuwaiti. Even if the story was not true, it reveals the fear and hatred of ordinary Moroccans towards the Arabs of the Gulf states.

A Prophet

The most important writer in Tangier in the mid-twentieth century was not a foreigner, nor a drug addict or a sex tourist, but the novelist Mohamed Choukri, who was born in the town of Nador but spent most of his life as witness to the rise and fall of Tangier.

When he died in 2003, Choukri was saluted by the king of Morocco, Mohammed VI, as the most famous and distinguished literary son of Morocco. In his lifetime, however, Choukri was mainly regarded as a pariah. He became notorious across the Arab world in the 1980s with his autobiography *For Bread Alone*, which told the story of how he had come to Tangier as an illiterate youth fleeing famine in the Rif mountains. He arrived in the city in the 1950s, at the height of its reputation as a glamorous playground for Westerners. Like everyone else he knew, Choukri sold his body to Western men for sex. The only other choice was starvation.

All of this is recounted in plain prose – itself an innovation in arabophone literature, which often prizes elaborate effects and an indirect, evasive style. By announcing himself as a realist in the mould of Zola or Hemingway, Choukri sent shockwaves through the Arab-speaking world. Moreover, he had revealed the family secrets of Moroccan life in the language of the enemy: the book had become a bestseller in the West, where it was published in 1973, translated and adapted by Paul Bowles, and in 1980 it appeared in French as *Le Pain nu*, translated by Tahar Ben Jelloun, who has since become the most distinguished Moroccan writer of his generation. The origins of the French text are unclear – Ben Jelloun has said that he never saw the full manuscript of the original Arabic version and presumably worked from the English edition. When an Arabic translation then appeared in 1982, Choukri was speaking to a whole generation, in the two major languages of North Africa, of what it meant to be 'the damned of the earth', and of why this experience had made him an atheist.

When I first met Choukri in the winter of 2002, he did not know that he was dying. He was in his sixties and one of the most infamous writers in the Arab world. All of my meetings with Choukri, through the winter and early spring, took place in the Café du Ritz, a run-down but friendly restaurant in the backstreets of downtown Tangier. I had first read Choukri while a student in Lyons in the 1980s. This was when the book was at the height of its popularity in France, at the very time that France was experiencing the first riots out in the *banlieues*.

It seemed to me then and now that reading his work was a way into understanding this revolt. Choukri's great theme was how the foreigners in Tangier, and in Morocco, had wiped away his sense of self; his career had been a way of rebuilding that identity. He had a divided opinion of France and the French, the effective masters of his country for most of his life. He could quote chunks of Rimbaud or Baudelaire at will and spoke self-taught, measured, classically calibrated French. He loved Paris, but he told me that he had never felt more alien and sometimes despised than during his visits there. He knew Moroccans in France and said that they either became French or had to somehow cover up their real identities. 'The French are not stupid,' he said. 'They know that they are the masters of the Arab world. That is how they are in Morocco. In Paris you just feel this even more.'[3]

We also talked a great deal about Tangier, and how the city had changed. Choukri's life was a palimpsest of the city's history. He had known nearly all of the gilded literary expatriates who came here, including Paul Bowles, William Burroughs and Tennessee Williams, as friends, clients or lovers. The only one he remembered with affection was Jean Genet. He said that Genet alone had never made him 'feel inferior'.

Genet had called Tangier 'the capital of treason', on the grounds that it was full of criminals, spies and homosexuals. Genet hated France – his whole life and career was predicated on this fact – and in Tangier he found the very opposite, or so it seemed to him, of respectable, bourgeois France. The fact that Tangier was not quite a colony, not quite Moroccan, also appealed to him; it was an in-between place, the perfect Genetesque combination of an erotic utopia and a den of thieves.

Choukri recalled Genet in his later years, wandering the corridors of Hotel Minzah in a Nembutal trance. He liked Genet, but thought he had a falsely romantic view of the city and knew nothing about the realities of life there. Where Genet saw freedom, Choukri saw exploitation. He told me about the first time that he performed fellatio on a rich foreigner in an expensive car near the seafront. He was in his late teens and starving. Afterwards, he went to sleep in a cemetery because he hated himself for what he had done. He was overcome with shame, and needed to sleep near his ancestors and pray to them for forgiveness. This was, said Choukri, a life that the French masters of Morocco could never understand.

By the time that I knew him, Choukri was a bitter old man, drinking heavily. He told me that by writing about the reality of Tangier life, he was accused of bringing *hchouma* (shame) to the city. After our drinks I sometimes accompanied Choukri to his apartment nearby. He was always worried about potential attackers, and was contemplating buying a knife, complaining that now he was older he couldn't defend himself. His book had made him famous but it was also banned in Egypt, Tunisia, Iran and Saudi Arabia. Since the Arab Spring, Choukri has become renowned as one of the first writers to speak openly about what it was truly like to live in a world of taboo and lies – almost a prophet of the revolutions to come.

In his life and work, Choukri marked the cultural distance between the Tanjawi and the foreigners who came to Tangier to fuck them. This is also clear in the diaries of the English playwright Joe Orton, who spent his summers here in the 1960s until his death in 1967 (murdered by his jealous boyfriend). When these diaries were published posthumously in 1986, the book was praised on both sides of the Atlantic for its witty and unashamed accounts of drug-taking and gay sex. Orton, and others like him, conceived of Tangier as a kind of anti-Britain, where they could do whatever they wanted, out of reach of the law and in the name of sexual liberation.

Orton loved flaunting his homosexuality and provoking any heterosexual tourist who dared to enter his space. In his diary, he recorded his pleasure at shocking a pair of staid American tourists who were eavesdropping on his conversation with friends at a table in the Café de Paris (the conversation involved sodomy, sperm and an expensive rug). When his friends nudged him to let him know that he was causing offence, he retorted loudly, cackling with camp glee: 'Fuck them! This is *our* country, *our* town, *our* civilization.'[4]

Orton could not have been more wrong.

22

Peaceful Penetration

Morocco is an old country. The oldest name for it is 'Marrakesh', synonymous with the great city in the south. The Turks know Morocco as 'Fez', in homage to the other great city, the capital of Moroccan spiritual life. It is foreigners who, over the centuries, have called the territory 'Morocco'. By the late eighteenth century, although the region was never properly charted, both Moroccans and Europeans had a clear idea of the borders of the land they called 'Morocco', running from the Mediterranean through the mountains of the Rif down to the Atlas range and the Sahara. If this was a nation, it was because the Sultan of Morocco – whose spiritual and political authority came from the fact that he was descended from the Prophet Mohammed – said it was.

By the late nineteenth century, Morocco was the only country in the region which had not been plundered or conquered in the scramble for African countries by European powers. This was partly because it was judged to be of little economic value – its largely dry and arid territory was difficult to exploit and was unpromising as an export market. It was also politically volatile: the sultan maintained order by moving between his royal cities – Meknes, Fez, Rabat and Marrakesh – often with an entourage of some 30,000 troops and courtiers, but his military authority did not extend into the hinterland, even though, as the Prophet's descendant, he was the Custodian of the Dar-el-Islam (House of Islam).

The British, who had long held Gibraltar as the first staging-post on the route to Suez and India, were keen to extend their influence over the African side of the Mediterranean. For this reason they had always packed Tangier, on the other side of the Strait of Gibraltar, with diplomats and spies. Meanwhile, in the late nineteenth century, Germany began to view the conquest of Morocco as a potential way of subverting the British Empire, and the Spanish feared any foreign influence so near to their home shores.

But it was the French who most coveted Morocco. Its conquest would extend French power and influence right across the region, effectively denying or controlling British access to the African Mediterranean. This argument was not quite enough, however, to convince the government in Paris. By 1900 enthusiasm for the great colonial projects of the previous century was on the wane. The greatest threat to French civilization came from the east, from Germany, and many politicians on the Right and Left argued that colonialism was a dangerous waste of industrial and military resources.

There was, however, the danger of a revolt in Algeria, a jihad launched from Moroccan territory, which could expel the French from Africa. French military commanders in Algeria described Morocco as 'the fireship on Algeria's flank'. For this reason, a plan was devised, not to launch a military operation, which would have been too risky and provoked European rivals, but to rule Morocco as a protectorate.[1]

The French effectively conquered Morocco by stealth. They encouraged the well-meaning but naïve young sultan, Mawaly Abdul Aziz, to take out loans with European (mainly French) banks, which the French authorities knew he could never repay. In private, high-ranking European diplomats sneered at Abdul Aziz for his apparent credulousness and his fascination with modern machines from 'civilized' Europe. And it is true that his palace at Fez was littered with the packing crates of a hansom cab, a grand piano, a barrel organ, a miniature train, an elevator (though he had a one-storey building), a camera made of gold and silver – expensive toys which shocked the puritanical inhabitants of Fez and made him look foolish in the eyes of Europeans. He rode a bicycle (having got over his fury at initially being presented with a women's model, which his advisers thought would be easier for him with his robes), but his pride and joy was a gasoline-powered tricycle. He had thirty black slaves to light a racetrack for night-time sorties and had photographs taken of him astride the contraption, rifle in hand, every inch the armed prince.

The sultan was introduced to these machines and gadgets by Gabriel Veyre, a native of the Isère, in eastern France, who had trained in cinematography with the Frères Lumière and travelled widely photographing the world. Veyre was hired as court photographer and documented this world in fast transition. Patronizing European diplomats considered Abdul Aziz as little more than a child and not far from a simpleton. One English diplomat described him in the following terms: 'His majesty was most affable, but I fear he is of very weak character. The way he clung to my hand and coat-tails and pleaded tearfully for advice was pathetic. In short, I was disappointed in him.'[2] But as Veyre testifies in his account of life at the court, Abdul Aziz was serious about his belief in modernity and progress. He sincerely wanted to take Morocco forward, both in terms of how it was governed and in improving material conditions for his people. The French bankers courted him with promises of investment for public works and, with this financial backing, the sultan drained the marshes around Fez, cleaned up the water supply and improved the hygiene in prisons, releasing many prisoners who had been falsely imprisoned. He also got rid of the elaborate diplomatic protocols which European diplomats found irritating or humiliating. Notwithstanding his good intentions, from 1901, when he first accepted a loan from the Banque de Paris et des Pays-Bas, Abdul Aziz was leading his country to bankruptcy.

As Morocco began the short slide into financial chaos in the first years of the twentieth century, the main cities and towns were beginning to fill up with European settlers, who came to Morocco for the same reason that they had flocked to Algeria: they were attracted to a new land ready to be cultivated and turned into capital. Ordinary Moroccans were obviously anxious about this influx of foreigners, whose numbers were unchecked and who took immediate control everywhere they settled. The same banks who had lent to the sultan on extortionate terms were offering cheap loans to small European companies prepared to bring technology and expertise to the country. Rumours began to circulate that the sultan had somehow been bewitched by the Europeans, dazzled by their toys, and was preparing to give the country away.

But there was no ideological opposition to the sultan and his failed policies in Morocco. A few tribal chiefs called for war against the Europeans, but they were disorganized and could not stand up to the more powerful caïds of the towns and cities, who were almost all pro-French. Salafism was a powerful force in the mosques. But still, Europeans, mostly French, swarmed all over the country, building what they called 'Maroc utile' (Useful Morocco), a replica France on the north-west coast of Africa. In the countryside famine and drought killed thousands of Moroccans in 1906 and 1907, and among all Moroccans who were not paid off by the French, resentment grew.

Their anger first erupted in Marrakesh in 1907, with the murder of a French doctor called Emile Mauchamp. He had been sent to Marrakesh as part of the French government's policy of winning hearts and minds by providing medical services across the country. Local medicine at this stage was an unscientific and usually painful affair, involving hot irons, lunar caustic, spells and incantations, but it was an integral part of Moroccan culture and identity. Modern European medicine clearly posed a threat to this identity. More than this, Moroccans began to believe that the '*roumi*' doctors had been sent to Morocco to poison the men who might one day lead an uprising against them.

In the spring of 1907 Mauchamp returned to Marrakesh from his annual leave in France and perhaps did not understand the heightened hostility towards Europeans coursing through the city. One of his projects was to make maps of the city, together with a geologist. To this end he set up a tall pole on top of his building. This soon brought him into conflict with the local *muqaddam* (a community leader), who told him that people thought it was a trick that was probably impious: they knew he was setting up a telegraph link to Frenchmen in Casablanca, who were giving him orders on how to control the local population. Mauchamp was sensitive enough to obey the *muqaddam*, but as he set off to dismantle the offending pole, he was approached by a stranger and slashed with a knife across the face and chest. He managed to stumble, bleeding, for less than a hundred yards, taking refuge in a blind alley, where he was stoned to death. Groups took turns to attack his corpse, his body was dragged several hundred yards and set on fire. The mob then set about looting his house. Mauchamp's effects, including a tennis racket and medical equipment, were soon on sale in the souk.

In Paris the authorities were stunned. There had been no sense that the policy of 'peaceful penetration', which was what they called the French conquest by stealth, could fail. In desperation, and partly as a knee-jerk reaction in the wake of the recent Dreyfus affair, the French Ministry of Foreign Affairs blamed the murder on a German Jew, Judah Holzmann, who been working for the local pasha. But there was never any evidence for this. The simple fact was that the 'natives' were not savage or superstitious innocents; they understood perfectly what the arrival of 'modernity' meant, and they used the only means available to resist it. Only the French military understood this. Generals talked among themselves about when, not if, the real violence would come, which would compel them to subjugate Morocco by force of arms.

When the story of poor, well-meaning Mauchamp reached Casablanca, it provoked predictable horror among the European population. They comforted themselves with the thought that Marrakesh was a long way away, almost another country, and that nothing of the sort could ever happen in Casablanca, the raw but busy economic capital of *Maroc utile*. The city was teeming will all-comers from France, Algeria and the Middle East, there to make a quick few hundred thousand francs. It was cheap to live there – in 1907 a palatial house could be rented for a few francs a month, a servant would cost ten francs (the same price as a donkey) and a horse could be bought for fifty francs. The empty countryside was full of game. The city was a raucous place, but it offered Europeans a high life which they could not have known at home.

At the time, Casablanca looked set to become the economic powerhouse of the future nation of Morocco. The Compagnie Marocaine, a French company financed by French loans, was already building a jetty for the harbour which would make this the most important port in Africa – in the minds of many Frenchmen, Casablanca was to be the 'New Algiers'. The experience of native Moroccans was very different. The winter of 1907 had brought no rains and the Medina – a modest enclave of the city near the sea – was overflowing with starving peasants, who brought the famine with them.

As the town grew and the European population swelled, the stable structures of Moroccan life – religious authority and social hierarchies – were all being swept away in the harsh and cruel drive towards 'modernity'. A highly visible image of this was the narrow-gauge railway which engineers from the Compagnie Marocaine had built in the harbour to deliver the stones to make the jetty. It was rumoured that many of these stones had been stolen from Muslim graveyards, even from the tombs of saints. On 28 July 1907 a delegation of tribesmen visited the local caïd, effectively the Muslim mayor of Casablanca, and asked him to put a stop to the Europeans' desecration of holy sites. They were most offended by the train's whistle – a sound of contempt in Morocco – hooting loudly as it passed Muslim graveyards. The caïd, named Sidi Bou Bekr Ben Bouzid, did nothing.

The Europeans began to note a new hostility among the Moroccans they came into contact with. They were often insulted, pointed at, stoned or spat at; this was quite frequent in the 'uncivilized' parts of Morocco, but was an entirely new phenomenon here in docile, domesticated Casablanca.

On 30 July, at around 1 p.m., a group of about 150 Moroccans placed a barricade of stones on the railway track. They shouted that the train's whistle was impious and that the French would pay the price. The train driver saw what was happening long before he approached the barricade and drew the train to a halt. In a panic, he started to run back to the town but he was caught, beaten and mutilated. The Moroccans then leapt over the walls into the quarry, where they killed nine unarmed European workmen, whose bodies were eviscerated and left to fry in the sun on the stone wall of the harbour, a warning to the entire city.

For the next few days, all was quiet in Casablanca, as Moulai el-Amin, an uncle of the sultan, took over from the wretched Ben Bouzid. El-Amin cleverly organized talks with the angry tribesmen outside the city walls, ensuring that at least there was no more conflict. As the talks stretched over days, the French authorities' response was both cynical and pathetic: they grew anxious and impatient to capitalize on the massacre and turn it into an international incident which could justify French military intervention in Casablanca. To this end, the French consul in Tangier, Auguste St Aulaire, wired the Quai d'Orsay, calling for warships to protect French lives in the region. He described the dead men as 'workers', to avoid objections from the anti-colonial Left in the National Assembly. To deflect predatory German complaints, he arranged for the sultan to write a letter calling for French aid, at the same time spreading rumours of mischievous German involvement. A warship, the *Galilée*, was summarily dispatched, arriving in Casablanca on 1 August 1907.

The problem, at least from the military point of view, was that the town was too quiet. Much of the French population had barricaded itself in the French consulate, and there was no violence on the streets. For the majority of the population of 25,000, life was going on as usual. Meanwhile, the *Galilée*, a dim, smoky haze on the horizon, had its guns pointed at Casablanca. This was not the situation that the sailors and soldiers on board the *Galilée* had anticipated.

For four long, hot days the ship rolled at anchor. The crew burned with rage, but Captain Ollivier stood firm as he awaited orders or reinforcements, or both, from Paris. But as he tried to parlay with local French officials, he was hissed at by his men, who shouted that 'he had trampled on the flag of France'. In a conciliatory gesture to these murderous sailors, he insisted that Moulai el-Amin deliver up the killers of the nine French workers. If not, he would send a landing party. In the meantime, Europeans in Casablanca stared at the distant ship, fantasizing that there were more behind it and longing for the invasion of Casablanca to begin.

Finally, at dawn on 5 August, three boats packed with armed sailors, steered through the open harbour gates towards the city. Those who saw them, Moroccan and European, could not believe that so few boats – and indeed just one warship – had been sent. Aboard the *Galilée*, the captain had miscalculated badly, believing that reinforcements were on their way.

The three Moroccan soldiers guarding the gates to the Medina were bewildered at the sight of the French sailors and quickly fled. The ensign leading the landing party heaved open the gates himself. It was still early in the morning and the narrow streets were busy with women and children fetching water from the wells. A Moroccan fired a rifle. This was enough to trigger the anger of the sailors, who charged up the narrow streets and alleys, shooting or slashing their bayonets into every human being they came across. The French consulate was only 250 metres away, but halfway there the streets were already piled with corpses.

Worse still, the sailors of the *Galilée* were welcomed into the consulate as saviours and heroes and, in a rush of euphoria, the signal was given from the roof of the building to begin the bombardment of Casablanca. This totally unnecessary act was driven by bloodlust and a desire to reinforce military supremacy. The city convulsed as the heavy naval shells slammed into the walls of the Medina. In the pall of smoke, amid the noise and general confusion, many Moroccans took to looting. The city gates were thrown open and Moroccans flooded in from the countryside to avenge their people and destroy all marks of the European presence. The French had managed to turn a minor colonial skirmish into a full-blown battle, which looked likely to end in massacre.

In the chaos the European food shops were left mainly untouched, as the Moroccans feared that the goods, particularly tinned goods, had been contaminated by pork. The Muslims took vengeance on the Jews, whom they blamed as collaborators with the French. The Jewish quarter of the Medina was under siege for several days; women were snatched by tribesmen who, months later, sold them back to the Jews from their camps in the countryside. Isolated Europeans who thought that they were safe in their large houses were also attacked. One contemporary account describes the assault on the house of a wealthy Spaniard:

> *'Ha! Those houses were beautiful. We of the country had never seen such wonderful things. We were afraid of them. Surely they must have been from the evil spirits. So we smashed and tore down all we saw . . . We wrecked and burnt and sang . . . Before they killed the Spaniard they took him to the room and showed him that which was his wife. Ay, the sight was not good. He bared his teeth and his eyes grew big and although he had no knife, many good Mussulmans knew pain before he fell with knife wounds that covered his body.*[3]

By 6 August reinforcements had arrived and the French were able to secure a barrier around all of the European consulates. The rest of the city was rubble, a bombed-out shell: 'the streets were a rubbish heap of cadavers,' one eyewitness recalled, 'enormous, blown-up with gas, their sex stiff in a monstrous erection'.

On 7 August the city was flooded with nearly 2,000 Senegalese sharpshooters and foreign legionaries from the ships that had just arrived. The battle was over, but the killing went on: the legionaries in particular saw it as their mission to punish any remaining inhabitants of the city; they stripped bare and shot anyone they found in the wreckage. Meanwhile the guns of the warships began seeking out villages in the hinterland, testing their range, almost as a game.

By 18 August Paris officially declared that 'order' had been restored in Casablanca. Moroccans were allowed to return to their homes, or what was left of them, after a humiliating interrogation by Arabic-speaking French officers carrying whips. All France's military and political objectives in Casablanca had now been achieved.

★

The real aim of the French who manipulated the disorder in Casablanca was to put pressure on the Mahkzen, the office of the sultan, who nominally still ruled the nation. What happened, however, was that by weakening the Mahkzen, they opened up the possibility of civil war between rivals competing for the throne. Official French policy was to let this struggle play itself out, but this only revealed how little the French understood the country that they were trying to conquer. The internal politics of Morocco were complicated, but its politicians were not naïve; at every step there was also the larger aim of throwing the French back out of the country. 'The French are like fish,' a saying went; 'they cannot leave the sea.'

For this reason, over the next few years, every French plan devised from the Quai d'Orsay was countered by an unexpected reaction in Morocco. Moroccan independence was already doomed, as European powers sensed the political weakness of the sultan and started to squabble over the pickings. In 1906 an international conference at Algeciras in Spain had guaranteed 'order, peace and prosperity in Morocco', which involved placing the administration of the country, its customs, banks and police force under 'European control'. Effectively Morocco was being handed over to France, and in 1912 the Treaty of Fez made Morocco a French protectorate. The Germans had been bought off by the British with colonial territory on the Congo River, but special concessions were made to Spain. The Spanish had made claims upon Morocco ever since the sixteenth century and their fortress outposts had hardened into the colonial towns of Ceuta and Melilla on the Mediterranean coast – which were officially parts of Spain. The Spanish also had great influence over the rest of northern Morocco and the southern extremities in the Sahara. In 1912, the French ceded a protectorate for Spain in both these areas. Although the city of Tangier was placed under international control, it contained enough of a European Spanish-speaking population to support a thriving Plaza de Toros.

Elsewhere the French had a free hand in Morocco; the Treaty of Fez guaranteed the religious authority of the sultan, and his secular sovereignty, but all other executive powers were now in the hands of the French.

23

French Friends

Although the French became the rulers of Morocco in 1912, they were still not in complete control of the territory. For one thing, the Spanish were agitating to hang on to their 'rights' in northern Morocco and parts of the southern Sahara. In Tangier, other European powers fought each other for a slice of the international pie, while paying lip service to the phoney sovereignty of the sultan. The internal politics of Morocco were even more complex: the tribal system was impenetrable to outsiders and although the French had military posts stationed across the country, they had hardly any influence on what happened.

The first task of the resident-general, Marshal Hubert Lyautey, was to impose French rule upon Morocco. His mission was made especially difficult by the fact that Moroccans resented and were openly disloyal to the proxy sultans he appointed. Lyautey's solution was to appoint political leaders who were loyal to the pre-colonial system and who could enforce their power with the authority of past tradition. This left him free to pursue the policy of a 'une tache d'huile', a 'slick of oil', by which he meant impressing the natives with French military power and technology, eventually winning them over to the benefits of European modernity. He admired British rule in Nigeria and India, which he saw as employing the same means. He also believed in the separation of Arab (and therefore mainly Islamic) values and Berber tradition, in line with the prevailing colonial theory that the Berbers were an independent-minded people who would one day follow the French creed of liberty, equality, fraternity.

Lyautey was an unusual and impressive man. He had been born into a devoutly Catholic military family from the Lorraine. From an early age, he combined military values with unorthodox views and a taste for literature. He served with great distinction as an officer in the French colonial wars of the late nineteenth century and rose quickly to the attention of the highest military authorities in Paris. He was not a good-looking man, but he was proud of his body, brisk in his movements, and seemed to be in perpetual motion. He supported Dreyfus during the cause célèbre which divided France in the 1890s, stating clearly that this was an anti-Semitic conspiracy and therefore a conspiracy against the Great Nation itself. He also criticized French colonial policy as inhumane, yet was devoted to serving France beyond the mainland. In one sense he was the quintessential Orientalist who revelled in the luxurious, ornamented way of life that he found in the Muslim world, as well developing a deep respect for its languages, politics and belief systems. He was a hard soldier who punished disobedience in all its forms with the utmost severity, but his actions were also driven by compassion and respect for the civilization he encountered – which he did not see as inferior to France's but simply as 'other'.

Until the 1970s Lyautey's biographers were oblique about his homosexuality, just referring to 'a sensual homophilia' or his 'Greek virtues'. In his own era Lyautey was openly homosexual, regularly seducing the best and brightest of his lieutenants as part of their military education. In Paris he frequented literary circles which included the likes of Jean Cocteau (Lyautey admired his erotic drawings of young men) and Marcel Proust (it was rumoured that Lyautey provided the blueprint for the pederast Baron de Charlus in *A la recherche du temps perdu*).

His homosexuality was an open secret. Georges Clemenceau is famously alleged to have said of Lyautey: '*Ça, c'est un homme admirable et courageux, qui a des couilles au cul. Dommage que ce ne soit pas souvent les siennes.*' ('That is an admirable and courageous man who has balls up to his arse. It's just a shame that they are not always his.')[1] It should be noted that Lyautey detested Clemenceau, just as he denounced most Parisian politicians as 'idiots'. Lyautey's wife Inès, nicknamed *la Maréchale*, was worldy wise about the life of a soldier; she is said to have addressed a group of young officers gathered round her husband by saying: '*Messieurs, j'ai le plaisir de vous informer que cette nuit je vous ai fait tous cocus.*' ('Well, gentlemen, I have the pleasure of informing you that last night I made you all cuckolds.')[2]

Lyautey identified with all manner of rebels. In Algeria, in 1904, for a few weeks he enjoyed a sexual friendship with Isabelle Eberhardt, a Russian Jew from Marseilles who had converted to Islam, disguised herself as a man, and was found sleeping in a tent outside Lyautey's encampment in the south Oranais. Later arrested as a spy, she was a delicious catch for a man whose own sense of style was predicated on transgressing all conventional Western forms of behaviour. The sex with Eberhardt was no doubt important for this man who prized physicality as a form of poetry in itself; but no less important was the sense of exile from Europe. Lyautey did not want to conquer North Africa so much as be absorbed into it, losing himself and distancing himself from Europe and its values. Much of his story reads like a version of André Gide's *L'Immoraliste* – the tale of a Nietzschean dandy who finds sexual enlightenment among the boys of North Africa.

In military and political affairs, Lyautey was a hard-headed strategist. Above all, he wanted to avoid what he saw as the errors of French rule in Algeria, and judged the pursuit of war to 'pacify' the territory as a waste of time and lives. Instead he made a great show of respecting indigenous institutions, although this did not necessarily apply to the incumbents (one of his first actions on his arrival in Morocco was to replace Sultan Mawaly Abdul Aziz, whom he distrusted, with the more firmly pro-French Moulay Youssef).

Beyond the cities and towns, Lyautey effectively ruled by cultivating good relations with the caïds, the tribal leaders who could raise an army; the *tariquas*, the spiritual Muslim brotherhoods; and the Berbers, many of whom were anti-Arab rather than pro-French. The French authorities controlled all the 'modern' components of governance: health, education, justice and finance were all directly administered by the French.

At the same time, Lyautey recruited Moroccan soldiers into the French army. The outbreak of the First World War interrupted Lyautey's subtle conquest of Morocco. At a meeting of rural chiefs held in Marrakesh in 1914, it was declared that 'We are the friends of France, and to the very end we shall share her fortunes, be they good or bad.' In the next few years, 34,000 Moroccan soldiers were called to fight in the killing fields of northern Europe.

In the wake of the First World War, the greatest challenge to French and Spanish rule came from the Spanish-controlled territories of northern Morocco, in the form of an insurgency in the heart of the stark, impassable Rif mountains led by a Muhammed Ibn'Abd el-Karim al-Khattabi, usually known as Abd el-Krim. The revolt in the Rif lasted five years, from 1921 to 1926, and cost the lives of tens of thousands of European soldiers. Its success has since been hailed by anti-colonialist leaders as the greatest defeat inflicted on a European army in Africa.

Abd el-Krim was a Berber who opposed Spanish, French and Moroccan rule and who aspired to a free state of the Rif. The insurgents had the military advantage of fighting in terrain that they knew intimately. By 1923, having wrecked the Spanish military presence in the region, Abd el-Krim had more or less established the foundations of a state. It was then that he turned his attention to the French.

Alarmed by the apparent efficiency and ruthlessness of Abd el-Krim, Lyautey went up to inspect his northern front. The Spanish collapse had left the French in an extremely vulnerable position: the mountain passes were undefended and the territory between the foothills of the mountains and cities such as Fez was porous. In 1924 Lyautey reported to Paris that this area needed to be occupied and defended quickly if Abd el-Krim's insurrection was not to catch fire in the French zone. Lyautey's alarm was not taken seriously – the French occupation of the Rhineland in 1923 had already overstretched the French military and it was inconceivable that the might of the French army could be challenged by an illiterate bandit.

Lyautey returned to Morocco both angry and frustrated. Inevitably, in 1925 Abd el-Krim began to attack the French zone. Along the way, his army mobilized the local tribal chiefs in a jihad against the unbeliever. The tribal leaders were convinced by Abd el-Krim's prestigious successes – the war was not only a matter of honour but Morocco could be free within days, so the arguments went. Within two months of the initial assaults, the French had retreated inside Fez's city walls, losing all their outposts in the countryside. In June 1925 Abd el-Krim made his camp just forty kilometres from the city, and began lobbying the religious leaders of that most holy of Moroccan cities.

The Fassi were not only Muslims but Arabs, and they could not support this Berber upstart from the mountains, who knew nothing of civilization or religion. Most importantly, the scholars argued, if the Rifi Berbers made allegiance with the Berbers who already enjoyed special status under Lyautey, then the whole apparatus of the spiritual world of Morocco – an Arab creation – was under threat.

In Paris Lyautey was dismissed as an incompetent for having let the Rifis flood into the French zone, even though he had given the government due warning. Despite French reinforcements, the military struggle went on. Lyautey was now in his seventies and exhausted. Philippe Pétain, the hero of Verdun, was sent to take command and a joint European force finally crushed the rebellion in 1926, with a massive surge of troops burying the insurgents in their mountain heartland. French rule continued.

Not all Frenchmen were supporters of the French or Spanish war in the Rif. In France the loudest and most powerful opponent of the war in the early 1920s was the French Communist Party, which not only enjoyed the prestige of supporting the recent Russian Revolution but also held enormous sway over the French working class. Arguably the rise of the Communist Party constituted the most dangerous and direct threat to the French social order. The Communists opposed the Rif war on the grounds that it was an aggressive act of European imperialism, aimed at subjugating, then economically exploiting a foreign people. With notable exceptions (such as the renegade Communists grouped around the journal *Clarté*), the Communists were ignorant of local politics, as opposed to French policy, in Morocco. They were indifferent to Abd el-Krim's status as a tribal chief and knew little or nothing about Islam.

Communist rhetoric was mainly couched in the language of classical Marxism. Young French workers had their first glimpse of the conflict from newsreels played in the cinemas. Outside, militants handed out pamphlets which exhorted young proletarians to 'join with their African brothers' and to 'raise the red flag and do not embark as corpses-in-waiting for African soil!' Communist leaders sent a telegram to Abd el-Krim, urging victory and saluting his war 'against bankers and industrialists'. The First World War was still vivid in the memory of the French population and it was easy for the Communist newspapers to shock their readership with accounts of 100-kilogram bombs, tanks, poison gas and aircraft being used against a population armed mainly with ancient rifles.

As the Moroccan war continued and the slaughter spread, the insurgents also found supporters in the unlikely form of the Surrealists. In 1925 this was an extremely young but influential movement of avant-garde iconoclasts who had come together with the stated aim of overcoming all previous forms of self-expression. Indeed, the original caucus of the Surrealists – more of a gang than a movement – led by the mercurial figure of the poet, essayist and polemicist André Breton, had been founded in 1924 to liberate the unconscious mind, thereby unleashing 'a revolution of the mind'. The Rif war was the first chance for these angry middle-class rebels to back a political cause of their own.

They did this in words and deeds. 'The war in Morocco surpasses in implausibility, stupidity and horror anything we can expect from those people,' wrote André Breton, who had seen the carnage of the Great War at first hand. 'After this who can still talk about writing poems and all the rest? No written protest is sufficient against such a thing. What is to be done?'[3] Breton and the other Surrealists were extremely wary of the Communists, dismissing their fetish for the proletariat as 'cretinous' and their belief in revolution as 'mysticism'. But, for a brief moment, Breton considered making common cause with them, and nineteen Surrealists showed their good faith by signing a petition organized by the Communist newspaper *L'Humanité*. Given that the popular press in France dubbed Abd el-Krim 'Abd el-Kriminel', giving public support to Abd el-Krim at that time was the rough equivalent of praising Saddam Hussein in Washington at the height of either of the Gulf Wars.

However, the prospect of collaboration with the Communists became an impossibility at an unlikely literary banquet held on 2 July 1925 at the Closerie des Lilas restaurant in Paris, organized by the journal *Mercure de France* in honour of the distinguished and now elderly poet Saint-Pol-Roux. The literary banquet was an old-fashioned mark of literary recognition, popular during the 1890s, and it had angered the Surrealists that such an 'outmoded' form of celebration should be held for Saint-Pol-Roux, whom they venerated as a Symbolist and a forerunner of Surrealism. It also happened to take place on the day when the petition in *L'Humanité* was published.

The banquet kicked off with Breton exchanging insults with art critics. Other staple provocations led some of the guests, sick of Breton's elegant barbs, to try to push him through the window on the second floor. This triggered a real brawl, with Surrealists hurling plates, glasses and obscenities. The police were called, but not before cries of '*Vive les Riffs*' and 'Down with France!' had attracted an angry crowd to the restaurant and passers-by started beating up Surrealist 'traitors'.

In truth, the Surrealists were anarchistic Romantics who, like the Communists, knew nothing of Morocco, the Rif or Abd el-Krim. They declared themselves to be against Western civilization and especially France, but really this was just an inverse Orientalism. None the less, the fiasco at the Closerie des Lilas was a significant moment in the history of the anti-colonialism of the French avant-garde. In the 1950s, at the height of the Algerian War, groups like the Lettrists and Situationists would deliberately provoke public anger with their pro-Algerian, pro-Moroccan and pro-Tunisian sympathies. For now, however, it was an obscure battle between élitist Parisian factions which no one in Morocco had ever heard of.

Throughout the 1930s, French *colons* settled in almost every part of Morocco where money could be earned. The illusion of a protectorate which would shelter Morocco's independence and autonomy fell away: although the legal status was different, by now this was well and truly a colony on the Algerian model.

As poverty forced Moroccans in the countryside to move to the cities (where they often ended up worse off), the complex political affiliations that held tribes and villages together began to crumble. Alongside this process, there were the first real stirrings of political resistance to the French.

One of the catalysts was a clumsy attempt by the French to divide the Arab and Berber population. In 1930 the French authorities announced a *dahir* (decree) which declared that Berber laws would hold in Berber-controlled parts of the country rather than the Sharia law which applied to all Muslims. The French had really only meant to pacify Berber aspirations. But across Morocco it was argued that this was the first step towards converting all Moroccans to Christianity, that the protectorate was a sham, and that this was another crusade by the Frankish infidels. This argument turned into a full-blown protest movement, with riots in every Moroccan city – easily quashed by French force of arms. Before long the most hard-line protesters went underground. Towards the end of 1930, a group of young men, some of whom had been educated in the French system and others in the Middle East, set up a secret society called the Zawiya (Assembly, or Group), and began to distribute a propaganda sheet, *L'Action du Peuple*. The cultural schizophrenia in Morocco was apparent in the Arabic name of the organization and the French title of the newsletter.

The demands made by Zawiya were relatively modest. In 1934 they called for reforms to governance and administration but did not dare even to suggest that the then resident-general, Charles Noguès, should leave. At times Moroccan politics seemed to be a perverse mirror image of what was happening in France. For example, as France exulted in the late 1930s in the worker-led Popular Front government, Noguès was obliged to legalize the Communist Party and trade unions, but Moroccans were forbidden to join them.

When Moroccans went on strike in mines in the south of the

country, Noguès sent in the army. Nationalists were rounded up and imprisoned. There was more rioting, but Noguès prided himself on his ruthless methods when faced with the mob; the Moroccans were not armed, they were disorganized and easily cut down by a bullet or a sword.

Towards Freedom

Everything changed with the Second World War. In 1939 the sultan explicitly sided with France and thousands of Moroccans scrambled to join the French army, as they had in the First World War. By 1940, with the Fall of France, over 47,000 Moroccans were enlisted in the French military, motivated by a desire to escape the poverty of their native land, curiosity for travel and adventure, and, occasionally, a skewed patriotism for 'France', a land that most of them had never seen.

One of the complications in the early part of the war was that Noguès sided with Vichy and came to an agreement with the Germans to maintain the protectorate. One of his first acts of defiance was to refuse to allow the Germans to round up Moroccan Jews. Under the protectorate, the Jews had no status as French citizens. The sultan cleverly saw this as a loophole – a perverse form of French anti-Semitism – to oppose both Vichy and the Nazis.

This gave the sultan high prestige with the Allied forces who landed on the Moroccan beaches of Casablanca, Safi and Kenitra in 1942 as part of 'Operation Torch'. Noguès ordered his troops to fight the Americans. Moroccans were confused by this, and wondered what had happened to French authority. More to the point, they saw that it could be challenged by force of arms.

In contrast to their despised status under the French authority, Moroccan Jews, who generally wore European clothes but were poor, noted that the Allied forces treated Jewish fighters with respect. There were tough Jews, some of them Zionists, who refused to be subordinate to the so-called superior races.

Moroccan Muslims were also impressed by the efficiency and glamour of the American troops. The French forces, shabby in comparison, who were in disarray and demoralized, were capable of offering only a token resistance to the Allied landings. By this time, Morocco was no longer the busy and fruitful colony that the French had built up since 1905: the phosphate mines had shut down, harvests were poor and food strictly rationed; there were epidemics of plague and cholera. Worst of all, in 1941, there was famine in the north, which was occupied by Spanish troops in the wake of the Fall of France. The Spanish were not, strictly speaking, participants in the Second World War, but they loosely sided with the Axis powers and were keen to grab as much land in Morocco as they could from the Allies. The real victims of this cynicism were the Moroccans, who went hungry as their former colonial masters fought over territorial rights.

For the Moroccans, the most momentous event of the war was the arrival in 1943 of Roosevelt and Churchill at Anfa, near Casablanca, to discuss the future. Although Roosevelt gave no formal word in support of Moroccan independence, it was rumoured that he had privately expressed his views to the sultan that the French in Morocco were a spent force. Meanwhile, the Nationalist movement gathered pace. On 11 January 1944, a new grouping, Istiqlal (Independence), published its manifesto for a free Morocco, led by the sultan, Sidi Mohammed V, with a democratic charter and a constitutional monarchy.

At the level of the street, this movement was given impetus by the encounter with the Americans: this was the first time that Moroccans had come into contact with a culture outside the Spanish or French-speaking world. After years of wartime shortages, they were dazzled by the chocolate, cigarettes, nylons and the jazz music that the Americans brought with them. The folksinger Houcine Slaoui celebrated this in his song 'Al Mirikane', in which he sings '*zin u l'ainaz-zarqajanabkulkhir*' (The beautiful blue-eyed ones brought us all good things), with references to '*shwing*' (chewing-gum) and English words such as 'OK, OK, come on, come on, bye-bye'. Most importantly, the Americans seemed bring with them the promise of liberation from the French.[4]

For their part, the French were naturally suspicious of the Americans. This mistrust intensified in 1947 when Moroccan Nationalists established the Office of the Arab Maghreb in Cairo – an organization that decided political strategy and took propaganda far beyond the reach of the French. Many in the French government saw in this an Anglo-American plot to destabilize French North Africa. Suddenly Morocco and Moroccan Nationalists were the most dangerous threat to the stability of the region.

The French were really only deluding themselves, as George Orwell had noted in his diary while convalescing in Marrakesh almost a decade earlier: 'When you walk through a town like this – two hundred thousand inhabitants, of whom at least twenty thousand own literally nothing except the rags they stand up in – when you see how the people live, and still more how easily they die, it is always difficult to believe that you are walking among human beings. All colonial empires are in reality founded upon that fact.' And Orwell wondered ominously: 'How long can we keep on kidding these people? How long before they turn their guns in the other direction?'[5]

Now it seemed that his questions were being answered by the sporadic violence which occasionally broke out in Morocco, with serious uprisings in Rabat and Fez in January 1944. Anxious to convince the British and the Americans that they still had a grip on the Muslim population, the French described the uprisings as pro-German rebellions. They were nothing of the kind. In 1947 sixty-seven people were shot dead in Casablanca by Senegalese sharpshooters. Again, this was dismissed as trouble-making and treason rather a real bid for independence.

At the same time, Mohammed V began making appeals to

the wider Arab world for support; in April 1947 he made a visit to Tangier, where he attracted international attention by proclaiming Morocco's ties to the Arab nation without making any reference to the French. This was expressly against the orders of the resident-general, a liberal named Erik Labonne. One eyewitness to the sultan's visit, Abou Bakr Lamtouni, a ten-year-old boy scout, described the European inhabitants of Tangier as being profoundly shaken by Mohammed's speech, which was delivered to Moroccans who had travelled from all over the country to hear this first open declaration of an anti-European strategy.

Moroccan Resistance

The French cracked down hard. They insisted first of all that Mohammed V disassociate himself from Istiqlal. He had no choice but to pretend to do so, even as demonstrations and clashes continued. One of the most unsettling mutinies, at least from the French point of view, took place in Tangier in 1952.

The riots began quietly enough. At around 1 p.m. on Sunday 30 March, a group of protesters gathered outside the Cinema Rex on the Grand Socco, chanting 'Istiqlal, Istiqlal!' They were soon joined by young lads from the district, eager to taunt the Europeans who often came to watch Hollywood films in the cinema (which occasionally showed *Casablanca* for whole weeks at a time). For young Moroccans, the cinema was not only a mark of the separation between rich Europeans and poor Moroccans but also a symbol of the barbarity of the Western world.

The crowd was being monitored fitfully by the French chief of security, François Wilbers, who was practically alone that weekend – all his senior officers and half his men were attending the final of a boules competition at Souk El Arba du Gharb. As the crowd grew, so did Wilbers' unease. There had been rumours in the Arabic-speaking community that something big would happen in Morocco on 30 March – the fortieth anniversary of the French protectorate. All morning, young Moroccans had been tearing around the streets of the city, carrying red banners and insignias. The European population was oblivious to all of this. When a shopkeeper on the Avenue d'Espagne lowered his shutters, warning of trouble, the police forced him to open up again.

Wilbers sent a pack of men into the crowd to try to get hold of the ringleaders, but the police were met by a hail of stones, bottles and iron bars. The crowds then moved to the Medina, smashing windows in the rue Semarine and rue des Siaghines. Shots were fired into the air. And then, as the police lined up a machine gun at the entrance of the Medina, automatic rounds were fired into the rioting young men. At least eleven rioters were killed and dozens seriously injured. By five o'clock the police had control of the town. Moroccans were in tears, lamenting the dead and fearful of more shooting, as they poured out of the city through Place de France and rue de Mexique. Most Europeans, who had spent the day as a holiday, had no idea what had happened and by early evening aperitifs were being poured as usual on the fashionable *terrasses* of the city.

Worryingly for the French, the disorder in Morocco was now starting to be matched by violence in Tunis. On 5 December 1952 La Main Rouge (The Red Hand), a French vigilante group allegedly close to the French secret services, murdered a Tunisian trade unionist called Farhat Hached, whom they had identified as one of the key leaders of the rebellion in Tangier. And then on 8 December, in Casablanca, police, colonial troops and the French Foreign Legion surrounded the shanty town known as the 'Carrières Centrales', where white-robed Nationalists filled the streets in protest. Light aeroplanes buzzed overhead, dropping tear gas. Some of those who managed to get out of the shanty towns attacked Europeans, wounding seven of them. Hundreds of Moroccans were arrested, beaten or killed. British

Pathé News, sensitive to the Cold War agenda of the period, described the insurgents as 'Communists' or 'simple-minded folk' who been 'led astray by Communists'. In fact, most of the rioters were angry young Muslims, living in wretched poverty, often literally starving. Among them were shoeshine boys, porters or newspapers sellers – '*yaouleds*', or street-kids. Most of them had never heard of Marx nor knew what Communism was. There was no official recognition in France or any other country that this could be a Nationalist anti-colonial rebellion.

24

Modern Times

The Casablanca massacre left many dead: the *New York Times* put the death toll as high as 400. The French believed that they had crushed Istiqlal and, having banned the Communist Party, proceeded with their plans to depose the sultan, Mohammed V, and to impose direct rule. The plot was crude and simplistic, aimed at satisfying the aspirations of the French settlers in much the same way as they had in Algeria. The strategy also created anger in Paris. At a meeting of the Académie Française, during which the Moroccan resident-general Alphonse Juin lavished praise on pro-French Moroccans, the distinguished Catholic novelist François Mauriac complained loudly that the protectorate and its officers were a 'masquerade' for colonial violence.

Most Moroccans of all classes, sickened by the Casablanca massacre, had become Nationalists in one form or another. These feelings intensified when the French launched their *coup* against the sultan and persuaded various mystical brotherhoods that, as a Nationalist, the sultan was effectively apostate. He was exiled to Corsica and then to Madagascar, while the French put their designated ally, Ben Arafa, on the throne.

The sultan's exile provoked fresh cycles of violence. Two new groups, born out of Istiqlal, led the way. In the countryside there was the Liberation Army and in the cities the Secret Organization. The first major act of resistance came from Abdel ben Abdellah, an unknown house painter from Casablanca, who launched a frenzied attack with a knife on the so-called 'French sultan' as he rode on horseback with the Royal Guard. Ben Arafa was unharmed and Abdellah shot dead.

The violence was matched by the Présence Française, a shadowy French terrorist group rumoured to be linked to the group called La Main Rouge, which was already operative in Algeria and Tunisia. No one knew for certain whether these groups really existed or whether they were a fiction invented by the French secret services (at the time of writing this is still unknown, as the archives have yet to be fully opened). Nevertheless, there was a spate of murders in Morocco which could not be properly attributed to any group but which mysteriously served French interests.

The response of the Moroccan resistance to these provocations was to escalate the violence. On Christmas Eve 1953 a bomb exploded in the Central Market of Casablanca killing twenty-six people. A former Istiqlal militant named Mohamed Zerktouni, a carpenter and a leader of the Secret Organization, was arrested. He killed himself with poison shortly after his arrest. This was the moment when the most peaceful Nationalist attitudes hardened into armed rebellion. Within weeks, Morocco became effectively ungovernable as riots, strikes and mutinies broke out spontaneously across the territory. French army squads patrolled the countryside. The parts of cities deemed 'troublesome' were sealed off. In Paris the French government wondered anxiously if the violence that was spreading through Algeria had infected Morocco.

'French Presence'

On 11 June 1953 the businessman Jacques Lemaigre-Dubreuil was shot dead on the steps of his Casablanca apartment building.

Lemaigre-Dubreuil was a financier and the owner of the newspaper *Maroc-Presse*. For the past five years he had been acting in Morocco as an intermediary between Paris and Rabat.

Initially he had been in favour of preserving and even strengthening the protectorate, and agreed that the deposition of Mohammed V was the way to achieve this. More recently, he had come over to the view that a middle ground could be found between Moroccan independence and French interests. These views were promoted in *Maroc-Presse*, much to the anger of extremist settlers. Lemaigre-Dubreuil had been intelligent enough to see, however, that the struggle in Morocco also had a geopolitical dimension: it was about France finding its place in the new world order after the Second World War. All of this was enough to condemn him to death in the eyes of the settlers.

The killing of Lemaigre-Dubreuil was a major blow to Paris. Firstly, the French government had lost a passionate and informed advocate in Morocco. Secondly, it looked likely that the fraught situation might become just as volatile and deadly as the war that was beginning in Algeria. The French Prime Minister, Edgar Faure, sent over a new resident-general, General Gilbert Grandval, a personal friend of Charles de Gaulle, to take a firm grip on the situation.

Grandval began by sacking senior police officers sympathetic to the pro-French terrorists, excluding from Moroccan territory the leader of Présence Française, and arresting the alleged murderers of Lemaigre-Dubreuil. He also released Moroccan political prisoners and began a dialogue with Nationalists.

Inevitably, these actions dismayed the *colons*. Whenever he appeared in public, Grandval was met with jeers and anti-Semitic insults. On 14 July 1953 a bomb exploded at Mers Sultan Square in Casablanca, killing seven Europeans. This was the provocation needed for retaliation by pro-French murder squads – gangs of young men who prowled the streets of

Casablanca on motorbikes and in black Citroën cars, gunning down Moroccans at random, dozens of whom were reported injured or killed. This level of violence exceeded anything yet seen in Algeria.

There were more riots and strikes. At Khourigba, a phosphate mine in the Middle Atlas, three hundred Europeans, including women and children, were massacred. The French army and air force counter-attacked, killing hundreds and possibly thousands of Moroccans in the countryside. Morocco was now in deep crisis. The response of Moroccan Nationalists was to press on and attack the French; briefly Moroccan and Algerian Nationalists were under a joint command. The insurrection threatened to become a war.

The threat of a war on two fronts, in Algeria and Morocco, forced the hand of the French: the protectorate was dissolved and Morocco finally gained its independence in April 1956. The French fled, leaving behind structures that were unworkable; the protectorate had effectively been the purest form of colony, in that it overlay the realities of Moroccan life with an administration that served only the settlers. Everything in Morocco had to be rebuilt, and this was not something which could take place overnight. Mohammed V, who had returned from exile in Madagascar to become king, was a shrewd man with a group of intelligent and sophisticated advisers. He promised to pull Morocco together as one nation, but his first priority was to establish order.

In the first months and years of independence, colonial law was universally disregarded, and the country he inherited faced massive economic and social problems. Ten million Moroccans lived in poverty, often on the edge of famine, while a French and Spanish minority owned the best land and held the best jobs. Anarchy was only a short step away. By May 1956 the Istiqlal party was divided, and Mohammed V himself conflicted over the way forward. For advice he relied on Mehdi Ben Barka, a former mathematics teacher who had evolved into a left-wing Nationalist. Ben Barka provided a counterpoint to the piety of Allal Al-Fassi, but the truth was that Free Morocco was a fragmented and unmanageable nation.

Mohammed V died in 1961 and was succeeded by his son Hassan II. At this stage the monarchy was still fragile and it was not expected to last; international observers, including the United States, anticipated a popular revolution mirroring the waves of Arab nationalism that had swept through Egypt and other Arab states. Hassan's first priority was therefore to ensure that he stayed in power. He did this by imitating the French strategies during the protectorate: controlling the army in the cities and buying off the caïds in the countryside. He asserted himself as the religious leader of the country and made a point of leading Friday prayers in Rabat, publicly slaughtering a ram to mark the beginning of the Aid El-Kebir festival.

He also declared himself 'amir al mouminine' (Commander of the Faithful) which made his very existence a sacred and inviolable fact; the Moroccan ulemas may have had a part to play in the organization of government, but it was the king who was the ultimate religious authority in the country. During the early 1960s, Hassan kept a tight rein on religious movements in Morocco by exercising this authority. Meanwhile, the Marxist Left was slowly dying, strangled by Hassan's repressive régime, which monitored and imprisoned all those who were a threat to the throne.

Through the 1960s and 1970s, Morocco remained a tense and unstable place. To the outside world, the country was known and celebrated as a counter-cultural paradise. The novels of Paul Bowles and William Burroughs and the activities of the Beats had given Morocco the reputation of a free-living society where drugs and gay sex were the norm. In an American guidebook published in 1971, clearly aimed at a hippie audience, the author compares the Moroccan Muslims, with their 'soul', to Afro-Americans: 'The Arabs are a trip,' he writes. 'They are soul people who practise brotherhood every day rather than just bullshit about it on Sundays'.[1]

The reality of Morocco from the inside was quite different: this was a society controlled by fear of the government and the police. There were frequent riots, killings and arrests, and two failed coup attempts by the military. During student riots in Casablanca in 1965, more than a thousand students were killed by the authorities. This was followed by more uprisings, strikes and insurgent actions – leading eventually to the declaration of a state of emergency. The period between 1965 and 1975 is usually referred to as '*les années de plomb*' (the years of lead). The truth about Morocco during that time could not have been further removed from the visions of the hippie dreamers who went there in pursuit of the exotic.

Darkness

The most notorious act of repression was the murder of Mehdi Ben Barka, the former adviser to Mohammed V, who became a leading figure in the Socialist Party. In 1963, having survived several assassination attempts, Ben Barka left Morocco for Europe. He was sentenced to death in absentia for allegedly plotting to kill the king.

In exile, Ben Barka proved to be a painful thorn in Hassan's side. He moved around constantly and relatively freely, arguing against Hassan's despotism and campaigning against the 'Gestapo-like' tortures which, he alleged, were taking place in Morocco. In 1964 Ben Barka was named as executive secretary of the Afro-Asian Solidarity Committee, with the brief of organizing the first Tri-Continental Conference, to be held in Cuba in 1966. He based himself in Geneva and, with growing support from Egypt and China, he looked set not only to rival Hassan as the public face of Morocco, but to overtake him as a leading statesman in Third World politics.

Ben Barka was constantly under surveillance by the Moroccan intelligence services but Hassan's policy was apparently to lure him back to Morocco, even promising him a hand in government. It is probable that Ben Barka was considering this when he mysteriously disappeared in France in October 1965. The details of what happened to him are still unclear. What is known is that he was invited to Paris by a publicist, Philippe Bernier, to discuss making a documentary film about decolonization. Ben Barka was told that Marguerite Duras had agreed to write the script and Georges Franju had agreed to direct the film; these were serious figures on the Parisian literary scene, with impeccable left-wing, anti-colonial views, and Ben Barka saw no reason not to take the proposal seriously.

Ben Barka arrived early for the meeting at Brasserie Lipp in St Germain-des-Prés, and was observed lingering around the bookshop opposite, La Hune, with a Moroccan student friend called Thami el Azemmouri. What neither of them knew was that a French intelligence agent, Antoine Lopez, had been alerted to Ben Barka's arrival at Orly earlier in the day by a Moroccan intelligence operative known only by the false name 'Chtouki'. Lopez was given orders to make sure that Ben Barka was delivered to 'a senior Moroccan personality' – most probably General Mohammed Oufkir, the Moroccan Interior Minister, who would later earn a fearsome reputation for his ruthless methods, including torture and murder.

Ben Barka and his friend were intercepted outside the bookshop by two men who identified themselves as French plain-clothes policemen. Reassured by their official IDs, Ben Barka got into their car with no resistance. He was then driven to a luxurious villa in the suburb of Fontenay, the property of Georges Boucheseiche, a well-known French gangster, who placed Ben Barka under the guard of his hired thugs. Still Ben

Barka saw no cause for alarm, as he believed himself to be under the protection of the French police. In the meantime, there was a flurry of calls from Orly to the Moroccan Ministry of the Interior. The next day Major Dlimi, chief of security in Morocco, flew to Paris, followed a few hours later by General Oufkir.

On his arrival, Dlimi told the gangsters that Ben Barka was to be 'liquidated'. This caused panic – they had signed up for kidnap but not for murder. None the less, Ben Barka was battered into unconsciousness and, according to a number of accounts, killed not long after. Oufkir caused further confusion when he told the gangsters and rogue intelligence agents that he had left Rabat too quickly to bring with him the agreed fee for 'taking care of Ben Barka' (allegedly a hundred million francs). No one really knows what happened next. A senior figure claimed to have seen Ben Barka's body dissolved in a vat of acid in Rabat shortly after his disappearance. Other sources claim that he was killed by the French or Moroccan secret services, or both, and buried on the banks of the Seine. In 1967 Oufkir, 'Chtouki' and the French gangsters were sentenced to life by a French court.

The Ben Barka affair became an international incident. Charles de Gaulle was furious that Oufkir should dare to act in such a criminal manner on French soil, and that his own intelligence officers had colluded with him. He sacked his head of counter-espionage and cancelled a state visit by Hassan. The Moroccan king in turn declared that de Gaulle was 'intolerable'. The affair still lingers darkly in the imagination of Moroccans, who have an obscure sense that this was their JFK moment – when their best and brightest hope for the future was extinguished in a French conspiracy.

In 1963 Morocco had been devastated by floods – a frequent occurrence in the central and northern parts of the country

– which left thousands homeless in the countryside and with no hope of rebuilding even their meagre lives. This was the cue for Hassan to promote the mass emigration of Moroccans to France. The rationale for this, it was understood, was that Morocco was a poor country with a broken infrastructure, which simply could not provide work or food for a significant part of the population. The French government was also keen to work with the Moroccans, partly because, after years of expansion since the Second World War, the country was suffering from a labour shortage. There was also a deeper strategy at work. From the earliest days of his reign, Hassan wanted to present Morocco as a stable, pro-Western power – the direct opposite of Algeria, in fact. Hassan himself spoke beautiful French, was openly pro-American, and friendly to Jewish interests and the state of Israel. He courted the French political establishment and flattered French businessmen into taking an interest, promising them that nothing like the Algerian disaster could happen in Morocco.

With the agreement of the French, the policy of mass emigration from Morocco to France got under way. The Moroccans immigrants during the 1960s were all men – usually from a rural background, from the Rif or the Sousse, and semi-literate at best. They arrived in their hundreds and then in their thousands. By the end of the 1960s an estimated 200,000 Moroccans lived and worked in France. The population grew even larger in the 1970s, when women and whole families arrived.

Part of the deal Hassan cut with the French was to actively discourage this population from seeking French nationality. When the migrants returned home every summer, a great fuss was made in Morocco about welcoming home '*les marocains de l'étranger*' (the Moroccans from abroad) – banners of welcome and special road-stops for weary travellers were all part of the propaganda. The Moroccan economy surged, boosted by the pay-checks of emigrant workers, but, discouraged or prevented from having dual French–Moroccan citizenship, they were also permanently disenfranchised.

For most of these workers, especially in the early days when car ownership was an impossibility, the journey north, in the cheapest trains or buses, was an annual misery. As they travelled through Europe, these young Moroccans would observe the affluence they saw all around them, only to arrive at their destination and find that life in the hostel or hotel felt much like life in prison. Most of them found work through agencies or touts, who set them up with lodgings where they were absorbed into the North African diaspora, which was spreading throughout all French towns and cities. It was a closed world of cheap hotels, cafés and brothels. The novelist Tahar Ben Jelloun drew up a list of prohibitions which defined the life of the new immigrant to France – it was meant as a parody but was not far from reality:

- It is forbidden to eat in your room (there is a kitchen at the end of the corridor)
- It is forbidden to have women in your room (there is a brothel called Chez Maribelle nearby)
- It is forbidden to listen to the radio after nine o'clock
- It is forbidden to sing in the evenings, especially in Arabic or Kabyle
- It is forbidden to slit the throat of a sheep (you must wait to return home for this)
- It is forbidden to masturbate in your room (go to the toilet for this)[2]

These men worked on building sites, sweeping the streets or in other lowly public services. There was also an alternative economy built around racketeering and prostitution. Newcomers to Paris, especially those from a rural background, were all too often ripped off by their compatriots. They were also wary of other nationalities, particularly Algerians, who were feared as unpredictable and violent revolutionaries. Many Moroccans knew that it was a good idea to distinguish themselves from Algerians in the eyes of the French, and so often avoided living in areas that were known to be predominantly Algerian, such as Barbès and, through the 1960s, the lower part of the boulevard Saint-Michel, which was nicknamed by racists 'Bougnoule Saint-Michel' ('Saint-Michel the Nigger'). For this reason many Moroccans made for Clichy and Gennevilliers; northern Moroccans tended to clustered around Gennevilliers, which they had heard about in Tangier or Tetouan.

In the south, Languedoc-Roussillon attracted many Moroccan workers, while others headed north, to work in the mines around Lille or Roubaix, or to eastern France. Lyons was to be avoided as an 'Algerian' city, as was Marseilles, which was also packed with pieds noirs and known as an uneasy place for Muslims.

Life was not easy for those who stayed behind in Morocco. Those who could not get to France made for Casablanca and the other big cities, dreaming of riches on an American scale. Inevitably, massive shanty towns grew up in the shadow of these cities. Morocco was now changing from a mainly rural country into another impoverished Third World mess. Hassan quashed resistance to this process by force, and exported to France the tens of thousands who were no longer needed in their home country.

During the 1970s Hassan only held on to power by courting Western support and crushing all opposition with his security services. There were rumours of secret prisons and torture. Left-wing and trade-union activists disappeared swiftly and mysteriously. Migrants returning from France often found that they did not recognize or understand their own country any more – in Europe they were displaced and had low status, but Morocco felt like a prison camp where no one dared speak the truth for fear of being 'disappeared' for ever.

There were sporadic outbreaks of violence throughout the 1970s, always brutally put down by the police and army, but the first signs of real trouble came in 1981 after the government decided to increase the price of oil, flour and butter by almost 77 per cent. The immediate effect was that thousands of people simply could not afford to feed themselves. In June 1981 the Hassan government looked for the first time to be shaken by the scale and the shape of the violence that took place in the cities of Oujda, Berkane, Nador and especially Casablanca.

The trade unions called for a general strike, which in Casablanca quickly became a riot when the police fired bullets above the crowd. The city erupted – the poorest quarters were the first to explode into fury as the news came through that people had been killed for demanding food. Tens of thousands took to the streets, marauding through the wealthier quarters, smashing windows, wrecking and burning cars. There was little or no looting: the rioters wanted food and justice, not consumer goods.

Aware of how precarious his position was, Hassan ordered tanks into the streets and helicopters buzzed over the crowds. This only further angered the rioters, as they saw how much the government invested in military hardware to control them. A state of siege was declared on 21 June, which gave the authorities to power to use snatch squads to pick off rioters. Officially, there were only sixty-six deaths, but everyone knew that this was a lie. Over the next weeks and months, residents of Casablanca reported that the ground had been dug up and bodies buried in wasteland across the city; one football team reported that they had been warned off their favourite pitch by the security services, who had buried an unknown number of corpses there. Cynically, Hassan invoked the spectre of the Iranian Revolution as a justification for his heavy-handed tactics. But these were not yet Islamists: simply a hungry and humiliated population.

The Islamic Call

The Islamist movement had been slow to catch fire in Morocco, largely because political Islam was at odds with the Moroccan home-grown version, which allowed for superstition, sorcery and saints. However, as in the rest of the Arab world, radical Islamism did eventually start to infiltrate mainstream religion.

The first Islamist group of any note in Morocco, Chabiba Islamiya (Islamic Youth), was founded in 1969 by Abdelkarim Mouti, a former inspector of primary schools who was born in the tiny town of Ben Ahmed and who hated the Left and the king in equal measure. Mouti would eventually flee to Libya in 1975 when he was accused of the murder of the prominent trade unionist Omar Benjelloun. Initially, the Chabiba concentrated on spreading propaganda through the universities. It was divided into two sections: one for preaching and the other for armed combat. In future years members of both wings would join legitimate Islamist parties in Morocco, or head towards the GIA in Algeria and ultimately to al-Qaeda.

The Chabiba were firebrands but they lacked convincing arguments. The Islamist movement really only began to take hold in Morocco with the group Al-Adl wal-Ihsan (Justice and Charity), led by the charismatic and cerebral figure of Abd al-Salam Yassine. Taking his cue from the Iran, Yassine began to attack Hassan in the 1970s as an arrogant despot unworthy of the throne of Morocco, arguing that Hassan was not even a Muslim. In 1974 he wrote an open letter to Hassan called 'Islam or Deluge', in which he said: 'God has warned you twice.' This was reference to the two failed coup attempts (the one led by Hassan's protégé General Oufkir had nearly cost the king his life). Yassine went on: 'This letter is a third warning.' For this Yassine was sent to a mental hospital for three years. Meanwhile his home in Salé became a place of pilgrimage for his growing number of followers. He emerged in 1979 at the height of the Iranian Revolution and immediately resumed his campaign against Hassan.[3]

In the wake of the riots and massacres of 1981, Yassine's prestige grew as Moroccans began to pit their experiences of poverty and injustice against the machinery of the state. There were more riots in 1984 – this time in the north of the country in Nador, provoked by a hike in the tariff which students had to pay to pass their exams. The response from the police and army was again merciless: officially there were twenty-nine deaths, but students also told of death squads and disappearances. This was when many of this generation began to turn away from Western ideas towards political Islam, a drift accelerated by the fact that many young people now sought their inspiration, in film, music and television, from the East rather than the West. One of the reasons for this was the sheer boredom and lies which made up the cultural output of the Hassan régime. The new influx of mainly French, affluent tourists also depressed ordinary Moroccans, who never saw any of this wealth other than what could be earned as a waiter or a hustler in the Medina.

25

Blank Generation

Mohammed VI came to the throne on 23 July 1999 to massive popular acclaim: the streets of cities, towns and villages throughout Morocco were packed with people from all backgrounds chanting, '*Yahla el Malik!*' ('Long live the king'). The hope was that Hassan's reign would be consigned to history and the new king, young, compassionate and generous, would finally lead Morocco to its place among the nations. This would be the '*génération M6*' (named after the trendy French TV channel M6) – a generation at home in Europe and Morocco, in touch with the past and the present, finally at ease in the world.[1]

The alternative nightmare scenario was already being played out in neighbouring Algeria, which had become a slaughterhouse as Islamists, the government and the military fought a three-way civil war which no one could win. A new cycle of violence had started in Morocco in August 1994, when, at the height of the tourist season, two Spanish tourists had been gunned down and killed in the foyer of the Hotel Asni in Marrakesh. This apparently random murder was the act of seven young men with French passports, Algerian and Moroccan backgrounds, who originally came from the *banlieue* of La Courneuve just outside Paris. They had equipped themselves with fake IDs that linked them with the FIS in Algeria, hoping to provoke an international incident between Algeria and Morocco, but in fact they were Maghrebi Parisians – the product of the dope-smoking culture of boredom and disaffection in the French suburbs. Their original plan had been even more grandiose – to shoot tourists on the beach in Tangier, to attack a synagogue in Casablanca and to mow down police in Fez; their aim was to convulse Morocco into a state of terror on the Algerian model. Even this small-scale attack nearly achieved this – the first instinct of the Moroccan government was to blame Algerians and tighten up the closed border.

It was the French and Moroccan secret services who revealed that the terrorist cell, operating out of Fez, was made up North African immigrants to France. The Moroccan authorities then insisted on treating the affair as a criminal case, while the French police pursued the line that a significant number of the would-be terrorists had been trained in Pakistan and Afghanistan. To follow this lead meant an investigation into the mosques of La Courneuve and Saint-Denis, where the ideology of jihad had been promulgated in response to the Gulf War, Palestine–Israel and Algeria. It was the French intifada in its purest form.

As a counterpoint to this violence, the king in Morocco was (and is still) held in very real affection. Mohammed styled himself 'le roi des pauvres' (the King of the Poor), and devoted much of his time to travelling around the country, often attending the humblest country fair or opening of a school. None the less, the challenges he faced were severe. The first was to reassure Moroccans and the outside world that Morocco was moving out of the darkness of Hassan II's reign towards something that, on the surface at least, looked like a Western democracy. This had to be achieved without disturbing the delicate structures of government, which Mohammed had inherited from his father, and without provoking a backlash from the still dangerous figures who remained in the court.[2]

The second challenge was to position Morocco as a power which, although friendly to the West, had not turned its back on the Arab world to the east. Mohammed openly courted Saudi influence, mainly a political manoeuvre which helped to demonstrate Morocco's fidelity to the Islamic sources of Arab culture. Unfortunately, friendship with the Saudis was not limited to the whoring and gambling in Morocco's casinos and designer hotels; Saudi-influenced Wahhabism, the puritanical version of Islam at odds with the homely Moroccan variety, entered the shanty towns and poorer quarters of the big cities.

The influence of Wahhabism was most clearly felt in the town of Salé, which lies just across the river from the capital city, Rabat. Its muddy streets and gloomy market are a long way from the French-influenced chic of Rabat or the bustle of Casablanca. Few foreigners come here, and those who do so are quickly made aware that they are barely tolerated. Nowadays only faded pro-Palestinian graffiti and a mural of the Al-Aqsa Mosque in Jerusalem at the entrance of the Old Town indicate that this place was a hotbed of Islamist activity, but until recently it was not unusual to spot Saudis in the street or for a neighbouring youth football team to acquire a shiny new kit with money from a mystery source. Amid the grinding poverty, it was easy for Saudis or their supporters to make friends in the area.

In 2002 Salé became notorious as the headquarters of one of the most daring and uncompromising Islamist groups in North Africa. The Salafi Jihadi (Salafist Combat) share not just their name with their Algerian counterpart, the Salafist Brigade for Combat, but also their ideology. Salafi Jihadi was founded in the early 1990s by forty veterans of the Afghan wars. It was part of a network linked to sister organizations in Algeria and to al-Qaeda, and for years its leader, the smiling and suave Hassan Ben Ali Kettani, taught here at the Grande Mosqueé, attracting followers from all over North Africa.

Late in 2002 the Grand Mosque was raided by police, with the aid of military helicopters. The police had discovered that Salafi Jihadi was providing logistical support to an al-Qaeda cell of Saudi militants who were plotting to attack the Strait of Gibraltar from Casablanca. Moreover, the group, which by then consisted of some 400 activists, was found to have links with a shadowy death squad, Takfir wal-Hijra. These two groups are alleged to have been responsible for 300 killings across Morocco.

'Franco-Moroccans'

During the 1990s the relationship with France was fundamental to securing Morocco's international credibility. This issue became even more acute in the aftermath of the attacks of 9/11, when it transpired that the first conspirator to be arrested and charged was a French Moroccan called Zacaria Moussaoui, whose family originally came from Meknes.

Moussaoui was in many ways a classic candidate for radicalization. He had been brought up in the *banlieue* of Narbonne, a sleepy, civilized town in southern France. He was a clever, sensitive student, who was easily bruised by perceived racism. The French intelligence services had been tracking him since 1996, when he came into contact with Islamist networks first in Rabat and then in London. During and after his trial in 2006, his mother complained loudly to the press that he was a victim of the French state and that he had been found guilty because he had publicly cursed 'America and the Jews'.

For all the press attention the Moussaoui case attracted in Morocco and France, the two countries had never been on friendlier terms. This was publicly marked in 2002 with the inauguration of the Place Mohammed V, just outside the Institut du Monde Arabe on the Left Bank in Paris. Mohammed VI, the grandson of the great leader who had brought Morocco independence, said that the square would be the symbol of 'ever stronger and permanent relations' between the two countries. This was followed up in the autumn of 2003 by a state visit to Morocco by President Jacques Chirac with six of his cabinet ministers.

There were, however, difficulties behind the scenes. The Moroccan government was wary of the bad press that it received in France. Liberalization after the death of Hassan II had given journalists in Morocco a free or at least a freer hand, to uncover the repression of his régime. There were regular articles in the serious French press and a plethora of investigative books about Morocco's recent past. The Moroccan government responded cautiously, but most of its citizens just felt insulted by this criticism from their former colonial master.

Confusion and anger also defined the mood of the third generation of Moroccan immigrants in France, who had come of age in the era of 9/11 and global terror. These emotions were caught in the short but piercing novel *Paris, Mon Bled* (*Paris, My Manor*) by the Rabati writer Youssouf Amine Elalamy, which describes the experiences of a group of young people on the outskirts of Paris who struggle to identify themselves as either French or Moroccan. At one level, this is a fairly standard comedy – the young people agonize over sexual adventures, take drugs, try to orientate themselves in a French-speaking world which is also being eroded by Anglo-American pop culture. But there is a more sinister undercurrent: the split identities are never properly resolved and the characters take sides one way or another. This is how, the novel tells us, the dope-smoking rap fan becomes an Islamist killer or the polar opposite – a spy for the French secret services, complicit in trickery and torture.

I met Elalamy several times in Casablanca: sophisticated, smart and fluent in several different cultures, he firmly asserted himself as a Moroccan who understood all of the conflicted identities in his novel, assuring me that this was the real story of the *génération M6*. 'You didn't have to leave Morocco to see this at work,' he said. 'It was here in the shanty towns, where everybody watched French TV and dreamed of leaving, and, because they couldn't, felt a mixture of desire, rage and humiliation.

★

The bombs all exploded around 10 p.m. on 16 May 2003. The explosions could be heard across Casablanca, like the sound of fireworks, and at first, on this mild, early-summer evening, nobody believed they could be anything else. But then the news footage came in of the carnage and it became clear that the first target was the Cercle de l'Alliance Israélite, where a nightwatchman and a policeman were killed. Near the Jewish cemetery alongside the Medina, another bomb killed three Moroccan passers-by.

Other targets were an Italian restaurant, the Positano, owned by Jews, and the al Farah hotel, owned by Kuwaitis. But the most savage attack was at the Casa de España on the rue Lafayette. This was a popular club where the dwindling and elderly Spanish population of Casablanca came on Friday nights for a drink, a chat and to play bingo. One of the bombers carried a scimitar, with which he sliced open the neck of a hapless security guard. He was trying to decapitate the man and, frustrated in his task, went on hacking away until finally – in front of an audience of appalled drinkers – he ripped off the guard's severed head in a fit of exultant anger. The two suicide bombers marched into the club and set off their bombs. 'You will lose you mind if you see what happened in here,' a policeman later warned the Spanish consul general, who arrived a few hours later to see what had happened. By the end of the night, forty-five people lay dead.

In the immediate wake of the bombings, there were demonstrations against terrorism and declarations of outrage. But what alarmed most middle-class Moroccans was the fact that the bombers were not foreigners, but came from Tangier and Casablanca. The news that one of the men held French nationality was initially greeted with delight, on the grounds that no Moroccan could have conceived of such a crime. But as it became clear that the other bombers were Moroccan, many commentators began to talk of a campaign of Islamist insurrection on the model of Algeria.

Mohammed VI went into a cold fury. He declared that the 'years of laxity' were over and invoked Algeria as the biggest threat to Morocco's hard-fought-for stability. The possibility of an Islamist insurgency in Morocco had first entered the public imagination a few years earlier, when reports from Nador, Rabat, Mohammedia, Tangier and Casablanca confirmed that disparate but organized Islamist factions, possibly under the influence of Algerian or Saudi-financed groups, were taking control of the slums and shanty towns. This was followed by regular stories that drinkers, prostitutes, drug dealers, policemen and others suspected of un-Islamic behaviour had been thrown into wells, stoned to death or had their throats cut. In the exclusive areas of Rabat and Casablanca, Moroccan women in Western clothes were assaulted at knife-point for not wearing the hijab.[3]

And now, in 2003, violence seemed to simmering all across Morocco. In Agadir, a cheap and popular holiday destination in the south of the country, a young man of twenty-three called Mohamed Agouirar, from the poor district of Dcheïra, walked into a seafront bar around 1 a.m. on 10 July and plunged a long knife into the bellies of the assembled. Those who had not been attacked were so stunned that they were unable to flee. Agouirar then stabbed himself to death on the beach. In Rabat two fourteen-year-old girls planned to firebomb a shopping mall and attack the royal family. In the north, magistrates and drug warlords were found to be arming Islamic extremists. There was no connection between these events, but it felt as if no place was immune from the violence.

26

Setting Europe on Fire

The morning of 11 March 2004 was clear and bright. As the city of Madrid awoke, a band of young men planted thirteen sports bags in four trains leaving from the outlying town of Alcalá de Henares. Each bag held a mobile phone. The men wore football scarves – in the colours of Real Madrid – as a light disguise and weaved between the trains, distributing the bombs.

This was all performed in a playful mood. At this time in the morning – between 7.00 and 7.15 a.m. – the trains were busy with early commuters, cleaners, labourers, shift workers and the packed carriages were alive with banter. One of the bombers stopped to chat up two pretty Romanian girls on their way to work, before hopping off the train, leaving behind a bomb in a rucksack. One of the girls, fancying her chances with the cheeky but good-looking Arab, called after him. Minutes later she was blown into pieces.

All the trains were heading towards Atocha, the main station in Madrid. At 7.39 a.m., as the first train went past the Calle Téllez, which lies no more than 500 metres from the station platform, the first bombs were detonated by a mobile phone. A few seconds later, four more bombs went off in another train heading into Atocha. Within minutes, two more trains were wrecked. By 8 a.m., the trains lay across the lines between

316

Atocha and the district of El Pozo del Tío Raimundo, a poor, immigrant quarter of Madrid. Between the station and the trains, the lines were scattered with bloodied, limbless trunks, arms, legs, and severed heads.[1]

The first Moroccans to be arrested were Jamal Zougam, Mohamed Bekkali and Mohammed Chaoui. The police had found one of the mobile phones used in the attacks and discovered that the SIM card had been sold on to other Moroccans, from Tangier and Tetouan, who worked in or hung around a *locutorio* called Nuevo Siglo (New Century) in the Calle de los Tribuletes, near the centre of Madrid. The Calle de los Tribuletes is in the district of Lavapiés – a former bastion of the white working class of Madrid which is now home to Africans, Arabs, Pakistanis, Sri Lankans and Indians. *Locutorio* is the Spanish word for the kind of cheap communications shop that exists now all over Europe, where immigrants from poor countries can call home at cheap rates, or simply hang out with friends and compatriots.

Shortly after the arrests I went to see for myself the *locutorio* where the massacre had apparently been plotted. When I got there, the shop was boarded-up, but the sign was still on the door. 'Those guys were not terrorists,' I was told by a Tunisian waiter at a nearby café who regularly served them coffee (he would not give me his name). 'No way. They were maybe rogues and did some bad stuff, but they were not killers.' This was a fair point; the fact that they had supplied the mobile phones used in the attacks did not make them guilty of anything more than dealing in stolen goods.

Jamal Zougam, however, was already well known to the Spanish security services. He had been picked up by the police in 2001, who found in his apartment videos of his Moroccan friends fighting in Dagestan, Russia. He also had videotapes of Bin Laden's speeches and books by radical imams – the paraphernalia of the apprentice jihadi.

Under Zougam's influence, the Nuevo Siglo became the place to meet with religious extremists and begin the journey towards radicalization. In recent years there have been numerous academic studies of how this works. The process is simple. The first step is to have a sense of belonging with other outsiders who feel displaced in their host society. Smoking *kif* (the Moroccan form of cannabis, traditionally smoked in a thin pipe called a *sebsi*), renouncing alcohol, singing old songs, watching videos, remembering the past, all contribute to a sense of family. The group also bonds over shared grudges and perceived slights – it could be a girl rejecting sexual advances because she was a 'racist', or a drugs deal gone wrong.

In this context, Islamic radicals present themselves as super-heroes, at war with the world of *Jahiliya*. Like all young men, the Islamic radicals are competitive and try to outdo each other with the ferocity of their faith, their denunciations of the West and their plans for destruction. The Spanish sociologist Rogelio Alonso, an expert on psycho-social stress in immigrant groups, has described this bonding very effectively: 'Terrorism is a group phenomenon,' he says; 'it is an action which is entirely determined by group dynamics.' In simple terms, this means that the radicals need each other: like football hooliganism, terrorism is violence as a game, a contest between competing egos to see who can wreak the most havoc.

There are two more steps towards murder. Firstly, you have to identify the enemy. For the young men at Zougam's *locutorio*, the enemies were the Spaniards they met every day, who not only denied them opportunity and wealth, but who were occupying the historic lands of Al-Andalus, which had once been Islamic territory. Police informers, who had been monitoring the group in the *locutorio* and in the nearby Restaurante Alhambra, reported that the Moroccans constantly referred to the 'occupation' and the 'Jews': they saw no difference between the Spanish 'occupation' of Ceuta and Melilla, which are on North African soil, and the lost world of Al-Andalus.

Secondly, in order to kill the enemy you must dehumanize him. This step towards terror takes the form of a linguistic sleight of hand. Zougam and his followers began by thinking that the Spanish *act like* the Jews in Israel. The experience of living in occupied Al-Andalus – the radicals in the *locutorio* argued among themselves – is directly equivalent to living like the Palestinians, displaced and lost in Israel and Gaza. The next step in this murderous logic is to imagine that the Spanish, the agents of dispossession, *actually are* 'Jews'. Police informers say that this was how the young men in Zougam's circle habitually referred to all the 'sub-humans' outside the *locutorio*. Beyond its doors, everything was *haram* – that is to say, forbidden by Islam and sinful. In this world, all Jews are the enemy, and all Jews are targets.

These young men in Madrid had no official affiliation to al-Qaeda. They didn't need it. This was al-Qaeda ideology as youth revolt.

The city of Tangier was central to the Islamist atrocity in Madrid. Not only were nearly all of the assassins of Moroccan origin, but most of them were from Tangier, only an hour away by ferry from the Spanish coast.

Although Tangier is in an Islamic country and in Africa, it is also part of the Spanish-speaking world. The neighbouring cities of Ceuta and Melilla, roughly a ninety-minute drive from Tangier, actually are Spanish territory – Moroccans need visas to get past the heavily policed border controls and a number of people have been killed trying to cross the borders illegally. The city of Tetouan, an hour away and a halfway house between Tangier and the Spanish enclaves, is in Morocco but looks like a Spanish city – it has the same plazas, the same architecture and street furniture.

But Tetouan is a desperately poor place and anything modern also looks half-wrecked. It is notorious as a lawless base for hard-line Islamists and many of the toughest gangsters in Tangier – experts in drug-running and people-trafficking – originate from here. I once stayed for a week in a hotel in Tetouan where the owners effortlessly combined pious prayers with an open drugs racket. With its whitewashed buildings, its Spanish-speaking population and its backdrop of high mountains controlled by drug-runners, Tetouan resembles nothing so much as a Mexican border town with an overlay of Islamic culture.

It also hides an eerie secret. Beneath the floor of the Medina are the Mazmorras (a Spanish word meaning 'silos') – a sub-terranean labyrinth of caves and grottoes that runs almost entire the length of the city. In the seventeenth and eighteenth centuries this was a vast underground prison, holding thousands of Christian captives at a time. Cervantes made reference to it in one of his comedies, comparing a dead marriage to being worse than the prisons of Tetouan. One of the entrances is in the rue al-Smitir, covered by a steel plate in front of a juice store and café. Under this spot was a Franciscan church, ministered by monks who came from Spain to barter for the prisoners, most of whom died here.

I was last in Tetouan the summer of 2013 to make a BBC documentary about Islam and I went to look at the steel plate in the Medina and say something about what it might mean for Christian and Muslims. As I stood there recording, I was cursed and hissed at by locals who, despite the best attempts of the Moroccan government to keep the Mazmorras out of public view, knew exactly what I was looking at. Later that day, all of my other interviews were cancelled at the last minute for no reason. I was told by a friend that the government was anxious about my presence in Tetouan and had decided that no one should speak to me. As I was leaving the city, I saw an angry demonstration by Islamists against Spain at the Spanish consulate. My Arabic-speaking companion said he could not make out what they were saying. To me it sounded like another curse.

The relationship with Spain in this part of Morocco is complicated. For one thing, there has always been a large Spanish population in Tangier and Tetouan – in Tangier they are called 'Tangerinos' to distinguish them from the 'Tanjawi', the Muslim inhabitants of the city. Even now, in the streets around rue Jebha al Watania, you can find remnants of a community of exiles who came to flee from Franco's Spain. This is a visibly ageing population but they still have barbershops and the kind of old-school tapas bars that you can't really find in Spain anymore. On clear days you can see the Spanish coast across the Mediterranean from almost any point in Tangier. Sometimes it seems so near that you can make out cars and houses.

One of the best views is from the Plaza de Faro, a square dead in the centre of the city on the boulevard Pasteur. During the late afternoon and early evening this place swarms with shoeshine merchants and low-level hustlers selling drugs or sex. Mostly, however, it is populated by young men hanging out, smoking dope, chatting with each other and staring out at Spain. The place is nicknamed Plaza de los Perezosos, 'Square of the Lazy', because it attracts the unemployed and the idle.

Nearly all young people have worked, or want to work, in Spain. This can be a fatal ambition. The bloated corpses of those who try to get across the Strait of Gibraltar illegally are regularly swept up on Spanish beaches. In the bars and cafés of Tangier there is a lot of black humour about this. The sea between here and Spain is casually called the 'graveyard'. There are jokes about the gullibility of the sub-Saharan Africans who perish there. These would-be immigrants come to Tangier and pay all they have to sail to their dream of Europe, usually at night and with no guide, in tiny boats called *pateras* – an old Andalusian word for a flat-bottomed fishing boat. They have little or no chance of survival. 'It's called "African tourism",' I was told by one late-night Moroccan drinker in the Bar Negresco. 'This is how it works: Don't See Europe and Die!'

In the 1990s there were several major crackdowns on the would-be emigrants. Many of them were rounded up and imprisoned in the old, disused Plaza de Toros outside Tangier. The Tanjawi gave the bullring a Spanish nickname – 'Matamoros' (Moor-Killer). When the sub-Saharan Africans began to outnumber the Moroccan prisoners, they renamed it 'Matanegros' (Nigger-Killer).

In the wake of the bombings in Madrid, and the very visible Moroccan involvement, the French-trained Moroccan security forces in Tangier, the Renseignements Généraux, began coming down hard on anyone suspected of association with terrorists, and the jails filled up. The mosques were empty. Overnight young men shaved their beards – the mark of the Islamist radical. People were frightened.

'We Make Jihadis!'

The con artists and hustlers of Tangier are world-class experts in the art of frightening first-time visitors to the city. They do this most often at the gates in the lower parts of the Medina, where the tourists get off the ferry and can be easily scared into handing over their cash to a group of tough-looking, dark-skinned lads who may or may not carry knives. The authorities have tried their best to clean the place up, but this part of town can be an intimidating introduction to the city. For many tourists, this is also their first introduction to the Arab world, and the Tangier hustlers, unwittingly following the Orientalist tradition, convince them that they are about to enter a new world of exotic and unknown dangers.

In fact, the most dangerous part of Tangier is not the relatively laidback centre, the Medina or the 'French' boulevards, but the outlying suburbs – an impenetrable forest of badly built, low-level apartment buildings. This is where most of the riots and other forms of violence – murders, muggings – take place. These areas are not unlike the French *banlieues*, the badlands of decaying public housing which surround all major French cities, although the suburbs of Tangier are far worse than anything you can see in Paris, Lyons or Marseilles.

I was told by a friend with inside knowledge of the political administration in Tangier that the apartments are often built by gangsters who are laundering money made from trafficking people or drugs. The buildings are badly built, prone to floods and even collapse. People have died as a result of the shoddy construction work. Because they were built at night by illegal labour, without regulation, many of these housing estates don't officially exist, but every time I drive down from the airport I am astonished at how quickly another forlorn, half-built rash of apartment blocks has sprouted out of nowhere. The Tanjawis call this '*hizam al-fakr*' (the belt of poverty).

Unsurprisingly, this is where the most radical Islamists have taken control of the mosques and the streets. It was here, in the early 2000s, in the suburb of Casabarata, that the preacher Mohamed Fizazi promised to send 'Islamic Brigades who would set fire to Europe'. Fizazi is now in jail for his involvement with the bombings in Casablanca in 2003, but he knew or had contact with all the Moroccans who bombed Madrid.

All of the eighteen bombers convicted at the trial in Madrid in 2007 had connections with Tangier. The ringleader, Jamal Zougam, had worshipped in Casabarata with Mohamed Fizazi. Zougam helped make the bombs and, according to three eye-witnesses, planted the rucksacks on the train in a smiling, relaxed mood.

Zougam was born in Tangier in 1973, in the rue Ben Aliyem, a rundown street in the upper part of the Medina. This is the poorest part of the Medina but only a few steps away from

the American legation, the former headquarters of the US
Diplomatic Mission, which has been here since 1821 and is now
an elegant museum. In the cafés further down towards the port,
where *sebsi* and tea are the main staples, Zougam is remembered
as a tough and witty friend. In the years since the bombing, at
least for some Tanjawis, he has also become a hero, a local boy
made good. 'Zougam showed that we can fight back,' I was
told by a heavy-lidded smoker. Nobody here had heard of Paul
Bowles, William Burroughs or any other bohemian expatriates,
but they knew all the names of the Madrid bombers and said
that they were proud that they came from Tangier. 'We should
be making famous footballers who can play for Chelsea,' I was
told by a guy called Rachid, who spoke English with a Cockney
accent as a result of his time spent in UK prisons, 'but we don't:
we make jihadis instead!' This was in the summer of 2012.

This perverse feeling of pride was far from universal across
the city; there were many who said that they were still ashamed
of the bombers. One of the hit songs of 2012 was a track by
DJ Muslim, a Tanjawi rapper, called '*Ana Muslim Mashi Irhabi*'
('I am a Muslim but not a Terrorist'). The smokers in the
Medina laughed when I mentioned this and said that DJ Muslim
was probably a stooge funded by the Moroccan government.
'DJ Muslim is not a rebel,' they told me. 'The real rebels are
somewhere else. They don't take money from the government.'

They meant rebels like Jamal Ahmidan, who killed himself in
April 2004 as the Spanish police began to lay siege to the house
in Leganés (a southern suburb of Madrid) where the plotters
had made the bombs. He was one of the key figures in the plot,
probably one of the most daring and hard-line figures, without
whom the bombing would never have happened. To many
young men in Tangier he is now a role model. His story is
like a video game, taking him from bad-boy gangster to Islamist
street-fighter and finally world-famous martyr.

Ahmidan was born in Tetouan in 1970 and arrived in Madrid

in 1990, by then already steeped in the low life of his native city and Tangier. He had the nickname '*El Chino*' (the Chinaman) because his features looked more Asian than Arab. Shortly after settling in Madrid, he married a Spanish woman, a junkie. He did this most probably to get papers, although he also fathered her son. He made a living by selling dope and forging documents, and he soon had his first experience of a Spanish jail when he was convicted in 1992 for drug dealing. He was arrested again in 1999 for the same offence, and this time was sent to a detention centre outside Madrid. With an Algerian cellmate, he started a fire in an attempt to break out. In 2000 he was back in prison in Morocco, having run someone over while drink-driving.

According to Ahmidan's brother Mustafa, this was the turning point when Jamal found Islam as the solution to his messy life. Mustafa testified to police that in prison Jamal gave up heroin, cocaine and alcohol and became a religious fanatic. On his release, however, this did not prevent him taking up his former career as a dope dealer. Only this time he was on a mission.

By now Jamal was an expert at negotiating the Madrid underworld and also a regular worshipper at the mosque in the Villaverde district of Madrid. This combination of criminal expertise and religious faith was toxic. He bought the explosives for the Madrid bombing with money made from his drug deals. For Ahmidan, this was a perfect and blessed exchange: to use the profits made from Western corruption in the holy war against the West.

One of the documents found by police in the *locutorio* on Calle de los Tribuletes after the bombings, described the bombers as 'most valuable young men who have changed history'. Certainly this is how they thought of themselves. They exulted in how the bombings in Madrid immediately divided Spain into two factions: the small minority in government who blamed the killing on the Basque separatist group ETA, who were no strangers to organized violence in Madrid, and the overwhelming majority of Spaniards, of all political views, who sensed a cover-up, a refusal to describe the bombing as an Islamist attack. In the days after the bombing their anger grew into a ferocious contempt for the government – obvious liars who were now mocking the dead by refusing to tell the truth. Spaniards with long memories claimed that they had never seen such heightened emotions on the streets since the Civil War of the 1930s.

For a brief moment, as Spain seemed about to split apart once again, the bombers must have imagined that the expulsion of the Moors from Al-Andalus was finally being avenged. Meanwhile in the radical mosques of Tangier, the worshippers exulted that it was Jamal Zougam from Tangier and his friend Jamal Ahmidan from Tetouan, the spiritual sons of Fizazi, who had divided the Spanish nation.

Outside Morocco, the attack in Madrid was seen as a blow against Europe, against Spain, the former colonial power. But it was also more complicated: it was part of a hidden Moroccan civil war – the long-standing conflict between Spanish-speaking Tangier in the north and the French-speaking élites of the south, Casablanca and Rabat. Nearly everyone in Tangier supports Spanish football teams. This is partly a provocation – they invoke Spain against France and French influence. At football matches between Tangier and the French-speaking teams, fans used to sing the Spanish national anthem or pro-Franco songs. Since the government banned this, they simply hum the tunes.

The north of Morocco has always been poorer than the south, to the extent that they sometimes seem to be two very different countries, with a largely Berber-speaking peasantry in the north, and in the south a metropolitan Arab class who use French easily, dress like the French (both men and women), and, if they have the money and visas, move easily between France and Morocco. In the north, where there has been little money and few visas, such a life seems impossible.

The hatred which inspired the Madrid bombing was not simply Islamist anger: it had a specifically Moroccan meaning. The bombing spoke directly to Moroccans; it was an act of revenge against the Moroccan French-speaking élites of Rabat and Casablanca who had wrecked Tetouan and Tangier and left its inhabitants to rot in squalor. As such it was an assault on the real mother of French-speaking Morocco – the hated nation of France.

27

The Neuilly–Marrakesh Express

In the early 2000s, in a place like the Café Arabe in the Medina of Marrakesh, it was possible to drink vodka and lime on the roof terrace, motoring on ecstasy or coke, surveying the roofs of this ancient city, while below most people lived on less than a euro a day. Mohammed VI had opened Morocco to the outside world as a glitzy destination. Marrakesh was the main focus, but other cities like Tangier and Fez also cleaned up their Medinas, got rid of the hustlers, imported 'tourist police' to ensure 'security', offered the 'Riad' experience, and presented the image of an exotic but ultimately sanitized and safe holiday destination

Morocco, and especially Marrakesh, became particularly attractive to French visitors. Jacques Chirac was a frequent and much feted visitor to the city, and he was followed by pop stars and film idols. Many Moroccans were proud to see the likes of Gérard Depardieu or Sophie Marceau on holiday in the country. But they were also proud of home-grown 'Franco-Moroccan' celebrities such as the comedian Jamel Debouzze or the singer Sophie Saidi, who had won a reality-TV singing contest and went on to become an actress. Morocco's status as a glamorous destination was confirmed when, in 2004, *Paris Match* published a thirteen-page cover story on '*Mohammed VI en famille*': the royal couple wore Western clothes and complained of how

cramped the king's quarters were at Salé and how they needed
to move to Dar Essalam, a huge estate of orchards and orange
groves, to bring up their family. It could have been the profile
of any Hollywood couple.

In 2007 President Nicolas Sarkozy came to Marrakesh,
lavishing extravagant praise on the king. It seemed then that the
links between the Moroccan royal family and the French élite
had never been stronger. These were apparently good times
for both countries; everybody was rich, or, at least, the French
and Moroccan media pretended that was so. Sarkozy's political
headquarters in Paris was the affluent suburb of Neuilly, also the
home of rock stars and the richest politicians. There were jokes
in the Moroccan and French press about the Neuilly–Marrakesh
Express – a connection which suddenly made Morocco
sound as chic and exclusive as its Parisian mirror image. Few
commentators in either country wanted to acknowledge,
however, a parallel trajectory, from the French *banlieues* back
to the *bled*, the poor heartlands of Morocco – journeys marked
by poverty, necessity and exile. These were two worlds which
could only meet in collision.[1]

Yet on the surface, during these years, Morocco did seem to
be undergoing a kind of cultural revolution. The word *nayda* –
with the meaning of 'awakening' – was used to describe what
was happening: a blaze of movies, music, art and literature,
all defined by their 'modernity'. Those who promoted *nayda*
compared it to the Spanish *movida* of the 1980s, the moment
when Spain ceased to the austere and miserable state under
Franco, a country adrift from the mainstream of political and
cultural life, and rejoined the Western world in a new wave of
nightclubs, rock bands and movies, proclaiming total liberty at
all costs, as exemplified by the films of Pedro Almodóvar.

One of the key markers of the *nayda* in Morocco was a
newly independent press, which wrote both in Arabic and
French. Leading the way was the magazine *Tel Quel*, edited by

Ahmed Benchemsi, a graduate of the Sorbonne and Sciences-Po, whose stated intention was to 'show Moroccan realities behind public declarations of intentions and the mystifications'. *Tel Quel*'s agenda was to break down taboos around sex, religion and politics. The tone was generally satirical but never wholeheartedly polemical. Above all, *Tel Quel* sounded a young note: its writers read French magazines such as *Marianne* and *Les Inrockuptibles*, which blended hip sensibility with serious cultural and political reporting.

The Arabic equivalent of *Tel Quel* was *Nichane*, which means 'direct' or 'the way it is' in dialectal Arabic. *Nichane* had the same agenda as *Tel Quel*, but its more conservative Arabic-speaking readership meant it was inevitably headed for conflict. This first controversy came in 2006 when the magazine published an issue on *noukates* (jokes) about sex, politics and religion. This provoked anger not only from Islamist groups but also in the government; eventually fines and prison sentences were handed down to journalists. The magazine limped on until 2007. Both *Nichane* and *Tel Quel*, sharp and ambitious as they were, represented wishful thinking rather than a real movement of change. Benchemsi left *Tel Quel* in 2011 to move to the United States. The magazine still exists, but its circulation has fallen and its influence is much diminished.

The biggest cause célèbre of this period, however, was the film *Marock*, directed by Leila Marrakchi, a teenage of rite-of-passage movie set in Casablanca in 1997, featuring a group of rich Moroccan school kids, educated at the élite French-speaking Lycée Lyautey. The film caused a scandal in Morocco not only because of its references to drugs and sex, but because the main character, Rita, falls in love with Youri, a Jew. This romance is set against the increasing radicalization of her brother Mao, who is turning to political Islam. All of this makes the film sound better than it is; in fact, it is quite dismal fare. What films like *Marock* demonstrated was that, for the majority, the hoped-for *nayda* was not much more than an illusion. *Nayda* belonged to the metropolitan élite which moved easily between France and Morocco, French and Arabic, lubricated by money and access to power. None of this applied to ordinary Moroccans in France or Morocco.

One film, however, did hit home in a more convincing manner. This was *Casanegra*, directed by Nour-Eddine Lakhmari and released in 2008. The plot is a typical crime scenario in which two young men, Adil and Karim, are out of their depth as they try to make a living scamming and hustling in downtown Casablanca, which they hate and refer to as 'Casanegra'. The film is fast, funny and violent – borrowing from Tarantino and Scorsese's *Mean Streets*. Aside from its international success – it won prizes across the world – it played to packed houses in all of Morocco's cities. Its depiction of the real life of Casablanca showed Moroccans for the first time how they actually lived.

In 2008, the year that *Casanegra* found its public, there were again stirrings of a mass protest movement, mostly directed against the increase in university fees, which in one fell swoop made higher education impossible for a generation. The students' anger was fuelled by the insanely high levels of unemployment across the country. It was bad enough that the universities, underfunded and poorly resourced, should be used to mask the reality of unemployment, but it was even worse to see to this fiction torn to shreds. On 14 and 15 May over a thousand police and military poured into the university residences of Marrakesh to put a violent end to the student protests against the privatization of the university. The police used tear gas, rubber bullets and brutality – there were claims that students were thrown off rooftops. For their part, wearing hoodies and throwing Molotov cocktails, employing tactics they had seen used in the French *banlieues*, the students fought the security services hard. They all remembered an earlier battle almost a year earlier at the village of Harbil, twenty-five kilometres outside Marrakesh, where security services crushed a demonstration against the demolition of the village to make way for tourist housing; the battle cry, then and now, was 'Who owns Marrakesh?'

The government was intent on ensuring that the answer to that question was not the native inhabitants of the city. By now Marrakesh had become known throughout the world as a kind of Arabia-lite, offering tourists a safe glimpse of the exotic Muslim world. But this hid harsher and deeper realities. French and other European visitors mingled in Djemaa el-Fna, the main square, with young people who would never earn a fraction of what the tourists had. Now the talk was of a new 'intifada' against the outsiders and the government that lured them here.

The heroine of the Marrakesh movement was a young woman, Zahra Boudkour, a twenty-year-old student who was arrested by police, stripped naked, and left for three days in a cell with other inmates, visibly menstruating. Other detainees in the police station claimed that they were tortured, treated as 'terrorists'. Zahra went on hunger strike and almost died. When she was finally released in 2010, the whole region exploded in joy and anger. In Djemaa el-Fna square, the crowds brandished portraits of Che Guevara, Lenin and Mao – these demonstrators were not the Islamist demons which the government complained were a threat to Moroccan democracy, but far-left militants protesting against poverty and injustice. All of this was watched by police, maintaining a steady cordon between protesters and tourists.

A month or so later, the demonstrations were followed by more violent clashes in the southern town of Sidi Ifni. The Al Jazeera television channel claimed that police had killed several people, but this was denied by the Moroccan authorities, who later imposed a punishing fine on the Al Jazeera office in Rabat. In the first few months of 2009, there were widespread and often violent demonstrations against Mohammed VI, his perceived pro-Western stance and in favour of Hamas. As ever, the protests were fuelled by conspiracy theories. The Russians had started to make their presence felt in Moroccan political life, and were proposing to establish a private English-speaking university outside Rabat. There were wilder theories that the Algerian and the Syrian secret services, with Russian backing, were seeking to provoke an Islamist uprising that would give Iran a foothold in the far west of the Muslim world. Such theories were given substance by the often mysterious financial backing for projects such as the so-called 'Syrian Mosque' in Tangier, hotels and other joint capital ventures.

Towards midday on 28 April 2011, a remote-controlled bomb exploded on the balcony of the Café Argana on Djemaa el-Fna square. This is one of the most popular tourist sites in the city, where visitors can take panoramic photos; like thousands of others, I had been there and done that with my own father and wife on a holiday to Marrakesh a few years earlier. The bomb killed seventeen people, most of them of French nationality. President Nicolas Sarkozy was furious and promised publicly that the killers would not go unpunished.

At first the Moroccan authorities claimed that the bomb was no more than an unfortunate gas explosion. This was dismissed straight away by security experts and eyewitnesses, who testified that the flames which ripped through the tourist crowd could only have come from a planned explosion. The term 'al-Qaeda' was then tossed about in the Moroccan press, but nobody really believed this: these were not al-Qaeda's methods, and the organization had no strategic interest in Marrakesh. Fingers were pointed at Islamists, recently released from prison, but again this did not really add up. The bomb had exploded only a few months after the revolution in Tunisia, but again the timing and execution of the massacre did not make sense in this context. Conspiracy theories – citing Syrian, Algerian or Iranian interests – abounded. The government had to react, and in October 2011 a certain Adil Al Atmani was condemned to death for the crime. Alleged accomplices were given light sentences. No one was convinced by this spectacle of justice, least of all the French families of those who had died, who accused the Moroccan judicial system of a cover-up. This was the darker side of the Neuilly–Marrakesh express, which no one in the French and Moroccan élite had wanted to see a few years earlier.

Of course there had always been a few dissenting voices, mainly on the Moroccan side. Chief among them was Ali Amar, an unrepentant controversialist who, with Aboubakr Jamai, founded *Le Journal Hebdomadaire* in 1997. As far the authorities were concerned, Amar's biggest crime as editor was to argue for transparency and accountability in the murkiest quarters of government. The bombing of the Café Argana was precisely the kind of 'mysterious event' that led him to suspect political intrigue. He always seemed to be just within the boundaries of the law. This did not prevent the government spreading rumours, via the PJD (Justice and Development Party), that Ali was a pro-Western agent who had even published the forbidden Danish satirical cartoons of the Prophet in his magazine (in reality he had published a photograph of a European looking at these pictures).

The *Journal Hebdomadaire* finally shut down in 2010, plagued by debts, reviled by Islamists and government alike. Aboubakr Jamai went to New York while Amar made for Paris as a safe haven, though he claims he had underestimated Sarkozy's close links to 'M6'; he found himself almost immediately deported to Casablanca on the orders of the Moroccan authorities. There he was arrested at the apartment of Zineb el Rhazoui, a feminist and fellow journalist (el Rhazoui had made herself notorious in Morocco for organizing 'picnics' at the height of Ramadan: for this she, too, was harassed and eventually locked up). On his arrest, Amar was beaten up, but was finally released. He now lives in France and Slovenia, where he claims that he is still regularly intimidated by the security forces.

The Suicide Solution

The Arab Spring never quite arrived in Morocco. The frustration had the same emotional force as in Tunisia or Egypt, but the rage never quite caught fire.

None the less, the early months of 2011 in Morocco, like everywhere else in the Arab World, were marked by demonstrations and protests, often spontaneous and often quickly turning violent. In February in Tangier, there were riots and demonstrations against French business interests, which were growing across the city. Mohammed VI had to make difficult choices: on the one hand he had to recognize the anger of the masses and concede ground on the constitution, making government more open and less opaque; on the other hand he could not afford to have the government undermined and overturned by the Islamist factions. The police, the military and the secret services kept a tight hold on all groups and individuals they perceived as a threat. Morocco's international reputation was not enhanced by rumours of collusion in torture and 'extraordinary rendition', while radical Islamists certainly saw the government of 'M6' not only as apostate but as an active collaborator with the hated forces of the West.

The hopes of ordinary Moroccans, which had been raised by events in Tunisia, quickly turned to despair. This found a new form of expression when demonstrators, realizing their impotence, began to make threats of collective suicide as a form of protest. These suicides started to happen in 2011 and 2012: there is disturbing YouTube footage of youths drinking and covering themselves in petrol in Casablanca and Rabat, before hurling themselves at police like human incendiary devices.

The main focus for the anger was Rabat, where regular

demonstrations were held outside parliament. These were well choreographed but began to turn into an empty ritual. 'The government has accepted that we are here and we can demonstrate more loudly than we used to, but still no one wants to hear us,' I was told this by Driss, a twenty-six-year-old postgraduate student from Fez who had come to Rabat to demonstrate. His mates soon started to chip in, keen to let the outside world know their story. 'Morocco is a prison,' they said. 'We are dying of boredom.' The most frequently repeated demand was: 'France must help us!' They hated the French for not doing more, and, like the young Algerians I had met in Algiers, they resented most of all the money and power of their own French-speaking élites.

But if Moroccans still look north to France, they avert their eyes with dread and fear from Algeria, their nearest neighbour in the east. With its art deco palaces and 1930s French colonial architecture, there is no city in the world which looks more like Algiers than Casablanca. Most Moroccans hope that the resemblance will stop there.

Part Four

TUNISIA,
MADE IN FRANCE

28

The Mysteries of Tunis

On 14 January 2011 President Zine Ben Ali finally fled his palaces in Tunis, heading for exile in Saudi Arabia. On the streets of Paris the mood that day was as festive as it was in cities across Tunisia. This was because the unthinkable had happened: Ben Ali had been in power since 1987 and seemed poised to stay in command for as long he liked – which, given his good health and vanity, could have been for a very long time – but, within a few short weeks, he was gone.

The catalyst for the angry demonstrations that led to his departure was the self-immolation of a twenty-six-year-old street vendor called Mohammed Bouazizi in the obscure Tunisian town of Sidi Bouzid. At 8 a.m. on 17 December 2010 'Besboos', as he was known locally, set up his cart of fruit as usual in the centre of town. At around 10 a.m. he began to be harassed by police officers who claimed that he did not have a permit and had no right to be there.

The reality was that Mohammed had simply not paid enough bribes and kickbacks to the local police, even though he had already put himself 200 dollars in debt by borrowing money to pay off officials. But Mohammed was in a defiant mood that day and stood his ground when a middle-aged female officer insulted him, cursed his dead father, and tried to seize his cart. When the officer grabbed his weighing scales, his most expensive piece of equipment, without which he could not conduct any business, the young man broke down. Angry beyond belief, unable to control his weeping, he ran to the local governor's office to complain at this vicious injustice. The governor refused point blank to see him. In a torment of frustration, Mohammed stood outside the governor's and threw a can of petrol over himself. To the horror of the small crowd that was gathering around him, he then set the petrol alight. His body was ablaze as he staggered in circles in mute agony. This was at 11.30, just an hour or so after the original row over his cart.

Mohammed died a few days later in hospital. His suicide has now gone down as the spark that lit the flame of the Tunisian revolution. As he lay dying, the ordinary people of Sidi Bouzid rose up against the petty bureaucrats who had held them in check until then. When the insurrection gained momentum, the military stopped trying to control the events and hundreds of thousands of Tunisians glimpsed that this was their first chance to oppose the authorities. Riots spread across the country and within a breathless few weeks, in the face of the hatred of his people, President Ben Ali was gone.[1]

In the meantime, riots and rebellions had spilled over into Algeria, Morocco, Jordan, Egypt and Yemen. This was the beginning of what would later be called the 'Arab Spring' or the 'Arab Revolution'.

It was the fairy-tale nature of the revolution which was celebrated on the streets of Paris on the day of Ben Ali's departure. France has a Tunisian population of more than 700,000 people, mostly concentrated in the Parisian region. Everywhere you went in Paris during the revolt in Tunisia, portable televisions blared at top volume in shops, takeaways and cafés, broadcasting a polyglot, polyphonic babble from Al Jazeera, Al-Arabiya and the French-speaking channels from the Maghreb. Everybody was excited and wanted to talk, especially the Tunisians themselves.

What was most stunning about these events – at least for those who did not know Tunisia – was that they had been set in motion in a country the West saw as a moderate, stable and apparently inconspicuous player in the politics of the region. Until this happened, the entire outside world thought of Tunisia as a downmarket tourist destination, with a servile attitude towards the West. All Tunisians knew that this view of their country was at best no more than wishful thinking and at worst a deliberate lie.

The bullying experienced by Bouazizi was the kind of thing which happened in Tunisia every day. It was directly connected to the people in power, who not only permitted but actively encouraged this low-level intimidation. When Mohammed Bouazizi set himself on fire, his action spoke directly to a nation ready to stake all for freedom. The president's flight into exile was justice long overdue. 'When Ben Ali left it was a beautiful moment,' I was told by a young woman who had been out on the streets to protest against him in Tunis. 'I did not know that such happiness was possible.'

In contrast to the jubilation of the Tunisian population in Paris that day, the mood of official France was sombre. The fall of Ben Ali was not at all what the French government wanted to happen. From the moment that he came into power in 1987, successive French governments had supported his régime, spurred on by him invoking Algeria and the threat of Islamist terrorism as a possibility in Tunisia. The French had taken Ben Ali at his word and turned a blind eye to all manner of abuses in the name of preserving 'stability' in Tunisia. They had also believed his hold on the country was unassailable.

'We were taken by surprise,' said Henri Guaino, special adviser to Nicolas Sarkozy with a particular brief for Mediterranean affairs. 'Nobody saw what was happening. It all happened very fast, a chain of events that degenerated very quickly.'

He also admitted, 'I had not been vigilant enough about the development of the régime and Tunisian public opinion.' This was putting it very mildly.[2] Since the late 1980s, successive French governments had become mired in compromising and contradictory relationships with Tunisia. French diplomats had reported on the brutal nature of Ben Ali's régime as far back as 1990, but the authorities in Paris had looked the other way.

Most disgracefully, on 11 January 2011, Michèle Alliot-Marie, the French Minister of State for Justice, Defence and Home Affairs, stood before the National Assembly in Paris and declared that the revolt in Tunisia was 'a complex situation' and that it was not for the French government to 'give any lessons to the régime'. It was hard to imagine a more arrogant and self-serving statement, as the people of Tunisia were fighting for their freedom. But there was worse to come: Alliot-Marie went on to offer the French military's 'world-renowned savoir-faire' to Ben Ali's régime, and to deliver this 'savoir-faire' to Tunis. The response, across all parties, was open-mouthed incredulity. Was the French minister really suggesting that French soldiers or police would fire on crowds in Tunis?

Sarkozy immediately distanced himself publicly from her – his adviser reported that Alliot-Marie had been giving her 'own personal analysis of the situation'. The Left was slower to react, partly because many on the Left, including the mayor of Paris, had their own issues with Tunisia. In the regions and in the *banlieues* of France, however, the speech provoked anger. In Algeria the daily newspaper *Liberté* made the point that, in her arrogance, Michèle Alliot-Marie 'has apparently no fear of awakening the memories of peoples who have already known historically the military "savoir-faire" of France. These memories are facts: regarding Algeria, we can recall 11 December 1960 in Algiers, in the quartier of Belcourt, and 17 October in Paris in 1961 – just to give two examples.' Tunisians bloggers – blogging was now the main form of communication in the country – were furious and sarcastic. '*Merci La France!*' was the response from a campaign on Facebook.

The controversy deepened even further over the next few days when it emerged that Alliot-Marie, who had close and friendly links with Ben Ali himself, had spent the Christmas of 2010 in a luxury resort in Tabarka, and had travelled there in a private jet belonging to an intimate friend of Ben Ali, who also happened to be criminal. It was then revealed that she had recently bought an apartment in the holiday complex of Gammarth, just outside Tunis. Meanwhile Tunisia went up in flames.

Few Tunisians were surprised at this French duplicity. In the past few years they had seen Ben Ali and his family and friends become extremely rich by plundering the nation. Tunisia was not a wealthy Arab country – for one thing, it has no oil money. But this did not prevent Ben Ali and his associates looting the country's resources and spending the money in France.

After the Revolution

When I arrived in Tunis in the autumn of 2012, I was practically the only Westerner landing that afternoon. I could see straight away that everything had changed since my last visit in 2011. I had been a fairly frequent visitor to Tunis from 2005 onwards, but had not been back since the revolution. Now it was the same city but a very different place.

On the short drive into town from the airport, the suburbs looked dirtier and more broken than they had before. The most obvious change to the cityscape was the absence of the huge portraits of Ben Ali, which, until the revolution, had lined every main road in and around the city. As we headed into the city centre, there was graffiti everywhere, often in several languages, not just Arabic; the graffiti in English, French and Spanish called for more revolution, declaring war on the West and all those who hated Islam.

A few days earlier the US Embassy in Tunis had been attacked and the American School had been burned down by a Salafist mob, apparently demonstrating against the provocative anti-Muslim film *The Innocence of Muslims*. Only days before this, the American ambassador to Libya had been murdered by a jihadist militia. In Tunisia, the Americans had pulled out all their staff and citizens to let the Tunisians know that they were not to be messed with. The atmosphere was made even more brittle by the publication in France of images of the Prophet in the satirical magazine *Charlie Hebdo*. As a consequence, the substantial French population of Tunisia had been frightened off the streets by death threats from the Salafists and stayed at home.

On my previous visits to Tunis, I had always thought that it was an easy place to work; it was safe and well organized. But despite its beauty and apparent order, there was always a secret and sinister side to Tunisian life. You were not exposed to the kind of violence and extremism which had so marked life in Algeria, nor was it as wretchedly poor as Morocco. Instead, Tunisia reminded me of my time in Romania in the early 1990s, where, even after the fall of Ceausescu, ordinary people were afraid to say what they really thought. Romanians described this as 'auto-censure' – self-censorship – and said that it was far more effective than the Securitate, the secret police. Nearly everybody I met in Tunisia before the revolution had adopted these habits of mind. It was a place where you could not really connect with anyone. The secret police were ever-present, listening and watching. But they were not really needed in a country where no one dared to criticize the government anyway.

When the journalist Christopher Hitchens came here in 2007 to write a piece for *Vanity Fair*, he wrote that his friend Edward Said had described Tunisia to him as the 'gentlest country in Africa'.[3] He was not disappointed by the stylishness of the Avenue Habib Bourguiba, the main artery in Tunis, the olive groves and the sheer gorgeousness of the island of Djerba (where nineteen tourists were killed in an al-Qaeda attack in 2002).

Hitchens found Tunisia to be a 'mild' place and, although he expressed disquiet at the twenty years that Ben Ali had been in power, the ubiquity of his image and the general reluctance of people to discuss politics, he was comforted by the availability of contraception, young people holding hands, and other clearly visible signs of 'Western values' and indifference to the puritan values of Islamism. Hitchens was obviously writing in good faith and reporting what he saw. This is what everyone saw when they first came to Tunisia. Below the surface there was, however, a bitter version of Tunisian reality at work within the nation's psyche.

As in Algeria and Morocco, one of the few places you could glimpse the inner rage of the Tunisians was at football matches. In September 2008 I watched a crowd of no more than a hundred fans of Espérance Sportive Tunis – the major team of the country – take on the riot police in the backstreets around Place de Carthage and Place de Barcelone. What impressed me most was how skilled and organized the 'hooligans' were – they were a quick-moving, agile force, constantly changing while remaining a solid phalanx. They smashed windows and roared through back alleys. They were completely in control of the situation and evidently enjoyed this battle with the foot soldiers of the régime. Later, in the Bar Celestina, a smoke-filled drinking den near the metro station, I spoke to a group of them. They were quick to make the point that they were not fighting other teams but only the police, which was the armed wing of the government. No one mentioned Ben Ali, but he was the obvious enemy.

So were the French. During the Ben Ali years, Tunisia was unofficially France's most favoured nation in the Maghreb. The links between Ben Ali and a succession of French presidents, from Mitterrand to Chirac and Sarkozy, were always firm and longstanding. Ben Ali travelled often to Paris, his 'real capital', where he lived lavishly and courted not only the French political élite but also the more dubious figures of the Trabelsi clan. Ben Ali's second wife Leila was a member of the Trabelsi family, a Mafia-like organization based in the most expensive *quartiers* of Paris and Nice that effectively ran Tunisia as their private fiefdom. All Tunisians knew that the fall of Ben Ali was not only due to the ideological sterility of his government, but also to the fact that his large-scale pillaging of the country in collusion with the Trabelsis was about to be exposed. That is why he fled Tunisia so quickly.

The New Tunisia

On a bright and sunny Friday morning in late September 2012, I set out to rediscover Tunis. I wanted see for myself what exactly had happened here since the revolution. I had arranged to meet friends and colleagues who had lived through the events. It seemed to me to be a rare and magical privilege to be in a place that had changed history, and to speak to the people who had seen it happen. I began my walk from my hotel near the Nelson Mandela metro station, heading for the Place Palestine and then the centre of town.

For all the low-grade tourist packages, Tunisia still struck me as a mysterious country for non-Tunisians. In fact, tourism had mainly served to visitors keep away from Tunisians and Tunisian life by herding them into so-called *zones touristiques* – phoney hotel complexes which, if you stayed in them for more than a day or two, felt like miniature prisons. When I left for Tunis, there were huge advertisements in the Paris metro promising commuters '*douceur et tranquilité*' (gentleness and tranquillity) on the beaches of Tunisia. The same advertisements were the first thing I saw at the airport in Tunis, even though it was heaving at the time with refugees from the chaos in neighbouring Libya.

Beyond these hotel complexes the country was pretty much unknown territory to foreigners. This was especially true of Tunis. The few foreign writers who had paid any attention to the city in the nineteenth century – notably Gustave Flaubert and Guy de Maupassant – saw it as either a museum or an exotic repository of Oriental treasures.

In the twentieth century Tunis remained a cultural backwater. The most famous writer to emerge from the city was Albert Memmi, a native of the Jewish quarter, who argued loud and long against colonialism. His writing was matched in Arabic by the likes of Tahar Guiga (who also wrote in Greek and French) and the poet Abou Kacem Chaabi. But none of these writers ever had the international reputation or readership of Albert Camus. Nor did they bring the avant-garde glamour to Tunis that Paul Bowles, William Burroughs and the Beats brought to Morocco. One of the greatest jazz tunes ever composed is called 'Night in Tunisia', covered by Charlie Parker and Miles Davies among others, but the title was a random accident. To this day, Tunisia has barely registered as a cultural or political entity beyond France and the Maghreb.

Yet Tunis remains one of the loveliest cities in French North Africa. The Avenue Habib Bourguiba cuts through the centre, starting at the Porte de France on the lake, near the rue Charles de Gaulle, in a straight line to the Medina. It is flanked by trees, shops and *café terrasses*. The architecture is the rich, creamy art nouveau you can find in Algiers or Casablanca, except that here it is on a smaller, more intimate scale. The Medina is elegant and cool, with wide paved alleyways that feel more Turkish than North African. The mosques, with their thin minarets and low domes, have a Levantine appearance. The nerve-centre of the city is the *quartier populaire* of Halfouine at the far end of the Medina. As I walked through this district, it seemed much poorer and more wrecked than I had ever seen it before.

The greatest surprise was that you could no longer walk freely through the city. I had constantly to keep changing my route, diverted by armed patrols and checkpoints. The mosques that I passed were surrounded by the military, all carrying heavy weaponry and tense in face of the provocations from the robed and bearded young men who were going to prayer.

I kept hearing the muttered insult '*Dégage!*' (the French term meaning 'Get out!') which had been the slogan of the crowds during the revolution. The bearded young men were yelling this in the faces of the soldiers of the post-revolutionary government. The soldiers flinched, cocked their weapons but did not respond.

When I got to the French Embassy and the Saint-Vincent-de-Paul Cathedral, I found the road blocked by barbed wire and tanks. Most sinister of all were the so-called 'Ninjas' – special forces dressed in black, wearing ski masks and carrying sub-machine guns. They were lined up in front of the embassy, spilling over into the arcades leading to the Place de la Victoire. From a safe distance, bearded young men made throat-slitting gestures. It occurred to me that this how it must have been in Algeria in 1992.

I mentioned this to my friend and colleague Imen Yacoubi as we drank coffee in the Grand Café du Théâtre, just a hundred metres away from the soldiers and Islamists. The café was part of the old, elegant Tunis: a direct counterpoint to the poverty and anger outside on the streets. I asked Imen how long she thought this could last and whether it really was like Algeria in 1992 all over again. 'We don't know yet,' she said, 'but there is a lot of fear of the Islamists. Everyone is scared that they will make a revolution within the revolution.'

Imen teaches at the University of Jendouba, a poor town less than a half hour's drive from the Algerian border. She had come to Tunis during the demonstrations that signalled the end for Ben Ali. She stayed with her sister and watched history unfold in the streets, willing the changes to happen. She is a direct person who is not given to exaggeration or hyperbole, yet she described the mass movements as 'beautiful', 'unbelievable' and 'mystical', and when she did so her eyes shone.

But now the revolution was entering a dangerous new phase. The current bogeyman was Abou Iyadh, leader of the Salafist group Ansar-el-Charia (Partisans of Sahria), who was then being hunted by the police for organizing the attacks on the US Embassy. Iyadh had followed an entirely predictable route for a jihadi, from Algeria in the 1990s, via Afghanistan and Britain. He had returned to Tunisia after the revolution vowing 'to sow discord'. His followers were now poised for action, he declared in the wake of the attack on the US Embassy. I had just come from the Mosque El Fatah, where he usually preached, which was now surrounded by soldiers in a stand-off with the faithful – not just '*les barbus*' but young men without beards, who could have been a football crowd from the French *banlieues*, wearing T-shirts and scarves over their faces.

Imen said she was 'ashamed' at what was happening. 'This is not Tunisia,' she said, 'this is not what we fought for.' However, Iyadh's star was on the rise: according to the Ministry of the Interior, the Salafists controlled nearly a quarter of the mosques in the country and had almost 100,000 hard-core supporters. A security expert from a Western embassy told me that what had been most shocking about the attack on the US Embassy was the scale and the savagery of the violence, and that this could quickly get worse.

In the eyes of the Tunisians, the real problems were unemployment and the sense that nothing had changed under the revolution, that life had in fact got worse. That evening I walked past the bars and semi-brothels in rue Ibn Khadloun and rue Oum Khaltoum. They were just around the corner from the quiet stylishness of Avenue Habib Bourguiba but were as hard-drinking and hard-core as any place in Algiers, Casablanca or Tangier. As darkness fell, men were literally falling over themselves in a fog of cigarette smoke, beer, and an all-pervading scent of piss. Everybody hated the Salafists, but they also hated the government, who they referred to as either 'Salafists in disguise' or 'the French'.

'We are not yet free,' I was told by a guy called Omar, who was chain-smoking out on the street but wasn't drinking. Omar asked me the time and we fell into conversation. He was obviously trying to hustle me but he also had a few things to say. I asked how he felt about the revolution. 'We thought that the Europeans would help us, that the French would give us money and aid. But instead they insult us.' (He was referring to the *Charlie Hebdo* cartoon.) He went on: 'The French who come here pretend to love us but really they despise us.' Like all Tunisians, he had not forgotten that at the height of the revolution, the French Minister of State for Justice, Defence and Home Affairs had almost offered to send French security forces to support Ben Ali. Still, Omar wanted to go to France, but he knew no one he could bribe for a visa and had no money anyway. Omar was not a Salafist, but by his admission he could easily become one. 'Why not?' he said. 'I can't get to France. There's nothing else here now. Why not fight for God?'

29

Stealing Tunisia

For most of its history, during the period of the French protectorate and after independence, the relationship between Tunisia and France has been defined by its inferior, often cowed position towards the European power. This dates back to the early nineteenth century, when Tunisia, like Algeria, was a fragile regency at the crumbling edges of the Ottoman Empire, vulnerable to attack by predatory European powers.

One of the first French visitors to Tunis was Jean-André Peyssonnel, a doctor from Marseilles who travelled to North Africa in 1724 on the orders of the French king Louis XV and 'in the interest of science' (he was particularly interested in finding a cure for plague, which eventually killed him at the age of eighty). Peyssonnel also visited Algiers, which he found to be much more sinister and dangerous than Tunis. He described Tunis as a place of limited interest, with buildings in the 'Turkish style' and a generally backward air, although he admired the climate and could see potential for agriculture. Peyssonnel had no strong political convictions but was sure that these savage and 'barbarous' states that he visited could only be improved by European domination.[1] Conflict inevitably followed. In 1770, Louis XV ordered Admiral De Broves to bombard the cities of Bizerte, Porto Farina and Monastir in response to Tunisian acts of piracy.

At this stage Tunisia did not exist as a nation state but rather as a family of squabbling tribes who were most of the time beyond the controlling authorities in the capital, Tunis. Until 1816 the main source of revenue for the government was piracy, but this melted away after a coalition of European navies signed the treaty of Aix-la-Chapelle, which sought to put an end to it. The panicked response of the rulers of Tunis was to levy heavy taxes on agriculture and trade; meanwhile the court in Tunis continued to spend lavishly, demanding luxury as the birthright of the Bey. But the real enemy for Tunisia was the ever-increasing pace of European industrialization, which had begun its long march across the globe in pursuit of goods and markets. By the 1830s, as the French began to settle in Algeria, the Tunisian government was seriously and irrevocably in debt. For advice, they turned to France.

This was partly to appease the country which had so swiftly and mercilessly invaded neighbouring Algeria, but the French had also been actively courting Tunisia as the logical extension of its North African empire. During this period Tunisia was ruled by Ahmad Bey, a reformer who believed in the project of European modernity and its potential to help Tunisia compete on its own terms with the more developed European nations. To this end, he set up an army on the European model, with a military academy and factories to manufacture its uniforms and weapons. Reform was a risky business – although Tunisia enjoyed a reasonable degree of autonomy from the Ottoman Empire and could make its own policies, the distance from Istanbul also meant that it was vulnerable to European political and military interference. The Italians and the British, as well as the French, were clearly keeping a predatory eye on Tunisia.

If Ahmad Bey underestimated the difficulties of modernization, one of his closest advisers saw them all too clearly. Khayr al-Din, one of the most important political figures in Tunisia, had been trained by French army officers in Ahmad Bey's new army yet remained faithful to the Islamic traditions of the Ottoman Empire. Having risen to the rank of general, he spoke French, Arabic and Turkish, and travelled widely through Europe and the Ottoman Empire. He saw that the only future for Muslim countries was to compete with European nation states as developed, industrialized nations. He wrote angrily about how Tunisian raw materials – wool, cotton and silk – were sold at rock bottom prices to Europeans, and then sold back to Tunisians at a high price once they had been processed into luxury goods. He called for investment in factories and a government intelligent enough to manage its own affairs.[2]

He watched in despair as Tunisia, instead of becoming a modern nation, slid into insolvency and ultimately the hands of European bankers. This process was accelerated by the spend-thrift ways of Ahmad Bey, who squandered several fortunes on the factories, arsenals and tanneries needed to supply his 'European' army. Ahmad Bey had other vanities: he built a palace at Mohameddia, south of Tunis, which he called the 'new Versailles'. Impressive though it was, before long the factories were shutting down and Tunisia became poorer than it had ever been before. Khayr al-Din now decided that the only way for Tunisia to preserve its independence was to play European nations off against each other, encouraging them to take rival interests in Tunisia, each of them cancelling the other out. He achieved some success with this policy, but it was only a matter of time before the French moved in.

In the 1840s the French made their presence felt by offering military advice to Ahmad Bey and his European-style army. This was both a logistical and financial disaster. Most of the equipment came from France at a high price. Ever more desperate, the government imposed heavier and heavier taxes on a population which simply could not pay them. Poverty soon led to violence and the Tunisian people seethed with discontent as famine and illness ravaged the countryside. This did not stop future Beys from building luxurious palaces and trying to impress European consuls with their wealth. By 1869 the country was all but bankrupt.

This was exactly what the French had been waiting for ever since the invasion of Algeria. But before the country could fall into their hands, the French had to negotiate a solution with other European powers – notably Italy, Germany and Britain – who each laid a claim to a share of the spoils. All of these countries had made substantial loans to the Tunisian government and now feared non-repayment. Accordingly, an international commission was set up to oversee Tunisia's financial affairs. There was resistance from ordinary Tunisians and their leaders, but effectively the country was handed over to France at the Congress of Berlin in 1878. In return for Cyprus, Britain agreed to let the French do as they wished in Tunisia. Italy, which had a geographical proximity to and cultural influence within Tunisia, remained a rival. As the Italian demands for supremacy became louder in 1880, the French decided to act.

In 1881 the French claimed that 9,000 Tunisian tribesman had raided Algeria – now French territory. This was purely cynical: the raid had in fact been encouraged and staged by the French. Within days, to the sound of fake outrage from Paris, the French sent an expeditionary force across the border, first to Le Kef and then to Tunis. Humiliated, the Bey signed the treaty of Ksar Said, which gave the French control over all Tunisian foreign affairs.[3] In a popular Tunisian song of the period, the Bey was said to have 'sold his people like vegetables'.

For a few years there was resistance, mainly from the countryside and the southern coast, but the Tunisian forces were tactically naïve and poorly armed. Over 10,000 Tunisians fled as refugees to Libya, to reorganize and plan a war against the French. Libya was initially a safe haven because the Tunisians and Libyans, despite tribal differences, regarded themselves as essentially

the same people. But it was impossible to fight the superior
military technology of the French army. Worse still, the Bey
was openly hostile to any uprising. By 1885, driven by hunger
and political indifference, most of the refugees had either died
or trickled back to Tunisia. In 1883 the Bey had signed the
Treaty of Bardo, which named the sultan as nominal sovereign
but enforced French colonial rule over all Tunisian affairs.

From this point on, there was a powerful drive to make
Tunisia a colony on the model of Algeria, which sometimes
turned violent. It began with the seizure of all lands to the south
of Tunis from Tunisians without title deeds. In one fell swoop
tens of thousands of independent farmers were reduced to the
status of landless day labourers. At the same time, taxation was
increased and government spending was used to promote the
cause of the settlers. Mining rights were handed over to French
companies. By 1900 there were 25,000 French settlers in Tunisia,
controlling all public administration, business and agriculture.

Early Resistance

The main stumbling block for French ambitions in Tunisia in
the late nineteenth century was the fact that the French were
outnumbered five to one by Italians, who considered Tunisia to
be their territory. Indeed the Italian prime minister, Francesco
Crispi, described Tunisia as 'an Italian colony occupied by
France'. There were occasionally violent clashes between French
and Italian settlers, who tended to be from tough European
stock on both sides. The Italians took confidence from the fact
that there were so many of them established in the towns and
the countryside; the French held a tight grip on governance,
but at the same time sought 'demographic allies' in the Maltese,
Spanish and Catalans, whom they encouraged to emigrate to
Tunisia, diluting the Italian population and building a genuinely
cosmopolitan populace on the model of Algeria. Meanwhile
Tunisians saw themselves dismissed as 'natives' – they were kept

out of government and administration and rarely achieved the basic levels of literacy needed to escape the poverty of rural life. Indeed the settlers actively petitioned the authorities to scale down attempts to educate the Tunisians, on the grounds that it would give them the means to argue back against their colonial masters. They produced 'scientific' evidence to justify the racial inferiority of the 'Muslim', which made the case that education would be a waste of time.

In the years leading up to the First World War, the most organized resistance to the French came from the Young Tunisians, a group of French-speaking Nationalists who published their ideas in a French-language journal called *Le Tunisien*. The Young Tunisians were intellectuals from wealthy families, and as such quite separate from the Tunisian peasantry and urban working class, who could provide the only real mass opposition to the French. At first, they were not revolutionaries but reformists, who really sought integration into French society. None the less the French saw them as a threat and crushed them when the opportunity arose. The first chance came in 1911 over an incident in Tunis, when the French-controlled council proposed a survey of the Muslim cemetery at Jellaz. A Young Tunisian and council member called Abd Al-Jalis Zaouche declared that this was an intrusion into the intimacies of Islamic life. This was less a call to arms than a statement of fact, though a series of riots duly followed. During one of these mutinies, a group of Muslims was herded into the Italian quarter, where shooting broke out and dozens of Tunisians and Europeans were killed. The Young Tunisians were accused of provocative behaviour, but none of them could be found guilty of direct intervention, despite the best efforts of the French police.

In the wake of the Jellaz riots, there was a growing hatred between Tunisians and Italians. A few months later a Tunisian child was run over and killed by an Italian tram driver in the centre of Tunis. The Young Tunisians declared a boycott of public transport and a strike against the council. This was the moment the French had been waiting for: they rounded up leading figures in the Young Tunisians movement, sending them to prison or into exile on the grounds of treason.

The movement was set back further at the beginning of the First World War, when the Tunisian Ulama went against the orders of the sultan in Istanbul, who had ordered a jihad against the Allies. The Young Tunisians hardened their views and swore to turn Tunis into a battleground. However, despite committing most of their resources to the killing fields of Europe, the French kept enough of a standing army in Tunisia to suppress any serious attempt at insurrection. At the end of the Great War, with the effective death of the Ottoman Empire, many Tunisian Nationalists preferred to remain in exile in Turkey or Switzerland. Their day had not yet come.

The political atmosphere in Tunisia continued to be tense throughout the 1920s and 1930s. This was partly because of the deepening mire of poverty in which most Tunisians now lived. As the French sought to recapture their pre-war markets, taxes and prices had increased, while ordinary Tunisians found themselves locked into a cycle of financial misery. There were famines and disease, which provoked strikes and riots, all met with a predictably heavy hand by the French authorities, who were experienced in the managing of their colonial subjects, from Indochina to Morocco. At the same time, the European settlers who returned to Tunisia after the First World War found that the law was entirely on their side when it came to displacing 'native' populations.

Tunisian discontent at this betrayal was channelled into a new party called 'Dustur' (Constitution). This movement began as the logical successor to the Young Tunisians: it was made up of young intellectuals who had often been educated at French universities and who cautiously argued for reform, not for revolt. At the same time, working-class Tunisians were beginning to organize themselves into trade unions and small militant parties, often inspired by European Socialist movements but also faithful to Islamic traditions. They were unafraid to face armed police or imprisonment, and their stance captured the political imagination of ordinary Tunisians.

Full-scale Tunisian nationalism emerged in 1930, when a series of political errors by the French sparked off loud and angry protests about the true nature of the protectorate. The first mistake was the decision of the Catholic Church, with the backing of the Vatican and the Tunisian and French authorities, to hold an international Eucharistic Congress at Carthage in May 1930. Pamphlets promoting conversion to Christianity were printed in Arabic and distributed throughout Tunis; Catholic youths led a parade dressed as Crusaders in the streets of Tunis and Carthage. Meanwhile, the papal legate described the Islamic era in North Africa as 'fourteen centuries of desolation and death'. This was not only a deep insult to Islam but an affront to the very core of Tunisian Muslim identity. The Congress brought all strands of Tunisian nationalism together, from the dockers in the port of La Goulette who launched wildcat strikes, to students at the University of Zitouna, which contained the most powerful mosque in Tunis, as well as students and schoolchildren from all social classes. In the *La Voix du Tunisien*, the party newspaper of Dustur, a young man of twenty-seven called Habib Bourguiba, recently returned to Tunisia from his studies in France, wrote how shocked he was that such a naked show of power could go unchecked. The same newspaper noted that the Congress was funded by the taxes of the protectorate, paid by all Tunisians. This was the sharpest form of humiliation.[4]

The furore was repeated in 1931 when the French authorities allocated massive sums to commemorate the fiftieth anniversary of the French presence – a presence which most Tunisians increasingly thought of as an occupation. The French president, Gaston Doumergue, became embroiled in the affair when he announced that the protectorate represented the highest humanitarian principles, a statement which not only provoked anger but also was contradicted by the incarceration of the loudest opponents of this view, all clustered around *La Voix du Tunisien*.

This mood of militancy was expressed in a new journal called *L'Amal* (*L'Action* in French), founded by Habib Bourguiba and others in 1932. One of the journal's key themes was that the French had no right to interfere in Islamic affairs. Before long, many so-called *'Musulfrancs'*, Muslims with French identity papers, began to renounce their French nationality; this was the key step forward which Tunisian Nationalists had been waiting for. In 1932 Dustur broke into two factions: the 'Old' Dustur, which was still essentially reformist, and the 'New' or 'Neo' Dustur, a group of younger, militant Nationalists, including the likes of Bourguiba, who argued that independence had to be the final aim of the Nationalist movement. The Neo-Dustur was an energetic group – they announced their arrival on the French and Tunisian political scene with a flurry of pamphlets, strikes, demonstrations and provocations. They angered the French resident-general, Marcel Peyrouton, so much that he had Bourguiba and other militants sent into internal exile in the deep south of Tunisia, which, of course, only increased their prestige in Tunis.

The revolt against France took its most physical form yet in 1937 and 1938. The electoral success of the left-wing coalition known as the Front Populaire in France in 1936 had raised expectations in Tunisia that the way might finally be open to independence. Equally aware of this possibility, the *colons* in Tunisia did everything they could to sabotage the policies of the Front Populaire.

Tunisian ambitions were at their highest when the Socialist Pierre Viénot, the French Secretary of State for Foreign Affairs, arrived in Tunis and began to talk of autonomy in Tunisia.

Bourguiba, who was brought back from exile in 1936, had already been to see Viénot in Paris and had presented him with a timetable for change.

The optimism did not last long. The Front Populaire collapsed in France in June 1937 in the face of an economic crisis. The *colons* were delighted and, with the return of Viénot to France, the Résidence Générale had a free hand to crack down on dissident factions, singling out the Neo-Dustur party as the main enemy. In return, the Neo-Dustur spurned the advances of the moderate Dustur party and became ever more radical, announcing 'an economic war' against the French authorities.

The first wave of revolts took the form of local strikes, culminating in the call for a general strike on 20 November 1937. In the face of open rebellion, the French authorities grew ever more ruthless – on 8 January 1938 six Tunisians were killed and dozens of others injured during a demonstration in the northern town of Bizerte. The Tunisian resistance hardened as strikes and street protests spread across the country. The French now began to arrest the alleged leaders of the rebellion, including the charismatic youth leader Ali Belhouane and the intellectual Slimane Ben Slimane, who were accused of inciting racial hatred and attacking French interests. The Neo-Dustur party demonstrated and eventually appealed to the Bey for their release. When this was met by silence, they called for a general strike in Tunis on 8 April 1938.

The protests began around 10 a.m., as the shops and cafés of Tunis pulled their shutters down and a crowd of demonstrators, many of them armed with small miners' pickaxes in their pockets, made their way through the area of Halfouine towards the Résidence Générale, where they converged with a similar mob who had come from Bab Menara, on the edge of the Medina. By 2 p.m., under the watchful eye of French soldiers, their rifles pointed at the demonstrators, a crowd of 10,000 finally assembled at the gates of the Résidence Générale. When the angry speeches of the Neo-Dustur leaders were shrugged off and ignored, another demonstration was called for 10 April before the crowd peacefully dispersed.

Before the planned protest, however, on the morning of 9 April, the angry students of the University of Zitouna began to call for direct action. Their natural leader was Habib Bourguiba, whom they petitioned for instructions. In the meantime, the police and army had already started firing on the crowds in and around the Medina. As the crowds gathered and demonstrators began arming themselves, a Zouave – a Tunisian soldier under French command – was stabbed while trying to defend the Palais de Justice in the Casbah. The French retaliated with machine-gun fire, which rattled mercilessly through the narrow streets of the Medina, cutting down everyone who stood in the way. Twenty-two people were killed and 150 injured. The resident-general declared a state of emergency in Tunis. Within hours the neo-Dustur party was made illegal. To escape imprisonment, its leaders now went underground. For the French, this was a far more dangerous proposition than arguing openly against a political party.

Occupation and Independence

Unsurprisingly, Tunisian Nationalists were exultant at the Fall of France in 1941, although they were taken aback by the speed and ease with which the Germans had achieved their victory. At the same time, they were wary of the Vichy government, which soon assumed control and was as hostile to Nationalist ambitions as any previous authority. However, the most important fact for the Nationalists was that the French enemy had been weakened; this offered a real chance to destroy the French occupying force for good.

With the Fall of France, Habib Bourguiba, who had been interned in France since the 'events' of 1938, was moved by the Italian authorities to Rome. The Italians hoped that he would support their claim to Tunisia. But since Bourguiba trusted the Italians even less than the French, and was an avowed anti-Fascist, he refused to co-operate, much to the frustration of his 'hosts'. Instead, he placed his faith in the Allies. Meanwhile Tunisia, his mother country, was set to become one of the most deadly, complex and strategically important battlefields of the Second World War.

Tunisia was the only country in North Africa to be properly invaded and occupied by the German army. The prelude to this was the deterioration of relations between France and Italy, leading to Italy's declaration of war against France on 10 June 1940. As part of his *casus belli* against France, Mussolini made an explicit claim on Tunisia. As an initial response, the French mobilized troops in the southern part of Tunisia and along the borders with Libya and Algeria. The Germans arrived, partly to support Italian aggression, on 9 November. They met a weak French force, whose high command was divided over tactics and strategy. The Germans swept through the eastern part of country, while the Italians occupied a swathe of central Tunisia.

The political consequences of the German occupation were uncertain for Tunisian Nationalists. Most of the group around Old Dustur gave their allegiance to the Germans, seeing the occupation as a chance to finally settle scores with the French. Supporters of Neo-Dustur were also tempted to throw in their lot with the Germans. Members of both factions helped with anti-Semitic propaganda and pro-German rants in Arabic on Radio Berlin. Bourguiba, however, now in Cairo, shrewdly kept faith with the Allies.

The status of Jews in Tunisia under the German occupation was precarious. Having taken the country by force of arms, the Germans wasted no time in making anti-Jewish laws a political priority. Prior to their arrival, Tunisia had a thriving Jewish community of some 100,000. As was the case in Algeria, the Jews in Tunisia were mainly Francophile and pro-European, feeling that France was their protector; suddenly, with collapse of French law, they were exposed to new, raw winds of hatred. They were made to wear yellow badges, had their property confiscated, and were sent to labour camps in Tunisia and Europe.

Not all Tunisian Muslims supported the persecution of the Jews. In the wake of the German occupation, Khaled Abdul-Wahab, a clever young Muslim from a wealthy and powerful family in the coastal town of Mahdia, played a role as translator and mediator between the Germans and the local population. When he learned that a group of German officers were planning to rape a young Jewish woman called Odette Boukhris, he was stricken by rage and compassion and took her with him to his farm in the countryside, where she hid with several other Jewish families until the end of the occupation. For his actions, Khaled was nominated by the Israelis as one of the Righteous Among Nations, an honour for non-Jews who helped save Jews during the Holocaust. He remains the only Arab to have been nominated for this status.

Initially, the end of the war brought very little change to the situation in Tunisia: the French took up the reins of the protectorate with renewed vigour, and were newly suspicious of all Nationalist factions, suspecting them of treachery and of having worked for the Axis powers. Even Bourguiba, who had openly published his thoughts on the Allies, was interrogated by the French authorities on the grounds of treason when he returned to Tunisia. On 25 March 1945 he secretly fled the country, setting off in the dead of night in a fishing boat from the tiny port of Kerkennah. He re-emerged shortly afterwards in Cairo, from where he worked ceaselessly to bring Tunisia's cause to the international stage. This would have been a pointless task, except that in the years after the war the French were feeling especially threatened by developments in Algeria and realized that they could not afford instability in tiny but influential

Tunisia. Negotiations began after the violent repression of a strike in Sfax in 1947. By 1950 the French were openly talking to Bourguiba about the way forward.

The French settlers began to organize resistance to what they saw as a sell-out by the French government. They armed themselves and planned for the civil war which they hoped to ignite. The French government wavered under the threat of insurrection, but the violence only intensified. The most deadly pro-French organization was the shadowy grouping known as La Main Rouge, effectively a death squad, which then and now was rumoured to be directly linked to the French government. Between 1952 and 1954, over forty Tunisian Nationalists were killed in mysterious circumstances.

The most well known of these was Farhat Hached, who was machine-gunned to death in an ambush on 5 December 1952. This came at a crucial point in the negotiations between the French authorities and the Nationalists – Habib Bourguiba had recently been imprisoned again and Hached was rumoured to be plotting armed attacks in revenge. Hached miraculously survived the first hail of bullets but was shot in the head and then dumped on the street beyond Radès, a suburb to the south of Tunis. In the weeks leading up to his murder, the pro-French press had been literally calling for his head, but the French authorities denied any knowledge of the assassination, blaming 'extremists'. The news of Hached's death provoked anti-French riots or protests in Casablanca, Cairo, Damascus, Beirut, Karachi, Jakarta, Brussels and Stockholm. The killing was denounced in France by leftist intellectuals such as Roger Stéphane and Daniel Guérin.

Following the murder of Hached, groups of *fellagha*, peasants and unemployed workers, began to organize themselves into small armed groups. Although they were not co-ordinated by any central movement, they were still able to paralyse the workings of the French protectorate in western and southern

Tunisia, attacking farms, sabotaging communications and killing policemen. By 1954 the *fellagha* were a force of several thousand men, often taking refuge in Libya, were they were provided with arms. They were also building political links with the Neo-Dustur. In response, the French population began openly to support the 'extremist' groups in their own ranks.

Fearing internal disorder and international censure, the French government sought to start talks about independence again. To break the stalemate, they released Bourguiba from prison and brought him back to Tunisia. He returned to Tunis on 1 June 1955 to a rapturous reception – he arrived by sea and was met by a huge crowd, which followed him as he travelled on horseback through the streets to meet the Bey. The euphoria intensified on 3 June when Bourguiba and the Bey accepted the Convention Franco-Tunisienne, which, although it maintained monetary union, granted Tunisia independence.

This was clearly a very limited agreement and it helped the cause of Bourguiba's enemies within the Nationalist movement, led by Salah Ben Youssef, who argued that Bourguiba was a stooge of the French and was betraying the cause of pan-Arab nationalism. Throughout 1955 Youssef led a guerrilla war in southern Tunisia with the aim of destabilizing Bourguiba and frightening the French back on to a war footing. He was supported by the Egyptians and the Algerians.

Bourguiba, however, had the confidence of his people and held steady. Tunisia became fully independent on 20 March 1956, and five days later Bourguiba was elected president. Youssef was assassinated in exile in Frankfurt in 1961.

Modern Tendencies

As he assumed power, Bourguiba had a clear understanding of the challenges ahead. Firstly, he set about building a legal and political framework to replace the overarching structures of the protectorate. In the elections of 1959 he was given a wide-ranging mandate, which included the power to nominate members of the government and civil service. Tunisia became effectively a one-party state, led by Bourguiba's party, now named the Parti Socialiste Destourien (PSD). At the same he initiated an extensive set of reforms to 'modernize' Tunisia – these included banning polygamy and encouraging women's education and civil rights. Bourguiba's model was clearly Mustafa Kemal (known as Ataturk), who, as president of the Turkish Republic, had fought to bring Turkey into the modern age in the 1920s and 1930s.

Bourguiba's second major priority was to limit the role of Islam in Tunisian political life, or at least to enforce a separation between the religious authorities and the state. This was no small task – Tunisia had always had a powerful religious tradition and indeed the city of Kairouan is one of the holiest cities in the Muslim world, and one of the most visited after Mecca, Medina and Jerusalem. The local tradition is the Malekite school of Islam, which is receptive to local folklore and customs and is deeply embedded in Tunisian daily life.

Bourguiba did not seek to displace Islam from its place in Tunisian society but to limit its constitutional influence. With this in mind, he established the Zitouna Mosque in Tunis as a department of Theology at the university, rather than as a separate entity, and even challenged the practice of Ramadan, making the wily argument that to be engaged in a jihad excuses the believer from Ramadan, and that all Tunisians were engaged in a jihad against underdevelopment. However, the most difficult and compelling task for Bourguiba was to pull away from the overweening influence of the French, who, although they had officially left the country, still treated it as their own fiefdom.

Resisting French interference was complicated by the fact that Bourguiba insisted on French as the main language of instruction. There were practical reasons for this – classical Arabic was not widely understood and did not serve the needs of a country that was trying to catch up with science and technology. The Arabic dialects were also either mutually incomprehensible or impossible to transcribe. Although the use of French was pragmatic, it meant that after independence, as was the case in Algeria, the educational sector in Tunisia continued to be maintained by a French or Francophile élite, which tended to promote the European language as culturally superior.

The tensions with France came to a head in 1961 in the northern Tunisian coastal town of Bizerte. By this stage in the Algerian war, the Tunisian border had become a constant problem for the French. The French kept over a thousand soldiers stationed at Bizerte under the treaty that had given Tunisia independence, to secure the border against Algeria and to keep a watchful eye on French oil interests further south. Sensing that the French were losing the war in Algeria and that the era of colonies was over, Bourguiba wrote directly to President de Gaulle in Paris to ask him to remove his troops. De Gaulle arrogantly ignored Bourguiba's handwritten message for over two weeks.

The Tunisian response to de Gaulle's silence began with a 'spontaneous demonstration', women and children rubbing shoulders with armed soldiers, which advanced on the French base to drive the Europeans into the sea. They sang songs and danced. Hardened to such scenes in nearby Algiers, the French opened fire without mercy, killing civilians and soldiers alike. In retaliation, the Tunisian militia began a heavy bombardment, blockading the French garrison by land and sea.[5]

De Gaulle was furious. All of this was happening on the eve of delicate talks with the Algerians and he could not afford to seem weak. Over 7,000 French paratroopers landed on Tunisian shores, while the harbour was rammed open by four warships. After three days of remorseless onslaught, there were twenty-four French deaths and over 2,000 dead Tunisians, most of them simple country folk who had come north to help their Muslim brothers across the border.

30

Holidays in the Sun

Bourguiba saw that Tunisia could play an important role in balancing out the various power-plays in the region. While resisting the French, he pursued an openly pro-Western policy, which set him apart from his peers. His main rival was Gamal Abdel Nasser in Cairo, who opposed British, French and American influence in North Africa and the Middle East, whereas Bourguiba publicly approved of American bombing in Vietnam and hinted that Palestinians should seek an agreement with Israel. In 1968 Bourguiba boycotted the Arab League, accusing it of playing into the hands of the Soviets.

It was unarguably a high-risk strategy. Bourguiba's foreign policy made it clear that he wanted to impress and court the West, but there were internal tensions as well as external threats. He was never quite in control of the army, and the failure of a whole series of Socialist economic plans meant that many Tunisians felt worse off under Bourguiba than under the French. The result was mass emigration, mainly to France.

Tunisians' initial experience of immigration was similar to that of their Moroccan or Algerian cousins. For most French people, Tunisians were first and foremost *maghrébins*, and had the same supposed racial and cultural defects of all North Africans, ranging from stupidity to criminality and a taste for violence.

As a minority within a minority, Tunisians found themselves working and living in the same ghettoes as Algerians and Moroccans, who enjoyed the protection of their own powerful families or clans.

For this reason, many Tunisian immigrants began to move away from the traditional 'Arab quarters', setting up their businesses – often as greengrocers or small shopkeepers – across towns and cities. By the early 1970s 'le petit tunisien' had entered the French lexicon as a by-word for a handy grocery store that was open all hours. Slowly, the word tunisien became slightly separate from maghrébin and, unlike algérien or marocain, it started to acquire a local, even homely meaning.

This was partly because, for all the loss of life, the Tunisian struggle for independence and its aftermath had been much less protracted than in Algeria or in Morocco. Indeed, although Bourguiba's government was publicly at odds with de Gaulle, throughout the 1960s Tunisia was a 'safe' destination for French visitors to North Africa. Many of these visitors came for an exotic adventure, but some, like the pieds rouges of Algeria, were driven by a mildly left-wing impulse to help the fledgling nation. In his novel Les Choses, Georges Perec describes the life of a young Parisian couple, Sylvie and Jérome, who come to Sfax for eight months to teach and learn about the world outside fashionable Paris. In the end, they are bored and return as quickly as they can to Paris, to all the 'things' that make up their world – the restaurants, the shops, the clothes, the magazines and concerts. As Perec describes it, it's not that they suffer 'culture shock' in Sfax, but 'non-culture shock'. This was not because Tunisia under Bourguiba and earlier lacked culture, but because Sylvie and Jérome, as Europeans and outsiders, simply did not know how to read it.[1]

Cheap, Essential Scenery

The separation between Europeans and Tunisians was also
actively reinforced under Bourguiba with the development of
the Tunisian tourist industry throughout the 1960s and 1970s,
following the successful model in Franco's Spain. Traditionally,
foreign visitors to Tunisia had been in the service of colonial
authorities or well-heeled literary types such as André Gide or
Aldous Huxley. In Spain Bourguiba saw how a cheap, mass-
market experience could make money from sun-starved north
Europeans, who were largely indifferent to the political context
of the country they were visiting.

The initial investment was not great – which allowed
mainly Tunisian companies to take control of the projects.
A plan was drawn up called *Les Perspectives décenalles, 1962–
1971*, which aimed to establish tourism as the central industry
in a country whose only other main product was phosphates.
Along the coast, in the modest towns of Hammamet, Sousse
and Monastir, more than five hundred hotels were built in
the *zone touristique* in the second wave of development in
the 1970s. These were complexes dedicated to the pleasure
of European tourists, and accordingly the beaches and bars
were patrolled by 'tourist police', who kept a tight control
on who could come and go. There was no pretence at luxury
in the 'palace hotels' – all built around swimming pools,
bars, restaurants and access to the sea – but they provided
a Mediterranean holiday for the mainly French or German
tourists who could not afford Saint-Tropez or Sorrento.
The tourists' experience of Tunisia, and therefore of the
Arab world, was confined to buying knick-knacks in the
Medina and a guided tour of some ruins. Little has changed
in the *zones touristiques* in the twenty-first century, except that
Russian and other East European holidaymakers predominate,
and the hotels, now more than twenty or thirty years old, are
beginning to crumble. In 2011 tourism still employed 10 per

cent of the population – a massive but precarious figure, given the disintegrating infrastructure and changing markets.

Beyond the confines of the *zones touristiques*, the real life and politics of Tunisia in the 1970s began to take on an ever-more convoluted shape. The defining issue of this period was the difficult relationship with Libya. Many Tunisians felt a close affinity with Libya – they spoke much the same language, worshipped in the same way and felt arbitrarily divided by borders which had been devised by Europeans but made no real sense on the ground. Thousands of Tunisians worked in Libya and vice versa. Right up to 2011, you could hire a taxi in the centre of Tunis which would take you all the way to Tripoli. It was a long drive, but one which Tunisians and Libyans made regularly.

There was, therefore, some logic to the proposal made in December 1974 by Colonel Muammar Gaddafi, the leader of the Libyan People's Republic, to unify Libya and Tunisia. At this stage Gaddafi was the brilliant army officer who had recently taken power in Libya and, as a fervent follower of Nasser, had seen how pan-Arabism and oil revenue could reshape the geopolitical map of the world. Gaddafi had already proposed the unification of Egypt and Libya – a move which rattled the Algerians, who were beginning to see themselves as the real superpower in the region. When the same proposal was put to Tunisia, the Algerians counselled against it. Publicly, Bourguiba was polite and diplomatic to the Libyan leader; he refused his offer and the millions of dollars that went with it. But privately he was furious and needed no encouragement from the Algerians to turn his back on Libya.

This was the beginning of a muted, low-level war of attrition between Libya and Tunisia which lasted until Gaddafi's death in 2011. In 1980 the Libyans were suspected of staging the attempted 'coup of Gafsa' – an armed insurrection launched against Bourguiba from the mining town of Gafsa in the south. In 1985 a Libyan pirate radio channel, La Voix de Vengeance et de la Haine Sacrée (The Voice of Vengeance and Sacred Hatred), broadcasting from Zouara near the Tunisian border, called on the Tunisians to massacre their Jewish population. The Tunisian army was placed on high alert and Bourguiba, furious at this provocation, raised the issue in talks between himself and President Ronald Reagan in Washington. It was reported that Libyan troops had been sighted wearing Tunisian army uniforms and preparing for an invasion of Tunisia. Shortly after the incident 30,000 Tunisian workers were expelled from Libya. This was a major catastrophe for Tunisia, which did not have the resources to offer work and money to the returning migrants.[2]

The Palestinians

Despite the tiny size of his country, Bourguiba was always ambitious about his position on the world stage. In 1982, when the Palestine Liberation Organization was bombed out of Beirut by the Israelis, he offered refuge in Tunis to the PLO leader Yasser Arafat and a headquarters for the organization. The aim was to establish the PLO headquarters alongside the Arab League, which now had a provisional base in Tunis, having left Cairo in disgust at Anwar Sadat's peace deal with Israel.

The Palestinians began arriving by boat in the port of Tunis in the dead heat of August, to be met personally by Bourguiba, waving from the dock. They brought with them over a thousand armed men as well as the military planning units of the PLO – eventually numbering 7,000 – and set up almost immediately at Borj Cedria, just outside Tunis. From this base they continued the long war against Israel, choosing targets and actions in Lebanon.

It was inevitable that this conflict would come to Tunisia. In 1982 Ariel Sharon threatened to bomb the newly established

PLO headquarters, but was appeased by Moroccan and American diplomacy. Israel's chance came again when three Mossad agents were killed in Larnaca, Cyprus, by a Palestinian group called Force 17, which was clearly operating out of Tunisia. The revenge attack on Tunis came at 10 a.m. on 1 October 1985; Tunisian radar gave only three minutes' warning. It was initially assumed that this was a Libyan offensive, but the Israelis soon claimed the strike as an act of self-defence. The PLO headquarters and the offices of Force 17 were wrecked and over sixty people killed. The Israelis had shown the world that they had the will and the means to operate far beyond the Middle East. None the less, the Palestinians stayed on in Tunisia through the first intifada, with the PLO directing events in the Middle East from Tunis.[3]

During the 1980s Bourguiba had domestic problems of his own. He was faced with a rising tide of anger in Tunisia as the population grew poorer. Tunisia had no oil money and the only way that many Tunisians could profit from the oil boom in the 1970s was to take low-grade and underpaid work in the Gulf states or Libya. In Tunisia itself much of this anger – at first manifest in strikes and protests – was channelled into the burgeoning Islamist movements, both home-grown and imported into Tunisia from other Arab states.

Zine Ben Ali, a notoriously ambitious hardman with a background in state security who was Minister of the Interior, cracked down hard on these movements, which became more violent as they went deeper underground, culminating in bomb attacks on holiday resorts in Sousse and Monastir in August 1987. Bourguiba insisted on the death penalty for the militants when they were finally rounded up and tried. Ben Ali, who had been promoted to prime minister in October 1987, argued that this would make them martyrs.

At this point in the stand-off, on the grounds of a threat to the state, Ben Ali declared Bourguiba unfit to govern due to his poor health. In November 1987 he was deposed and placed under house arrest in his home town of Monastir. It was true that Bourguiba was by now an elderly and sometimes quite frail figure. Having had Bourguiba's state of health verified by physician, Ben Ali took office himself, at first on a provisional basis and then – so it seemed – for ever.

Ben Ali was, of course, no friend of the Islamist militants. But the spectre he invoked of increased Islamist violence, and even an Algerian-style insurrection, was more than enough to win over the friends he needed in the high command of the military. Ben Ali declared his seizure of power 'the Historic Change'.

31

Miracles

Ben Ali began his career as a dictator with a series of liberal reforms which he claimed would help modernize the country. They also helped to distinguish him from Bourguiba, presenting himself as a believer in social justice and political openness. His first major act was to declare a policy of National Reconciliation and in his first six months in office he released over 5,000 so-called political prisoners.

Certainly during his first years in power, most Tunisians did well under Ben Ali. Political censorship was relaxed and opposition parties were allowed to stand for election. Ben Ali changed the name of the ruling party to the Rassemblement Constitutionnel Démocratique (RCD) and established elections every five years, though he maintained the ban on the party Hizb Nahda (Party of the Awakening), and there were frequent clashes as he sought to establish control over the most influential mosques, including the Zitouna Mosque, the most prestigious in the country. During the early 1990s, there were constant rumours of plots and attacks on all sides, and the Tunisian government kept a wary eye on its porous border with Algeria. Meanwhile, Tunisian Islamists began to move between Tunis, Afghanistan and Pakistan to visit 'training camps' on the model of their Algerian brothers.

Soon after taking power, Ben Ali began to reverse Bourguiba's implacably anti-French foreign policy. Ben Ali made his first state visit to France in 1988, a clear signal to both Tunisians and the outside world that France had special status as an ally and friend. This relationship was quickly cemented by Tunisia and France jointly lobbying the United Nations Security Council to condemn Israel for the murder on Tunisian soil of the Palestinian militant Abou Jihad at Sidi Bou Said in 1988. This had the dual effect of raising France's profile as a defender of the Muslims in the region, while allowing Tunisia to flex its muscles and show its Arab brothers that it was quite unafraid of the West.

Most significantly, as a result of this first contact, Ben Ali, who had been trained as an officer in France, was able to secure huge amounts of military aid from the French. The aid took the form of special advisors and special forces, who claimed to be experts in counter-terrorism and able to extinguish the Islamist threat, but also millions of francs, to be spent on upgrading Tunisian military hardware to European standards. Sandwiched between volatile Algeria, which was fast disintegrating into civil war, and the madness of Gaddafi's Libya, Tunisia somehow had to be made safe. Moreover, the French saw investment in the Tunisian military as a key diplomatic victory, a new way of entering into the power play in the region. The two countries were now locked together in a 'special relationship' as political partners.

The slow disintegration of human rights in Tunisia really began in the early 1990s. It was hard for French foreign-policy experts to understand exactly what was happening as Ben Ali clamped down on the Islamist opposition with increasing ferocity. On the one hand, this seemed to be a logical and appropriate response to the growing threat of Islamist forces in Algeria, but at the same time Ben Ali had a tendency to denounce all dissident voices as de facto Islamists and act accordingly. By the time of the revolution of 2011, there were simply no opposing forces left, save for the Salafists who had endured throughout the years of repression.

In 1994 Amnesty International complained about a wave of mass arrests and trials, which involved some 3,000 people loosely described as 'Islamists'. Amnesty denounced the treatment meted out to the detainees as 'cruel, inhuman and degrading'. More specifically, the report detailed instances of rape and torture – the alleged 'Islamists' or 'political prisoners', male and female, were often raped by criminal prisoners who were bribed or encouraged to punish these 'enemies of the state'. Torture methods included 'beatings, especially on the soles of the feet, sometimes when the victim was suspended by the ankles; suspension for long periods in contorted positions, often accompanied by beatings; semi-suffocation with cloths drenched in dirty water or bleach; sexual abuse with sticks and other objects; and electric shocks'.[1]

Only twelve months after the Amnesty International report, in November 1995 Jacques Chirac, France's newly elected president, made his first official state visit to Tunisia. In a photograph published in *Jeune Afrique*, Chirac poses in front of Ben Ali's palace in the company of the Minister of Interior, Jean-Louis Debré; the president of the National Assembly, Philippe Séguin (who was widely known to be a close friend of Ben Ali); and the Minister for Foreign Affairs, Henri de Chavette. Sixteen years later, when the Ben Ali régime imploded, Henri de Chavette insisted that support for Ben Ali had been entirely logical, that France had no other choice. But he also admitted that the French allowed themselves to 'drift' into complying with a dysfunctional and dangerous régime.

None the less, Chirac publicly hailed what he described as the 'Tunisian Miracle' – by which he meant that Ben Ali had somehow managed to construct a modern Francophone state out of the wreckage of colonization, a model for the entire region. This was a myth. The reality was that 'stability' in Tunisia had been imposed by force of arms and the systematic use of torture: its 'Francophone' identity was undermined by the fact that few Tunisians could ever get to France, and those who did often found themselves living in worse conditions than they had known at home. However, the French needed Tunisian intelligence on Algeria, Libya and Morocco, and even used Ben Ali as a channel to communicate with Yasser Arafat, who was resident in Tunis until 1995.

When the Socialists came to power in France in 1997, Lionel Jospin was quick to distance himself from Ben Ali. The days of presidential visits to Tunis were suddenly over, but this did not stop the mayor of Paris, Jean Tiberi, from holding a magnificent reception for Ben Ali at the Hôtel de Ville, with Ségolène Royal and other luminaries in attendance. The former president of the National Assembly, Philippe Séguin, presided over a speech made by Ben Ali at the Grande Arche de la Défense, attended by thousands of Tunisians resident in France. Jospin hosted a dinner at the Matignon.

Ben Ali's Tunisia had become a tough and ugly place, but it was still a cheap and popular holiday destination for European, especially French, holidaymakers. Along the strip of coast south of Tunis, often in partnership with French travel firms, the government invested millions in the *zones touristiques*, which grew ever more lavish and grotesque.

The government boasted that living standards were higher than in all other comparable nations, but the price to pay for this was a devastating paralysis of thought and action among ordinary Tunisians. All the young people dreamed of Europe, and thousands died as they tried to turn the dream into reality by attempting to get across the Mediterranean. This was the same story I had heard from Tangier to Tunis. Imen Yacoubi told me of a young man, a friend who enjoyed swimming at night in La Goulette, the port of Tunis, where he could see the tantalizing lights of distant Italy. One night he swam right out and never came back. He was a member of a generation who were literally dying of boredom.

England Away!

The outside world first caught a glimpse of the secret inner life of Tunisian youth when England played Tunisia on 15 June 1998 at the FIFA World Cup, which was being held that year in France. The violence of the Tunisian youths on the streets of Marseilles seemed to come out of nowhere, at least for non-French observers who had no idea of the realities of Tunisian life in France or Tunisia.

The most dramatic fighting erupted on the Quai des Belges in the centre of Marseilles on the evening of Sunday 14 June. The match was scheduled for the Monday, which meant the English fans had a whole weekend to drink their way down to the South of France. It is still unclear who started the fighting, but on the Saturday night in La Canebière, in the heart of Marseilles, English fans had burned a Tunisian flag, made Nazi salutes and jeered at Tunisians and other North Africans as 'Pakis'. The young Tunisians were not afraid, however, of these fat, stupid white men. They buzzed them on mopeds, threw beer glasses back at them, and, whenever they could pick one off, beat them into the ground with kicks and blows.

By Sunday night the Tunisians were joined by Moroccans and Algerians. The general feeling was that the English needed to be taught a lesson. This was not about football or football hooliganism anymore. The English had come to Marseilles and strutted around as if they owned it. To Tunisian eyes, their behaviour was disgusting – they walked round half-naked, bloated bellies pink in the sun, and were mostly drunk and chanted like animals. For their part, the English had no idea who or what they were fighting and were surprised to be so effectively hammered over the three days of combat. Their defeat at the hands of Tunisian youth bred even more hatred: 'We didn't lose that much money really, as we had already drunk most of the money we had on us,' remembered one English fan, 'but I tell you, there was no way we was leaving without giving some Arab shit a good hiding.'[2]

The events in Marseilles were barely reported in the Tunisian press, and certainly there was no reference to disaffected youth. The French press, having had some experience of what was happening in big French cities, got nearer the mark: almost everywhere the battle of Marseilles was reported as the French *banlieues* against the rest of the world.

Images and Illusions

Although there were enormous posters of the oily visage of Ben Ali plastered all over the country, nobody in Tunisia ever really knew anything about the man himself. There was a legend that the 'Supreme Combatant' had been born in Monastir in a *zaouïa* – a holy building that, according to local folklore, was often the birthplace of Muslim saints. This rumour was started partly because Bourguiba was known to favour the natives of Monastir. But the reality was that Ben Ali was born in the countryside between Gabès and Médenine in the south of Tunisia, one of eleven children in a family of modest means. His father had served in the French navy. His mother and grandmother hoped that he would become a primary-school teacher.

But Ben Ali never finished school and never gained the baccalaureate (*le bac*), the leaving certificate which was the basic requirement for any civil-service job. In later years, Ben Ali was nicknamed in the French press '*bac moins trois*' (three years short of a *bac*) as an explanation for his stubbornness and stupidity. Indeed, Ben Ali never lost a sense of insecurity in the company of 'intellectuals', saying that he preferred to be with the 'simple people' of Tunisia. This never stopped him from claiming in the French press that he had a degree in law from the University of Tunis.

Ben Ali's career began in the years after Tunisian independence when he was one of a group of young army officers selected to train at Saint-Cyr, the French military college in Brittany. This meant he had a thorough education in the French art of war and, as much as anyone of his generation who went through that process, he respected law, order and discipline. He gained a reputation for ruthlessness and severity as a military commander. Beyond this, he revealed no taste or interest in culture or history. His training at Saint-Cyr was followed by a brief stint in the United States, studying Intelligence and Security Issues in Baltimore.

In her sickly and self-serving autobiography, published as an apologia in 2012, Ben Ali's second wife Leila paints a portrait of a man driven by duty to the Tunisian people, displaying the same sense of responsibility towards them that he showed towards his children.[3] But he emerges in this book, too, as a singularly colourless individual, lacking any political ambition beyond survival. From this point of view it is easy to believe the rumours that Ben Ali's ascent to power was manipulated by the Italian and Algerian secret services to ensure nothing more than security in Tunisia. Certainly, in the years to follow he never made a political statement of any note.

He was undoubtedly paranoid and it was this quality which drove his realpolitik and, in 1999, compelled him to turn against and humiliate the veteran French journalist Jean Daniel, hitherto a self-identified 'friend of Tunisia'. Daniel had been wounded in the conflict at Bizerte in 1961 and since then had professed nothing but admiration for the country. Daniel's 'crime' was to have noted in his published diaries the importance of Ben Ali's 'cult of personality' in Tunisian politics. His punishment was to find himself attacked in the Tunisian press and immediately excluded from the charmed circles of political contacts. When

I spoke to Jean Daniel in 2013, by then a frail old man in his nineties, he snarled at the mention of Ben Ali.

The politics of paranoia were also played out on the larger world stage. The attacks of 9/11 were a gift to Ben Ali (as they were to many other equally dubious Arab leaders). He was now officially one of America's best friends in the Arab world, the official face of the anti-terrorist Arab order. From his palaces in Carthage Ben Ali took it upon himself to lecture the Western world on 'laxity' in the war against terror, singling out London, or 'Londonistan', as the capital of radical terror (it was no accident that London was also home to a generation of Tunisians in exile). In the pages of *L'Express* in France, Ben Ali was praised as the potential saviour of the Maghreb, and the paper was unable to resist the play on words in the headline 'Ben Ali against Ben Laden'. Shortly afterwards, the 'good democrat', as he was described, made himself President for Life.

In April 2002 al-Qaeda launched an attack on the synagogue on the quiet isle of Djerba in southern Tunisia, which left over thirty dead. In the wake of this attack, the Tunisian authorities clamped down. But still the violence grew; in 2006 a shoot-out between police and a suspected al-Qaeda cell in the Tunis suburb of Grombalia killed thirty people. The Islamist revenge was to be swift and cruel: a planned attack on embassies and tourist hotels on Cap Bon in 2007. When the plot was uncovered, the Tunisian army was called in to deal with a terrorist cell armed with rocket launchers. Battle raged for an afternoon in a suburb of Tunis. The leader of the group 'Sassi', shot through the brain by a sniper, was found to be Tunisian-born and educated in France.

In the meantime, Ben Ali's stranglehold on Tunisia grew even tighter. There were, of course, a few dissenting voices. In 2000 a magistrate, Mokhtar Yahyaoui, wrote an open letter to Ben Ali complaining that he was ashamed to work in such a rotten legal system. He then disappeared. The writer and journalist Taoufik

Ben Brik started a hunger strike in Tunis, which he then took to Paris – much to the irritation of Ben Ali. He ended up in prison on trumped-up charges. When he was released in 2010 he took his message about Ben Ali's wickedness to Paris. He claimed that France had to intervene, that France owed Tunisia a debt – as former colonizers who had left behind 'native colonialists' – but no one was really listening.

There were others who spoke out: lawyers, teachers and journalists, including Radhia Nasraoui, Hamma Hammami, Sihem Bensédrine, Moncef Mazouki, Mohamed Bouebdelli. These names were pretty much unknown to the outside world. But on trips to Tunis and other cities, crude evidence of Ben Ali's totalitarian machine was never far from view. Like all visitors to Tunisia who were not holidaymakers, I was immediately an object of suspicion. My female Moroccan colleague, Fatima Ahloulay, was accosted and insulted by men in dark glasses and leather jackets – the secret police – when we walked the city streets together. They followed us everywhere. We would joke about it and she would reply with insults in Spanish, which they didn't understand. But we never really found it amusing. When we mentioned this low-level harassment to Tunisian colleagues, they simply shied away from the subject. They knew that, for all its stability and alleged prosperity, Ben Ali's Tunisia was a diseased and rotten place.

Gangsters

In its last years, the Ben Ali régime was marked by criminality and farce. One of the more notorious scandals was the involvement of Imed Trabelsi, nephew of Leila Ben Ali, in the theft of a yacht from the Corsican port of Bonifacio. Trabelsi normally described himself as a politician and businessman – he was mayor of La Goulette, dominated the construction industry in Tunisia and managed the French DIY franchise called Bricorama.

In 2006, at the age of thirty-two, he was also a spoilt and

sleazy playboy. 'I've got Ferraris, limousines,' he once said, 'but nothing gives me a hard-on, not even my wife, like a boat. It's like an uncut diamond.'[4] On the morning of 5 May 2006, in the port of Sidi Bou Said, he was seen at the helm of the yacht *Beru Ma*, a top-of-the-range vessel worth a million and a half euros.

The problem was that the yacht actually belonged to Bruno Roger, the multi-millionaire banker, head of the Lazard Brothers banking group. Roger also happened to be a personal friend of Jacques Chirac and Nicolas Sarkozy. The yacht was tracked down by Jean-Baptiste Andréani, a former French police officer working as a private detective, who used his contacts with the French secret services to identify Imed and the boat. Andréani also reported that Imed was a 'well-known hooligan who could act with total impunity'.

In her book Leila Ben Ali recounts that she had no idea why Nicolas Sarkozy personally telephoned Ben Ali, asking him to release the two Corsican crew members of the *Beru Ma* who were being held in Tunisia. She adds that her charming nephew had been a victim of his own innocence and gullibility and the real villain was an Algerian yacht thief whose name no one could remember.[5]

Unsurprisingly, the visit of the French President Nicolas Sarkozy in April 2008 provoked divided opinions among Tunisians. Many ordinary people felt flattered that Sarkozy had bothered at all, and the papers were full of pictures of his wife, the glamorous Carla, consorting with the great and good of this small North African country. There were others, however, who argued that Sarkozy was primarily on a mission to do deals and make money for France. Ben Ali could do whatever he wanted – imprisonment without trial, even assassination – as long as it was in the name of the struggle against Islamic terror.

Much to the satisfaction of French diplomats, the Sarkozy visit to Tunisia went off quietly, with no mention of the Trabelsis. The truth was that the French wanted as little fuss as possible.

Leila herself was conspicuous by her absence, having most likely been ordered to keep out the way. In 2009, to the stupefaction of all observers, the charges of 'organized theft' made against Imed Trabelsi in a Corsican court were suddenly dropped, and the pair were released to face trial in Tunisia, where, as Leila put it, due to 'an excess of zeal', the Tunisian judge acquitted them both.

This had all the elements of high comedy, except that at stake was the integrity of the French government at the highest level. It was a sorry state of affairs; the French ambassador had recently commended the Ben Alis to his American colleague as 'leaders who are in touch with the people', who were making steady progress with their human-rights issues. The French turned a blind eye and refused to take action against corruption, which encouraged worse acts of theft and piracy. In December 2010 the Trabelsi clan reunited in Dubai, a favoured destination, where they were sent 500 million dollars from Tunisia. This was aside from the 1,500 kilos of gold which Leila had openly stolen from the Central Bank of Tunisia. As the country stood on the brink of a revolution which would shake the Arab world to its core, the ruling élite of Tunisia systematically pillaged the country for every penny they could lay their hands on.

These were the people, it is worth remembering at this late stage in the drama, to whom the French Minister of State for Justice, Defence and Home Affairs, Michèle Alliot-Marie, was shortly to offer French military and police assistance.

The end for the Ben Ali régime came all of a sudden on 14 January 2011. According to Leila Ben Ali, the family was the victim of a plot by greedy and selfish politicians to depose the noble Ben Ali and seize power for themselves. In reality, in the classic mode of revolutions, the turning point was that the military had decided to serve the people and not the regime, in order to 'protect the revolution'. The Ben Alis became aware of this when the military attacked their own security forces.

This was a direct threat. The model for this, as far I could see, was the Romanian revolution of 1989, when Nicolae and Elena Ceausescu were summarily tried and executed by a people's court at the height of the revolutionary fervour. The Ben Alis had no desire to go the same way. Frantic phone calls bought them the promise of exile in Saudi Arabia, after the French had refused asylum to their oldest and closest friends in the Arab world.

A plane was chartered and flights hurriedly organized, first to Malta and then to Riyadh. The convoy to the airport was a tense affair, heightened by Leila Ben Ali's demands that the Central Bank of Tunisia should give the family a further 1,500 kilos of gold from the country's gold reserves. This was refused – the first time ever that the bank had stood its ground.

The Libyan security services, on the direct orders of Colonel Gaddafi, provided cover and protection on the way to the airport. The colonel would shortly go on Libyan television to accuse the Tunisian people of folly and call for the return of Ben Ali.

The mutiny lasted no more than four weeks. But it changed everything in Tunisia and indeed across the Arab world, as ordinary people from Morocco to Yemen felt inspired and fearless enough to take on their rulers. The uprising would eventually lead to the fall of Hosni Mubarak in Egypt and the violent civil war in Libya, which culminated in the killing of Gaddafi. Other revolts in Algeria and Morocco began to unsettle governments. In Jordan, Iraq and Bahrain, there were protests, disturbances and deaths. In Syria the protest movement unleashed a brutal civil war which, at the time of writing, is not yet over and has the potential to engulf the region.

None of this could have been predicted the day after Ben Ali left Tunisia and the streets were filled with happy crowds, melting together in euphoria and disbelief. There was, however, an undercurrent of violence. The main railway station in Tunis was firebombed and militias set up as neighbourhood protection units. Gunfire was constant. The breakout of some 1,000 prisoners from the main jail at Mahdia, and then from other prisons across the country, introduced a new, harsher edge of fear into the atmosphere. Those who were left in power were cautious about going too near to the edge of anarchy. A state of emergency was established, which effectively meant that the military was in charge. An interim government was soon in place, including opposition figures and old hands from the Ben Ali régime, but was soon removed from power as street protests continued. Free elections were promised within sixty days. The Ennahda party, the moderately Islamist grouping that had been banned under Ben Ali, led by the human-rights activist Moncef Marzouki, took power with 41 per cent of the vote.

But Tunisia does not yet feel safe. Salafists are threatening to turn the country into the 'new Pakistan' – a nation making total war with the West, from only a few hundred kilometres from the European mainland. Credible security services estimate the number of radicals ready to take up arms at around 3,000. In a country of 10 million people this is a dangerous statistic. Worse still, the numbers of young people who feel enough hatred and contempt to kill is growing fast.

Most Tunisians, not just the Salafists, now feel twice betrayed by France, the country which has dominated and shaped Tunisia's political and cultural identity for over a century. Whether they wanted to or not, they grew up believing that France was their mother county, and that at the very least the French had the Tunisians' best interests at heart. During the heady days of the revolution, France was in fact revealed as a cynical and corrupt enemy.

On the evening of 14 October 2008, there was a friendly football match at the Stade de France between France and

Tunisia. The French government had been anticipating trouble for months. Ever since the riots in Clichy-sous-Bois in 2005, all matches with North African teams had become potential triggers for trouble in Paris. Still, Tunisia was held to be a less volatile and dangerous place than either Morocco or Algeria and Tunisians in Paris are not seen as gangsters or Islamic radicals. But to defuse any possible tensions, the authorities had decided that the teams should mix together as they lined up and that the 'Marseillaise' should be sung by Laam, a young R&B singer of Franco-Tunisian extraction.

As soon as Laam picked up the mike, the hissing started, rising quickly to a high-pitched crescendo of whistling which carried through the stadium like bad feedback. The young girl looked around for help but none came. She fought on through the blizzard of white noise, but it was hopeless. When she finally stopped, Tunisian fans were laughing and high-fiving as if they were 3–0 up on the home team. 'Where did it come from, this wall of hate?' I asked a Tunisian bloke next to me in the bar where I was watching the match. He smiled goofily and slugged back the remains of his beer: 'Made in France!'

Part Five

PRISONERS OF WAR

32

Muslims in Prison

The first time you enter a prison is a shock. It doesn't matter
how many films you've seen, or how many books you've read.
Nothing can prepare you for the moment when the keys turn
and the bars crash down behind you.

On my first visit to Fresnes Prison, to the south of Paris, in
October 2011, the guards told me that this is when prisoners
often break down and weep. Sometimes this is with relief, even
from those who have resisted captivity with maximum force.
In a side room adjacent to the barred gate, they are given a
blanket, toothbrush, toothpaste, soap, tissues and a comb.
The guards can sometimes be tender here. They told me that
prisoners are by now usually glad to be away from the police
and the courts of justice. In a military conflict, this moment is
often described as 'the shock of capture', a psychological state of
extreme disorientation, when prisoners may start crying for no
reason because they do not know what is coming next. Military
interrogators seek to prolong these feelings to their advantage, a
subtle form of torture. In Fresnes, the prisoners also cry because
from now on there is no turning back. I was told by the regional
Director of Prisons: 'This is when the prisoner sees for the first
time that the wall is real. Now there really is no way out.'

To get into Fresnes as a visitor is no easy matter. It took

months of argument and persuasion on my part before the government authorities would grant me a visit. I argued that I was investigating the theory that the prison system is the engine room of Islamic radicalism in France, so I needed to test this theory in a real prison, talking to prisoners, warders, psychiatrists, doctors and managers. Most of all, I wanted to see what prison meant for all of these people, and how this made them feel.

My guide to Fresnes was the regional Director of Prisons, whom I will call here J.N. Having been introduced to each other at a party at the British Embassy in Paris, we met several times and liked each other – we shared literary tastes (Céline, Camus), an interest in football, and an educational background in Lyons in the 1980s. He is a small wiry man, with the physical discipline that comes from a military background and a dandyish penchant for tailored clothes and expensive watches. He would say things like, 'In prison I am not afraid of anything – not the toughest criminal. I have no fear of dead bodies or suicides.' I believed him. Crucially, J.N. could see the significance of my work – the present book – and wanted to help me.

As we drove to Fresnes on a sunny autumn afternoon, I noted that it was only a couple of kilometres up the road from the worst parts of Bagneux, where I had investigated the killing of Ilam Halimi in 2008. I imagined the lads I had interviewed, now a few years older, maybe deeper into drug habits, maybe they had escaped the *banlieues*, and maybe some of them were in Fresnes. I mentioned this to J.N., who said he did not doubt that some of them would be there, which was 'bound to make things worse'.

The prison itself is set in what almost seems to be a country park. It is surrounded by villas built for the guards in the nineteenth century, which are still quite pleasant, with small gardens and stone walls (and still inhabited by the prison staff). After walking a hundred metres on crunchy gravel, you enter the prison, handing over kit and documents, and emerging into an empty exercise yard. You enter another building, an imposing edifice of grey-green stone. More documents are handed over, papers stamped. Then a warder with an enormous key – it seems more theatrical than anything else – opens the lock on the huge barred gates to where the prisoners are kept. He pushes the gates open. They slide easily. And now, all of a sudden, you are inside.

The prison smells very clean but is also very noisy. From the entrance I catch my first glimpse of the inmates, high above me on the prison wings, half-hidden by the nets to catch suicides. They prowl on the wing, hang out, gossip, smoke, and shout. They are indifferent to our presence. You can understand this. They are captives. The freest thing that they can do is to ignore us, their captors.

At the latest estimate, the prison population of France is thought to be 70 per cent Muslim. No one can know the exact figure because under French law it is illegal to distinguish individuals on the grounds of their religion – this is the principle of *laïcité*, the specifically anti-religious concept which is meant to guarantee the moral unity of the French nation. Given this constraint, the only way that prison administrators can make an intelligent guess at who they are guarding is by compiling statistics on dietary requirements and practices such as fasting. These are far from reliable, as many non-Muslim prisoners find prison food so disgusting that they buy Halal food.

'Everybody with a grievance claims that they are Muslim,' I was told by Madame la Directrice in her elegant book-lined office at the entrance to Fresnes. I was there with J.N. to discuss the problem of Islamic extremism in prison and the radicalization of youths from the *banlieues*. 'Islam is the best and most effective way of calling into question the entire system,' she said. She went on to give an example of a Russian gangster who had been disciplined for having sex with a prostitute during visiting hours. He claimed his human rights as a Muslim were being abused. No one could prove that he was not a Muslim. Within hours the prison was on the edge of a riot.

The biggest challenge for the authorities, right up to government level, is that they simply do not know how to handle their Muslim population. I spoke to the guards about this. 'They are not like the European prisoners,' I was told by one of the senior officers. 'You can't really see them as proper criminals or a political gang. You can speak to the Basques or the Corsicans, have a laugh; you could be friends on the outside. With the Muslims, it's like they're a secret army, working against you. You can never know what they're thinking, but you know they hate you. They spit in our faces – we're in danger of catching their illnesses ... They constantly threaten us and swear revenge.' I was not allowed to speak to any prisoners in this category. The few prisoners from other categories I did speak to said that the guard's account was true.

Islam in prison has a strange status in France; everybody knows that it is a significant force, but everyone denies it. It is hard to find imams who will work in prisons, for fear of recrimination in their own communities. So the 'street Islam' that is practised becomes more political, more war-like. The blindness of the French legal system to Islam in prison does not help. The prison library I saw at Fresnes was unmonitored and easily manipulated by radicals, transmitting pamphlets and cassettes in a variety of unlistened-to languages.

J.N. did not challenge in any way my assertion that prisons were now the engine-room of Islamist radicalism in France. As a result of the uncontrolled growth of radical Islam in French prisons, 'what we are faced with is a totally new situation,' he told me. 'This is not about criminals or even political prisoners, like the Basques or Corsicans, who have a cause. It's about people who hate our civilization. It's a totally new kind of war fought by a totally new kind of enemy.'

★

The word *prisun* or *prison* is one of the oldest words in the French language. It entered the language at roughly the same time as *donjon*, or *dongeon* and to describe the place where you kept those who had been *pris* – literally 'captured'. The first *prisoniers* were almost exclusively prisoners of war, usually kept against a ransom in a *donjon* or *prisun*. In this sense, the rulers of twelfth-century France were arguably the first to invent (and then export to the British Isles) the *prisun*.[1]

However, it was not until the early Enlightenment that a prison was conceived of as a place to keep criminals and other moral transgressors separate from society. The transformation of the *donjon* or *prisun* into the modern form of 'prison' was by no means consistent across Europe or France. Even the Bastille, the most totemic prison in French history, was only one of many *bassetilles* (military fortifications) which stood at the gates of most French cities. This was still effectively its status at the dawn of the French Revolution: its *prisoniers* were mainly religious or political dissidents (including the Marquis de Sade) rather than criminals.

The idea was to contain 'anti-social' forces rather than to punish them. Physical punishment was reserved for true criminals, including 'death, judicial torture, flogging, banishment'. In his classic history of the French prison system, *Surveiller et punir: Naissance de la prison* (*Discipline and Punish: The Birth of the Prison*), Michel Foucault lists (with more than a touch of lip-smacking relish, it has to be said) the varieties of capital punishment available to the authorities in the sixteenth century: they included 'having tongues cut out or pierced, then to be hanged; to be broken alive and then to die on the wheel, after having had limbs broken; to be burnt alive, to be strangled, to be burnt alive after first being strangled, to be drawn by four horses, to have heads cut off and heads broken'.

Foucault's book, first published in 1975, is still read as a key textbook by future directors of French prisons at the Ecole

Nationale d'Administration Pénitentiaire (ENAP), a handsome rural campus near Agen in south-west France. The students come here after taking a competitive exam and go on to study criminology, law, social sciences, psychology and, most crucially, the political history of prisons. Foucault's big idea in *Surveiller et punir*, still admired as the cornerstone of modern penal thinking, is that the development of the prison in France throughout the eighteenth and nineteenth century was not brought about by reformists with humanitarian ideals, but as a result of power shifting from the sovereign to the state.

From this point of view, the prison, as an institution of social control, was the precursor of the hospital, asylum, school and the Church. It easy to see how this argument appealed to the 1960s generation of libertarians, who thought that society itself was a kind of prison. This, of course, echoes the fall of the Bastille in 1789 – the ultimate act of rebellion against oppressive authority and the founding moment of the French Republic.

Fresnes is an old prison, one of the oldest in the French system. It is one of the three main prisons in the Paris region, along with Fleury-Mérogis, the largest prison in Europe, which is also to the south of Paris, and La Santé, which is in the centre of the city, on boulevard Arago in the 14th arrondissement. Fresnes was built in 1895 by the architect Henri Poussin, a specialist in prisons, whose main concerns were hygiene, comfort and functionality. It is constructed on the so-called 'telephone pole' model – this means that the cells extend on either side of a single long corridor, which gently ascends and takes you to the Maximum Security area. This is a terrifyingly small space. The guards are huge black guys with gentle, soft faces and arms that could twist you into pieces. 'When you see these babies, you know you're in trouble,' commented the genial pipe-smoking psychiatrist accompanying my visit.

Poussin's idea was that a kind of community would grow

here. In the spirit of the age, he regarded prison not merely as a place to punish criminals; it was also to serve a 'hygienic' function for society at large. This concept is carried over into the neat and tidy pebbled pathways which lead right up to the main complex. As you pass into the prison proper, the first thing you see is the execution yard, where generations of prisoners condemned to death were either guillotined or, more often, shot. The last guillotine in France – nicknamed '*La Veuve*' (The Widow) – was moved here in 1978, and this was the last prison in France where executions could legally take place. The last man to be guillotined, Hamida Djandoubi, a Tunisian immigrant accused of the murder of a young Frenchwoman, was executed in Marseilles in 1977. The death penalty was finally abolished in 1981 – France was the last European country to renounce the punishment. The guillotine is still here in Fresnes, housed in a discreet part of the psychiatric ward.

Fresnes was much praised in its day as an innovative and enlightened prison. It soon became the model for prisons across France and beyond, including Les Baumettes in Marseilles and Riker's Island in New York. These days, it is a *maison d'arrêt* – a holding centre for prisoners waiting for trial or to be sent to a *centre de détention* (a detention centre for illegal immigrants) or a *maison centrale* (a high-security prison).

In its own way, Fresnes is also a *lieu de mémoire*, a site of collective French historical memory. During the Second World War, the prison was used by the Nazis to imprison and torture members of the Resistance and British secret agents. At the end of the Second World War, it housed the Gestapo and pro-Nazi collaborators, most notably the journalist and broadcaster Jean Hérold-Paquis, and Pierre Laval, chief architect of the Vichy régime. Both of them were shot here. The industrialist Louis Renault, another suspected collaborator, died here in circumstances which remain mysterious to this day.

The most notable literary inmates of Fresnes were Jean Genet and Robert Brasillach. Genet effectively began his literary career here, while serving time for theft in 1942. This is where he began writing the long poem '*Le condamné à mort*' ('The condemned man'), an erotic meditation dedicated to his friend Maurice Pilorge, who was guillotined in 1939 at the age of twenty. For Genet, prison had an 'erotic charm' and an 'aura' which he thought encouraged homosexuality. This first poem is sometimes incoherent but also evokes brilliantly the special quality of insomnia in a prison – 'the prison sleeps standing in the dark of a dead man's song'. Most importantly, it was in prison that Genet learned his particular brand of hatred, defining his enemy as bourgeois society and all those who collaborated in its hypocrisy. Ultimately this would lead him to champion everyone who attacked this society in art, politics or terrorism. He praised the Black Panthers and the Baader-Meinhof gang, and was commissioned by Yasser Arafat to write a book for the Palestinian cause. This book, *Captif amoureux* (*Prisoner of Love*), written after he had witnessed the massacre of the Palestinians by 'Christian' militants at Sabra and Chatila in 1982, is one of his most complex, uncompromising and beautiful works. When he died in 1986, he was buried at Larache in Morocco, far away from the West and from France – the mother country that had betrayed him.[2]

Genet's anti-patriotism stood in direct contrast to the ultra-Nationalist Robert Brasillach, the highly intellectual and viciously anti-Semitic poet, novelist, film critic and editor of the pro-Nazi journal *Je Suis Partout*. A coalition of leading figures in Paris, including Jean Cocteau and Colette, personally petitioned Charles de Gaulle for clemency when Brasillach was charged with collaboration in 1945. De Gaulle refused to listen to them and Brasillach was shot on 6 February 1945. In prison he had been working on his history of the cinema and a series of poems known posthumously as *Les Poèmes de Fresnes*. In recent years there have been attempts in right-wing literary circles to rehabilitate Brasillach as a kind of Ezra Pound figure – a misguided genius who just happened to choose the wrong side. The poems are certainly moving ('a world has disappeared here/in the black sun of pain' reads one fine poem). But in 1945 de Gaulle had no other choice than to destroy his most intellectually able opponents in the fragile free France of the period. For this 'crime' de Gaulle is still vilified in French right-wing circles.

During the Algerian War, Fresnes housed leaders of the OAS (Organization of the Secret Army), including Claude Piegts, Albert Dovecar, Roger Degueldre and Jean Bastien-Thiry, who were all shot for treason in the nearby forest. The leaders of the FLN (National Liberation Front) and future leaders of Algeria were also held here. In June 1961 there was a famous breakout when five commanders of the FLN got over the walls. In November that same year, the Algerian detainees launched a hunger strike to gain political status. Since then the prison has entered Algerian folklore as the place where the French refined their torture practices – the Abu Ghraib of its day. The physical layout of the prison has changed very little in the past hundred years. What has changed is the prison population, which now has a Muslim majority, mainly made up of Algerians.

After the shootings in Toulouse in March 2012 by Mohamed Merah, his brother Abdelkader arrived at Fresnes on 26 March and was immediately put into solitary confinement. The official line, reported on television and in the press, was that this was to protect his safety. This was not quite true. The reality was that for many of the prisoners in Fresnes, and indeed across the French prison system, the name of Mohamed Merah was an inspiration. What the authorities feared was that the sight of his brother might inspire a mutiny or even a riot. By the time he was locked up, Merah's name was already written in French and Arabic graffiti all over the prison. For his admirers, he was now a prisoner of war, the newest and most implacable enemy of France.

Renegades

The new enemies of France include the likes of Lionel Dumont – blonde, blue-eyed and a working-class *souchard* (a native Frenchman) from Roubaix. Dumont is also one of the most powerful and influential Islamist radicals currently detained in the French prison system. In the flesh, he is a tough, handsome man, clearly highly intelligent and possessed of a charisma which seems to reduce his guards to an almost homoerotic awe worthy of Jean Genet. The Director of Prisons, who knows Dumont well, described him to me as a 'fascinating man. You could almost imagine him as a friend. He is certainly worth knowing.'

Dumont is presently serving twenty-five years in the prison of La Santé for terrorist activities. He is moved around constantly because his very presence in a prison convulses the Muslim population there into an ever more rebellious mood. He speaks broken Arabic forcefully and is unafraid to complain publicly and loudly in French to the guards about the plight of '*Nous, les musulmans*' ('We Muslims'). He is almost universally admired by Muslim prisoners – those I spoke to who had been in prison with him called him the 'French Osama'.

He first came to the attention of the French press in 1997, when he was arrested for plotting to explode a car bomb during a G7 meeting in Lille, among other crimes. The press described him as '*le ch'ti d'Allah*', an expression that is hard to translate exactly – 'the Northerner of Allah', perhaps – but its meaning reveals much about the changing shape of the French intifada.

The term *ch'ti* has a double sense in French. On the one hand it is a cosy word used to describe the 'simple people' of the north of France, who are meant to embody down-to-earth northern values. The bestselling French film of all time, the 2007 comedy *Bienvenue chez les ch'tis* (*Welcome to the Sticks*), recounts the comic adventures of a sophisticated middle-class Frenchman from the south who goes to live among these earthy folk, with their chips and beer and unemployment. On the other hand *ch'ti* can often be an insult. The north of France is the poorest part of the country and has the highest rates not only of unemployment but also of alcoholism, drug addiction and paedophilia – all marks of social dysfunction. The *ch'timi* are often despised as a stupid and vicious underclass. In 2008, when Lens, a big French football team from a poor mining town, came to Paris, the Parisian supporters famously unveiled a banner which read: '*Pédophiles, chômeurs, consanguins, bienvenue chez les ch'tis*' ('Paedophilia, unemployment, inbreeding: welcome to the sticks'). This was a harsh joke even by the standards of the sharpest Parisian ironist.

The poorest town in the north of France is Roubaix, which also has the country's largest Muslim population. This is where Dumont dropped out of journalism school and began attending the local mosque in the rue Archimède in the mid-1990s, after a stint serving in the French army in Somalia. He claimed that Somalia was the turning point – this is where he saw honest Muslims heartlessly massacred by a cynical European killing machine. On his return to Roubaix, he still wanted to be a soldier, but decided to change sides. He made his way to Bosnia and joined the Mujahideen. In Bosnia he linked up with another comrade from Roubaix, Christophe Caze, and thrived on the battles against the Serbs. Both Caze and Dumont were further radicalized by this experience and when they eventually returned to the north of France they led a criminal gang – the 'Gang de Roubaix' – which carried out a series of murderous bank raids to finance terrorist activity. The police were astonished to find themselves under fire from heavy military weapons – rocket launchers and Kalashnikovs – for the first time on French soil, and being apparently used by experts.

All the members of the gang were either killed or arrested in 1996, except for Dumont, who again made his way to Bosnia, where he was sheltered by his jihadist brothers. He continued with robberies and bank raids, until he killed a Bosnian police officer and was sentenced to twenty years in jail in Zenica. He escaped from this prison and, with a fake passport, made his way to Japan. He had allegedly become a key al-Qaeda operative by the time he was eventually arrested in Japan and extradited to France, where he was sentenced in 2005.

In the past, French converts to Islam tended to be rarefied intellectual dandies, for whom Islam represented an exotic counterpoint to the mysteries of Catholicism. Prominent among this group are the Orientalist Louis Massignon – sometimes known as the 'Catholic Muslim' – and Réné Guénon, the aesthete and metaphysician much admired by the Surrealists. Recent well-known converts include Roger Garaudy, who died in 2012, once one of the official 'philosophers' of the French Communist Party, but better known for his 'negationist' views as a Holocaust denier.

However, there has also been a wave of white, working-class conversions to Islam. These include Franck Ribéry, the footballer who has played for Bayern Munich, Marseille and the French national team. Ribéry is often portrayed as a gormless clown in the French press – he speaks ungrammatically with the *ch'ti* accent of his native Boulogne. He converted to Islam for the gentlest and most sincere reason – to please his Moroccan wife Wahiba – and often speaks of his love for the Maghreb and its people.

This phenomenon is not so rare as it sounds, particularly in the north of France, where the white working class often feel closer to their Muslim neighbours than they do to the metropolitan élites elsewhere in France. It is easy to see how a young lad like Ribéry, whose mates are mainly Muslim, could fall in with the culture, in the same way that he falls in love with hip-hop, Nike and football. Above all, it is a conscious rejection by the white working class of the 'universalist' France which has left the *banlieues* behind.

Lionel Dumont once declared that he fought for Islam and

against France because Communism was over and the Muslims were the only people 'still fighting for justice'. Not all young white Muslims have the same rage as Dumont, but he is far from being alone.

Ghosts

There is no neat or tidy conclusion to this book. I make no prediction or prophesy about the future of France and the Arab nations. To do so would be a betrayal of the complexity of the subject matter and the singularity of my encounters in France and the Maghreb. What I have aimed to present here is an accessible analysis of current tensions on both sides of the Mediterranean, informed by an account of the historical circumstances which have brought us to where we are.

In Paris, in early 2013, the year has begun with the coldest weather that the city has known in over twenty years. This did not stop the nightly car-burnings and low-level skirmishes taking place in the *banlieues*; these events have become unremarkable facts of life in the suburbs of the big French cities. In my own district of Pernety, the frequent disturbances are regularly marked by a police lock-down of the council estates which skirt the *quartier*. The police, usually the heavily armed CRS riot police in Robocop gear, set up checkpoints at rue de Plaisance and Porte de Vanves (normally a centre for street prostitution). Arab and black kids are frisked before they can pass.

At the time of writing, France has launched a military intervention in Mali, striking against the mainly Algerian Islamist forces which have been rallying in the northern part of the country. The French had little choice but to attack as the Islamists ratcheted up their provocations against France and threatened to set off an insurgency in the southern part of Algeria, which shares a border with Mali. Publicly, the Algerians are furious about what seems to be another neo-colonialist war being fought in their back yard. Secretly, they welcome and support the French. The risk is that the Islamists destabilize the whole region, from Morocco and Algeria to Tunisia, and take the war across the Mediterranean. They are armed with high-grade weapons from the wreckage of Libya and they have a plan to bring the Afghan wars to Europe. My contacts in British and French counter-terrorism and intelligence have been worrying over the intervention in Mali for months. Their biggest fear is the blowback in France. In North Africa their fears were confirmed in the days after the first French air strikes, when an Islamist group launched a deadly assault on a BP gas plant in eastern Algeria on 16 January 2103, killing foreign hostages. Immediately France's conflict in Mali took on a new, dangerous global dimension.

Back in the *banlieues* little has yet changed. There is a lot of anger and a lot of young men willing to turn themselves into soldiers for God. Most importantly, the rioters, wreckers, even the killers of the *banlieues* are not looking for reform or revolution. They are looking for revenge.

Their rage is often expressed symbolically: appropriating the language of the intifada, which was originally a spontaneous and legitimate uprising against oppression; speaking Arabic slang; waving the Algerian flag; provocatively wearing the veil. These are all acts directed at subverting the French Republic. For many French people, for all these reasons, the *banlieues* represent 'otherness' – the otherness of exclusion, of the repressed, of the fearful and despised.

Until this ceases to be the case, the unacknowledged civil war between France and its disturbed suburbs – one of the most complex and fragile front lines in the Fourth World War – will go on. The positions and tactics of the immigrants of the *banlieues* – their identification with Palestine, their hatred of France – reveal the struggle to be part of the 'long war', just like those caught up in the conflicts in Iraq and Afghanistan. It is a short journey from symbolic revolt to real action in the minds of those who are so bitterly disenchanted with and excluded from French 'civilization'.

In the nineteenth century, Charles Baudelaire wrote of Paris being haunted by its past, by 'ghosts in daylight'. In the early twenty-first century, the ghosts of colonial and anti-colonial assassins continue to be visible in the daylight of the *banlieues*. It may be that what France needs is not hard-headed political solutions or even psychiatry, but an exorcist.

Notes

Introduction: 'Fuck France!'

The texts consulted in this section include:

Christopher Caldwell, *Reflections on the Revolution in Europe: Can Europe be the Same with Different People in it?* (Allen Lane, London, 2009)

Alain Finkielkraut, *Qu'est-ce que la France?* (Stock, Paris, 2007); *La Querelle de l'école* (Stock, Paris, 2007)

Gilles Kepel, *Les Banlieues de l'Islam: Naissance d'une religion en France* (Seuil, Paris, 1987); *La Revanche de Dieu: Chrétiens, juifs et musulmans à la reconquête du monde* (Seuil, Paris, 1991, 2003); *A l'ouest d'Allah* (Seuil, Paris, 1994, 1995); *Jihad: Expansion et déclin de l'islamisme* (Gallimard, Paris, 2000); *Chronique d'une guerre d'Orient* (Gallimard, Paris, 2002); *Fitna: Guerre au cœur de l'Islam* (Gallimard, Paris, 2004); *Quatre-vingt-treize* (Gallimard, Paris, 2012)

Tariq Ramadan, *To be a Western Muslim* (Cambridge University Press, 2009)

Justin Vaisse and Jonathan Laurence, *Intégrer l'Islam* (Odile Jacob, Paris, 2010)

1. See, for example, articles in *Le Parisien, Le Figaro, Libération, Le Monde*, 28–9 March 2007
2. This formula is defined and then turned on its head by the memoir by the Congolese rapper Abd al Malik, *Qu'Allah bénisse la France* (Albin Michel, Paris, 2004), p. 208
3. Interview with author, Paris, 21 May 2012
4. *Ha'aretz*, 18 November 2005
5. *Le Nouvel Observateur*, 24 November 2005
6. Interview with author, Paris, 10 June 2013

Part One: State of Denial

The texts consulted in this section include:

L'intelligence d'une ville: Vie culturelle et intellectuelle à Lyon entre 1945 et 1975, matériaux pour une histoire (Bibliothèque municipale de Lyon, 2006), p. 309

Alain Bertho, *Temps des émeutes* (BMP, Lyon, 2010)

Ludovic Frobert, *Les Canuts ou la démocratie turbulente: Lyon, 1831–1834* (Tallandier, Paris, 2009)

Michel Houellebecq, *Platform*, trans. Frank Wynne (Vintage, London, 2003)

Jean-Paul Sartre, *Portrait d'un anti-semite* (Gallimard, Paris, 1947)

1 Murder in the Suburbs

1. This is the account as given in *Libération* and other press sources, 1 March 2006
2. Jean-Paul Sartre, *Réflexions sur la question juive* (P. Morihien, Paris, 1946)
3. Louis-Ferdinand Céline, *Journey to the End of the Night*, trans. Ralph Manheim (Alma Classics, London, 2012), p. 115
4. See Abd al Malik, www.rap-2-france52.skyrock.com/2238704711-Abd-Al-Malik-Celine.html
5. Michel Houellebecq, *Platform*, trans. Frank Wynne (Vintage, London, 2003), p. 198

2 The Secrets of Lyons

1. See *Le Trésor de la langue française*, pp. 233–53
2. *Le Point*, 23 July 1993
3. Jules Michelet, *Le Banquet: papiers intimes* (Calmann Lévy, Paris, 1879), p. 154
4. *Le Monde*, 17 April 1981
5. Quoted in Mustafa Dikeç, *Badlands of the Republic* (Blackwell, London, 2007), p. 48; see also pp. 40–45
6. Henri Rousso, *Le Dossier Lyon 3* (Fayard, Paris, 2004)

3 A Soldier for God

1. This case was widely covered in the French press. For an account in English, see Andrew Hussey, 'France: A Country at War with Itself', in *New Statesman*, 30 March 2012
2. *Le Monde*, 10 May 2012

Part Two: Algeria, Prisoners of Love

The texts consulted in this section include:

F. Abécassi and G. Meynier (eds.), *Pour une histoire franco-algérienne: En finir avec les pressions officielles et les lobbies de mémoire* (La Découverte, Paris, 2008)

Charles-Robert Ageron, *Histoire de l'Algérie contemporaine (1871–1954)*, vols. 1 and 2 (Presses Universitaires de France, Paris, 1979); 'L'évolution politique et l'Algérie sous le Second Empire', *Politiques coloniales au Maghreb* (Presses Universitaires de France, Paris, 1972); *'L'Algérie algérienne' de Napoléon III à de Gaulle* (Sindbad, Paris, 1980)

Augustin E. Berque, *L'Algérie des années trente: Rapport à la direction des Affaires Indigènes* (Fayard, Paris, 2012)

Martin Evans and John Phillips, *Algeria: Anger of the Dispossessed* (Yale University Press, New Haven, 2007)

J. Frémeaux, *De quoi fut fait l'empire: Les Guerres coloniales au XIXe siècle* (CNRS, Paris, 2010)

D. Guignard, 'Conservatoire ou révolutionnaire? Le sénatus-consulte de 1863 appliqué au régime foncier d'Algérie', *Revue d'histoire du XIXe siècle*, no. 41, 2010, p. 81–96

Mohammed Harbi, *Le FLN, mirage et réalité: Des origines à la prise du pouvoir* (Jeune Afrique, Paris, 1980); *L'Algérie et son destin: Croyants et citoyens* (Editions Arcantère, Paris, 1993)

Alistair Horne, *A Savage War of Peace: Algeria 1954–1962* (Macmillan, London, 1977)

J. House, N. MacMaster, *Paris 1961: Les Algériens, la République et la terreur d'état* (Tallandier, Paris, 2008)

Charles-André Julien, *Histoire de l'Algérie contemporaine*, vol. 1: *Conquête et les débuts de la colonisation 1827–1871* (PUF, Paris, 1979)

François Maspero, *L'honneur de Saint-Arnaud* (Seuil, Paris, 2012)

G. Pervillé, *La France en Algérie* (Editions Vendémiaire, Paris, 2012)

C. Phéline, *L'Aube d'une révolution: Margueritte, Algérie, 26 avril 1901* (Privat, Paris, 2012)

A. Rey-Goldzeiguer, *Le Royaume arabe: La Politique algérienne de Napoléon III, 1861–1870* (SNED, Algiers, 1977)

D. Rivet, *Le Maghreb à l'épreuve de la colonisation* (Hachette, Paris, 2002)

J. Ruedy, *Land Policy in Colonial Algeria: The Origins of the Rural Public Domain* (University of California Press, Los Angeles, 1967)

D. Sari, *L'Insurrection de 1871* (SNED, Algiers, 1972)

410   Notes to pp. 66–79

C. Scheffer, *L'Algérie et révolution de la colonisation française* (Editions Honoré Champion, Paris, 1928)

Benjamin Stora, *Histoire de l'Algérie coloniale, 1830–1954* (La Découverte, Paris, 2004)

S. Thénault, *Violence ordinaire dans l'Algérie coloniale: Camps, internements, assignations à résidence* (Odile Jacob, Paris, 2012)

4 The Walls of Algiers

1. Alfred Sauvy, *L'Observateur*, 14 August 1952
2. There are several convincing and accurate accounts of this period in Algerian history. See, for example, Martin Evans and John Phillips, *Algeria: Anger of the Dispossessed* (Yale University Press, New Haven, 2007), pp. 177–215; Robert Fisk, *The Great War for Civilization* (Vintage, London, 2005), pp. 631–720; Luis Martinez, *La Guerre civile en Algérie* (Karthala, Paris, 1998); Hugh Roberts, *The Battlefield: Algeria 1988–2002* (Verso, New York and London, 2003); Mohammed Samraoui, *Chroniques des années de sang* (Denoël, Paris, 2003); James D. Le Sueur, *Between Terror and Democracy: Algeria Since 1989* (Zed Books, London, 2010); Youcef Ziram, *L'Algérie, la guerre des ombres* (GRIP, Brussels, 2002)
3. See Frantz Fanon, *The Wretched of the Earth*, trans. Constance Harrington (Penguin, London, 2001), pp. 27–75

5 Conquest

1. This account is based on Stora, *Histoire de l'Algérie* (La Découverte, Paris, 2004), p. 13. See also Jérome Louis, *La Question de l'Orient sous Louis-Philippe* (Sciences de l'Homme et Société, Paris, 2011), pp. 29 and 31. Eyewitness accounts include Nicolas Loverdo, *Extrait du journal d'un officier supérieur attaché à la deuxième division de l'armée d'Afrique* (Chez Anselin, Paris, 1831). See also Jean Serres, *La politique turque en Afrique du Nord sous la monarchie de Juillet* (P. Geuthner, Paris, 1925)
2. See Louis, *La Question de l'Orient*, pp. 31–6
3. For a full account see Roland Courtinat, *L'Algerieniste*, no. 113, March 2006. Also mentioned in Jean-Toussaint Merle, *Anecdotes historiques et politiques pour servir à l'histoire de la conquête d'Alger* (Hachette, Paris, 1831), pp. 43–4
4. See Evans and Phillips, *Algeria*, pp. 12–20

5. Filippo Pananti and Edward Blaquière, *Narrative of a Residence in Algiers: Comprising a Geographical and Historical Account of the Regency* (Henry Colburn, London, 1818)
6. Guy Antonetti, *Louis-Philippe* (Le Grand livre du mois, Paris, 2002)
7. Merle, *Anecdotes historiques*, p. 29
8. See *Walls of Algiers: Narratives of the City Through Text and Image*, ed. Zeynep Celik, Julia Clancy-Smith, Frances Terpak (University of Washington Press, Seattle, 2009), p. 25. Tulin is noted in Joelle Redouane, 'La présence anglaise en Algérie de 1830 à 1930', *Revue de l'Occident Musulman et de la Méditerranée*, 1984, p. 15
9. Merle, *Anecdotes historiques*, p. 62

6 The Secret World of the 'Algerines'

1. Merle, *Anecdotes historiques*, p. 207
2. Pananti, *Narrative of a Residence in Algiers*, pp. 153–81
3. Ibid. pp. 307–26
4. See Fontenelle, *Entretiens sur la pluralité des mondes pour qualifier la Régence d'Alger* (Paris, 1668). The name was officially adopted on 14 October 1839 by Antoine Virgile Schneider, French Minister for War

7 New America

1. Djamel Kharchi, *Colonisation et politique d'assimilation en Algérie, 1830–1962* (Casbah Editions, Algiers, 2004), pp. 71–89
2. Stora, *Histoire de l'Algérie*, p. 4
3. Joelle Hureau, *La Mémoire des pieds-noirs* (Académiques Perrin Editions, Paris, 2002), pp. 40–1
4. Achille-Hippolyte Blanc Saint-Hypolite, *De l'Algérie: Système du duc de Rovigo, en 1832: Moyens d'affermir nos possessions en 1840* (Hachette Livre BNF, Paris, 2013)
5. See Bruno Etienne, *Abdelkader* (Gallimard, Paris, 2003). Also Abd el-Kader, *Livre des haltes*, trans A. Penot (Dervy, Paris, 2008); *Écrits spirituels* (Seuil, Paris, 1982, 2000); *Lettre aux Français*, trans. René R. Khawam (Phebus, Paris, 1977)
6. Kharchi, *Colonisation*, pp. 40–44

8 The French Kingdom of the Arabs

1. Maurice Arama, *Delacroix: Un voyage initiatique* (Editions Non Lieu, Paris, 2006)
2. See Pascal Blanchard et al., *Le Paris Arabe* (La Découverte, Paris, 2003), pp. 28–9
3. Ibid. p. 28

9 Latin Africa

1. Ernest Renan, *De la part des peuples sémitiques dans l'histoire de la civilisation*, Discours au Collège de France (Michel Lévy Frères, Paris, 1862)
2. Celik, *The Walls of Algiers*, pp. 25–6
3. Hureau, *La Mémoire des pieds-noirs*, pp. 272–8
4. Ibid. pp. 217–18. See also Paul Siblot, 'Cagayous anti-juif', *Mots*, 1987, pp. 59–75
5. The so-called '*Marseillaise antijuive*' was given words by the pseudonymous 'Charles le Téméraire' and set to the tune of the original 'Marseillaise' by Rouget de Lisle. It was distributed in Paris and other French territories at the height of the Dreyfus affair. See www.dreyfus-affair.org/6_BIB_chansons.htmhttp://www.dreyfus-affair.org/6_BIB_chansons.htm
6. Reprinted in www.djazairess.com/fr/elwatan/18210
7. See Seth Graebner, *History's Place: Nostalgia and the City in French Algerian Literature*, 'After the Empire: The Francophone World and Postcolonial France' (Lexington Books, New York, 2007), p. 37
8. Ibid. p. 36
9. Ibid. p. 38

10 Awakenings

1. James McDougall, *History and the Culture of Nationalism in Algeria*, Cambridge Middle East Studies (Cambridge University Press, 2008)
2. Ibid. p. 45
3. Blanchard et al., *Le Paris Arabe*, pp. 140–41
4. Ibid. p. 45

11 Enemy States

1. Kharchi, *Colonisation*, p. 326
2. McDougall, *History and the Culture of Nationalism*, pp. 122–44
3. Martin Evans, *Algeria: France's Undeclared War*, Making of the Modern World series (Oxford University Press, 2012), pp. 41–3, 55–6
4. McDougall, *History and the Culture of Nationalism*, pp. 71–2
5. Albert Camus, *The First Man*, trans. David Hapgood (Vintage International, London, 1995), pp. 72–3
6. Interview with Catherine Camus, Loumarin, 21 May 2013
7. See Evans, *Algeria: France's Undeclared War*, pp. 57–67

12 Switching Sides

1. Evans, *Algeria: France's Undeclared War*, pp. 76–7; Kharchi, *Colonisation*, p. 391
2. Brian T. Edwards, *Morocco Bound: Disorienting America's Maghreb, from Casablanca to the Marrakech Express* (Duke University Press, Durham NC, 2005), p. 56
3. <http://www.bbc.co.uk/history/ww2peopleswar/user/70/u593170.shtml>
4. Edwards, *Morocco Bound*, p. 38
5. Alistair Horne, *A Savage War of Peace: Algeria 1954–1962* (Macmillan, London, 1977), p. 536
6. Ibid. p. 23
7. Ibid. pp. 23–8; see also Evans, *Algeria: France's Undeclared War*, pp. 86–9
8. Albert Camus, *Chroniques algériennes* (Gallimard, Paris, 1958), p. 95
9. Quoted in Horne, *A Savage War*, p. 27

13 The Reconquest

1. Horne, *A Savage War*, pp. 90–94
2. www.cinemadocumentaire.wordpress.com/2013/01/25/la-chine-est-encore-loin-malek-bensmail
3. Horne, *A Savage War*, p. 98
4. Ibid. p. 98
5. Ibid. pp. 119–23
6. Ibid. p. 119

7. Ibid. p. 1
8. www.babelouedstory.com/cdhas/31_20_08_1955_suite/massacre_el_halia.html
9. Dr Boigey, 'Psychologie morbide: Etude psychologique sur l'Islam', *Annales Médico-Psychologiques* (Masson, Paris, 1908)
10. Général Aussaresses, *Je n'ai pas tout dit: Ultimes révélations au service de la France* (Editions du Rocher, Paris, 2008), p. xx
11. Camus, *Chroniques algériennes*, pp. 167–87
12. Quoted in Olivier Todd, *Albert Camus: A Life* (Knopf, 1997), pp. 330–31. Also interview with Olivier Todd, Paris, 22 May 2013
13. Horne, *A Savage War*, p. 501
14. Todd, *Albert Camus*, p. 337

14 Capitals of Madness
1. Ali Haroun, *La 7e Wilaya: La Guerre du FLN en France, 1954–1962* (Seuil, Paris, 2005), pp. 67–77
2. Horne, *A Savage War*, pp. 183–7
3. Ibid. pp. 188–92
4. Ibid. p. 186
5. Ibid. p. 200
6. Ibid. p. 201
7. David Macey, *Frantz Fanon: A Life* (Granta Books, London, 2000), pp. 290–99
8. Horne, *A Savage War*, p. 205

15 De Gaulle and the French Civil War
1. Horne, *A Savage War*, pp. 359–61
2. Ibid. pp. 296–7
3. Ibid. p. 318
4. Ibid. p. 363
5. Interview with Harold Chapman, Kent, June 2012
6. Horne, *A Savage War*, p. 501
7. Ibid. p. 432

16 An Experimental Nation
1. Stora, *Histoire de l'Algérie*, pp. 126–7
2. Horne, *A Savage War*, pp. 537–40; Abd el Aziz Méliani, *Le Drame des Harkis: La France honteuse* (Libraire Académique Perrin, Paris, 1993), pp. 84–5

3. *Le Monde*, 11 July 2000
4. Interview with Zinédine Zidane, Madrid, 16 February 2003
5. Evans and Phillips, *Algeria*, p. 83
6. Ibid. p. 97
7. Ibid. pp. 77–8

17 The Algerian Intifada

1. Evans and Phillips, *Algeria*, pp. 140–46
2. Ibid. p. 128
3. Ibid. p. 111
4. Ibid. pp. 113–14
5. Ibid. p. 164
6. Ibid. p. 165

18 The New War with France

1. Evans and Phillips, *Algeria*, p. 175
2. Ibid. pp. 178–9
3. Ibid. p. 175
4. Ibid. p. 190
5. Lounis Aggoun and Jean-Baptiste Rivoire, *Françalgérie, crimes et mensonges d'états*, Paris (La Découverte, Paris, 2005), pp. 448–9
6. Ibid. p. 453
7. Ibid. p. 450
8. Evans and Phillips, *Algeria*, pp. 212–13

19 Mysteries and Martyrs

1. Aggoun and Rivoire, *Françalgérie*, pp. 475–89
2. Nesroullah Yous, *Qui a tué à Bentalha?* (La Découverte, Paris, 2000), quoted in Evans and Phillips, *Algeria*, p. 241

20 Family Secrets

1. Interview with Aimé Jacquet, Clairefontaine, 11 May 2006
2. Evans and Phillips, *Algeria*, p. 250

Part Three: In Morocco

The texts consulted in this section include:
Abdelhadi Alaoui, *Le Maroc et la France 1912–1956: Textes et documents à l'appui* (Fanigraph, Rabat, 2007)

Eugène Aubin, *Le Maroc dans la tourmente: 1902–1903* (Paris-Méditerranée, 2004)

François Broche, *L'Assassinat de Lemaigre-Dubreuil: Casablanca, le 11 juin 1955* (Balland, Paris, 1977)

Jean-Louis Cohen and Monique Eleb, *Casablanca, Mythes et figures d'une aventure urbaine* (Belvisi Hazan, Paris, 1998)

Julien Couleau, *La paysannerie marocaine* (CNRS, Paris, 1968)

Ignace Dalle, *Le Règne de Hassan II 1961–1999: Une espérance brisée* (Maisonneuve et Larose, Paris, 2001)

Guy Delanoë, *Lyautey, Juin, Mohammed V: Fin d'un protectorat* (Eddif, Paris, 1993)

Philippe Jacquier, Marion Pranal and Farid Abdelouahab, *Le Maroc de Gabriel Veyre* (Kubik, Paris, 2005)

Henri Terrasse, *Histoire du Maroc des origines à l'établissement du protectorat français* (Editions Frontispice, Casablanca, 2005)

Pierre Vermeren, *Histoire du Maroc depuis l'Indépendance* (La Découverte, Paris, 2002)

21 Queer Tangier

1. Oliver Harris, ed., *The Letters of William S. Burroughs 1945–1959* (Penguin, London, 1993), pp. 336–7
2. Ibid. p. 319
3. Interview with author, Tangier, 22 February 2002
4. Joe Orton, *The Orton Diaries*, ed. John Lahr (Methuen, London, 1986), p. 187

22 Peaceful Penetration

1. Douglas Porch, *The Conquest of Morocco: A Savage Colonial War* (Farrar, Straus and Giroux, 1982), pp. 5–6
2. Ibid. p. 63
3. Ibid. p. 156

23 French Friends

1. Porch, *Conquest of Morocco*, p. 131
2. Ibid, p. 134
3. *La Révolution Surréaliste*, Paris, 1927, quoted in Mark Polizzotti, *Revolution of the Mind: the Life of André Breton* (Bloomsbury, London, 2005), pp. 236–7

4.   Edwards, *Morocco Bound*, p. 59
5.   George Orwell, 'Marrakech', *New Writing*, December 1939

24 Modern Times
1.   Edwards, *Morocco Bound*, p. 247
2.   Tahar Ben Jelloun, *Les Yeux Baissés* (Seuil, Paris, 1984), p. 56
3.   Okacha Ben Elmostafa, *Les Mouvements islamiques au Maroc: Leurs modes d'action et d'organisation* (L'Harmattan, Paris, 2007), pp. 56–83

25 Blank Generation
1.   Marvine Howe, *Morocco: The Islamist Awakening and Other Challenges* (Oxford University Press, 2005), pp. 10–12
2.   Ali Amar, *Mohammed VI: Le Grand Malentendu* (Calmann-Lévy, Paris, 2009), pp. 15–23
3.   Andrew Hussey, 'The Tipping Point of Terror', *Observer*, 4 April 2004. Also Howe, *Morocco*, pp. 323–53

26 Setting Europe on Fire
1.   Giles Tremlett, *The Ghosts of Spain* (Faber, London, 2006), pp. 246–80. Also Howe, *Morocco*, pp. 352–7

27 The Neuilly–Marrakesh Express
1.   Amar, *Mohammed VI*, p. 297. See also Ali Amar and Jean-Pierre Tuquoi, *Paris–Marrakech: Luxe, pouvoir et réseaux* (Calman-Lévy, Paris, 2012)

Part Four: Tunisia, Made in France
The texts consulted in this section include:

Samir Aounallah and Mounir Fantar, *A la découverte du Cap Bon: Guide historique et archéologique* (Agence de mise en valeur du patrimoine et de promotion culturelle, Tunis, 2006)

Nicolas Beau and Jean-Pierre Tuquoi, *Notre ami Ben Ali: L'envers du 'miracle tunisien'* (La Découverte, Paris, 2002)

Habib Bourguiba, *La trace et l'héritage*, ed. Michel Camau and Vincent Geisser (Karthala, Paris and Aix-en-Provence, 2004)

Michel Camau and Vincent Geisser, *Le Syndrome autoritaire: Politique en Tunisie de Bourguiba à Ben Ali* (Presses de Sciences Po, Paris, 2003)

Mounir Charfi, *Les ministres de Bourguiba (1956–1987)* (L'Harmattan, Paris, 1989)

Béatrice Hibou, *La force de l'obéissance: Économie politique de la répression en Tunisie* (La Découverte, Paris, 2006)

Sadri Khiari, *Tunisie: Le délitement de la cité* (Karthala, Paris, 2003)

Olfa Lamloum and Bernard Ravenel, eds., *La Tunisie de Ben Ali: La société contre le régime* (L'Harmattan, Paris, 2002)

Reporters sans frontières, ed., *Tunisie: Le livre noir* (La Découverte, Paris, 2002)

28 The Mysteries of Tunis

1. See Olivier Piot, *La Révolution tunisienne* (Les Petits Matins, Paris, 2011). See also Lamloum and Ravenel, *La Tunisie de Ben Ali*
2. Lénaig Brédoux and Mathieu Magnadieux, *Tunis connection: Enquête sur les réseaux franco-tunisiens sous Ben Ali* (Seuil, Paris, 2012), pp. 12–13. See interview with Henri Guaino at <http://www.liberation.fr/politiques/2011/01/24/-_709542>
3. Christopher Hitchens, 'At the Desert's Edge', *Vanity Fair*, 1 July 2007

29 Stealing Tunisia

1. Jean-André Peyssonnel, *Voyage dans les régences de Tunis et d'Alger* (M Dureau de la Malle, Paris, 1838), pp. 56–7
2. Kenneth J. Perkins, *A History of Modern Tunisia* (Cambridge University Press, 2004), pp. 39–65
3. Ibid. pp. 67–9
4. Ibid. pp. 89–90
5. Ibid. pp. 142–4; also Horne, *A Savage War*, p. 455; Nicole Grimaud, *La Tunisie à la recherche de sa sécurité* (Presses Universitaires de France, Paris, 1995), pp. 70–77

30 Holidays in the Sun

1. David Bellos, *Georges Perec: A Life in Words* (Harvill, London, 1995), pp. 342–3
2. Ibid. pp. 123–6
3. Ibid. pp. 173–6

31 Miracles

1. See Lamloum and Ravenel, *La Tunisie de Ben Ali*, pp. 154–7
2. Nigel and Colin Cawthorne, *Football Hooligans: No One Likes Us and We Don't Care* (Robinson, London, 2011), p. 56
3. Leila Ben Ali, *Ma Vérité* (Editions du Moment, Paris, 2012), pp. 114–15
4. <http://www.leparisien.fr/crise-tunisie/tunisie-imed-trabelsi-un-proche-de-ben-ali-est-vivant-21-01-2011–1237618.php>; <http://www.lejdd.fr/Societe/Justice/Actualite/L-affaire-des-yachts-voles-refait-surface–125225>
5. Ben Ali, *Ma Vérité*, pp. 165–6

Part Five: Prisoners of War

32 Muslims in Prison

1. *Le Trésor de la langue française*, pp. 3445–6
2. Edmund White, *Genet* (Vintage, London, 1996)

Acknowledgements

Given the nature of this book, and the times we live in, there are a good number of people on all sides without whom this book could not have been written, but who will not want to be named. Among those who helped, whom I can thank here, are Fatima Ahloulay, Hicham Aidi, Abdelatif Akbib, Khalid Amine, Mohamed Benaboud, Geoff Bird, Collette Brown, Catherine Camus, Jason Cowley, Nick Danziger, Sir Graeme Davies, Jane Ferguson, Alain Finkielkraut, Gill Gillespie, Allen Hibbard, Chris Hickey, Les Hodge, Gill Hunter, Jeremy Jacobson, Deborah Kapchan, Gilles Kepel, Mohemed Laamiri, Louise Lyle, Samia Mahiddine, Steve and Ali McNulty, Jeffrey Miller, Anne Mitchell, Touria Nakkouch, Sophie Nellis, Ruaridh Nicoll, José Manuel Goñi Pérez, Kate Pullinger, Stephen Regan, Martin Rose, David Trotter, Claire Spencer, Lamia Tayeb, Francis Whately, Imen Yacoubi and Amin Zaoui.

Of course this book would not have happened without the inspiration of Andrew Wylie, Sarah Chalfant, Luke Ingram and Stephanie Derbyshire at the Wylie Agency. Nor could it have been made without the editorial wisdom of Mitzi Angel, Laura Barber, Sara Holloway, Daphne Tagg.

Most of all I thank my dad, John Hussey, with love for his ideas, arguments, digging out sources, and smoking cigars over a pint at Pernety.

Illustration Credits

The author and the publisher have made every effort to trace the copyright holders. Please contact the publisher if you are aware of any omissions.

1. Paris, France: A man throws a metal object during riots at the Paris Gare du Nord railways station, 27 March 2007. Copyright © Francois Guillot/AFP/Getty Images.

2. Policemen arrest a man during riots at the Paris Gare du Nord railways station, 27 March 2007. Copyright © Jacques Demarthon/AFP/Getty Images.

3. 'Nick la Police' photograph copyright © Jamie H. Gibson.

4. Jean Gabin in *Pépé le Moko* (1937)/Paris Film Production. Founded by brothers Robert and Raymond Hakim. Photo courtesy of the British Film Institute.

5. Fighting between the Algerian and French Troops in front of the gates of Algiers, c.1830 (colour litho), French School (19th century). Copyright © Bibliotheque des Arts Decoratifs, Paris, France/Archives Charmet/The Bridgeman Art Library.

6. Portrait of Abd el-Kader (1808–83) (oil on canvas) by Jean

Baptiste Ange Tissier (1814–76). Copyright © Château de Versailles, France/Giraudon/The Bridgeman Art Library.

7. *Les Femmes d'Alger/Women of Algiers in their Rooms* by Eugene Delacroix (1798–1863): 1834. Paris, Louvre. Oil on canvas. cm 180 x 229 – © 2013. Photo copyright © Photo Scala, Florence.

8. Poster advertising the International Overseas Exhibition, Paris, 1931 (colour litho), Desmeures (fl.1931). Copyright © Bibliotheque Historique de la Ville de Paris, Paris, France

9. Photo of cover from *Les Races Humaines* reproduced courtesy of Newspapers-collection.com.

10. Cover from *La Lanterne de Cagayous*.

11. In the main street of Algiers, the rue Michelet, French 'Gardes Mobiles' try to stop young demonstrators opposing a peace plan with France. Copyright © Nicolas Tikhomiroff/ Magnum Photos.

12. General Charles de Gaulle (centre) riding through street in Algiers. Copyright © Loomis Dean/Time Life Pictures/Getty Images.

13. 'Ici On Noie Les Algeriens': Guerre d'Algérie: vue d'un pont à Paris. Copyright © Jean Texier/Mémoire d'Humanité, Archives de la Seine St Denis.

14. Morocco under French Colonial rule – "La France va pouvoir porter librement au Maroc la civilisation, la richesse et la paix". (Allegory of the benefits of French rule). Colour print. From *Le Petit Journal*, vol 22, Paris, 19 November 1911. Photo copyright © akg-images.

15. Morocco, town of Tangiers. Moroccan writer Mohamed Choukri, 1987. Photo copyright © Harry Gruyaert/Magnum Photos.

16. Tunisia – April 28: French president Nicolas Sarkozy and Mrs Carla Sarkozy's arrival at the airport of Tunis Carthage and the reception by Mr Zine El Abidine Ben Ali president of Tunisia on April 28, 2008. Photo copyright © Olivier Sanchez/Gamma-Rapho via Getty Gamma-Rapho via Getty Images.

17. A man holds a poster showing a photo of Tunisian president Zine El Abidine Ben Ali and reading 'Down with the dictator in Tunisia', on January 13, 2011 in Paris, during a demonstration to protest against the repression against demonstrators in Tunisia. Photo copyright © Joel Saget/AFP/Getty Images.

18. Fresnes prison/Interior of cell. Photo copyright © Collection Dupondt/akg-images.

19. France – March 14: Aerial view of Fresnes prison in Fresnes, France on March 14, 2003. Photo copyright © Pool le Floch/ TRAVERS/Gamma-Rapho via Getty Images.

Index